ALLIONS IN COLLIN COUNTY

ollin McKinney Home.
aac Graves Home.
oees and Truett Law Office — Once
hrockmorton's Office, our Governor
f Texas.

1. Throckmorton, site of the very first settlement in county, 1842 (7-D)
2. Buckner—site first post office, fort, store. Estab. by Jack McGarrah, 1843 (5-F)
3. First Indian Massacre, 1843. (4-D)
4. Battle at Buckner—settlers and Indians, 1843.
5. Cedar Springs—Bonham road, through Buckner. Travelers, stagecoach. (2-K to 11-B)
6. Bogard's stage station. (7-E)
7. Sugar Hill—1852 (12-F)
8. Site of old covered bridge. (5-F) 1877 to 1919.
9. Foreman's Store—Site—1852 (5-J)
10. Site of Muncy's family massacre by Indians, 1844. (4-I)
11. Site where Joe Rice was killed by Indians, 1844.
12. Camp of "Spotted Tail," the Indian who protected early settlers from Plains tribes. (4-11)
13. Mantua—ghost town where once stood important settlement. (7-A)
14. Ardath—another thriving settlement, now gone. (9-F)
15. Eureka—another ghost town. (9-J)
16. Shepton—ghost town. (2-J)
17. Rock Hill, ghost town. (2-F)
18. St. Paul, ghost town. (7-J)
19. Fitzhugh Mills (Tonkawa Indian village prior to 1840). (8-I)
20. Cherokee Indian village prior to 1840 (7-E)
21. Delaware Indian village prior to 1840 (7-F)
23. Bell's oil well, 1st in county, 1910 (8-E)
A. Ballew hanged this site, 1872. (6G)
B. Shack, a Negro hanged here—1882. (6-F)
C. Estep hanged—1922. (6-F)
24. Roland (Liberty Springs)—famed Camp Meeting ground—(5-O)
25. Site of town of Clear Lake. (10-J)
26. Site of Springtown. (10-I)
27. Foncine (3-G)
28. House of Collin McKinney, pioneer, signer Tex. Independence (9-B) Medallion Home.
29. Elm Grove Camp Meeting ground (9-3)
30. Roseland (3-C)
31. Erudia (a ghost town)—(1-F)
32. Bethel Camp Meetin Ground (1-G)
33. Covered Bridge

EARLY SCHOOL SITES:

2. Pleasant Hill School (12-J)	44. Faulkner—(6-I)	86. Martin Box—(9-B)
3. Sabine School—(13-J)	45. Lovejoy—(6-H)	87. Pleasant Hill—(9-H)
4. Harris School—(13-I)	46. McDonald—(7-G)	88. Carmel—(11-B)
5. Aston School—(13-H)	47. Bois D'Arc—(5-F)	89. Bosby (Negro)—(6-D)
6. Brushy School—(14-H)	48. Ash Grove—(6-D)	90. White's Grove—(5-G)
7. New Liberty—(13-G)	49. Lone Elm—(5-D)	91. Wetsel—(5-H)
8. Union School (13-F)	50. Helm—(5-C)	92. Fairview—(7-B)
9. Red Oak—(13-F)	51. Coffman—(7-C)	93. Little Creek—(11-J)
10. Arnold School—(13-E)	52. Kelly—(6-B)	94. Richardson—(2-E)
11. Dixon School—(12-D)	53. Warden—(6-A)	95. Pedigo—(12-K)
12. Callis School—(13-C)	54. Betheny—(3-I)	96. Brown—(5-J)
13. Empire School—(11-I)	55. Rowlett—(3-H)	97. Faulkner—(6J)
14. Prairie Grove—(12-I)	56. Bush—(3-G)	98. Possum Trot—(3-F)
15. Neathery—(12-H)	57. Upper Rowlett—(3-G)	99. Hobbins—(9-H)
16. Spring Hill—(11-G)	58. Pleasant Ridge—(3-F)	100. Glenn—(12-D)
17. Rock Quarry (11-G)	59. Bowlby—(4-F)	101. New Hope—(7-F)
18. Hickman (12-F)	60. Walnut Grove—(3-F)	102. Long Neck—(9-F)
19. Hornett —(11-F)	61. Bloomdale—(4-F)	103. Corinth—(4-D)
20. Moreland—(12-C)	62. Franklin	104. Asa Walker—(12-A)
21. McMinn (12-I)	63. Cottage Hill—(4-D)	105. Foncine—(3-G)
22. Cairo—(10-I)	64. Bilderback—(4-C)	106. Rose Hill—(12-G)
23. Cotton Belt—(9-J)	65. Alla—(3-B)	107. Heard Ranch—(9-G)
24. Clear Lake—(10-I)	66. Lone Star—(5-B)	108. Prairie View—(3-I)
25. Mesquite—(10-J)	67. Sunbeam—(3-A)	109. South Church—(12-K)
26. Thompson—(10-J)	68. Barnsdale—(I-J)	110. Cowskin—(13-H)
27. Sister Grove—(11-G)	69. Lebanon—(2-H)	111. Cliff—(11-K)
28. Viney Grove—(9-F)	70. Hutcherson—(1-E)	112. Old Copeville—(11-I)
29. Midway—(11-F)	71. Shain's Chapel—(1-B)	113. Bois D'Arc—(13-J)
30. Womble—(10-F)	72. Rosemond—(9-B)	114. Bear Creek—(11-J)
31. New Life—(10-E)	73. Climax—(10-F)	115. Hackberry—(5-F)
32. Routh—(10-C)	74. Donna—(10-C)	116. Stinson—(7-J)
33. Cramer—(9-K)	75. Red Oak—(11-D)	117. Wilmeth—(6-F)
34. Lone Elm—(8-J)	76. Flowers—(11-D)	118. Trinity—(7-B)
35. Morris—(8-I)	77. Rhymer—(9-D)	119. Willow Springs—(8-I)
36. Winningkoff (7-H)	78. Ticky—(9-H)	120. Viney Grove (Wilson)—(8-F)
37. Bishop—(7-H)	79. Martins Box—(9-H)	121. Sedalia (Independence)
38. Milligan—(7-G)	80. Graybill—(10-B)	— (10-A)
39. Woodlawn—(7-F)	81. McWherter—(3-B)	122. Stats—(14-F)
40. Stiff Creek—(9-E)	82. Crossroads—(3-C)	123. Branch—(9-I)
41. White Rock—(9-D)	83. Emerson—(2-B)	124. Johnson—(10-F)
42. Parker—(6-J)	84. Berger—(1-B)	125. Shields—(8-C)
43. Cottonwood—(5-J)	85. Skaggs—(2-A)	127. Chambersville

COLLIN COUNTY, TEXAS

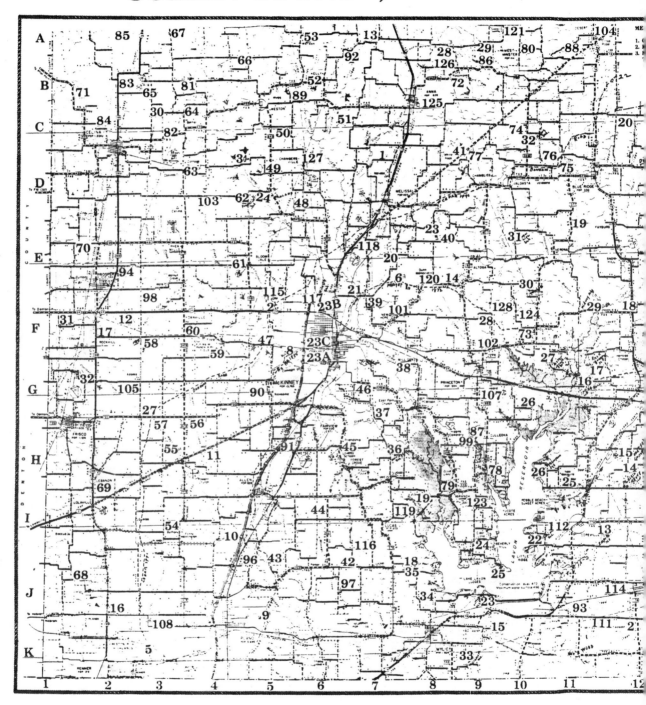

COLLIN COUNTY

COUNTY

Pioneering   In North Texas

By Capt. Roy F. Hall
And Helen Gibbard Hall

Published 1994 by

HERITAGE BOOKS, INC.
1540-E Pointer Ridge Place,
Bowie, Maryland 20716
(301) 390-7709

ISBN 0-7884-0037-1

A Complete Catalog Listing Hundreds of Titles
on Genealogy, History, and Americana
Available Free on Request

To Roy

Whose zest for living,

whose thirst for knowledge,

and whose lively interest in

all things, living or past,

made of life an exciting adventure.

Acknowledgments

In trying to assemble the thousands of pages of material my husband had written about Collin County, I was faced with many choices. What should be included? What left out of this particular book? He had notes that would make several books. I hope I chose the right things to include so that it will be most helpful to the most people. Without the encouragement of everyone, I could not have gotten it all together.

My special thanks go out to the many, many people who responded to my newspaper request for family histories. The response was wonderful. I wish that every family in the county could have been in the book, but family history is such a personal matter that I felt I should use only the stories sent to me or those Roy had already written. Every pioneer was important in the formation of Collin County, each contributing in his own way.

I want to thank all the news media of the county for the use of their space to publicize my need for family histories. Without the help of the newspapers and radio station, I could not have reached so many people. Radio Station KYAL has given me time and publicity, as has the Examiner and Courier-Gazette of McKinney. Their interest in the project I was undertaking and many kindnesses have made working with them a pleasure.

I want to express my thanks for the courteous help the people at the McKinney Library have given so freely. They start uncovering the machine that enlarges the microfilmed newspapers as soon as I arrive! Their knowledge of where to look for information has been most helpful.

To the photographic shops I owe a special thanks for making a special rate at the time I was gathering family information. This made it possible for treasured old family pictures to be copied for me to use at a nominal cost.

To everyone who helped in any way I am grateful. And for the many new friends this work has brought my way, I truly appreciate.

Digging into the past brings many rewarding experiences. My thanks to Roy Hall Jr. for his work in getting materials researched and typed.

Sources used in this book include:

Roy's articles and notes.

Microfilmed copies of old newspapers at the Library.

Old clippings from newspaper biographies at the death of pioneer citizens.

Biographical Souvenirs of Texas loaned by my neighbor and friend, Mrs. George Lacey.

Boxes of old letters sent to Roy by people over the years.

Materials acquired from the Archives at Austin.

Biographies sent me by people from several states, along with treasured photographs.

PREFACE

The people of Collin County have a rich, robust and unique heritage. This heritage is directly related to the black fertile soil and our geographic location on the upper reaches of the watershed. It covers the period from the first settler who worked from sun to sun with a wooden plow drawn by oxen in order to break the native sod, on one acre of land, worth approximately $1 in the market place. He was barely able to feed and clothe himself and family.

Our heritage is still agricultural. Today our farmer climbs on a tractor, adjusts the tension on his over-stuffed seat, adjusts the angle and height of the steering wheel, tunes an AM-FM radio, sets the thermostat on his air conditioner, starts a diesel engine and in eight hours, while listening to the news from around the World or from outer space, plows 100 acres of land which is worth, in today's market, $200,000. While doing this, not only feeds and clothes himself and his family, but fifty other people.

Agriculture is still our heritage. It was the heritage of the Indian who pre-dated the pioneer. Captain Roy F. Hall believed that the young people of this county, when properly informed, would appreciate their heritage and that their lives would be enriched by a study of the lives their forefathers lived. He was born March 6, 1887, the son of Stuart Holland Hall and Princess Annie Thompson Hall. He was born in the home of his grandfather, J.B. Wilmeth, two miles north of McKinney. His grandfather was one of the first settlers of the county. He helped survey the McKinney townsite.

After a colorful and distinguished army career, during which time he served in quelling the Moros uprising in the Phillipines, the Boxer uprising in China, acted as body guard for President Teddy Roosevelt, and served with the famed 90th division in the army of occupation in Europe during World War I, having won countless medals for sharp shooting and representing the United States Army in world wide marksmanship competition in Switzerland and establishing a record which still stands; he returned home and spent the balance of his life in Collin County. Stambaugh and Stambaugh, in publishing their excellent history of Collin County; George P. Brown in writing the county's history, as remembered by early day settlers; Walter B. Wilson, who compiled the scrap books covering two generations in our early history; Harold Beame who did his Masters thesis at the University of Texas on the Collin County history; Claude Elliott in writing *Leathercoat,* the Life of James W. Throckmorton; John Wilson Bawyer and Claude Harrison Thurman in compiling the Annals of Elder Horn, Early Life in the Southwest; and Grace (Moran) Evans who spent eighteen years collecting and compiling data on the early families in the Nevada, Lavon, Millwood and Copeville communities; all did much to preserve our heritage. None of them surpass the effort or the contribution that Captain Roy F. Hall has made. He filled the gap from then to now. He lived our history. He made our history live. His widow, Helen Hall, 811 Barnes Street, McKinney, Texas, is continuing his work today.

ROLAND BOYD

The Successor Of Capt. Roy Hall
As Chairman Of The Collin County
Historical Survey Committee And
Presently Vice Chairman In Charge
Of Special Projects Of The Collin
County Historical Survey Committee

Dated June 1, 1975.

ABOUT THE AUTHOR
CAPT. ROY F. HALL

Roy Franklin Hall, son of Stuart Holland Hall and Princess Annie Thompson Hall, was born in the home of his great-grandfather, J.B. Wilmeth, who settled two miles north of present McKinney in 1845.

This grandfather had perhaps the most influence on the life of the small boy and much of the stories he later wrote were told to him by this pioneer who was here from the beginning of the settlement of Collin County, helping to survey the present town of McKinney, establishing churches over much of North Texas, and establishing one of the first schools in the area.

Roy grew up on the adjoining farm (now the McIntyre farm), and worked along with his father to clear the land of the huge virgin forest that covered it. He attended Wilmeth School that stood on land which in 1975 was a part of the Job Corp grounds.

While still underage he joined the Army and was sent to the Philippine Islands to help subdue the Moros who were proving a source of trouble to the soldiers occupying the Islands. Later he was sent to China for the latter part of the Boxer Uprising. While stationed in Washington he was chosen to go to the White House as one of President Teddy Roosevelt's bodyguards, going with him on a special train used for his campaigning for re-election.

After the enlistment ended, he signed with the Cincinnati Red Legs only to have his baseball career cut short when he was struck by a streetcar, breaking his shoulder.

Back home in McKinney he was a motorman for a while on the old Interurban and later a dispatcher at Plano. One year he worked on the XIT Ranch in West Texas. He later taught school at Bowlby and at Bloomdale.

At the outbreak of World War I he was called back into the Army, training at the First Officer's Training Camp at Leon Springs. He served in the 90th Division as a Captain and at the end of the war stayed on in the Army of Occupation in Germany.

After retiring from the Army he became a feature writer for the San Antonio Express and did photographic work for them. Later came back to McKinney to live on his farm

at Stony Point. With time to devote to it, he became active in gathering all the facts about local history that he could find. He wrote four different columns at the same same time for the McKinney Daily Courier-Gazette, "Farming in Collin County—50 Years Ago," "Way Back Yonder," "Seen About Town," and "Over the Wing in Collin County," an assignment that took him constantly over the county.

He was a columnist for the McKinney Examiner for over 15 years, writing stories and articles about local history, interspersed with stories now and then about "Uncle Tom," the hill-billy uncle who came from Tennessee to live with the family while Roy was a child. All the stories were actual happenings that reflected the times as they were then.

He organized the Collin County Historical Committee in 1956 and worked with them as long as health would permit. He was a charter member of the Jimmie Geigas American Legion Post of McKinney, a member of the Mockingbird Chapter of the Texas Poetry Society, was the volunteer Weather Observer for 15 years, served as Mayor of McKinney for two years and was a Lion's Club member for 15 years.

He was first married to Mattie Lou Rowe and to them were born five daughters, Maxine, Doris, Ann, Madelon and Jessie Mina.

All preceded him in death except Ann, Mrs. Leo Fox of San Antonio.

In 1936 he married Helen Gibbard of Durant, Okla. Their five children are Sidney Ann Cahill, Roy F. Hall Jr., Nancy Hall Munger, David Hall, and Stanley Hall. He has two sisters, Mrs. Ora Craft of Sherman and Mrs. Sue Walker of Pronghorn, La.

A heart ailment cut short his writing activities and he died August 24, 1970 and was buried in Pecan Grove Cemetery, a fitting resting place since his grandmother, Kitura Melvina Wilmeth Thompson, was the first person buried there years before it became a cemetery. Kitura died at the birth of Roy's mother and when her father, J.B. Wilmeth, went to bring her body home, he was struck by the beauty of the area shaded by huge trees, some of the most beautiful in his beloved Collin County.

HELEN GIBBARD HALL

(The material for this History of Collin County by Capt. Roy F. Hall was published posthumously. The manuscript that Capt. Hall had gathered and written over the years was edited after his death by his wife, Helen Gibbard Hall, and prepared for publication. Mrs Hall also collected the family histories found at the conclusion of Capt. Hall's history.)

HELEN GIBBARD HALL was born on the old Chisholm Trail in the heart of the Pottowatomi Indian Nation. Her parents had moved there when everyone except the Indians had to pay the government a yearly sum for the privilege of living there.

Her parents were Emma Hart Gibbard and Isaac Franklin Gibbard, both descended from early Texas pioneer families. Her mother's family settled in Bosque County and her father's family at Wills Point.

She spent her childhood in Durant, Oklahoma, graduated from Southeastern Oklahoma State College and later did graduate work at North Texas State University in Denton. She was a history major in college and the fascinating story of Oklahoma also made her a life-long history buff.

Following her marriage to Capt. Hall on July 15, 1936, she moved to Texas to live. The first two years of their married life were spent "on the road," as Capt. Hall researched and located the sites of every battle fought on Texas soil for a book he was in the process of writing.

Roy and Helen Hall had five children, Sidney Anne, Mrs. David Cahill of Roswell, New Mexico; Roy F. Hall, who married Rita Taylor and lives in Melissa, Texas; Nancy Wilmeth Hall, who married Ken Munger and lives in Irving, Texas; David Gibbard Hall, who married Ora Morrison and teaches at the University of Texas at Austin and Stanley V. Hall of Dallas.

Mrs. Hall retired from the teaching profession after eight years with the McKinney public schools.

TABLE OF CONTENTS

1

Geology of Collin County

CHAPTER I

Geology Of Collin County

Before we take up the history of man in Collin County, let us go back, briefly, and see how the very ground we now live on happened to be here before the white men came, or any form of man.

It is not known just how old this earth is, but what we can gather from rocks and fossils we are pretty sure that a billion years must have passed since the earth cooled to a point where some form of life would be possible. The top soil of this county, from which we glean our daily bread, is close to 100 million years old.

Roughly, there are four great ages in the history of the earth. In Geology they are known as the Archean Time, which was the beginning almost without life, save a few crawling things that appeared at the close of the period. Then came the Paleozoic Time, in which life expanded and took shape as fishes, insects, and trees. This was the age in which coal was formed on earth.

The third age was the Mesozoic and in this period life reached its greatest magnitude. It spanned about 100 million years, ending some 60 million years ago.

This was the age of the mighty lizard called Dinosaurs, some standing up to twenty feet and measuring eighty feet long. For about 100 million years they overran the earth and there were untold millions of them. This was the age when the whiterock of Collin County was formed. This was the age when our earth became covered with trees and other plant life.

The fourth age is the Cenozoic, in which we now live. The great lizards became extinct and other animals appeared on earth. Many of these first animals were much larger than their modern-day counterpart.

This was the age when palm trees and other seed bearing trees spread over the land.

Toward the end of this Cenozoic age a new animal appeared on earth. This newcomer was man himself. So far as we can find out man made his appearance about a half million years ago. It may have been longer. We have evidence of him through bone fragments as far back as five-hundred thousand years ago.

Excavations made during the building of the Lavon Dam in Southeast Collin County unearthed the site of an ancient village whose history is lost in antiquity.

Every white-rock creek, and they are everywhere in the county, abounds in fossils that tell the story of what life was like before the coming of man.

Great oceans covered this part of Texas in ages past, and these oceans contained a multitude of animal life, both large and small. In dying, these small creatures sank to the bottom of the seas, decayed and left their shells and bones. In the course of millions of years these became the whiterock as we now know it. As the whiterock or, as it is called, Cretaceous formation, is up to 1,500 feet in thickness here, it must have taken millions of years to build it to its present depth.

Several million years ago this part of the state emerged from the sea, exposing the white slime made from the shells and bones of the sea-dwelling animals, and finally dried and hardened into our present whiterock or limestone. Weather dissolved the surface of the linestone into fine particles, in which hardy plants found root. When these plants died they added fertility in the form of leaf mold to the limestone, gradually changing its white texture to the dark humus we now recognize as our soil.

All the top soil of Collin County is composed of the underlying limestone, mixed with the rotted blades of grass, leaves and trunks of trees. The county lies in the belt of Houston Black Clay, a strip of very fertile soil, averaging fifty miles in width, and reaching from near Sherman to south of Austin.

At the time of the first settlement in Collin County all the valleys were covered with a very heavy growth of hardwood trees, which covered slightly more than half the area of the county. The rest of the county, chiefly west of the East Fork of the Trinity, was carpeted with native grasses, blue-stem and buffalo grass. Little of the native grasses now grow in the county.

THE SITE OF Collin County's first county seat, Fort Buckner. The Fort was built by Texas Rangers about 1845-1848. Trees are "Tree of Heaven," brought here as a gift to a friend by the hero of Texas War for Independence, Ben Milam. Ben Milam was engaged to Collin McKinney's daughter at the time of his visit to Collin County. She later married Ben Milam's brother.

2

Pioneer Settlers, 1841-1845

TEXAS GOVERNOR JAMES W. THROCKMORTON—1866-67
. . . native son of Collin County

(Photo courtesy Texas State Archives)

CHAPTER II

Pioneer Settlers, 1841 To 1845

It is possible that there never has been a country possessed of more scenic beauty than this particular section of the state when the first settlers arrived. The land lay mainly level, with a gentle slope to the southeast, and rolling ridges dividing the forests along the streams, and streams flowing the year around, clear and swift.

On the prairies were herds of deer, a few buffalo and countless numbers of prairie chickens and quail. In the forests were panthers, bears, wolves and an abundance of smaller game. The five lakes of the area were covered, in season, with thousands of wild geese, ducks, swans and cranes. The streams abounded in catfish, white bass, shad, crappie and eels. Game was so plentiful and tame that deer and bears were pests. To rid the vicinity of smokehouse raiders and pig stealers, the settlers on Sister Grove Creek put on a bear hunt in 1849 and killed 52 bears in one day.

Ancient Indians doubtless inhabited the area, as skeletons have been found over the county, but the only Indians here when the first settlers came were a few bands of Tonkawas, Cherokees and Delawares, plus a few Kickapoos. In 1841 a camp of Delawares were at the big spring which was later Fitzhugh Mills. A small village of Tonkawas was located two miles north of present McKinney and another Tonkawa village seven miles northeast. In all, there were not over 200 Indins then in the county.

The Cherokees and Delawares were crop raisers when they came to this section in early 1820, but while in present Collin though, they did not grow crops, but lived as did the native Tonkawas on wild fruit and game. Save some minor thieving by the Tonkawas, none of these Indians caused the first settlers in the present county any trouble. Their Indian fights were with the plains Indians, raiding in from the west.

Until 1841 there was no white man living in present Collin County. Some land was already owned though, but the owners had never seen their property. In a few cases up to 1,280 acres or slightly more, had been given to those who fought in the Texas Revolution against Mexico in 1835-36. These were called grants, and in practically all cases those to whom the grant was made sold or traded it off without ever seeing it. They had selected their grant from crude maps in the General Land office at Austin. Almost all the land in the present county, though, was owned by the Republic of Texas, and was free to settlers.

Fannin County was organized in 1838, and that county then included all the territory of present Collin County. Fort English was the capitol and general headquarters for all the settlers in this part of northeast Texas at the time, and people living there had heard of the fine land lying on the East Fork of the Trinity River, through hunters and trappers. A party was organized at Fort English—later Bonham—to look at the virgin territory.

This party, composed of Daniel Rowlett, Jabez Fitzgerald, Edmund Todd, Pleasant Wilson—for whom Wilson Creek is named, Dr. William E. Throckmorton—

father of James, who later became governor; William R. Garnett, and Littleton Rattan left Fort English the first week in November, 1841, and explored the country as far as present Rowlett Creek.

The men so liked the beautiful country that they returned to Fort English and brought out their families and household goods, intending to make their homes here. With them this time came three additional men and their families. These three men were Garrett Fitzgerald, M.C. Westley and Bluford Clements.

They selected land seven miles north of present McKinney on what became Throckmorton Creek, erected log cabins and built a stockade around them. This, in January, 1842, was the first white settlement of now Collin County.

During the summer of 1842, Benjamin White, Archie White, William Pulliam, Peg Whistler, John M. Kincaid, Joe Wilcox, David Helm, and Joe Harlan came to Throckmorton. In November, John McGarrah, Samuel Young, William Rice, and J.E. Blankenship brought their families and stopped there. The settlement now had a population of about 90 people, old and young. It was Christmas, 1842.

Shortly after the first of the year, 1843, the settlers began spreading out to their claims; Young, who was single, Westley Clements and Peg Whistler and their families located on Honey Creek—then called Hurricane Creek—just above present Roland. Late that year both Whistler and Clements were killed by Comanche Indians, but their families managed to escape back to the Throckmorton settlement.

Joe Wilcox, David Helm and Joe Harlan settled on Wilson Creek, two miles south of present McKinney. Here, on Christmas Day they were attacked by the same band of Comanches that had killed Whistler and Clements, but fought the savages off until nightfall from their log cabin, and then escaped up East Fork to Throckmorton.

John (Jack) McGarrah located three miles northwest of present McKinney with William Rice and family, and built log cabins on their claims. Rice moved, a year later, to his other claim just east of where McKinney now is, and in August his son, Joe, rode out toward Rowlett Creek looking for stock. The boy and a companion were attacked by Comanches and Joe was killed.

In February of that year, while McGarrah, J.H. Wilcox, David Helm, Joe Harlan, Asa Blankenship and William Rice, were completing a building on McGarrah's survey to be used as a store, Dr. Calder of Cedar Springs, now in the city of Dallas, rode up, saying he was on his way to Bailey English's—now Bonham.

He was killed 400 yards north of McGarrah's by 40 Comanches who then attacked the men in the incompleted building. The savages made several attempts to have the men in the cabin to fire so that they could overpower the settlers before they could reload. The 40 or more Indians milled around until noon, but were afraid to come close to the rifles and shotguns protruding from between the logs of the partly-finished house. At nightfall the settlers slipped out down a ravine to Wilson Creek, and made their way to join their families at Throckmorton.

The next year Jeremiah Muncy, his wife and three children, and McBain Jameson, all of whom had located on Rowlett Creek, where Highway 75 now crosses the creek, were killed at dawn, December 31, by a band of Comanches.

Every adult living in Texas during 1835 could claim 4,600 acres if married, and 1,534 if single. This class did not have to even see their claims in order to own the land. There were few of them, but some were famous. For instance: J.C. Neil, who commanded the Texas artillery when Ben Milam stormed San Antonio in 1835, was granted a square mile of land seven miles northeast of present McKinney, and another half section farther north. James Fisher, William Dabbs, Richard H. Lock,

Calvin Boles, Samuel Sloan, Grizzel Kennedy, Carter T. Clifft, William B. Williams and Jonathan Douthitt were all veterans of the Texas Revolution and all owned big land holdings in this county. There were others.

The second class of land claimers were those who came in like the Throckmortons. They could take up about as much land as the first class, but had to live on their claims in order to own the land. This class included most of the settlers who came to the area in 1842 to 1844, and they located, mainly, to the north and west of present McKinney.

The third class were those who were granted land here by the Peters Colony. In August, 1841, President Lamar, of the Republic of Texas, entered into a contract with W.S. Peters and others of Louisville, Kentucky, and Cincinnati, Ohio, to settle at least 600 families on vacant lands in north Texas. This company, called the Texas Emigration and Land Company, secured a great section of territory covering several north Texas counties as they now exist, along Red River and south to Ellis County, west to Wise and including all of present Collin.

The company promised each settler a cabin, musket and ball, and each married person could take up 640 acres, a singe person, 320. By the end of 1845 Peters Colony had brought in 341 families. Peters' contract was ended in 1848, but he was responsible for the rapid settlement of the east and south part of the county. Most of the early settlers of Collin County came from the states of Missouri, Kentucky, Tennessee and Alabama, and all of them, of course had to come overland for at least part of the way in wagons and on horseback, for there were no railroads in this part of the nation at that time.

INDIANS OF COLLIN COUNTY

Ancient Indians inhabited this area as skeletons have been found all over North Texas, but the only Indians here when the first settlers came were a few bands of Tonkawas, Cherokees, Delawares, and Kickapoos. In 1841 the Delawares had a village at the big spring which later became Fitzhugh Mills. A small band of Tonkawas lived in a small village two miles north of McKinney, and the Cherokees and Tonkawas lived together in a town seven miles of present McKinney. These were the Indians seen by the first settlers. None of them were hostile, and the only trouble the settlers encountered from them was thieving by the "Tonks," as the pioneers called the Tonkawas.

The Kickapoos and Tonkawas were more or less native to the area, the Cherokees had migrated here from their native Georgia in 1820. Just where the Delawares came from is lost in obscurity. They were a fine proud race and possibly the most handsome of all American Indians. The Cherokees and Delawares were farming Indians and did not depend on wild game as did the Kickapoos and Tonkawas. They built houses of poles, interlaced with switches and reeds and never used teepees. The main crop was corn, though pumpkins, squash, and melons were grown. Our hominy came from the Cherokees and one of their favorite hominy dishes was "Pashofa." Another was "softy" made from corn ground up with a stone pestle.

The Indians in Collin County all spoke different tongues, but had no trouble talking to each other through use of the sign language.

Seventy years ago there were three locations where one might pick up Indian artifacts, the Delaware village north of McKinney, the Cherokee village southwest of old Squeezepenny (near Indian Creek), and the Fitzhugh Mills site. All the arrow points that I have seen from these sites were of the same flint and the spear heads were of very fine workmanship.

We know from ruins unearthed in making the dams around the county that Indians occupied this area for thousands of years but who these ancient tribes were is not clear. A half mile southwest of the Branch store, an ancient village was unearthed when excavating was done to build the Lavon Dam. The skeletons showed the race to be not more than five feet in height. They were fish and clam eating people as the bits of shells found with the bones. No artifacts were unearthed with them.

Marine fossils abound in all Collin County whiterock creeks. You can pick up fossils of mollusks, fishes and insects dating back a hundred million years. Two insect fossils to be found in the whiterock are ancestors of our present scorpion and the household pest, the cockroach.

In looking for fossils you will find them mostly on the floor or bed of the stream. Some of the fossils are quite large, more than 12 inches across. The ancient sea was full of worm life also and you can find fossil worm cases or tubes. These fossils may be found in any place in the county where the layers of whiterock have been disturbed, whether by a stream cutting downward, or by the various rock pits made when the rocks are hauled away for commercial purposes. They make a nice collection for anyone interested in preserving a part of our past from 60 to 100 million years ago.

CHIEF SPOTTED TAIL
By Capt. Roy F. Hall
(Written for *McKinney Examiner,* whose permission I have in a letter to use.)

Early settlers of Collin County owe a great debt to this old Indian. He kept the plains Indians out of the area.

I have written several times in this column of the Kiowa Indian Chief, Spotted Tail, who aided and protected the early settlers of this county. Spotted Tail was in bad with the U.S. troops. Up in Kansas and Nebraska he gave them some trouble, which led to his taking up his place of abode down here in Texas.

The first we have on the chief was in 1845, when he attended a Fourth of July celebration at old Buckner. He came to the fandango with a few of his sub chiefs and got completely and absolutely drunk, as did several of the settlers. At this time, Spotted Tail and his band of around 200 were encamped on the hills east of the Flats, or Little Elm Valley, between the present towns of Frisco and Prosper, about a half mile south of the latter. In the succeeding years the chief made his fall and winter village in various places in west Collin, from near present Lewisville in Denton County to present Cottage Hill in Collin, but he never pitched camp any farther east than the places named. The Kiowas were prairie Indians and hated the timber land that lay to the eastward.

We have a pretty good description of Spotted Tail. Ed Stiff, who married one of Jack McGarrah's girls, and lived a while at the McGarrah store at old Buckner, said that the chief was a little below medium height for a Kiowa, which would make him around five feet ten inches, as the Comanches and Kiowas were among the tallest men in the world at the time. Comanches, especially, most of whom stood six feet and over.

Spotted Tail had a perfect Indian face, according to other accounts; Roman nose and piercing eyes, long straight black hair which he kept in two braids down his back. His war bonnet had a whole string of feathers. Each feather in a warrior's bonnet, as you may know, stood for an individual deed of bravery performed by the wearer. The war bonnet was worn only on ceremonials and when on the war path. George Henry Herndon said Spotted Tail's string of feathers reached from his forehead over and down to his heels. Too bad we do not have a history of the old chief, other than what we know of him here and from official reports of the U.S. Army, who fought Spotted Tail and other chiefs on the plains of Kansas and Nebraska.

He was a friend of the Kiowa Chief, Yellow Hand, who was killed by Buffalo Bill in a knife duel in the middle of a river. Spotted Tail's band was not large, numbering usually less than 300, counting bucks, squaws and children, but they seemed to be powerful enough to keep the rest of the wild Indians out of Collin County. Spotted Tail came to west Collin in the fall of 1845, so far as we know, hunting buffalo for winter meat. After he took his stance here there were no more Indian massacres in this county.

The chief had three wives, according to Edd Stiff, but not a child. Stiff, as a child, spent many days in the Indian village and came to know many of the braves by name. Too bad no record was kept of all this, but the fact is that nobody thought much of an Indian in those days, and many people distrusted all Indians whatsoever, including Spotted Tail's band. So far as known, this tribe did no harm here at all, save beg around the trading post run by Jack McGarrah.

McGarrah said that Spotted Tail would sit around at the store all day long waiting for somebody to give him a drink of whiskey. There used to be a part Cherokee Indian here who knew Spotted Tail before the first white man came to this section. The Cherokee's name was Frank House—translated into English, and old Frank did not think too highly of Spotted Tail. Frank, being part Cherokee, would work, something no wild Indian ever did. He didn't think much either, of Spotted Tail's fondness for roasted dog.

The Cherokees, as you possibly know, were one of the Five Civilized tribes of Indians brought from Georgia and Alabama in 1832 and settled on reservations in the then Indian Territory, now Oklahoma. The Cherokees tended fields and built houses of sorts, but anyway they raised their own food mostly, and did not depend totally on the chase as did the plains Indians. Old Frank could use fairly good English; Spotted Tail had command of only a dozen words or so.

Spotted Tail lived around the settlements until 1873, when smallpox got him and he lies in the old Buckner graveyard, three miles west on Highway 24. His services were especially valuable to the colonists during the Civil War, 1861-65. The war took almost all the able-bodied men of the county, leaving the very old and the very young to defend settlements against Indian raids. Indians raided up and down from Red River through Denton County to the south, but Spotted Tail kept them out of Collin.

In the years following the war Spotted Tail became a fixture in McKinney, where he could be seen almost every day, begging a drink at a saloon here and there. He generally got his drinks, too. Everybody remembered how he saved the early settlements and old Spotted Tail was called "The Big Drunk." He would beg a quart of whiskey, take a stiff drink and make for Ford's livery stable and wagon yard, where the present Ford automobile house is now on East Louisiana. It just happens that the names are the same.

Andy Ford would have a stall cleared out, fresh hay spread down and the old chief would go in and get soused. Ford would not allow anybody to bother the Indian, and he would often sleep a whole day and night. Suddenly, he would be gone. He found that he could get about the same results from drinking bay rum, and he begged bottles of that. Bay rum, in those days, did not have the bitter deterrent in it that it has now and many drunkards used it when they could not get the real stuff.

Another favorite drink of Spotted Tail's was paregoric. G.A. Foote, who operated the first drug store in McKinney where the McKinney Drug is now, said that he would estimate that the old Indian consumed enough free paregoric from his store to float the courthouse. Despite all his later-day failings, I think the old chief deserves a monument, and I am going to try to bum one from the State Historical Committee. Failing in this, maybe we can contribute enough among ourselves to place a marker for him, maybe on the courthouse lawn.

In 1854 the State of Texas established an Indian reservation up near Camp Cooper on the Brazos and all wild Indians were herded onto it. James W. Throckmorton interceded however, and Spotted Tail and his band were allowed to remain in west Collin for a while. A few years later the reservation Indians were moved to the Indian Territory and most of the Kiowas under Spotted Tail went with them voluntarily. This was due to the fact that the Indians had found that they were to be fed by Uncle Sam and would not have to work, even to hunt for their food.

Spotted Tail though, with his wives and a few others stayed on Sherman's Prairie for years. The others drifted away to the Indian Territory reserves, but Spotted Tail stayed. It was during this period that the old Kiowa gave his best service to the settlers. He had not over a score in his camp, but the wild Indians never attempted to pass him and come into Collin County. Don't know why. Some Indian agreement, I suppose.

After the Civil War, Spotted Tail got an old Federal Army coat somehow, and that was his principal raiment for years. Most of the time he would wear the blue coat with brass buttons, and have on no trousers at all, just a gee string and moccasins. He wore this army coat until it actually got so filthy and stiff that it would crackle when moved. It finally fell to pieces, but so far as anybody knew, Spotted Tail never once removed it from his back until it was worn completely out.

His band, before the Civil War, was armed with guns, mostly U.S. Army muskets of the Harper Ferry model. Frank House said they got the firearms in combat with U.S. Troops on the plains. All his bucks were mounted, some had horses with the Army Quartermaster brand on them, and many had army saddles. Altogether, his band had about 100 horses, good and bad, and fifteen or twenty army muskets. The rest were armed with spears and bows and arrows. These were taken away by the state when Indians were removed to the Indian Territory, which accounts for Spotted Tail's losing most of his tribe. They were allowed to retain their bows and arrows, but not firearms.

Buffalo had disappeared from the west part of the county by the time of the Civil War, and deer could not be chased down on horseback like a buffalo, so Spotted Tail's band were soon near starvation and had to join the other Indians in the Indian Territory. But the old chief himself decided to pitch his fortunes with the settlers, which he did by begging almost altogether. And too, the U.S. Government had a price on the old fellow's head, and if he went back to the reservations he would probably have been brought to account for some of the things he did on the Republican River in Kansas, and on the Platte in Nebraska. Texans, especially Throckmorton, saw to it that he was not molested here.

After the Civil War, when Throckmorton was elected Governor of Texas, Capt. Tom Scott, of Melissa, who had been the Confederate Indian agent in the Indian

Territory, got permission from the Indian agency of the U.S. to allow Spotted Tail's band to pay Throckmorton a visit. In full war regalia about 60 braves came down from across Red River, joined Spotted Tail near Rhea's Mill and rode into McKinney.

From his home on the branch near the old Thompson place, Captain Tuck Hill met the band and led them into town. Even with Captain Hill heading the calvacade, a great deal of excitement was created. No untoward incident marred the occasion however, and the Indians assembled in the front yard of the Throckmorton home, which was south across the street from the present Memorial Library.

Throckmorton knew they were coming and had a banquet spread for them. Most of the prominent people of the county were there, and Spotted Tail delivered a long, eloquent speech, which, as it happened, nobody could understand, as it was in the Kiowa language. This was Spotted Tail's last public appearance, unless his appearances at the various saloons around town could be so classified.

THIS IS ONE of the last remaining Peter's Colony log cabins in all Collin County. It seems incredible to us that big families grew up in these little one room cabins.

THIS OLD HOUSE was built by Samuel Bogard in Woodlawn Community. Mr. Bogard was the first elected Representative from the county to the Republic of Texas. This house became a freight stop for the big wagons that hauled freight from East Texas. Here they found food, water and rest.

THIS PIONEER DWELLING of one of Collin County's famous citizens is located in Finch Park in Southwest McKinney. It is not typical of the period for most of the people had log cabins. This house was one of the first ones built here from lumber freighted in from Jefferson. It was completed in 1854. Collin McKinney was one of the signers of the Texas Declaration of Independence. Both Collin County and the County set of McKinney are named for him.

3

Farming
and
Free Land

CHAPTER III

Early Settlers

The reason for the influx of the early settlers into what is now Collin County was due to several conditions existing in this section, and in the states from which they emigrated. The main reason was free land. In the states of Kentucky, Missouri, Tennessee, Georgia and Alabama, from which most of the first settlers came, good free land had all been taken up, and was selling for five to twenty dollars an acre. Some of the early settlers had been land owners before emigrating, but most of them had been tenants, owning only a wagon and team, a few farming tools and household supplies. To all these pioneers, the ownership of a square mile of virgin land in the new country was attractive enough to outweigh the hardships incidental to the long journey in covered wagons, and the danger of Indian attacks after they arrived on the frontier.

A great majority of the first settlers came into Texas by way of the ferry at Lane's Port, later Harris' Ferry in the northeast corner of Red River County, then through Clarksville, Bonham, then called Fort English, and to present Collin County. After 1845 many came down through the Indian Territory, crossing Red River north of present Denison at Colbert's Ferry. A few, coming from Missouri, turned west in the Indian Territory and entered Texas at Preston, ten miles upriver from Colbert's Ferry. Those coming from Alabama, Mississippi and Georgia came in by way of Shreveport, and some through Texarkana.

Those arriving in the area with the first settlers, and within a year or two thereafter, merely stepped off their land, drove stakes down at the corners and attached their names to them. This was called, "Staking out" a claim. Within a reasonable length of time, a year or so, these claims had to be registered at the General Land office in Austin, Texas, or with the Peters Colony headquarters near present Farmer's Branch in now northern Dallas County. A small amount was charged for this "filing," usually less than ten cents an acre, in most cases less than five cents.

In some cases a settler, through ignorance of the land laws, would locate a block of land, build a cabin and call it home, without registering his claim. Later, when he was informed of the filing requirements, he would register. Some refused to do so and were known as "Squatters." There were few of them in this section, and all lost their claims due to others filing for it.

A few of the early settlers became discouraged and returned home, selling their claims for a few dollars, or even abandoning it altogether. Dr. Tony Hunn, on an exploring trip to this section in 1845 to 1848, acquired 11,000 acres of land through buying up these claims. Dr. Hunn later abandoned this land himself, saying it was not worth the $22.00 tax due on it. His land lay down on both sides of east Fork, southeast of present McKinney.

Of course this sort of "staking" claims would include many errors as to boundaries, and when George White, a surveyor from New York, came to Buckner in 1847, he was appointed county surveyor to permanently locate all claim lines. White found plenty to keep him busy for ten years. While most of the claimers had run their boundaries north and south, he discovered many running any which way. White re-located them all.

Land taken up by a settler was called a "headright," which was different in name only from the "grants" given the same kind of settlers for service he had rendered the Republic of Texas during the War of Independence of 1835-36. A headrighter had to live on his land to own it; a grantor did not.

Up to the year 1845 immigration into this section of Texas was slow, and was confined mostly to people who lived around Fort English, Pin Hook—now Paris, and northeast Texas. A few also came into this present county from Arkansas. By the end of the year, 1844, the population of present Collin County numbered about 200, including men, women and children.

But in the year, 1845, however, the situation changed rapidly, and due, mainly, to the activities of the Peters Colony promoters. They blanketed the states east of the Missisippi River with circulars, describing the rich, fertile land on the headwaters of the Trinity River, setting forth that it was free and that the Peters Colony would build a log cabin for each family, and furnish a gun and ammunition for each settler's household. All the claimer had to do was to get to the land and stake it out. Before the end of that year 500 families were on the way to present Collin County from Missouri, Kentucky, Tennessee and farther north.

By June, 1845, 114 covered wagons had arrived at Buckner and at Throckmorton, where they camped while the men spread out to locate a land claim. Please remember that this present county was, at that time, a part of Fannin County, and, when Collin County was organized the next year it contained only 886 square miles, as many of these settlers took up a square mile—some two, it can readily be seen that free land was soon to be a thing of the past.

Toward the close of the year 1845, free land ran out in present Collin County, and those locating thereafter had to purchase land from a dissatisfied headrighter, usually at about a dollar an acre, or take over a headright from an original settler who was returning to "the old states" due to homesickness or other reasons. This last was called a "quitclaim deed," so called because the first headrighter transferred the deed to someone else without cost. On the General Land Office map, showing the original headrights of Collin County, many of these who got their land through quitclaims are shown as original settlers. They are, but they purchased their claim, or else it was transferred to them after being located by another party.

Below is a partial list of those who got their land free, or who purchased it at a very low figure, up to 1845. Many of those named will be quickly recognized as having had a definite influence on the later development of the county. The list follows, together with the general location of the pioneer's headright:

Wm. E. Throckmorton	Throckmorton
James W. Throckmorton	Throckmorton
Daniel Rowlett	Altoga
Pleasant Wilson	Chambersville
Bluford Clements	Northeast of McKinney
Benjamin White	Weston
S.M. Pulliam	Rowlett
John Kincaid	West of Anna
Joe Wilcox	Rowlett
David Helm	Weston
John McGarrah	Buckner

William E. Throckmorton	1842	Throckmorton
James W. Throckmorton	1842	Throckmorton
Daniel Rowlett	1842	Altoga
Pleasant Wilson	1842	Chambersville
Bluford Clements	1842	Clements Creek
M.C. Westley	1842	Roland
Benjamin White	1842	Weston
Marshall Pulliam	1842	Rowlett
John M. Kincaid	1842	Anna
Joe Wilcox	1842	Rowlett
David Helm	1842	Weston
John (Jack) McGarrah	1842	Buckner
Peg Whistler	1842	Roland
Samuel Young	1842	Lebanon
William Rice	1842	Bloomdale
J.E. Blankenship	1842	Pike
Archie White	1842	Went back, 1843
Joe Harlan	1842	Went back, 1844

The above list is complete. It contains all the white males in present Collin County up to the end of 1842, over 18 years of age, most of whom were married and had brought their families with them. Below are the names of the most influential settlers immigrating later, not all of whom headrighted land.

Tola Dunn	1843	North of McKinney
Jeremiah Muncy	1843	Rowlett Creek
McBain Jameson	1843	Rowlett Creek
King Custer	1843	Buckner
George Wash Ford	1843	Buckner
Henry O. Hedgecoxe	1843	Rowlett
Littleton Rattan	1843	Throckmorton
John Wells	1843	Throckmorton
George A. Wilson	1843	Clements Creek
James M. McReynolds	1843	Foote
Alfred Chandler	1843	Buckner
Asa Blankenship	1843	Pike
William Culwell	1843	Cottage Hill
William Davis	1843	McKinney
Thomas Rattan	1844	Throckmorton
Leonard Searcy	1844	Foote
Solomon Fitzhugh	1844	Plano
John Coffman	1844	Anna
Hogan Witt	1844	Allen
David Melton	1844	Rowlett
William G. McKinney	1844	Van Alstyne
Ashley McKinney	1844	Van Alstyne
Samuel Bogart	1845	Clements Creek
William Snider	1845	Forest Grove
Joseph Russell	1845	Plano
Jeremiah Horn	1845	Walnut Grove
Lindsey L. Lewis	1845	Melissa

John Westley Kirby	1845	Forest Grove
Comfort A. McMillen	1845	Murphy
John Fitzhugh	1845	Fitzhugh Mills
Gerald A. Foote	1845	Buckner
Benjamin Baccus	1845	Lebanon
Charles Rector	1845	Frisco
William Snider	1845	Forest Grove
Joseph Russell	1845	Plano
Jeremiah Horn	1845	Walnut Grove
Lindsey L. Lewis	1845	Melissa
John W. Kirby	1845	Forest Grove
Comfort A. McMillen	1845	Murphy
John Fitzhugh	1845	Fitzhugh Mills
George Fitzhugh	1845	Forest Grove
Gabriel Fitzhugh	1845	Forest Grove
James M. Feland	1845	West of McKinney
Gerald A. Foote	1845	Buckner
Benjamin Baccus	1845	Lebanon
Charles Rector	1845	West Collin
Henry H. Tucker	1845	Bloomdale
Godfrey S. Baccus	1845	Lebanon
Joel F. Stewart	1845	North of McKinney
Jesse Stiff	1845	Northeast of McKinney
P.F. Kindle	1845	Buckner
James M. Graves	1845	Throckmorton
James Maxwell	1845	Murphy
Lewis Marshall	1845	Murphy
Lanson Clark	1845	Southwest Collin
Meredith Ashlock	1845	Foote
Mrs. Ann Hurt	1845	Buckner
John D. Brown	1845	Cottage Hill
Joseph Russell	1845	Plano
J.P. Dumas	1845	Fitzhugh Mills
Collin McKinney	1846	Van Alstyne
Joseph B. Wilmeth	1846	North of McKinney

In filing, or registering for his claim the settler did not always do so in his own name. There were several instances in which the name of his wife was used, and often the name of the eldest son. Many times too, the land claimer neglected to file with Peters Colony headquarters for several years after he had actually located and built a cabin, leading to confusion in the land records. Those named above, though, lived in present Collin County at the end of 1845.

There were many more living here who did not take up land; deeming it as practically worthless. Their names are not included in the above list. Note that most of the land claimers of the period took up land in the western edge of the area. The reason, of course, was the big forests which covered most of the eastern and southern part of present Collin County. The huge trees presented a problem the settlers did not care to cope with, while the prairies were ready for the plow.

Below are the names of most of those settlers who came in during 1846, and who contributed most toward the development of the county. Unlike the first, this list is not complete, or is it intended to be. Only the leading settlers in a particular locality are included, as the list would be too long to tabulate here. Free land played out this year, and many of those named secured their land by quitclaims, or, as in some cases, by preemption; wherein the original claimant abandoned his land, and the later settler located on it.

While the settlers of 1846 and for a few years thereafter, were not the true pioneers, as were those who came before that year, they must be, in every sense, classified as first settlers.

John Beverly	Plano
James Ledbetter	Weston
John S. Huffman	Rowlett
Mrs. Ann S. Hurt	Forest Grove
George Fitzhugh	Forest Grove
Gaberiel Fitzhugh	Forest Grove
John M. McKinney	Forest Grove
Joseph Russell	Plano
Sam P. Brown	Rowlett
John D. Brown	Rowlett
Sam P. Brown	Honey Creek
William A. Brown	Honey Creek
William C. Quigley	Honey Creek
Robert H. Brown	Honey Creek
Elisha Chambers	Rhea Mills
Collin McKinney	Van Alstyne
Sol Fitzhugh	Plano
Hugh Thompson	Lebanon
Garland R. Martin	Lebanon

THE PETER'S COLONY

Peter's Colony was instrumental in bringing many settlers to this county and others around us. The organization was called Peter's Colony, but was officially the Texas Emigration and Land Company. It came into being when the Republic of Texas, through its Legislature, authorized the president of Texas to contract with W.C. Peters and others of Cincinnati and St. Louis for the settlement of certain public lands of the Republic. The contract was awarded by Pres. Lamar in August 1841 with Peters agreeing to settle 600 families on the land set aside for the Colony. The company agreed to give each family a section of land—640 acres—if married and half as much if a single man. They were also to build cabins for the settlers, furnish them guns and ammunition, and certain other supplies.

Collin County was then only a part of Fannin County. The outskirts of the grant started over on Mineral Creek in Fannin County, south to the South border of present Collin County, and west 22 miles, then north to Red River, then down that river to the starting point. This was the first grant. This did not include present McKinney. The second grant was made in November 1841 and took in all of Collin

County, Dallas County, Hunt and Denton, as well as parts of other counties. A third grant was given the company in January 1843 which extended the boundaries as far as Gainsville. McKinney was now pretty close to the center of Peter's Colony holdings.

By 1843 the settlers were a disappointed lot. They claimed the company had not provided all that was promised and they felt the land was too slow in settling. Up until 1844 Peters had brought in 197 families, 42 of them in Collin County. By the middle of 1848 over 1,400 families had been settled in the grant, over 300 of them in the Collin County area, about 2,000 cabins had been built, 1,900 rifles and muskets had been furnished the settlers, 150,000 rounds of ammunition had been given them. The Peter's Colony reserved every other section of land for themselves and the vacant land was filling up by settlers who did not bother to pay the $30 filing fee so were not legally a part of the Colony. Peter's Colony did not have the legal right to remove the squatters and could not have anyway for they only had one agent for the entire area, Henry Hedgecoxe, whose headquarters were then in Denton County.

In 1844, when it was seen that Texas was going to unite with the United States, a Constitutional Convention was called in Austin to draft a State Constitution. Collin County area was represented by James W. Throckmorton, who was appointed along with others to look into the affairs of the Peter's Colony.

The Texas Legislature stepped into the picture, and proceeded to mix things up thoroughly. By an act of law they agreed to give each settler who had arrived before July 1, 1848 the section of land and allowed them to settle on the land they had already given to the Peter's Colony! This aroused such a storm of protest that in January 1850 the Legislature again stepped in and passed an act that read in part: "Certificates of ownership issued by the commissioner of Peter's Colony may be located on any land within the limites of the colony not otherwise appropriated." Now believing that the new law authorized them to do so, settlers settled on any land that appeared to be vacant, whether government land or that given to Peter's Colony.

Peters' contract expired in 1848 and in spite of all the trials and errors, the settlement of Collin County was now assured.

THE HEDGECOXE WAR

The Hedgecoxe War was a war in name only, but it was quite a disturbance in the Peter's Colony. In March of 1841, William S. Peters, head of the newly organized Texian Emigration and Land Co. of Louisville, Kentucky, contracted to settle 600 families in an area covered by 18 counties in North Texas.

Field headquarters of the land company were established at Farmers Branch in 1845, while Peters stayed in Louisville and continued to distribute literature about the free land in Texas. Henry O. Hedgecoxe was the agent for the Peter's Colony in Texas and his small cabin was called Stewardsville. During the spring of 1845 more than 1000 came from the old states and settled around McKinney and around Farmer's Branch, and in the village of Dallas.

From the first there was trouble between the colonists and those in charge at Stewardsville. Instead of the comfortable houses they had expected, Hedgecoxe had had one room log cabins built. If the people had taken the trouble to read their contracts, they would have seen that this is exactly what they were supposed to get. It also irked the settlers that they had to pay to have their own land surveyed and as time went on they were so angered by this that they elected a delegate to go to Bonham and get their contracts with the Colony nullified. Nothing ever came of this and the dissatisfaction grew.

In 1845 an armed band of about 40 men rode out of Dallas bound for Stewardsville to expell Hedgecoxe and take over the Peter's Colony records. But Hedgecoxe was warned of their intention so he promptly took flight with all the records. The lynchers had to return empty-handed to Dallas and Hedgecoxe established a new headquarters seven miles southwest of McKinney.

The trouble really went much deeper than the reasons given. Pres. Sam Houston favored the Peter's Colony people because Peters had aided Texas in many ways during its fight for independence. Houston was trying to return the favor. In 1849 the Peter's surveyors were in this area surveying the land and ordering the settlers to move to other locations. These earliest settlers wanted no part of the Peter's Colony land and decided to resort to armed resistance.

With the feeling at fever heat, they met in Dallas and sent a delegation to go to Hedgecoxe and demand to see the records. The committee was met by several armed surveyors, and the settlers were forced to go back to Dallas with mission not accomplished. In Dallas, on the morning of July 16, 1852, about 100 armed men gathered on the banks of the Trinity River and elected John G. Good to command them in a march on Hedgecoxe headquarters and take over the records. A mounted courier had been dispatched to McKinney the night before, asking that a Collin County posse join the Dallas force south of Hedgecoxe's at noon on the next day.

Not much was done in McKinney since the messenger arrived after midnight and when J.M. McReynolds, Robert Fitzhugh, Alf Johnson and others were gathering a company on the morning of the 16th, another messenger arrived from Dallas and said that the Dallas posse led by John M. Crockett would march to McKinney and all would go together and take over the headquarters. (Crockett later became Lt. Governor of Texas in 1861.)

Crockett's company arrived in McKinney at 2 p.m. and was joined by the McKinney company led by Judge Robert Fitzhugh, in all about 50 armed men. They met at Whitley's Saloon (where Penny's store now stands) and had several rounds of drinks before going into battle. In the meantime, J.W. Throckmorton (later Gov. of Texas) heard of the plans, and wishing to avoid needless bloodshed, sent a mounted man to warn Hedgecoxe. The posse headed out at 4:30 in the afternoon. They took the new Alton Road, crossed Wilson Creek at the ford and turned south on the high ground, heading for Hedgecoxe's headquarters. This building stood just west of the Dallas road near Rowlett Creek on the present Foncine Road. Warned by Throckmorton's messenger, Hedgecoxe had hidden all the records in a corn field just north of his building, and hid there himself. Fitzhugh's company deployed in the corn field and Crockett led his men south and came up through the trees along Rowlett Creek. At the first shot from Crockett's gun, both companies charged the building, yelling. They crashed in, front and rear, shotguns, rifles, and pistols in readiness.

The shack was empty. A few pieces of worthless paper lay on the floor, but no records, and no Henry Hedgecoxe. The war party returned to McKinney. All the time, Hedgecoxe lay in the corn field with the records, scarcely 200 yards from the house.

That night Hedgecoxe bought a horse and wagon from George Herndon, loaded the records in it, and took the Buckner-Bonham Road and pulled out. He went to Shreveport, Louisiana without any trouble and once there, he shipped the records to St. Louis and came back to Dallas. And so ended the so-called Hedgecoxe War, a war in which not a shot was fired in anger and no person injured. But it had aftermaths. The records were lost, apparently, forever. Nothing much has been found of them since. As these records contained all the proof the settlers had of ownership of the land many were left with no proof at all. Most settlers were affected. Only the ones who settled here before Peter's Colony days were not affected.

The affairs of the Peter's Colony were so muddled that Throckmorton went to Austin and prevailed upon Houston to untangle the mess. This he did. He got the Peter's Colony people to relinquish their claim on the land here in exchange for land in another area of Texas. The Legislature ended the matter Feb. 4, 1853 by granting titles to the colonists who had lost their deeds when the records dispapeared. This is why many land deeds read from 1843 to 1852. This is why, too, that some of your forefathers came here earlier than you might suppose.

COLLIN COUNTY'S FIRST SOLDIERS

THE BUCKNER VOLUNTEERS

On July 4, 1846, Ft. Buckner was the scene of a picnic that drew all the settlers in the vicinity. Andrew Stapp, who lived at Buckner, used the gathering to enlist Collin County's first soldiers.

Mounting a stump, Stapp called the meeting to order and said, "Men of Collin County, we are now a part of the great state of Texas, and Texas is at war. The United States is at war with Mexico and needs soldiers. I am authorized by the governor of the state to raise a company of volunteers here and now to march across the Rio Grande River. I want men, real men, to come into the store and put your names down as the first soldiers Collin County ever had. Who will be first?"

Stapp got his men. They knew all about it beforehand and came prepared to join up. In an hour, 60 men had signed and many more were turned away. Many now living in Collin County will recognize the name of an ancestor in this group of pioneer soldiers.

> Captain Andrew Stapp, age 44 years.
> Thomas J. McDonald, Lt., age 30.
> Thomas A. Wilson, 2nd Lt., age 26.
> John Fitzhugh, 1st Sgt., age 50.
> Henry H. Turner, 2nd. Sgt., age 30.
> Langdon C. Searcy, 3rd Sgt., age 31.
> William C. Lewis, 4th Sgt., age 30.
> Martin Langston, 1st Corporal, age 37.
> James Lampkins, 2nd Corporal, age 24.
> John Myrick, 3rd Corporal, age 24.
> Larkin McCarty, 4th Corporal, age 33.

> Privates: Jonathan Allen, age 45.
> Ellis Alexander, age 24.
> William Boiles, age 20.
> Robert H. Brown, age 20.
> John Bartum, age 28.

William C. Brown, age 40.
Edward Bradley, age 40.
John Crutchfield, age 23.
Dixon Crutchfield, age 20.
Barnett Collier, age 25.
John Clay, age 20.
Alfred Chandler, age 26.
Joshua Dillingham, age 27.
Daniel J. Franklin, age 26.
S.W. Forman, age 26.
James M. Graves, age 27.
John Horn, age 24.
Richard Knight, age 24.
George F. Lucas, age 30.
James Lovelady, age 33.
Lindsey D. Lewis, age 29.
Peter Lucas, age 36.
John J. Mounts, age 26.
Benjamin McNeal, age 22.
George McNeal, age 24.
James McReynolds, age 28.
Josiah Nichols, age 23.
C.L. O'Brien, age 26.

Abner C. Perkins, age 26.
Marshall M. Pulliam, age 28.
Horace R. Pinnel, age 24.
Samuel L. Prichitt, age 25, the bugler.
Thomas Phillips, age 29.
Pascal H. Rice, age 27.
William Rice, age 40.
John Roberts, age 30.
Charles Rice, age 19.
W. Richman, age 29.
Christopher Searcy, age 33.
Joseph R. State, age 40.
John Scott, age 22.
James Stiff, age 21.
Jesse Stiff, age 40.
E.F. Springer, age 28.
M.L. Stinton, age 26.
Malachi Tucker, age 25.
A.H. Tucker, age 25.
Fontaine H. Vance, age 26.
William Wilson, age 35.
Coleman White, age 25.

Many of these volunteers were married and some of them were big land owners in the county. Fourteen of them failed to return from the war, and for these 14 we hope to erect a monument at Buckner, a marker designating them not only as pioneers but as the first of thousands of soldiers Collin County was to give in later years to the cause of liberty and justice. In this list of Stapp's men are to be found the names of men who later became leaders in the county and whose descendents now compose a great cross-section of the county's population.

The year 1849 marked the beginning of records being kept relative to land values and tax records. In 1848 George W. Barnett, agent for the A.M. Alexander Co., rendered $3,000. in merchandise. The only other merchandise rendered was $300. by J.M. Bounds and $1,000 by John Lovejoy, agent for J. Dillingham. Slaves were valued at $360. on the average. Total tax collections were $718.83 for 1848.

Renditions for 1849 were:

134,117 acres of land valued at $90,000. Negro slaves, 107 in number valued at $38,300. Horses and Mules, 365 in number, valued at $19,680. 681 cows were rendered at $5,656. Merchandise in stores, $4,300.

Land rendition was about 68 cents per acre. A list of the largest land owners in 1849 follows.

Name	Acres
Wm. H. Pulliam	6,814
M.R. Roberts	4,776
Alfred Johnson	3,756
John C. Bates	3,100
Joe Fisher	2,827
Wm. C. McKinney	2,308

B.H. Martin	2,121
Jonathan Allen	1,920
R. Fitzhugh	1,920
Gallatin Searcy	1,796
William Davis	1,720
Peter Fisher	1,680
Joseph Wilcox	1,462
John McGarrah	1,420

McKINNEY CROWD, 1907.

THE CENTER BUILDING was once the toughest place in Collin County. All three buildings were saloons and quite notorious, but the center one was the best known and was called the Rock Front Saloon. Since they were on East Virginia Street near the railroad they attracted their trade from the railroad and the people coming in by means of them. This saloon was the favorite hang-out for the James Boys and their friends when they came to McKinney to let things cool off up north.

THE ISAAC GRAVES home, marked by a medallion.

THIS OLD LIVERY STABLE was operated by Coffey and Kendell right after the Civil War and still stands, although the coming of the automobile put it and other Livery Stables out of business. Here Frank James stabled his horses. (McKinney)

THE LITTLE HOUSE still on the Graves Ranch where Steve Hall took his bride.

FRANK JAMES, past 70 years, and his favorite horse, a pacer named Dan.

4

Life
And
Customs
of the First Settlers

CHAPTER IV

Life And Customs Of The First Settlers

Among the early settlers in this county, horses, mules and vehicles were almost worth their weight in gold. Practically all the pioneers brought their wagons and teams with them, but not quite all. Some took the steamboat route down the Mississippi, up Red River to Jefferson in east Texas and then overland the best way they could find. Almost all those coming from Missouri, Tennessee, Alabama and Georgia came in wagons driving horses.

Few made the journey in ox wagons. Mostly they came in trains made up of several wagons and carriages, and oxen would have been too slow to keep up with them. There generally were no roads from the "old states," and the travelers had to wind across country, seeking the most level ground and a route to avoid as many large rivers as possible.

Those early wagons were practically all of one type: high wheels, with steel tires an inch and a half in width, and all wagons were covered with a wagon sheet. Two horses or mules hauled the wagon, which was called the "Kentucky wagon," due to its being built in that state. This was the same wagon used here until the coming of automobiles and trucks. The "Conestoga" wagon you have read about in stories, never came to this section. It was a huge vehicle, pulled by several teams, and had wide tires to travel on the soft ground of the northern and western states.

Many carriages were brought along. These were not the type of carriages popular here around 1900, being big and strongly built, and called, due to their being slung on leather straps instead of springs, "Rockaways." They were used by the settlers to haul the women and children, thus making room in the main wagon for household goods and farming tools. Very little food was carried by the travelers. They depended on their firearms for game.

Oxen were used to an extent after the colonists arrived, but mostly for farming purposes. The people did not like to ride behind an animal so slow. Travel about the area, unless a heavy load was to be transported, was done on horseback. Not that this was best, but because there were no roads.

Nobody thought of trying to clear off the heavy forests for growing crops. In fact, up until 1849 there practically was no cultivating of the soil done in the county. People lived as the Indians had lived; on wild fruit and game. The first attempt at crop growing was in 1846, when J.B. Wilmeth and his sons ploughed up the prairie on top of the high hill a mile west of the Throckmorton stockade, and planted twenty acres to wheat.

They made a good yield, but owing to the difficulty of having it ground into flour, most of it was distributed among the settlers to be eaten whole. In some cases a tree was cut off level near the ground, the top hollowed out with fire, and wheat and corn placed in the depression and pounded to powder with a wooden pestle. The nearest grist mill was at Bonham, but the settlers preferred doing without meal rather than to attempt the 40-mile journey through the wilderness.

In 1848, however, John L. Lovejoy got in a small supply of hand-operated steel mills, somewhat like a coffee grinder, and sold them to the pioneers. This helped a lot. The people ground their own corn, sifted out the finer parts for meal and used the rest as hominy. Flour was practically unknown until after 1850.

I have a door leading upstairs, rescued when the J.B. Wilmeth home was razed. It was painted with paint made by boiling bear grease, walnut chips and Bois d'arc. The color is still good, though 120 or more years old.

Bear grease was used for shortening, and it was excellent. Bear meat was salted down and used as bacon, and when this was fried they took the grease, crumbled cornbread in it and put in water and made a fried dish called "Poor Doo." Coffee could not be obtained. Many a meal was eaten with only cornbread and coffee made from corn meal.

Pumpkins and honey, copied from the Indians, made up a great part of the settlers' diet. The pumpkins were stewed until done, removed from the rind, meal added and the whole worked up into a dough. This was baked in small, thin cakes called pumpkin bread.

Some settlers brought kitchen utensils with them, but most used gourds for dishes. One particular gourd, called "Fat Gourd" would hold almost a half bushel. Another, known as the "Spanish Gourd" was large at both ends and small in the middle. These were used like canteens are now used, and could be easily carried on horseback with a thong fastened to the middle. The settlers milked their cows in gourds, drank water from them and used pieces cut from the Fat Gourd as dishes.

Most everyone dressed alike: home-made dresses, woven on the few looms some had hauled out from the old homes, homemade hats, shoes and skirts. Few wore coats, and those few had brought the garment to this area with them.

Dresses were mostly of wool until after 1850, when cotton was grown for weaving. Many had brought sheep with them, driving them behind the wagons, and almost everybody owned a small flock within a few years after Throckmorton was established. All women knew how to card and spin, as they had been taught this from childhood. When cotton was raised, the burden was eased a little, so far as wearing woolen clothing in summer was concerned. But the cotton lint had to be picked from the seed by hand as there were no gins anywhere in those days.

The cotton and wool was woven on the few looms in the county, and dyeing was rather easy. Walnut and bois d' arc chips were boiled for dyeing the men's clothing, and settlers grew their own indigo for the women's dresses. Indigo, of course, is a deep blue, and bois d' arc chips boiled with the cloth gave them a dark yellow. These were the only colors sported by the pioneer women of Collin County for ten years after the first settlement.

Straw, mostly prairie hay, was pleated and woven for hats in summer, while old jeans were worked over for winter head covering. Ropes and thongs were made of strips of dear hide, often pleated. Most shoes were homemade, usually from deer hide with the raw side outward, which custom gave us the name "rawhide."

Furniture consisted of a bedstead, usually one, no matter how large the family, and it had one leg, its other supports being two walls of the room. The bedstead was also homemade, and the support for the mattress was rawhide strung back and forth across the rails. This mattress was either made of corn shucks or prairie hay, more commonly of shucks. Chairs were mostly of big wheels sawed off the end of a log, with pegs for legs. Tables were made from big logs, split into thin slabs and fastened together with wooden pegs.

There were no stoves in this county until after the Civil War of 1861-65; all cooking being done on an open fire outside in summer, and in the fireplace in winter.

Every log cabin had a fireplace, usually built of the white limestone in the vicinity. Some, though, were constructed of short logs stacked up like a pig pen with the open places filled with clay or other mud.

On coming to the new country, each housewife had seen to it that a skillet was brought along. Most also brought a deep pot, holding a gallon or more, to boil meat and stews while hanging from a pothook over the fire in the fireplace. Fire was kept going at all times. In winter in the fireplace; in the summer outside, usually by igniting a big log near the cabin. Fire once lost had to be borrowed from a neighbor.

The houses of the first settlers were almost all alike. They were constructed of logs ten to fourteen feet in length, hewn down square with an adze and a broadaxe. The adze resembled a grubbing hoe and the broadaxe looked like an ordinary axe, except that it was twice as broad. Both were kept as sharp as razors.

The squared logs were notched at the ends and dovetailed into each other so that very little chinking had to be done to make them practically airtight. Two of these square rooms were erected six to ten feet from each other, and the roof between them another room. Doors and windows were sawed out, usually one on each side of the room, and rawhide stretched over them as doors. Some cabins had wooden doors made of slabs, but not many.

Roofs were made of four-feet long shingles split from a sawed-off log of oak. Red or black oak was mostly used, as they split easily. A tool called the fro was used for this. It had a blunt splitting edge and an upright handle to hold to while the instrument was driven into the end of the log, splitting off a one-inch slab called a "shake." Shakes were from three to ten inches in width, and were held on the roof poles by other poles reaching across the roof on each row of shakes.

The better cabins were floored with "puncheons," a log split and smoothed with an adze. They were not fastened down, but placed firmly on the straight logs used as sills. Most of the cabins had natural earth floors, which were, in many cases, far better than a puncheon floor. There were log cabins of the pioneers still in use in this county until around 1900. Many are still in use, but have been sealed in by building over them so that they became a part of a re-modeled house.

During the first days of the settlements, water was obtained altogether from springs, of which there were many in this county. Most of the log cabins were erected near a spring in order to avoid having to carry water long distances for household uses. The spring was the life blood of the early settler. Not only did the family use its water for drinking and cooking, but it was also used for the family washing, bathing, cooling milk and to water livestock. Trees always grew around a spring, making it an ideal place for the family gatherings that were so popular with the early settlers. Many were famous, as Shirley Springs, Liberty Spring—now Roland, Hart Spring, Spring Hill, Throckmorton Spring, Walnut Springs, Spanish Spring and others.

But as the county gained in population, a time came when there were not enough springs to go around. The people followed the custom, then, that they had used in the old states. They dug cisterns. Dug them in the limestone if possible, but if they lived where the whiterock was too far below the surface, they dug them anyway and walled them with rocks. A cistern was a huge hole in the ground, twenty feet or more across at the bottom, narrowing to three or four feet at the top. They were made to catch water draining from house roofs. After McKinney was founded, in 1848, the town was supplied by two big cisterns; one on the southeast and the other on the northwest corner of the square.

Sickness, especially among children, plagued the early settlers. Malaria, whooping cough, scarlett fever, measles, diptheria, typhoid, smallpox and other diseases took the lives of at least half the children of the early settlers. There were no doctors in the settlements, and there was no cure for any kind of serious malady.

Not until 1845 was there a doctor in Collin County. In the summer of that year, however, 22-year-old Dr. G.A. Foote came to Buckner on an exploring trip. People begged him to stay, but he said he had to return to his practice in Mississippi. He did stay though; not because of the pleadings of the settlers, but due to a young lady. He fell in love with pretty little Eliza Jane, daughter of John McGarrah, founder of Buckner, and married her when she came of age, two years later. Dr. Foote stayed, ministered to the needs of the pioneers until his death, 57 years later.

5

Collin County—

Organized And Growin'

CHAPTER V

Organization Of Collin County

And The First Post Office

In November, 1842, John (Jack) McGarrah came from Arkansas with his family and headrighted 680 acres three miles northwest of present McKinney. Early the following year he built a log cabin on his claim and moved his family there from the Throckmorton settlement. Later that year McGarrah's sons-in-law, Tola Dunn and George Herndon, settled near him, and McGarrah's brother, George McGarrah, located three miles to the southwest.

Late in the summer Talton Cunnius, who lived near present Bloomdale, hauled two wagon loads of merchandise and blacksmith tools from Wright's Landing on Red River to the McGarrah settlement. With the tools Cunnius started a blacksmith shop under an arbor of tree limbs, and John McGarrah opened a small store in his cabin with the merchandise. These were the first business concerns in present Collin County. During the following six years, Buckner, as the settlement was called, was the only place within forty miles where merchandise of any kind could be purchased, and McGarrah's stock of general merchandise was small.

On December 29, 1845, the Republic of Texas ceased to exist, due to annexation to the United States on that date, and the Texas Legislature immediately took steps to organize all the new states into counties. At the time Nacogdoches and Fannin counties covered a great part of north Texas; present Collin lying within Fannin County.

Collin McKinney, who had moved from Bowie County, in northeast Texas, to three miles southeast of present Van Alstyne, in January, 1846, recommended to the Texas Legislature that all new counties in northern Texas be surveyed out as near thirty miles square as possible, with boundaries running due north and south, instead of following natural features of the locality, such as rivers and streams.

This recommendation was adopted, and on April 3, 1846, an act was signed by Governor J. Pinckney Henderson creating Collin County. Section 4 of that act reads as follows:

"Be it further enacted, that John McGarrah, J.C.M. Hodge, Thomas Rattan, Ashley McKinney, and Pleasant Wilson be, and they are hereby appointed commissioners, whose duty it shall be to find the centre of said county and select two places within three miles of said centre, having due respect to the donations that may be offered by individuals for a town site for the use of the county. The commissioners shall then proceed to hold an election, and the place receiving the greatest number of votes shall be the county seat, and the place so elected shall be known and called by the name of Buckner, and the commissioners shall proceed to lay off said town and sell the lots therein at public auction on a credit of twelve months."

And so, Collin County was created. On July 4, that year, a meeting of everybody in the county who could attend, was held at Buckner to debate the question. A speech was made, a flag was raised, and a grand dance took place at night. Nobody had any idea as to the location of the county boundaries, and it was decided that as

Buckner was the only town in the new county, and was probably within three miles of the center, it was voted county seat.

The people ignored the requirement of the act calling for a vote between two selected sites, but this amounted to nothing, as it shortly was ascertained that Buckner was not within three miles of the center of the county, and had to be moved anyway.

Andrew Stapp took advantage of the meeting to organize and enlist a company of volunteers for the Mexican War which had just started. Stapp was elected captain, Thomas J. McDonald was elected as lieutenant and John Fitzhugh as first sergeant. This company was called into Federal service for a duration of six months on July 24, 1846.

On August 1, 1846, John McGarrah donated fifty acres of his land for a town site and the commissioners then laid the town off in lots 80 feet square, with a public square in the center for a court house. On September 1, that year, lots were sold to the highest bidders, entirely on credit. Eight lots were sold, and on October 18, 1846, the Honorable John T. Mills of Fannin County opened the first term of District Court at Buckner. November 25, 1846, the U.S. Postmaster established a post office at Buckner with John McGarrah as postmaster, and the first capitol of Collin County was on its way.

The first election held in Collin County took place at Buckner on July 13, 1846, when Zachary Roberts was elected Chief Justice—now County Judge, Moses G. Wilson was elected District Clerk, Tola Dunn, county clerk; King Custer, Sheriff; John Fitzhugh, Godfrey Baccus, Peter F. Lucas and John A. Wilson, commissioners. William W. Butler, Jacob Baccus and Joel F. Stewart were elected as Justices of the Peace for the three precincts.

In January, 1847, George White, a surveyor from New York, came to Buckner and was appointed county surveyor by Justice Roberts, and instructed to find the center of the new county. In June, White reported that so far as he could find out, the center of the county was seven miles southeast of Buckner on the banks of East Fork creek.

This was a shock to the settlers, but the law was plain. The county seat had to be within three miles of the center of the county. The Chief Justice then appointed J.B. Wilmeth, Meredith Ashlock and John Crutchfield as commissioners to select the two sites called for in the law. These were to be voted on for the county seat on November 1, 1847. Ashlock could not serve, so Crutchfield selected as one of the possible sites Sloan's Grove, three miles south of present McKinney, while J.B. Wilmeth selected the present site of McKinney.

Not many votes were cast. It had been raining several days and those settlers south of Wilson Creek and east of East Fork could not get across, due to high water, and those living in the western part of the county took no great interest, as they thought the county seat would remain at Buckner, law or no law. The final ballot was ten to one for Wilmeth's selection, Ben Baccus came in just before the polls closed and finding that Wilmeth's selection had ten votes and Sloan's Grove, cast a ballot for the latter, merely, he said, for "devilment," as his was the last ballot for the day.

Due to Indian raids in Denton County the state authorized a ranger company from Collin County to patrol the frontier and to protect settlers. This company was enlisted at Buckner with William Fitzhugh as captain, Thomas J. McDonald, Joshua Dillingham and Alfred Chandler as lieutenants. It was sworn into the ranger service for a year, on July 3, 1847.

John L. Lovejoy moved from Sister Grove Creek in southeast Grayson County to Buckner in late 1846, and opened a drygoods store in a small frame building constructed from lumber hauled down from the steamboat landing on Red River. This was the first frame building in Collin County. It was about twelve feet wide and fifteen feet in length, one room.

As nothing had been done about moving Buckner to a new site, Lovejoy took matters in his own hands. He engaged two men with oxen to drag the structure on skids over the prairie, and to where the new county seat was going to be. The building was hauled down, placed on the northwest corner of the present square on May 3, 1848, and Lovejoy opened it for business on May 6, 1848. This was the first store in present McKinney.

A month after John L. Lovejoy opened his store, Sam Reynolds built a log cabin where the First Baptist Church is now, and George W. Barnett erected another log cabin to use as a general merchandise store near the southwest corner of the present square in McKinney. About the same time Joe M. Bounds built a cabin fifty yards northeast of Lovejoy's and put in a small stock of merchandise. All the merchandise sold in the three stores had to be hauled by wagons from Red River, north of Bonham.

On May 31, 1848, the U.S. Post Office Department changed the name of the new county seat from Buckner to McKinney, saying there was another Buckner in the state. Now that the new town was assured, people came in rapidly. Cabins and shacks sprang up everywhere . The post office, however, remained for the time at Buckner, with Joel F. Stewart as postmaster.

July 31, 1848, Peter's Colony contract with the state expired, and all land deals were henceforth to be made with the State of Texas. Settlers, though, could keep the land they had.

Henry Wetsel and his sons came to McKinney in August, 1848, and started to build a grist mill on now South Tennessee Street, and a furniture shop west of Barnett's store. That same month the people of the county met and built a log-cabin courthouse on the southwest corner of the present square. At the end of the June, 1848, term of the District Court at Buckner, Judge John T. Mills announced that the next term of the court would open in McKinney, November 10, 1848, the post office was moved from Buckner to John L. Lovejoy's store, with Lovejoy as postmaster. McKinney, the new county seat, was on its way: population 35.

December 15, 1848, William McKinney, John Fitzhugh, James M. McReynolds and J.B. Wilmeth were appointed commissioners to survey and plat the townsite. William Davis and his wife, Margaret, who had headrighted 3,000 acres where McKinney now stands, donated 120 acres for the site of the town on March 24, 1849. With the help of George White and Etheldred Whiteley, surveyors, the town platting was completed by the commissioners in April, 1849, and a sale of lots was announced for August 24th.

Jonathan Allen bought the first lot, Number 19, Block 3, on the northwest corner of the square, south across the street from Lovejoy's store. Allen paid $49 for it. Whiteley bought the lot south of this for the same price, and later opened a saloon there, McKinney's first.

January 16, 1849, the Grand Lodge of Texas granted dispensation for Masonic Lodge No. 51 at McKinney, the first fraternal order in Collin County. In the summer of that year John M. McKinney, driving ten oxen, broke out gardens for Dr. G.A. Foote and I.D. Newsome in the new town, and Dr. Foote put a few acres in

34

cultivation a mile northwest of the Lovejoy store. This plowing was the first land broken around McKinney.

In 1849 the gold fever from California overcame many people in Collin County and many from the settlements went west seeking their fortunes. John McGarrah, the founder of Buckner, Tola Dunn, McGarrah's son-in-law, Thomas J. McDonald and G.W. Ford left Buckner late that year, going to California overland. Two years later, returning, McGarrah died of yellow fever while crossing Mexico, and Tola Dunn died of the same disease in Louisiana. Both men left widows with several small children.

The Act of April 3, 1846, creating Collin County from Fannin County specified that Collin should be represented in the Texas Legislature as a part of Fannin County until Collin County had population enough to have representatives of its own. At that time Collin and Fannin counties were represented in the Texas Senate by William M. Williams, and in the House by Samuel Bogart of Collin County. In 1848 Collin, Grayson, Dallas, Henderson, Kaufman and Van Zandt counties were placed in the 4th Senatorial District and Grayson, Collin and Cooke in the 6th Representative District. In the Election of August 6, 1849, A.G. Walker was elected Senator, and Samuel Bogart from Collin was elected Representative.

Under the Act of January 16, 1850, Collin, Grayson, Cooke, Denton and Dallas counties were placed in the 3rd Senatorial District, and in the same Act Collin, and Denton counties were placed in the 25th Representative District. In the election of August 4, 1851, Samuel Bogart was elected Senator, and James W. Throckmorton, Representative. For the first time, Collin County had its own representatives in the Texas Legislature.

By the first of 1849 Collin County had a population of 1,086, divided as follows: Males, all ages, 559; females, all ages, 447. In the above were 80 slaves who were not enumerated as to sex. Collin County itself was young, and its population was young. Of the 1,086 persons, only 42 of them were over the age of 45. Note the high proportion of females to males; almost three-fourths. The settlers of the county brought their families to the new country with them, for they had come to stay.

Up to about 1849 almost everyone in Collin County subsisted almost entirely on the natural resources, wild game, fish, and fruits. There was little incentive to work and little was done. There was inducement to hunt, however, for deer skins, bear skins and those of oxen could be shipped to Jefferson and from there to New Orleans where there was a ready market.

Collin County has had several courthouse buildings to house its courts of justice. The first was a little log cabin on the southwest corner of the square. Owing to a constant disagreement as to whose duty it was to make the fires, a meeting was called in the summer of 1849 and the people agreed to build a new courthouse of pine lumber that could be freighted from Jefferson in East Texas. The new one also had two rooms with a roof made of shingles cut from the bottoms of East Fork Creek near town. On Christmas a big ball was held in the new structure to celebrate its completion, with Lucy Baccus and Alfred Chandler leading the grand march.

In the year 1859 McKinney was incorporated. Joe Steele graded the new streets with ox teams and for a year or so they were impassable. Thomas Lowery was the postmaster with the post office located on the west side of the square. At this time post offices had been established at several points in Collin County, at Farmersville, Plano, Millwood, Rock Hill, Roseland, Mantua, Lone Tree, Highland, Rowlett Creek and Weston.

Hostile Indians became active in late 1859 and the governor of Texas called for a regiment of volunteers to patrol the frontier. Of this Regiment Collin was to furnish one company, with William and Gabriel Fitzhugh to recruit it. This company of 60 men was soon recruited and left in March of 1860 for Ft. Belknap. They were sent on a prolonged scouting trip up into Indian Territory and far up the Canadian River. They were discharged at Ft. Belknap in October 1860.

In September 1859 the Sawyer Brothers started their stage line from Clarksville through McKinney to Austin. They drove six mules to the coach with stations fifteen miles apart where they could change to fresh teams. They carried passengers, mail and some merchandise.

In 1859 Collin County decided to build a better courthouse. The frame building that stood in the center of the square was put on wooden wheels and hauled down to the site of the old jail. Rock for the new building was hauled in from several places around Texas and dumped on the square, where it lay for 15 years. The Civil War stopped all building. Court was held during this period in the old one they had hauled away.

In October of 1860 the first real County Fair was held in the County Seat, McKinney. It was called the Agricultural and Mechanical Science Fair and was located on the old fair grounds in east McKinney. Thomas Llewelling was president, Isaac Graves vice president and George Herndon was secretary with George White treasurer. Prizes were offered for home-made dishes, blankets, thread, for all kinds of fowl, garden produce, fruit, and for such mechanical things as wagons, bridles, shoes, plows and tools. Also prizes were given for the best cow, sheep, jack, jenny, and horse. Prizes were given for ladies horsemanship, gents, and for breaking horses. Twenty cents was the admission, children ten cents.

Law and order was coming to Collin County in the 1850's. In 1850 David Stiff was appointed tax collector and elected to that office in 1851. Tax collectors were not well accepted at first in the frontier times. We have record of Stiff being fined 50 cents for "striking one Boswell with his fist" after an argument in his office over the tax being collected.

In September, 1853, Dr. G.A. Foote was fined fifty cents for fighting with Thomas J. McDonald. Dr. Foote was the only participant fined since McDonald lived three miles away in the Wilmeth community and it was too far to go fetch him in. Several men were fined for failure to show up to help work the roads. The first homicide in McKinney was January 4, 1854. Alfred Johnson and Joe Peake got in an argument in a saloon where the Ritz Theatre now stands. When Peake made a threatening movement, Johnson shot him. Johnson was found not guilty as he acted "totally in self defense."

EARLY COLLIN ROADS

The very first road of any note was the Cedar Springs-Buckner-Bonham Road. This road had its south end at Cedar Springs, now Dallas, and ran north along the high ground 6 miles west of present McKinney, past the old James Herndon home, on north to Ft. Buckner, and northeast across Honey Creek and East Fork and out through the present Trinity community. It passed just north of the old Sheldon Mimms home, ran due east, turned slightly northeast and ran by the Hatler home. It passed Stony Point where there was a stage stop at a big spring. The road kept to high ground all the way, passing Lebanon. Several places along the road, wheel marks are clearly visible. One place is on Hart Spring Ridge five miles northwest of

THE LONG ABANDONED Cedar Springs—Buckner—Bonham road, showing wheel marks made by freight wagons. Seven miles northwest of McKinney, Texas.

McKinney, where deep ruts cut across the land.

This is the very first road that could be called a road in the county. It started in 1843 and came to an end as a road in 1857, when a road was opened from Dallas to McKinney. Since McKinney came into being in 1848, it was manifest that they needed roads. Settlements had grown up in Denton County and it was decided here to build a road over into Denton County, mainly to the small town of Alton. The road was laid out in 1852, leading out roughly where Cole Street is in McKinney now, and following the Foote Road out past the Old Thompson homestead. 400 yards west of this home, the road veered off southwest and wound around the foot of the hills, crossing Wilson Creek at a ford. This old road can still be seen where it turns off Foote Road to the southwest. This was the main road west until 1925 and was known as the Alton Road.

Going to and from Dallas one had to take the Alton Road to the old Cedar Springs trace, and then turn south into Cedar Springs (Dallas). In 1857 a new road branched off from the Wilson Creek crossing and turned due south, going up a steep hill near the Singleton farm. This was the main road to Dallas for 10 years. In 1878 a covered bridge was placed over the creek and a road turned south to cross the bridge and then on up the Singleton Hill. This covered bridge, the only one in Collin County, was dismantled in 1921.

In 1858 the Sawyer brothers started a stage route from Dallas, through McKinney, and on to Bonham, and decided they needed a shorter route than the Alton Road provided. From Plano they laid out a road across the Prairie east of the old Dallas Road just mentioned. It wound up over the high ground, marked at first by stakes, and came to the valley of Wilson Creek by the old Buck place, 3 miles southwest of present McKinney. It crossed Wilson Creek just above the old iron bridge site built later. This ford was remarkable for its pure white sand on the east bank, found no other place. This place, so troublesome caused the people to build a log bridge 50 feet below the crossing in 1861. This log bridge washed away several times and was finally replaced by an iron bridge in 1878. This road was called the

New Dallas Road and also the Buck Road. It was a main road as late as 1915, even though better roads had then opened to Dallas. It was on this road, at this crossing, that the great county-wide picnics were held between 1898 and 1905. These were the largest gatherings ever held in Collin County with as many as 20,000 people attending during the four days picnic. The picnics were held on a grassy plain just north of Wilson Creek, and on a scale never before seen in Collin County, nor since. Important men of the state always attended, the governor, and other state officials. This was called Benge's Park.

During the Civil War, a road of sorts was opened farther down the creek but could only be used in fair weather. It was not used much for the high water in rainy seasons kept sweeping the bridges away. It was 1870 before this road became a thoroughfare. About 1867 the road was opened from Wilson Creek to reach Wetsel.

In 1882 the Collin County Prison (jail in McKinney) was built from stones shipped here from Shreveport. The stones were uncut, being huge pieces of stone so they had to be cut and shaped right at the building site. The small pieces of stone not used were used to surface the Buck Road on the north side of Wilson Creek. Most of the stone has long since been covered by mud in overflows, but some can still be seen. This was the first surfaced road in the county.

The first road eastward out of McKinney was the freight road to Jefferson, in East Texas. This never was a planned road, but was formed by the big freight wagons hauling goods to and from McKinney to the steamboat landing in Jefferson. Leaving McKinney it wound around the brow of the hill in the southeast part of McKinney, turning south near the old Eastline Railroad bed. From there it turned east and crossed East Fork. The first recorded use of this road appeared about 1854. We have accounts of Emerson's big wagons having trouble on a steep hill just east of East Fork.

This road is still there, though the iron bridge placed there in 1878 is gone. The road runs just north of the Camp Fire Girls' encampment, just west of East Fork. Owing to the steep hill on the east side of the creek, this road was the most dreaded in the county, but it was the only road east at the time.

A branch of this road turned off at the old East Line and went south to Millwood, a distributing point for lumber all over North Texas. It was called the Millwood Road and still goes by the name. Most of the road is still used.

This was the most traveled road in the county then. Most of the fine old homes in the county were built from lumber hauled over that road by ox-drawn freight wagons. Millwood and McKinney were the distributing points for the lumber hauled by these lumbering old wagons.

When the Sawyer brothers started the stage line in 1857, they had no road to the northeast, except the old Buckner Road up through the Trinity settlement. They started a new one simply by driving out by way of present Woodlawn and marking the best route they could find by "blazing" trees along the way. This trail more or less followed the present Woodlawn Road, except it left that road after crossing East Fork and went by the Throckmorton place, a mile north of there. Throckmorton had built a fine home there two years before in order to get away from the threat of Indians in his old settlement seven miles north of McKinney.

As J.B. Wilmeth had a lane that led from his home two miles north of McKinney into town, the stage line followed this lane in dry weather. In bad weather they followed this lane, but turned east on the old Buckner Road and went on to Melissa. As the stage went to Bonham, both of these roads were known as the Bonham

THE FIRST ROADS IN Collin County were surfaced in 1915, but it was much later before all the roads were passable in wet weather. This picture of Capt. Roy F. Hall made in 1920 when he attempted to go up Wilmeth Lane to his old home, is typical of conditions even in the 20's.

A COMMON SCENE on any mud road of Collin Co. in 1928.

COVERED BRIDGE on Wilson Creek west of McKinney on the Alton Road. Picture sketched by Roy F. Hall. It was still standing when he was a child.

Road, the one by Woodlawn was the Lower Bonham Road, and the one by the northern route was the Upper Bonham Road. The old Highway 75 north out of McKinney follows the Upper Bonham Road fairly closely, while the Lower Bonham Road is still known as the Woodlawn Road, as far as East Fork.

In 1842 Sam Houston had a road surveyed and laid out from Cedar Springs (Dallas) to Coffee's Station on Red River. This road later became known as the Preston Road, but it was never an actual road. In going through the woods the surveyors cut the trees so high that a wagon axle could not pass over them, and the few who took that route out of Texas made no attempt to follow the trace, but wound around among the trees seeking a path of their own. Coffee's Station was too far west and most people entering Texas came by way of Colbert's Ferry on Red River or by the more eastern route. The danger from the plains Indians was still too great in the western portion of Texas. So Preston Road never amounted to much.

This is a condensed account of the early roads of Collin County. There were, of course, many lanes and trails but they were short, usually connecting one community or settlement with another. It is the intention of the Historical Society to mark everyone of these early roads. I have them marked on the big map I will include in the book.

HOW THE COLLIN COUNTY STREAMS WERE NAMED

When the first settlers came into the section that is now Collin County, none of the landmarks had a name. The settlers named them, and named them from something that they knew or something that happened. Many of the places went by several names over the years and some of the old names have disappeared completely.

As most of the early settlers came in from the northeast Collin section, they blazed the trails for those who came after them. Over at Ft. English in Fannin County, Daniel Rowlett who had come to Collin with Throckmorton on an exploring trip, drew a map of the new country which he sold to immigrants coming in for a quarter each. These maps were very sketchy indeed, as Rowlett had made only the one trip here in 1841. He only went as far as the Rowlett church location then back to Ft. English. In coming into this section he had come along the north boundary of Collin turning south toward Anna and on to Rowlett. Rowlett Creek bears his name.

On Rowlett's map he shows the upper end of Sister Grove Creek, but he called it Six Mile Creek, because it was about that distance from Pilot Grove. He shows the East Fork of the Trinity as East Fork, for John H. Reagan had named this creek when he surveyed north of present Dallas a year or two before Rowlett came here. Actually East Fork is not a fork of the Trinity but a creek that flows into the Trinity. For many years after settlers had built homes on the upper branch near the Grayson County line it was called Spring Creek, named of course, for the many springs that fed the creek. Around McKinney it was always called East Fork, but this was a common practice, for the head of a creek to go be one name and farther down another. All over the county there were creeks named Spring Creek, called so from the huge springs all over the county. The only Spring Creek now is the one that flows southward from west of Plano.

When Throckmorton came in 1841 to explore there was with him a rudy-faced man by the name of Pleasant Wilson. A giant of a man, good natured, a true explorer, he was the ram-rod of the expedition. He discovered a lot of game on Ten Mile Creek, so called because it was believed to be ten miles from the Throckmorton camp, later a settlement. This was his best hunting ground and he talked so much about it that James Throckmorton gave the creek the name Pleasant Wilson's Creek. This change was made after 1851 because I have a map from the land office showing Ten Mile Creek in 1851. Later the name was shortened to Wilson's Creek and later the "s" was dropped and today it is Wilson Creek.

Honey Creek had a number of different names at first—Wild Horse Creek, Bear Creek, White Rock, and finally Honey Creek, due to the enormous numbers of wild bee trees in the forests nearby. Wilson's love of hunting gave the little creek into East Fork north of present Chambersville its name. While hunting one day he surprised a mother bear and her two cubs. The big bear charged him and his only way of escape was to hit the water of the creek and swim. He later said that he "hit that water like a hurricane." From that day, his creek was and is called Hurricane Creek.

Down in the southeast corner of the county is a small creek that still bears its original name, Brushy Creek. In 1841 Sam Houston ordered a road be surveyed from Dallas northward to Red River. The surveyors got lost in the great thicket by going too far east and they wound up on the brushy little creek that they called Brushy on their map.

The name Whiterock Creek is only born by one sizable creek in the County although all creeks originally ran over clean whiterock. This one is located in the southwest part of the county near Renner.

Down between Wylie and Plano are two small creeks that take the name Muddy and Maxwell's Branch. Maxwell Branch took its name because the creek flowed for several miles across the headright of James and Henry Maxwell. Muddy was named for the nature of its valley, which was virtually a swamp for many years after John

Mitchell and Moses Sparks headrighted the land on its banks.

There were many Panther and Bear Creeks in the early days, but only one of each retains its name. Panther Creek, running west into Little Elm valley north of Frisco, and Bear Creek just west of Nevada. Both got their names from the great number of these animals to be found there in early days.

Bear Creek is especially notable. In 1849 a great bear hunt was staged by Peters Colony settlers and in that one day more than fifty bears were killed on this creek. There used to be a Panther Creek up near Cottage Hill. Someone killed a panther high in a tree and it could not be dislodged and the bones hung there for some time.

Sabine Creek rises in the extreme southeast part of the county and turns eastward to become the boundary between Texas and Louisiana. Just north of Josephine, and running into Brushy, is a small creek called Cowskin. The Honakers, early settlers in that vicinity, had so much trouble with bears and panthers killing their cattle that they hung up a dry cowskin to frighten them away. One of the men would tie the crackling cowskin behind his horse and drag it rapidly along the branch, hoping to frighten away any marauder.

Indian Creek, close to Snow Hill, got its name from the same source as Desert Creek—the Indians. There was an Indian village in the creek when the settlers first came, or rather the remains of one. This village was a half mile north of the crossing on Indian Creek. Indian Creek used to be the prettiest little creek in the county.

Most of the smaller creeks in the county got their names naturally, as Oak Creek, west of Blue Ridge, Elm and Bois d'Arc Creeks in the southeast part of the county. Many were named for an early settler, as Stover Creek near Rheas Mill was named for Joseph Stover, a pioneer who came to the area in 1843. Gray's Branch, near Foote, was named for Joseph R. Gray, who headrighted on the land at an early date. Stover Creek is unique in that it has the deepest valley in the county.

Stiff Creek, west of Altoga, was named for Jesse Stiff, who settled on its headwaters in 1850. Ticky Creek, west of Stiff Chapel, was named for the great number of ticks that inhabited the creek area. There are numerous other small creeks all over the county, and each played a big part in the settlement of the county.

BRIEF HISTORY OF COLLIN COUNTY AGRICULTURE

The soil of Collin County originated from the basic limestone, which was layed down by oceans over 60 million years ago. It consists of eroded limestone mixed with decayed vegetation; trees, leaves and grasses. The soil of the county is known as the Houston Black clay, in several compositions, and is extremely fertile for most staple crops.

Since the first cultivation, beginning around 1860, the soil has eroded badly, especially on slopes, and this erosion continued rapidly until conservation methods were inaugurated beginning in the 1930s.

In general, the eastern half of the county was originally in timber, the western half prairies. Though there was plenty of timber along streams in the west portion and some prairie land in the east half. The forests consisted of oak, ash, hackberry, bois d'arc, elm, walnut, cottonwood, pecans and lesser trees. The prairies were usually of buffalo grass, or gramma grass. The buffalo grass has totally disappeared from the county, as it was a poor seeder.

The first settlers came to the area in 1842, settling seven miles north of present McKinney. Settlement was rapid from that time up to the time of the Civil War in 1861, when the population of the county was about 8,000. Following that war the settlers came in rapidly until the county reached its maximum population in 1900. Free land had all been taken up by 1855, save some few hundred acres of railway land in the northwest part of the county.

The Peters Colony, of Tennessee, were the instigators of most of the first settlers, having rights to colonize all the county and give each land grantee a section of land if married, or a half section if single. The colony also built log cabins for the first settlers and furnished them with guns and ammunition.

The first crop grown in the county was at the old Throckmorton settlement, seven miles north of present McKinney in 1848, when the settlers at Throckmorton planted about 20 acres to wheat. The next cultivated land was on the present Cameron place, at the northwest edge of present McKinney.

The big forests were too much for the settlers and no attempt was made to clear any land of forests. Instead, what land that was placed in cultivation before the Civil War was prairie land, and that broken out with a heavy "prairie plow," usually pulled by six oxen. Corn was the main crop, outnumbering wheat and oats three to one. Emphasis was placed on gardens for the colonists had to make their own living from the soil. Every farm had cows, horses, hogs and poultry. Slaughtered meat was salted down for the year's supply and vegetables were canned and dried. There was little or no markets for farm produce until after the Civil War.

During the Civil War, 1861-65, agriculture came almost to a standstill in the county, as, out of a population of some 8,000 the county sent over 2,000 men to that war. All farms were run by women and for those who had them, slaves. There was no progress in the county during the war.

After the war trading opened with East Texas via wagon trains, especially with Jefferson, the head of navigation on Red River. The wagon trade had started during the mid-1850's though most of this was between Jefferson and Millwood, in southeast Collin County. From the latter place lumber—principally—had been distributed over North Texas, by individual wagons.

This wagon-train trade reached its maximum in the early 1870s, when several wagon trains hauled goods in and took some produce out to Jefferson.

From 1865 to 1870 some tobacco was grown, though lack of markets soon ended this attempt. Freight to and from East Texas was one dollar a hundred pounds and few could profit by shipping farm produce in that manner. Some cotton was grown, but as in the case of tobacco, lack of shipping facilities held its growth back. Corn was the main crop. Some few hundred acres of wheat were grown but all for local use. Four mills in the county ground meal, but until 1873 there was no flour mill in the county.

In 1872 the Houston & Texas Central Railroad reached McKinney, builded from Harrisburg, or present Houston, from which place it had started—to be stopped—when the Civil War started. From 1855 to 1872 there was little change in the agriculture picture of Collin County. Several hundred acres of the prairie land had been turned over by plows to be planted in corn and wheat, but the big timbers had not been touched.

After the railroad reached the county there occurred a great spurt in building. Wages went to ten dollars a day for carpenters and farm wages went up somewhat also, though most farmers tended their farms with the family. Little outside labor was hired, save for occasional corn hoeing and the like an this was little indeed. All the farms were self sustained.

The new railroad hauled out supplies at a fraction of the cost of the old wagon freights and, in 1875, several hundred bales of cotton was shipped out. This proved

THE OLD COTTONSEED Oil Mill was built in East McKinney in 1892 and revolutionized the whole cotton industry here. Prior to the coming of the mill there was no market for the seed and much of them were discarded as waste. Some gins required the farmer to haul them away and tons of seed were dumped into the ditches along county roads, but by 1898 cotton seeds were bringing $12. a ton. J.S. Heard was president of the new company. They produced 300,000 gallons of oil, employed 40 people. 1892

to be a money-making venture and in 1876 there were over 10,000 acres of cotton planted in the county, though corn continued to be the chief farm crop. The average production of cotton was one bale per acre.

By 1880 cotton was the king of the crops of the county, for the first time eclypsing corn as the main farm crop. Some wheat was grown west of McKinney and proved to be such a success that the following year 6,000 acres were planted. The steam thresher had superceded the horse-power thresher and, as the price of wheat rose to 80 cents a bushel in 1881 much new land was broken out on the prairies in the western part of the county and sown to wheat and oats, mostly wheat.

In the year 1885 about all the arable prairie land was in cultivation, save that in the "Flats," as the valley of Little Elm Creek was then called. This valley, near two miles wide and reaching from present Celina to present Frisco, was one vast swamp, covered with high Gramma grass, with a few trees here and there. In the eastern part of the county most all the prairie land was under the plow, and some clearing of the forests had been done. This clearing of the woods was rather minor, compared to the whole area, and was usually confined to small patches around homesteads.

Farmers came into their own after the building spree collapsed in 1874, and prices returned to normal, and often below. Normal wages were a dollar a day for men; half that for boys big enough to work. About all the work that required labor, from 1874 to 1880 was the few laborers employed seasonally on farms, such as threshermen and cotton choppers. The county was, at the time, almost purely agricultural.

Around 1890 cotton was undisputed king of the crops in the county, Collin County producing up to 50,000 bales a year. This was about maximum for the land in use, for only prairie land was planted to crops at the time. The big forests stood as nature made them, untouched, practically, by man. Their only use was for fuel as log cabins had ceased to be built after the railroad came through in 1872, and brought cheap lumber to the area. At that time, though, there were many log-cabin homes in the county.

Beginning in 1891 a weak market opened for cordwood in the county, Northern buyers paying $1.25 a cord for it delivered to the railroad at McKinney, Plano, Melissa, Anna and Caruth Switch. Only a small amount—some 100 cords—were so purchased, and the market died in the spring of 1891 when warm weather returned. However, it revived in the fall of that year, the Northern buyers asking for all the cordwood that could be delivered.

Cotton, the freighting of buffalo hides and bones, had kept the economy of the county at a fairly high level from 1886 to 1891. When the advent of the railroad ended the freight wagon trains from East Texas, these wagon owners turned to freighting buffalo hides from as far west as Fort Griffin to shipping points on the H & T.C. railway. McKinney was the main shipping point in the county, and over 200 thousand dollars worth of buffalo hides were shipped from the town from 1886 to 1889. Then a market opened for buffalo bones to make buttons and this added another 100 thousand dollars to the county's income.

When it was proven as a fact that the market for cordwood was endless, everybody on the farms, and a great deal of hired help, started clearing the forests from the land. Cordwood went to $2.50 a cord and remained there until most of the cordwood trees in the county had been cut and sold. Land, which had cost around $2.50 an acre with trees on it, paid for itself several times over in cordwood cut from it. Only the unusable trees were left as a rule; water elm, cottonwood, willow and sycamore, were left standing. As these were comparatively few, they were, in most cases, deadened and eventually removed and the land placed in cultivation. This bottom land proved to be rich as the black soil of the upland and land prices went up to fifteen to twenty dollars an acre for cut-over land.

When it was found that this bottom land was superior to the upland for corn growing, corn was mostly removed from the prairie soil and became the main crop in the bottoms—as the low timberland was called. This freed the upland and more cotton was planted, a market for which was apparently permanent. The bottom soil would grow cotton as well as corn and yields of two bales of cotton per acre were common.

It was found too, that alfalfa would do well on the bottom land and several thousand acres were planted from 1895 to 1909. By 1898 the agricultural economy of the county was booming. So well indeed that by 1900 Collin County was rated as 14th in the agricultural counties of the whole nation. This was reflected in the growth of the towns. McKinney, for instance, in 1900 was rated as the richest city, per capita in the United States. Cotton, corn, wheat, alfalfa, horses and mules made the agricultural aspect of Collin County the envy of the nation. In 1904, for instance, over 100,000 bales of cotton were sold in the county.

There were few insect pests to damage crops, though the cotton boll worm (corn worm) did some damage in the low lands, and a common yield per acre was over a bale of cotton, 80 bushels of corn and 60 bushels of wheat. From 1895 to around 1907 was the heyday of the farmer in Collin County, though the boll weevil came in 1903 and severely cut back the yield of cotton. Land that had been producing as much as two bales of cotton per acre dropped in the one year to as much as a fourth of that. There was, at the time, no way to combat this pest. Today, with regulated dusting and spraying some well-tended soils produce up to two bales of cotton per acre, though there are few of these farms in the county. Many farmers turned their cotton land to alfalfa and some grew wealthy, but the financial yield was a little over half of that of two bales of cotton per acre.

THIS IS A VIEW of the "Flats" as the low plains of western Collin County are known. So different from wooded, low rolling terrain of the rest of the county. It was formed by the Balcones Fault that is west of McKinney.

WHERE INDIANS used to find their abundant game on the prairies, lazy Herefords enjoy the abundant grass.

WITH COTTON no longer the big crop, farmers began to diversify. Poultry, onions, dairy farms—all helped the economy.

MELISSA COTTON GIN, 1947.　　　　**SAW MILL AT CLEAR LAKE, 1950.**

AS COTTON CEASED to be "King Cotton" in Collin County, cows became a big source of income, especially fine stock. Mr. C.L. Haggard, near Lebanon, 1952. Black Angus have become a popular breed on local ranches.

THE LAST OF THE old steam threshers at work on the Perry Wilson farm near Danville.

WHEAT GROWING was a lucrative operation in the "Flats" for years. Collin County was famous for its "White Billows" flour, milled here from Collin County Wheat.

THE TYPICAL "Cook Shack" that went with a threshing crew from one farm to the next. This one belonged to Joe Crutcher. Good, hearty food, flowed freely from all these cook shacks.

THE FIRST RAILROAD

The biggest thing that ever happened to Collin County was the coming of the first railroad in October 1872. The Houston and Texas Central was built through the County in 1872, having already been completed from Harrisburg (Houston) to Hempstead when the Civil War stopped all construction in Texas. After the war the road was completed up to Red River. This road was always known here as the H. & T. C. Later the East Line ran through McKinney to Jefferson, but nothing so changed the face of McKinney as this first railroad.

Until the coming of the railroad through the county, we were a lot of shabby little towns with slab huts and log cabins. The railroad changed it all and changed it even before they got here. There are only two houses still standing in McKinney that were here as they are now, before the coming of the railroad. This is the Graves home in Northwest McKinney, and the old Taylor home on South Chestnut Street. The Graves home was built in 1857 and the Taylor home in 1863. No commercial house or business establishment in McKinney has the same building still in use that they had before 1872. In the county there are not more than a dozen original buildings older than 1872. There were some built from lumber freighted in from Jefferson, like the old Collin McKinney home now in Finch Park in McKinney, but originally stood near Van Alstyne. It was built in 1854.

In 1871 the contractors for the railroad arrived in the county and hired every man they could get to start building the road bed. A man got ten dollars a day, an unheard of thing here, and a man with a team of horses got fifteen. The roadbed was laid out in one to three mile sections and a contractor was responsible for his part of the bed. For instance a contractor by the name of Mullins had the section from McKinney north to East Fork. Mullins hired his own men and teams, plows and scrapers, called slips. A man with two horses or mules to a slip, using another man to handle the horses made up a team. The entire road bed was built in this manner, slow in our modern thinking, but with a thousand men working a three mile section, the work here was finished in a little over a month. It was like this from Plano north to Red River, the whole road being thrown up at the same time in a month, using 40 contractors.

As soon as the roadbed was finished the contractors were given the task of getting out crossties for the railroad and usually the same men stayed on for the job. The crossties for the section handled by Mullins were cut from land around the present McKinney Country Club, and from there were hauled by wagons to Melissa. All the crossties were of Bois d 'Arc trees, as the builder, C.P. Huntington, specified, and few of those old ties would pass muster today in railroad building. Some were straight but most were crooked since this is a characteristic of the tree. All had to be scaled with an axe so the tie would have two flat sides. It was specified that all ties must be cut from green Bois d 'Arc as nails cannot be driven well into seasoned wood of this type.

The grading of the roadbed was completed just before Christmas of 1871 and the bed was allowed to remain untouched, to "sit," for five months so it would completely settle. In the early spring of 1872 the surveyors and topping crews came along and leveled the roadbed to receive the crossties, which had been scattered along the roadbed to both sides. Behind the topping crew came the droppers who paced the ties roughly in place. By August of 1872 the head of the track was as far as Wilson Creek. This consisted of the work-train and the crews to lay the rails on the crossties. This track-laying crew was an efficient one. Huntingdon, who had just

ABOVE IS A picture of a bois d' arc fence on the Mallow farm. This was built more than 155 years ago by slaves on the farm.

CORN CRIBS, barns, and sheds were all fashioned crudely of logs.

completed the Union Pacific across the nation, brought his track crews with him, and they were good. There were about 100 men, mostly Irish, Chinese, and Italians. They were divided into three sub-crews; the draggers, who dragged the crossties up the grade and placed them, the tiers who set the crosstie firmly in place, and the layers. The last were real men. A road engine pushed two flatcars loaded with the steel rails ahead of it on the finished track, while the layers ran the rails off the front end of the leading car, placed it down on the crosstie and spiked it firmly. My grandfather who had land on both sides of the new roadbed north of McKinney, said that the layers could put down the new rails about as fast as a man could walk. Bridges had already been built, so they could move along fast. A finishing crew came along behind them and straightened out any kinks.

The regular trains started on Oct. 2, 1872, when a celebration was held attended by state dignataries, including the Secretary of State. This is a brief account of the coming of the oldest railroad west of the Mississippi River.

The coming of the railroad changed the economy in Collin County. Where there had been no opportunity to make money at all, suddenly 2,000 men of the county were making ten to fifteen dollars per day. The county began to bustle, demand for new goods reached a new high, and for the first time Collin citizens had good clothes. Women blossomed out in Calico in brilliant hues, the men discarded their home-made jeans and to don clothing made in England. Fine homes were built all over the county with this new spurt to the economy and business boomed.

Collin County was at last coming of age.

Pioneers everywhere make ingenious use of the resources at hand. The great forests of trees they found in Collin County furnished materials to build homes and all the other things they had to have.

THE CIVIL WAR ERA

The presidential election of 1856 was the forerunner of the great conflict that tore the United States apart and inflicted wounds that have not completely healed to this day.

While slavery was not what the war was fought over, it was certainly the talking point that led up to the actual war. Up to the Mexican War of 1848 there were few hotheads on either side over the question of slavery, either in North or South. What few there were made themselves heard. The great majority of people in the North where there was no slavery looked upon it as an unfortunate part of the American way of life but something that would have to remain until some satisfactory way could be worked out to eliminate it.

Opposition to slavery did not, at first, belong to any particular political party. Some slave owners were Democrats and some Whigs. But throughout the South the people believed the Republican party favored taking away the slaves without recompense to the owners. Feeling was running high before the 1856 election and had a Republican been elected, war would have come then. James Buchanan was elected and with a Democrat in office, people felt the war was averted for four years at least, and it was.

In the election of 1860, Abraham Lincoln was elected as the Republican candidate and eleven (11) southern states immediately left the union. There is no doubt that had there been a fair and calm expression of opinions in the South, the vast majority would have voted against secession. There was no calm discussion anywhere. Hot heads and those too old to go to war shouted long and loud that the North was trying to steal the slaves and the owner would get nothing in return. Overlooking the fact that the North had the South outnumbered in man power 3 to 1, and in industrial power 100 to 1, speakers everywhere bellowed that one Southerner could whip five Yankees and the war would be over in three months. Feeling ran high in both North and South, but there were many prominent people in both places who proclaimed that the government had no power to coerce the South into submission.

President Lincoln was sworn in as President of the United States March 6, 1861, and the Southern states made good their threat to secede from the Union.

Here in Collin County the feeling was 4 to 1 for staying in the Union, one of the few counties that voted to stay in. James W. Throckmorton was our representative at the secession convention in Austin and voted against secession. Collin County was not Republican by any means but there were many men here of high calibre who feared the South had little chance of winning against the North with its manpower and industrial readiness. Those who voted against it were not voting for or with the North, but voted to remain one nation and try to work out our differences by argument rather than war.

Fifteen days after the news of the bombardment at Ft. Sumpter came to Collin County, Throckmorton started raising troops around McKinney and the County, with the purpose of taking over the forts in the Indian Territory, and this was accomplished with little incident.

In the fall of 1861 all the young men of the county were required to drill on Saturday. Out of this grew the first group called the Martin's Texas Partisan Rangers, and they were sworn in July 5, 1862, and camped seven miles North of McKinney at Shirley Springs. Thomas B. Estes was the Adjutant. In the fall they went into the Indian Territory, camped near Colbert, then to Ft. Washita. In October they went to Ft. Smith where they stayed until Christmas. They swam the Arkansas River and marched 70 miles to join the main army forces. Their arms were mainly muzzle loading rifles using No. 1 buckshot. A few had double-barrel shotguns, and a few Sharps rifles.

Those of us who went through the last two wars and found the fighting tough should read a really good history of the Civil War and see what fighting can really be like. Losses in battle were terrific, considering the numbers engaged. Capt. Alf Johnson of Collin Co. took 144 men to the war and brought back 22 of them. Over 2000 men went from Collin County and barely half came home at the end. Capt. Bingham said later, "I commanded Good's Battery and three times during the war I lost 100 percent of my men."

The fighting, of course, was in the open, trenches and breastwork were not used until 1863, and not then unless in a long seige. The men won by walking or running toward each other in lines, firing until one side fell back. The Confederate soldiers were handicapped by having so little food, and by the latter part of the war, they were in rags, over half fought barefoot. The standard ration of the Confederates for a day was one-half an ear of corn, to be parched or eaten raw. It took a mighty will and a powerful spirit to carry the South through four years of war, and, as Mr. Watus Pendergrass of near McKinney said after the war, "They overpowered us, but we're not whipped."

In the fall of 1861 the Confederate Government passed laws requiring all able bodied men between the ages of 18 and 35 to register and hold themselves in readiness for service with the confederacy. This law was not enforced for a while since all the men of the South rushed to join, and conscription was not needed. As the war progressed, it became hard to find enough men to make up a company and the Texas Legislature passed the Conscript Law in 1862 requiring all men between 18 and 50 years of age to enroll in service. Collin County did not have many men left. Seventeen Collin Co. regiments were already in the field by 1863.

After the forts of the Indian Territory had been occupied, Col. Wm. C. Young organized a regiment to aid the Confederacy. Two companies from this regiment, then called the Alexander Regiment and later the 34th Texas Cavalry, were from Collin County. They were Captained by W.N. Bush and James W. Throckmorton. Throckmorton's regiment later returned to Collin County to become part of Throckmorton's original outfit, the 6th Texas Cavalry.

The Company commanded by W.N. Bush (originally the Straughan Co.) later became Company C of the 34th Cavalry was in battle in Mississippi and in Puisana and were mustered out of service in Hempstead in May 30, 1865. Below is a list of all the men present when they were organized into a company and up until it became a part of the 34th Texas Cavalry in March of 1862.

Collin County sent seventeen companies of cavalry to the Civil War and one of Infantry. This Infantry Company was that of Captain Joseph Dickenson, a McKinney lawyer. He was killed at Shiloh in 1862. Other companies were:

2. Captain John M. McKinney
3. Capt. J.W. Kolfus
4. Capt. J.D. Naylor
5. Capt. G.H. Fitzhugh
6. Capt. Hazekiah Warden
7. Captain J.R. Briscoe
8. Captain Alfred Johnson
9. Capt. John K. Bumpass
10. Capt. T.H. Bowen
11. Capt. David C. Haynes
12. Capt. T.H. Brown
13. Capt. Jordon O. Straughan
14. Capt. Coleman (Coley) White
15. Capt. W.M. Bush
16. Capt. J.G. Vance
17. Capt. James W. Throckmorton
   and F.M. Board

In most cases these captains were displaced by others later on, due to promotion, retirement or battle casualties. But these were the company commanders when they left Collin County for the war. Out of a population of slightly less than 10,000 Collin County furnished almost 3,000 soldiers for the Confederacy.

RECONSTRUCTION DAYS IN TEXAS

Times were hard in Texas during the Civil War, and when the war ended in 1865 the cold hand of misery and want laid hold of Collin County. There was little to sell, though a few farmers grew corn and tobacco, but there was no way to ship it to a market. There was no money anywhere, an unknown thing in Collin County. McKinney was a town of shanties and huts, not a two-story house in town, save a brick store being built on the southeast corner of the square.

After the war ended and the slaves were freed, offices were created by the Federal Government over the South to see that the Negro got his rights. These were called Freedmen Bureaus and the officials there were called Bureau Agents. Throughout the north, in order to gain the support of the colored men, it was proclaimed in the North that the Negro would never have to work if they were freed and the North won the war. Once free, the Negros flocked into the towns in the

South and created new problems. The North promptly forgot them, and had not their former owners chipped in, many would have starved for there was no work.

The oath of allegiance was called the "Iron-clad oath," and it excluded the Southerners. The unfairness of the situation gave rise to the Ku Klux Klan.

Here is the "Iron-clad oath":

> I (name) do solemnly swear, in the presence of Almighty God, that I will henseforth faithfully support, protect, and defend the Constitution of the United States, and the union of the states thereunder, and I will in like abide by and faithfully support all laws and proclamations which have been made during the existing rebellion with reference to the emancipation of the slaves, so help me, God."

The last part of the oath about supporting the laws and proclamations was the sentence that excluded all Texans from voting. Some of these laws and proclamations were so worded that anyone from the North could, on making a sworn statement that the Rebel was still a rebel, could then take over the property of the so-called rebel. This is where the "Carpetbagger" came into his own. If he could not obtain a job as an official in the new regime, he could swear that any certain person he wished was still loyal to the South and against the North. The property was then handed over to the Carpetbagger.

On August 20, 1866, President Johnson issued a proclamation saying that the rebellion in Texas was at an end. The Reconstruction Act became a law on March 2, 1867, and Union soldiers were sent to Texas and the South and Military rule began. Texas and Louisiana were in the Fifth Military District with Gen. Phillip Sherman in command.

Unfortunately, the Radical Republican element was in control in Washington and they held the firm belief that the South had to be "Reconstructed." President Lincoln had formulated a plan of reconstruction that was not punitive, but would really have put the South back on its feet. President Johnson tried to put Pres. Lincoln's plan into operation but not for long. The radical wing soon outlawed the plan of reconstruction, but not before the president had managed to appoint several provisional governors for some of the Southern states. Among these was A.J. Hamilton, Provisional Governor of Texas.

Hamilton was a good, honest official. He had been a Texan, but not favoring secession, had gone to New Orleans, and finally into the Union Army as a Brig. General. Before Hamilton reached Texas the Union General, Gordon Granger, landed at Galveston on June 19 and at once proclaimed the slaves free and independent. That is why June 19th is a day of celebration for our Negro citizens. Granger declared all acts of the Governor and Legislature since secession to be illegal.

On call of Hamilton, a convention was called to convene in Austin in February 1866, and wrote a new constitution. An election for all state officers was held in June. James Throckmorton, McKinney, defeated E.M. Pease, the Union candidate, for Gov., four to one. Texas now appeared to be on the road to reconstruction. Throckmorton took office in August and the newly elected legislature met that month. Things looked rosy, for Texas was once more in control of their own affairs. But this was not to be for long. The Congress was controlled by the radicals and they insisted the South should be punished for their secession, so they refused to seat the newly elected representatives. They then put into force the military rule outlined earlier, and said the military rule should exist until a suitable government could be established. Before Congress would approve any plan of government in

56

the South, the state had to ratify the 15th Amendment, giving the Negro full civil rights. A new oath of allegiance was required, which outlawed all men in Texas who had served in the Confederate Army, or had, in any manner, supported the Confederate Army. This was the lowest ebb in Reconstruction days, Texans considered this worse than the war itself.

Collin County was very lucky during these reconstruction days since no Union soldiers were stationed here. Collin County was under Major G. McClellan, who had no troops with which to control the vote, as did so many localities. The Major was a fine man, well liked by people here.

E.M. Pease, who had been beaten for the Governor's seat by Collin County's Throckmorton, was appointed by the Radicals as the Provisional Governor in July of 1867. Sheridan said that Throckmorton was still loyal to the Southern cause and would not cooperate with him, so he removed Throckmorton. Pease was a Republican, an able and honest man, but he was outnumbered by the more radical sector of his party and was forced to issue orders that were repugnant to him. Pease did his best but when he saw that he could accomplish nothing, he resigned the governorship in September 1869. When E.J. Davis was then elected governor, Texas saw that resistance was hopeless, so ratified the 14th and 15th amendments and was admitted to the Union once more, March 1870.

Here in Collin County the days of reconstruction had ended several years before. From the end of the war they had held their own elections since McClellan refused to interfere in the ballot. The reconstruction days were never much trouble here. Twice a year a patrol came this way from Ft. Richardson but never found anything to take action on. Collin County Negros gave no trouble during the war or afterward. Many of them had a hard time for a while. Throughout the Civil War the Negroes remained loyal and faithful to the families of which they were a part, many refused to leave their old homes and lived out their lives with the people they knew best.

CLEANING OUT THE BUSHWHACKERS

W.W. (Bill) Warden who was Deputy Sheriff under Jim Reed in 1864 was a mighty deputy who harbored two hates—horse thieves and bushwhackers. There were few horses left in the county as the army had taken them all but there was a surplus of bushwhackers. These were the men locally who took to the woods to avoid conscription to fight in the Confederate Army. They stayed alive by slipping back at home nights, if they lived here, and by robbing travelers or stealing from the farms where all the men were away and the women were unprotected. Some of them had been prominent citizens before the war and a very few attained respectability again after the war was over, but when the Confederate soldiers came home they regarded these men as scum, to be shot on sight.

During the Civil War they got so daring around McKinney and other Collin towns that the citizens here appealed to the famed Charles Quantrill who was camped at Sherman. He rode down to McKinney with about 100 men including our own Capt. Tuck Hill. They surrounded the Bushwhackers who were in hiding in Jernigan's Swamp (now Finch Park) and after capturing 42 of them, they were hanged from the limb of a Cottonwood tree on the Southeast corner of the square. (Blood from the hangings so polluted the big cistern below that supplied McKinney with water, that it was sealed over and a new one dug on the Northwest corner of the square.) This ended the bushwhackers in McKinney but the rest of the county continued to suffer from their depredations.

From Melissa eastward they were especially bad. Melissa was not there at that time, but the big thicket stretching from there to Blue Ridge became a vast camping ground for the Bushwhackers. They fully expected the North to win and were biding their time until that day to come out of hiding, claiming to be northern sympathizers.

Another encounter happened October 3, 1864 when Sebe Hatler east of Melissa reported Bushwhackers taking his horse. Bill Warden quickly assembled a posse of 30 men, mostly Confederate soldiers who happened to be near and rode to Hampton Mills (Squeezepenny). They learned that about 30 Bushwhackers were camped on a hill near Stony Point but were riding that day to join others at Blue Ridge. Warden and his men took up positions near Sister Grove. As the column of Bushwhackers rode near, one of the possemen's horses snorted. Instantly the Bushwhacker leader whirled his horse, followed by his men, but Warden was ready for this. The Bushwhackers were caught between two lines of fire from men who had already fought three years in the deadliest war of our time. Smoke filled the area as shots were fired at close range, three volleys. Twenty men died in less than five minutes. Only five Bushwhackers got away due to the fact that their horses stampeded off through the trees at the first volley. The posse took off in pursuit and two were killed near Blue Ridge and three just west of Farmersville. None escaped.

This broke the back of organized Bushwhacking in Collin County, though many men who had joined them had to remain in hiding long after the war had ended in 1865. Bill Warden was elected Sheriff in 1874, after years as a colorful deputy.

THE LEE-PEACOCK FEUD

The years immediately following the Civil War, or from 1865 to 1870, were perilous ones in this section of Texas. An influx of Carpetbaggers overran the country; bringing not only the Carpetbaggers themselves, but also many discharged Union soldiers, attracted at the prospect of taking over the land and property of Ex-Confederates, as had been halfway promised them. These were the years of the Reconstruction in the South.

Heavy taxes were slapped on the citizens by the Federal Government and having nothing but worthless Confederate money, they were unable to pay them and thousands of acres of land were sold for taxes. Federal soldiers were quartered at Sherman, Greenville, and Bonham to enforce the orders issued by the military authorities and by the edicts of Hardin Hart of Greenville, who had been appointed judge by General J.J. Reynolds of Austin, commanding the Union occupation forces in Texas.

Unwilling to lose their lands, the farmers resorted to the guerilla tactics resorted to by the "bushwhackers" during the war. This is, they took to the thickets and fought back, some even took to banditry by preying on the Carpetbaggers, the Jay Hawkers from Kansas, and the scallawags—the fellow who had hid out as a Union sympathizer during the war. In Northeast Collin County, with Blue Ridge as about the center, this warfare reached its peak in the Lee-Peacock feud, in which a good many men lost their lives. We will take a typical case of this feud and follow it through.

William Penn, a youth of 19, lived in Kentucky Town, in Grayson County, and operated a freight line from Jefferson to Bonham, to support his widowed mother and family, whose father had served in the Home Guards during the war. Charged with fighting a Freedman, he was taken to Sherman and placed on bond. When his case was called, his wagon became bogged in a creek and he was late at appearing for his trial. His bond was forfeited and from that day forward he became a fugitive from the military in Texas.

Together with another young man, Dow Witt, Bill Penn joined the forces of Capt. Bob Lee of the Lee-Peacock feudists. Lee had been a captain in the Confederate Army and found him beset by the Union League when he returned from the war. He took to the brush and organized his forces, to carry on the fight. This organization became so powerful that a reward was posted in McKinney, Greenville, Bonham, and Sherman by the Union forces offering $1,000 for any member of the Lee group delivered at Greenville.

On the morning of March 29, 1869 a military posse from Sherman rode into McKinney and asked that the Sheriff, George A. Wilson, help him go North a few miles and capture the outlaws, Penn and Witt, who were in hiding at the home of Col. William Fitzhugh, a short distance south of Melissa. Sheriff Wilson delegated Deputy William C. Hall to organize a posse and go with the Union men. The posse left McKinney about 10 o'clock that night, a very stormy night, with 25 or 30 men in the posse.

The posse went to Col. Fitzhugh's home and searched it, but found no bandits. They rode north a mile and surrounded the home of Mrs. Lewis, a widow, and demanded that the wanted men come out. Mrs. Lewis came to the door, lantern held high, and told them no one was at her home except her own family. A blast from a posseman's gun drove her inside. Hall and Short, two deputies, dismounted and prepared to open fire on the house.

At this point, a horseman, later found to be Witt, rode out of the woods south of the house and fired at the posse with a shotgun. He then rode into the woods with the posse in pursuit. While crossing Clements Creek, swolen by the rain, Witt's horse was shot from under him, and he was badly wounded. Witt took a stand behind a mound east of the creek, but was soon killed by the soldiers who had come up behind him. The posse rode back to McKinney in a downpour of rain.

The next morning, the posse again took to the field and Col. William Fitzhugh's home. Within 100 yards of the house, Penn and the other "outlaw" named Hayes ran out of the house and into the thicket east of the place. Sheriff Wilson and Deputy Hall ordered a charge into the brush in pursuit. All hung back, so the officers rode in pursuit, accompanied by one other man, James Johnson.

They were met by gunfire and Hall was hit four times. The others were forced to dismount and the outlaws took their horses and guns. The two men escaped. Johnson, the soldier who had gone into the thicket with the officers, was wounded, but not so seriously as Hall, who had to be carried back to McKinney on an improvised stretcher.

Hall died of his wounds a month later and orders were issued to get Penn and Hayes dead or alive. A month after these orders were received in Bonham that Penn and Hayes had been seen just north of that town in a farmhouse in a river bottom. On the night of April 20, 1869, a posse made up of the military from Sherman, and from men from Grayson, and Fannin County rode to the farm house at the mouth of Bois d' Arc Creek and surrounded it.

Like Witt had done before him, Penn came out with guns blazing while his pal,

Hayes, escaped and was never captured though the rumors have it that he was the man who commited suicide on a farm near Van Alstyne in September of that year.

Penn was shot down and in his dying moments raised his pistol and sent a shot to graze the ear of Sheriff Bill Everheart of Grayson County, who was bending over him, so William Penn died in his 22nd year, a soldier by chance, a farmer by choice, and an "outlaw" by circumstance.

Lewis Peacock was killed from ambush on June 14, 1871, and Bob Lee died the same way on the morning of May 24, 1869. Both had been leaders in the feud, and both were good men but with widely divergent views. This story is a cross section of that famous feud, about which this writer knows a lot more that he dares not print. One side has been named by reconstruction forces as "outlaws," the other side was called by the Lee sympathizers "Radicals" there was a lot of right and a lot of wrong on both sides, but, as stated before, these were perilous times in Collin County.

Collin County has furnished brave soldiers in all the wars of our nation, including the present Viet Nam War. Some who have attained greatness in rank are Gen. W.S. Scott of Melissa, who served as Chief of Staff of the U.S. Army, Admiral Henry Wiley of McKinney was in charge of the battleship division of the U.S. Navy. Audie Murphy (deceased) of Farmersville, was World War II's most decorated hero. Thousands of Collin County soldiers have given their lives—"Dead, Sir, on the Field of Honor."

ADMIRAL HENRY WILEY

EARLY SCHOOLS IN COLLIN COUNTY

A history of the schools in Collin County is really a history of its people, for no other institution so truly reflects a community and its people. These little school-houses of the past were not just dispensers of knowledge, but were the heart and soul of the community and always the social center and general meeting place. In many cases the building doubled also as a church for one or more denomination. In gathering materials on early schools I received many hundreds of letters from people who attended a pioneer school and one has only to look these letters over to see that these little schools hold a warm spot in the hearts of everyone.

Collin County can point with pride to the fact that our pioneer ancestors provided some kind of school for the young of a community almost as soon as their log cabins had been completed, many teaching their own and neighbor children in the home with whatever books were at hand. In the period from 1848 until about 1853 most of the schools were taught in the homes by a member of the family. One of the first free schools taught outside a home was one established by J.B. Wilmeth in a log cabin that he built just north of the present powerhouse north of McKinney. (1848) He and his sons and daughters taught in this school until 1855 when he moved it to the upstairs of his newly built home. Sometimes Anson Mills and E.W. Kirkpatrick taught in this school also. In 1856 Anson Mills, who later became a General, opened a paid school on a lot where the First Methodist Church now stands in McKinney. This school taught most of the subjects taught in the average High School and many of the prominent business people of Collin County passed through its doors. This was the first school in McKinney.

In the fall of 1858, R.L. Waddill employed A.L. Darnall to teach in a school situated in a small building in his back yard. His home stood just north of the present Methodist Church in McKinney. This was a free school, but not a public school, but was certainly the beginning of free schools here. This school was abandoned at the beginning of the Civil War in 1861, but reopened a year later for a year under Professor Charles Carlton, who later founded Carlton College.

This same year in 1858, J.S. Muse opened his Mount Pleasant College in his home on North Waddill Street in McKinney. This school operated for 10 years and practically all the higher branches of learning were taught here. The two-story home still stands at 1306 North Waddill and has been mentioned for a Historical Medallion.

The first Negro school in the county was opened in 1866 and stood on the same location as the Doty School now stands. John Garrett was the first teacher.

A college was founded at old Mantua in 1859 and was called the Mantua Seminary. It was a co-educational college and taught about the same subjects as Muse's college. The school operated in a lodge hall for several years, then in 1865 the building was completed. As many as 80 pupils attended and the tuition was from $10 to $20. for each of the two terms. Eight teachers made up the faculty.

Other county schools started before the Civil War. One of the first was near Westminister and was called Martin Box and was established in 1860. Another began at Walnut Grove in 1856 and was known as Swayback. None of these can be classified as a public school, since a fee was charged for attendance. Practically every school closed during the Civil War since there were no men left to teach.

In 1873 George White opened a campaign in McKinney for public schools. He organized the McKinney Academy Association and sold shares in the project for $10 per share. Enough money was raised in this way to erect a school on the five acres set aside by the Association. It stood on the land now occupied by the Middle School on the corner of Louisiana and College Streets. It was completed and opened for classes in 1874 with Nathaniel Somerville as principal and operated as a pay school. This building with two rooms upstairs and two down was built at a cost of $1,850.

In the 1880s the newspapers in McKinney began a campaign for a public school, and in 1883 the City of McKinney purchased the Academy from White's Association and began making plans for a public school and school began there in 1883 and was now called the Central Public School. This was the first free public school in McKinney. Teachers were paid partly by the state and partly by local subscription but tuition was free.

In 1883 the Plano Institute was started in that city and classes began in the Christian Church but soon moved to a building owned by W.F. Mister, the teacher. He was paid by charging tuition from his pupils. This institute conferred degrees and was operated by various owners until 1891 when the City of Plano bought the property and began a public school system.

The Westminister Institute was founded at Seven Points, now called Westminister in 1886. It was named The Seven Points College at first and later it was changed to the Westminister Institute, and functioned as such until it was purchased by the Collin County Methodists and they opened it in 1896 as the Westminister College. They soon outgrew the location and sold it and moved to Tehecu. In 1902 it was purchased by the Collin County Baptist Association and used it as a training school for teachers and preachers. This was the only real college Collin County ever had and the imposing old building still stands in the north edge of Westminister. (Razed in 1974.)

There were many institutes in McKinney from 1870 to 1890, but all of them were private schools operated by individuals—like Mrs. Bradley's School for Young Ladies, in an old church building on West Virginia Street in McKinney in 1877. She charged $2.00 per month per pupil and had as many as 75 in attendance at the time. At the same time Professor Looney and his sister taught a private school on South Tennessee Street. In 1884 they opened a Male and Female School at the same location.

McKinney's first real school was the McKinney Collegiate Institute opened in September of 1889, with Prof. J.W. Melton as teacher and President. It was co-educational and non-denominational and taught from primary grades right on through college and commercial subjects. Its main purpose was to prepare pupils for commercial work or for the universities. Over 100 stockholders subscribed to the building fund, and the structure was erected on land purchased from G.A. Foote. It was one of the finest buildings in Texas when it was completed, a two-story brick building with nine rooms and an assembly hall. It was heated with hot air flues, the first in McKinney. It opened in 1889 with Mr. Melton the president, Miss N.M. Wakefield, the principal, Miss Fanny Shipe, principal of Primary education, Miss Alma Anderson, Music, Miss Miria Saddler, Art, with the teachers boarding at the old dormitory on Foote Street for $10 per month. The school ran until 1898, when it was sold to C.C. Perrin, who ran it as Hawthorne College until 1902. It stood empty until 1904 when Prof. F.G. Jones leased it and ran it as the McKinney Training School. He taught commercial courses and generally prepared pupils for entry into a university. In 1908 it was purchased by the city of McKinney and it became a part of the McKinney School District. It was used for a number of years as J.H. Hill Central Ward School.

(If no date is given, they are "Free Schools" after 1880.)

Superintendent's Office.
1. Alla—established and financed by Dr. and Mrs. Moses Hubbard.
2. Allen
3. Altoga
4. Anna
5. Arnold (also called Freegrass)
6. Asa Walker
7. Arnold Creek
8. Ash Grove
9. Aston Chapel
10. Backbone
11. Barksdale—1860
12. Barlow—1858
13. Barnett
14. Bear Creek—1870
15. Bethel—1855
16. Betheny—1877
17. Bilderback
18. Bishop
19. Bloomdale
20. Blue Ridge
21. Barlow
22. Bass—1869
23. Bois d' arc (in West Collin)
24. Bois d' arc (S.E. Collin)
25. Bosby
26. Bowlby
27. Boggy
28. Branch
29. Boxtown (also called Fairfield)
30. Brushy
31. Brown
32. Burger (called Shain also)
33. Bush
34. Celina
35. Chambersville—1853
36. Clay Thomas—1850
37. Clear Lake
38. Clift (called also Monkey Run)
39. Climax
40. Coffman
41. Collins
42. Cold Springs
43. Copeville
44. Corinth
45. Cottage Hill
46. Cotton Belt
47. Crossroads
48. Cotton Wood—1863
49. Cow Skin (also called Harris)
50. County Line
51. Cox
52. Culleoka
53. Crossroads
54. Desert
55. Dixon (also called Frognot and Frognod)
56. Donna
57. Dublin
58. Empire
59. Enloe—1858
60. Erudia
61. Fairfield
62. Fairview
63. Falkner (called Hog Waller)
64. Farmersville
65. Farmer's Schoolhouse
66. Fayburg
67. Foote
68. Foncine
69. Flowers
70. Floyd
71. Forest Grove
72. Frankfort
73. Frankford
74. Franklin
75. Frisco
76. Grassy Lake
77. Gray Bill
78. Green Viel
79. Grounds
80. Hackberry—1860
81. Harmony (Klondike)
82. Harris (Cow Skin)
83. Heardville
84. Hedgecoxe
85. Helms
86. Hickman
87. Higgins
88. Honey Creek
89. Hopewell
90. Hutchins
91. Haggard—1858
92. Hideout—1868
93. Hocker—1854
94. Hobbins

95. Hampton—1860
96. Highland—1871
97. Illinois
98. Independence
99. Jewel
100. Johnson
101. Josephine
102. Kelly
103. Ketch Any—1860
104. Klondike
105. Kreymer
106. Lavon
107. Lebanon—1875
108. Liberty
109. Liberty Hill
110. Lick Springs—1871
111. Lick Skillet
112. Little Creek
113. Lone Elm (west Collin Co.)—
114. Lone Elm (S.E. Collin)
115. Lone Star
116. Long Neck
117. Lovejoy
118. Lower Rowlett
119. Lucas (Willow Spri gs)
120. Mantua
121. Massie—1860
122. McDonald
123. McKinney—1872
124. McMinn
125. Melissa
126. Merit
127. Mesquite
128. Midway
129. Milligan
130. Millwood
131. Moreland
132. Mississippi
133. Morris
134. Mt. Carmel
135. Mount Olive—1855
136. Mt. Pisgah (called Cairo)
137. Murphy
138. Mustang—1851
139. Muse College—1866
140. Neathery
141. Nevada
142. New Albany
143. New Hope—1866
144. New Liberty

145. New Life
146. Oak Grove (Callis)
147. Old Egypt—1852
148. Palmer
149. Parker
150. Pedigo
151. Perryville
152. Petersburg
153. Pike
154. Pilgrim
155. Plano
156. Prairie Grove
157. Prairie View
158. Pleasant Hill (Spanish Pup)
159. Pleasant Ridge (Possum Trot)
160. Princeton
161. Prosper
162. Renner
163. Rhea Mills
164. Rhymer
165. Richards
166. Richland
167. Rivers (Lone Elm)
168. Rock Hill
169. Rock Quarry (took in Henley Chapel)
170. Rock Rest—1871
171. Rosemond
172. Rose Hill
173. Routh (Donna and Flowers combined)
174. Ruth
175. Russellville
176. Rowell
177. Rowelett
178. Sabine
179. Sedallia (Independence)
180. Sellers
181. Sache
182. Shain's Chapel
183. Shady Grove—1861
184. Scantles—1856
185. Sheilds—1855
186. Scott—1862
187. Spring Creek—1857
188. Sister Grove
189. Snow Hill
190. Spring Hill
191. South Church
192. Stats (Old Liberty)

193. Stiff Chapel—1870
194. Scott
195. Searcy—1853
196. Stiff Creek—1856
197. Stinson (Who'd a Thought it)
198. Squeezepenny—1855
199. St. Paul
200. Stony Point
201. Swayback (Walnut Grove)-1853
202. Tirkey
203. Ticky (Hopewell)
204. Thompson
205. Trinity
206. Throckmorton
207. Union
208. Upper Rowelett—1861
209. Valdasta
210. Verona
211. Vineland (Hackberry)
212. Viney Grove No. 1
213. Viney Grove No. 2
214. Waddill
215. Warden
216. Water Ridge
217. West
218. Weston—1855
219. Whiterock (Rhymer, Stony Point, and Wood Dale combined 1917.)
220. Wetsel
221. Westminister (Martin Box and Seven Points consolidated)
222. White's Grove
223. Whiteley—1856
224. White Elephant
225. Wilkins
226. Willow Springs (Lucas)
227. Wilmeth
228. Wilson (Called Big Viney Grove)
229. Wilson Creek—1871
230. Winningcoff
231. Womble—1871
232. Wooddale
233. Woodlawn
234. Wylie
235. Young—1867

The first real school organized in Collin County was by Anson Mills in 1857. Mills had failed at West Point and made his way to Texas, coming by steamboat to Shreveport and walking the rest of the way to Collin County. In McKinney, Robert L. Waddill got him to organize a school in a small house that stood on the Plemmons lot about where the Methodist Church now stands in McKinney. He taught there one year and was followed by A.L. Darnall who taught until the Civil War began. This was a fine school attended by many of the prominent citizens of the county.

OLD WESTMINISTER COLLEGE

THIS PICTURE of a school group, taken on the North side of the Hutcherson School (White Elephant) that stood for several years in the Southwest corner of the pasture on the John Settle farm, about 2½ miles Northwest of Prosper, Collin County, Texas. The photo was made about 1897. Front row, left to right, Jim Jones, Jerry Moore, Etta Jones, Mary Paddock, Deloma Settle, Willard Settle, Flossie Settle, Tolliver (Tod) Settle (griping hat), Lizzie Hutcherson, Effie Moore, Annie Couser. Second row, left to right, Maud Maynard, Willie Moore, — Anderson, Mr. Vade Burkett (teacher, hat in hand), Charley Shipley, Carl Paddock, Lollie Cocanougher, Edgar Twitty. Third row, left to right, short row, Ernest Couser, Wick Settle, Horace Maynard. Fourth row, left to right, Varner Settle, John Moore (hat on), Will Cunningham, Albert Settle, Bud Nance, Rome Shipley, Fayette Cunningham, and Rube Shipley (last).

OLD RECEIPT FOR money received by R.L. Wise. A subscription school charging $1 per month.

About the only amusement open to young people in pioneer times was the square dances and parties, known as "Play Parties." As dances were frowned upon by a large percentage of the parents, fewer of them were held. In winter especially, scarcely a week night went by that there was not a play party announced somewhere within riding distance. No invitations were given, two or three neighborhood boys would gain permission from some family to have a party at their house and mount their horses and ride through the community passing the word of the party. Here is a strange fact most people do not now know. Girls and boys did not have a "date" to attend. Girls usually went with a brother or friends and at the party the young swain would ask to "See her home." It was not until the advent of the buggy that a young man called for a girl to go places with him, and even that was looked upon with high disapproval by the older generation, at first, for they were well aware of the romantic situation brought about by the buggy ride home, soft moonlight, the call of the Whip-poor-will, the purr of the buggy tires in the soft dirt. Cupid got in his best licks right here and many marriages were planned on these leisurely rides home from a party. In fact many marriages were performed at the minister's home, with the couple sitting in the buggy!

Like Americans today, those early settlers were extremely fond of music, and in nearly every home at least one person played some kind of music and sometimes the entire family could play something. There were few young people back then who could not play either the organ, banjo, guitar, mandolin, French Harp, or even the lowly Jews Harp. That age produced the great American "fiddler," a product that is as typically American as turnip greens and hog jowl. The skill of some of these fiddlers was astonishing, and it was they who set the stage for the carefree and rollicking abandon of the square dance. The young people of Collin Co. then were, as they are now, always looking for something exciting and daring. On one occasion the young people held a square dance at the bottom of a newly dug cistern (19 feet across at the bottom) on the Taylor farm east of Melissa. Another time an enormous oak tree was cut at Squeezepenny and the top of the stump was so large that a square dance was held on the stump, with lanterns hung in the nearby trees for light.

This was the period when America was at her lustiest and finest. To attend one of these pioneer parties was inspiring. To see one of the pioneer youths sitting at a piano or organ pounding out sweet music with hands gnarled and callused by swinging an axe all day in the forests or holding the handles of a "new ground plow," from sun up to sun down, made a fellow's heart swell with pride and joy of being an American.

One of the really big outings of the year was the trip to the State Fair in Dallas. Going by wagon was fun for the children, with parents trying to make Whiterock Creek by lunch time, then on to a wagon yard in Dallas by nightfall. Next morning, everyone boarded a horse-drawn car for the Fair grounds, a good two hour trip with the little mules pulling 20 or more people on a car. The little car was on the same rails that the electric street cars later ran on.

In summer when crops were "laid by" the protracted meetings sprang up all over the county. Most people called them "Camp Meetings" since people came from all over the county and camped for several days. Even families living close enough to go home at night usually camped with the others in order to enjoy visiting old acquaintances. During the day the people enjoyed big dinners all spread together on

THIS PHOTOGRAPH SHOWS a group of Wilmeth Community young people off for a day of fun at the Old Settler's Picnic. These picnics were the biggest event of the year, held on Wilson Creek in a grove of mighty trees, the event went on for days and whole families came and camped for the entire week. Some of Texas' great politicians spoke at these gatherings that numbered in the thousands.

WHILE THE FIRST airplane flight in Collin County was back in 1912, planes still drew big crowds of spectators when air shows were staged at the Old Settler's Picnic. Wing walking, loop-the-loop flying and other daredevil stunts left spectators in awed silence. (1923 photograph.)

the ground, shooting matches, wrestling matches, or even fishing, as these meetings were always staged on a river or big spring. The preaching was at night with several preachers alternating in preaching the gospel. Records show that 137 joined on one night at Morris Springs. Pioneers took their religion very seriously, but to the children, a camp meeting was a joyous affair.

Another event that afforded both children and grownups alike with fun and change was the coming of kin folk. It was not unusual for a covered wagon to drive up at a pioneer home loaded with a large family come to spend a month with the kin. The days were spent in visiting, cooking, with all women joining in the work, hunting and fishing for the men and carefree days of play for the children. Sleeping was no problem, for every household had extra bedticks folded and packed away for just such emergencies. It was the children's job to take them to the hay stack or barn and fill each tick with fresh sweet-smelling hay or shucks from the corn crib. Everyone hated to see them leave for it was always a welcome break from the routine life of the pioneer.

Women looked forward to the all day quiltings that were not only necessary to any woman with a large family to keep warm in winter, but was a welcome way to visit with neighbor women without having a feeling of guilt about being idle while visiting. (Idleness among the early settlers was almost a cardinal sin.) Many writers refer to them as "Quilting Bees," but the term was never used locally, as in the north. It was in America that quilt making reached its highest stage in feminine design and workmanship and many of these old quilts are still treasured mementos of days that are gone.

Fishing, then as now, was a popular sport with the men and boys as soon as the work of the fields would allow them to go. All the streams and sloughs were situated in a lovely setting, big trees, whiterock beds for the water to flow over, and plenty of fish, buffalo, perch, cat fish. Hunting, too, afforded the men a break from the work of the farms and kept their families fed with fresh meat.

It was not until much later that such amusements as the circus, Buffalo Bill's Show, and others came to Collin County.

In the 90's Collin County was well into that period of history called "The Gay Nineties." The economy was booming. Clearing of the forests and selling the cordwood had paid for the farms with money to spare. King Cotton was coming into his reign, and the hard times of the pioneer days were almost forgotten. In this period of opulence a social order came to life in old Collin. Every town had newly rich people who had made a fortune in freighting, selling buffalo hides, and buffalo bones, and in their newly found leisure, they established a social order par deluxe. Gracious living came into its own. McKinney had an Opera House and many of the famous people of that day appeared on its stage.

Some of the early Women's clubs were The Chautauqua Circle, organized in McKinney in 1890 for self improvement and literary culture, the first literary club in McKinney. The Owl Club was organized in 1893 to work for school improvement. Eidelweiss Club was organized in 1898 to work for city improvement and to get a town clock, improve sidewalks, and beautify surroundings. The Pierrian Club was organized to do charitable work. The Entre Nous Club was organized to improve schools and city. The Delphian Club was organized to promote charitable work among the poor. The Art Literature Club was to study both art and literature. Mother's Clubs, a fore-runner of the PTA, were formed to better conditions at the schools and to promote cooperation between the teachers and the parents. The Scott-Dixon Chapter of the UDC had the responsibility of furnishing the dinners the

Confederate Veterans enjoyed from time to time and to look after the interest of ailing veterans. The City Federation of Women's Clubs was organized along civic and charitable lines. They secured Finch Park, started manual training at the high school, started inspection of foods sold here, and in 1911 secured the statue of Gov. Throckmorton that stands on the Court House square.

The McKinney Rotary Club was organized May 30, 1919 with 24 members. Dr. A.E. Booth, pastor of the First Baptist Church, was its first president. (Daily Courier Gazette, Sept. 22, 1921)

Empire Lodge, Odd Fellows was organized in 1852 and dissolved in 1916. At that time the W.C. Burrus Lodge was organized.

The Rebekahs organized in 1890 as an auxillary of the I.O.O.F. Dr. T.W. Wiley was the Grand Master of the Texas Grand Lodge.

Brotherhood of American Yoemen organized about 1917 with J.M. Davis the foreman. It went under the name Perkins Homestead.

The Old Settlers and Confederate reunion was organized at a meeting April 28, 1883 at the court house.

The Camp Fire movement started in McKinney in 1927, when Miss Lois Largent's class at old Central school felt the need for diversion in leisure hours.

A Possum and Tate Club was organized Dec. 4, 1901 with E.W. Kirkpatrick as president and Jim Dockins as keeper of the records.

The Prosper Masonic Lodge, No. 435, was organized at Rheas Mill with W.M. Miller, W.D. Davis, and Alexander Newman the officials. (Complete story in *Daily Courier Gazette, June* 25, 1925.)

The Lions Club was organized in McKinney in Nov. 10, 1920, with J.L. Chapman as President. (Story in DCG Nov. 11, 1920.)

The very first lodge in Collin County was when the Grand Lodge of Texas granted a dispensation for Lodge No. 51 at McKinney in Jan. 16, 1849. (From Grand Lodge of Texas, Vol. 1, P. 276.)

The Empire Lodge No. 68 was organized at McKinney in May 5, 1857 and was one of the most active lodges among the Odd Fellows of Texas.

The Chamber of Commerce was organized at McKinney Oct. 3, 1913 with F.B. Pope as President, Avery Dowell as Vice-President, F.D. Perkins, Secretary, and Sam Massie, Treasurer.

The County Federation of Women's Clubs was organized at McKinney, Nov. 16, 1915, with Mrs. M.H. Garnett the chairman, and Mrs. K.D. Thompson the Secretary. Fourteen clubs from all over the county participated. Some of the women present for the first meeting were Miss Hattie Neatherly of Farmersville, Mrs. Robert Holsonbake of the Culture Club, Mrs. Kimbrough of the Entre Nous Club, Mothers Club of Farmersville sent Mrs. W.P. Herron, Mrs. J.T. Foster and Mrs. J.L. Greer represented the McKinney Mothers Club, Mrs. McDonald from the UDC, Mrs. W.B. Carson from Celina Civic Club. Mrs. John L. Lovejoy was elected President (DCG Nov. 18, 1915.)

Roland W.O.W. organized by J.D. Alexander of Garland, May 31, 1901. (DCG Feb. 27, 1936)

Collin County Alliance met Feb. 20, 1886 and a flour mill was pledged to turn out flour from 1000 bushels of wheat daily. The six towns involved were McKinney, Weston, Farmersville, Melissa, Allen, and Plano.

Modern Woodmen of America was organized in 1908 in McKinney with its Auxillary, the Royal Neighbors of America.

The Order of Eastern Star, auxillary of the Masonic Blue Lodge, was organized Sept. 1911.

The Roland W.O.W. was organized in 1901.

The I.O.O.F. Lodge of Prosper was the old Rock Hill Lodge, one of the oldest in the county. New building was dedicated in 1903.

The Elks organized Jan. 24, 1903 with M.S. Metz as Exalted Ruler.

Knights Templer No. 34 K.T. instituted in 1900, with J.S. Heard and Eminent Commander.

St. John's Lodge, A.F. and A.M. No. 51, instituted Jan. 24, 1850 and by 1906 owned their own building, with H.S. Wysong Worshipful Master.

Haggai Chapter, No. 55, R.A.M. was instituted June 24, 1856.

Odd Fellows, Empire Lodge, No. 68, I.O.O.F. was instituted in May 5, 1857.

The Knights of Pythias, Defiance Lodge No. 28, was instituted in 1886.,

The W.O.W. Magnolia Camp No. 431. W.O.W. started in 1886.

Secret Orders:

B.P.O.E., Lodge No. 827, Org. Jan. 24, 1893. Membership, 175. J. Ed Rhea, E.R.; John Penn, E.L.K.; Joe Burton, E.L.K.; Tom Goodner, Treas.; W.T. Oglesby, Secty.; Roy Largent, Tyler, Mgr.; S. Wiseman, G.W. Fox and J.P. Thomas, Trustees. Meets Elk Hall, 301-03 N. Ky. St.

Masonic: Commandry No. 34. H.Q. Smith, E.C.; J.R. Gough, Gen.; T.J. Cloyd, C. of G.; S.J.B. Plemmons, E.P.; L.A. Scott, Treas.; R.F. Dowell, Recorder; M.S. Metz, S.W.; E.E. King, S.B.; G.E. Abernathy, J.W.; A.E. Smith, W.; V.M. Keene, Sentinel. Meets Masonic Hall, 217 N. Ky. St.

St. John's Lodge, No. 51., A.F. & A.M.; R.A. Abernathy, W.M.; J.A. Garrison, S.W.; A.L. Gerrish, J.W.; E.E. King, Chaplain; W.B. Newsome, Treas.; R.F. Dowell, Sec.; J.H. Hill, S.D.; S. Lamdsdale, J.W.; W.C. Gerrish, S.S.; A.J. Allen, J.D.; V.M. Keene, Tyler. Meets Masonic Hall.

Haggai Chapter, No. 53. J.H. Taylor, H.P.; W.M. Shirley, E.S.; G.E. Abernathy, E.K.; S.J.B. Plemmons, C of H; S.T. Hammond, R.A.C.; T.J. Cloyd, P.S.; H.Q. Smith, Treas.; R.F. Dowell, Scribe; W.R. Dowell, G.M.; 1st V; J.K. Wilson, G.M., 2d V; J.M. Woody, G.M., 3rd V; V.M. Keene, Guard. Meets Masonic Hall.

K of P, DeFiance Lodge, No. 28. Org. 1882. G.M. Alsup, C.C.; C.A. Turrentine, P; O.M. Goddard, K of R.S.; T.J. Melton, M of F; H.L. Davis, M of E; Meets K of P southeast cor square.

W.O.W. Woodmen Circle; No. 736. Mrs. Quinnie B. Koch, Guardian; Mrs. Beatrice Padgitt, Clerk; D.M. Padgitt, Banker. Meets K of P Hall.

Magnolia Camp No. 431. I.E. Rives, C.C.; D.D. Marley, P.C.C.; R.L. Worsham, A.L.; L.W. Crouch, Banker; L.J. Truitt, Clerk; E.C Meadows, Escort; S.H. Stalcup, W.; Frank Hendricks, Sentry; Dr. W.C. Bryant, Phys. W.N. Griffin, W.L. Yarborough and S.E. Walker, Managers. Meets K of P. Hall.

International Barbers' Union of America, Loca. No. 346. Members 20. Meets in Palace Barbershop, east side square. Jack Gocher, Pres.; J.W. Jones, Sety.

I.O.O.F. Empire Lodge No. 68. Membership 202. Org. May 5, 1857. E.G. West, N.G.; T.C. Andrews, V.G.; G. Adams, Secty.; J.L. Franklin, Treas. Meets Odd Fellows Hall, northeast cor square.

McKinney Rebecca Lodge, No. 85. Org., Feb. 25, 1887. Mrs. Emma W. Moreland, N.G.; Mrs. Eppie De Shields, V.G.; Miss Allie Rogers, F.S.; Miss Emma Pearce, R.S.; Mrs. Ed West, Treas. Meets Odd Fellows Hall.

Collin Co. Home Relief Assn. Org. 1901. Membership 2,000. M.G. Abernathy, Pres.; McCarty Moore, V.P.; W.B. Carnes, Secty.; H.H. White, Treas. Meets 1st of each Mo. in Commercial Hotel Club Rooms, 217 North Ky. St.

Commercial Club of McKinney. Org. Nov. 1, 1907. Membership 160. R.E. Carpenter, Pres.; Dick Allen, 1st V.P.; A.L. Anderson, 2d V.P.; L.W. Crouch, Treas.; W.B. Carnes, Secty.; Giles McKinney, W.H. Matthews, Howell E. Smith, McCarry Moore, Geo. Wilcox, Walter B. Wilson, J.L. White, G.M. Alsup, Alfred Scott, C.W. Smith, Sam Massie and Dr. E.L. Burton, Directors. Meets once a Mo. Commercial Club Rooms, 217 N. Ky.

Civic League of McKinney. Mrs. K.D. Thompson, Pres.; Mrs. P.H. Lawson.

COLLIN COUNTY AND THE
SPANISH-AMERICAN WAR—1898

For a small war, the Spanish-American War had a great impact on Collin County as well as the rest of the nation. It came during that period of history known as the "Gay Nineties," and they were gay. The hardships of pioneer days were behind us, people everywhere were prosperous and the tragedy of the Civil War strife was well past.

Spain had owned Cuba for several hundred years, off and on, and now the Cubans had revolted against Spanish rule and taken to the jungles and were fighting a bitter guerilla warfare, not only against Spain, but against any authority whatever. The Spanish Army commanded by Gen. Wyler a soldier of fortune, retaliated by herding the Cubans into stockades and starving a good many of them. At first the Americans did not pay too much attention to the situation until the newspapers took up the cry. The President, William McKinley, did not wish to mix into the affair, but finally, egged on by the newspapers, he took action, against his wishes. He asked Congress to look into the matter.

The matter was taken out of his hands on Feb. 15, 1898 when our big battleship, The Maine, was blown up in the Havana Harbor, taking the lives of 264 American naval officers and men. Immediately the cry resounded from one end of the land to the other, "The Spaniards destroyed the Maine. Let's blow the Dons out of Cuba." Our torpedo boats cruised along the shores of Cuba, capturing every Spanish craft they saw. The president called for 100,000 volunteers and 200,000 joined. Congress declared War against Spain April 19, 1898. Only one real battle was fought, at Santiago and the American forces won. Very few of the volunteers ever got out of the country, the war was fought mostly by the regular army and navy.

As soon as the call went out for volunteers, plans were made to raise a company in Collin County. A meeting was held at the courthouse and James F. Rhea was selected to organize a company of infantry as soon as possible. In three days Rhea had his company. Rhea was elected Capt., H.F. McDonald, 1st Lt., and C.C. Provine, 2nd Lt. Counting the officers, there were 120 men on the roster. Capt. Rhea drilled his men on the square in McKinney every night and soon left McKinney on a special train for Camp Ball in Houston, where they were mustered into the Regular U.S. Army July 12, 1898 and designated as Company C, 4th Texas Infantry. Those in the company besides the officers already given were:

Abernathy, W.R.	Cooley, W.F.	Fordyce, Arch
Allen, John M.	Corbett, J.H.	Foreman, Edgar
Anderson, A.L.	Cox, W.F.	Franklin, Wm.
Beauchamp, J.E.	Crockett, James	Gates, H.D.
Bechett, I.L.	Cullingham, G.R.	Gerrish, M.E.
Beckett, R.O.	Daugherty, Joseph	Greer, W.A.
Bell, M.J.	Davis, T.H.	Greer, W.T.
Board, E.M.	Derrick, R.K.	Hall, John
Burnett, F.C.	Duncan, J.O.	Hamilton, J.B.
Burrage, R.W.	Dunn, Durrett	Harper, J.R.
Calhoun, H.S.	Dunn, H.B.	Howard, J.S.
Carr, J.D.	Evans, W.A.	Huff, N.D.
Chancellor, F.L.	Fain, J.E.	Hulse, T.B.
Childress, W.B.	Forbes, J.R.	Hutchinson, R.E.
Coleman, W.F.	Forbes, J.T.	Kendall, W.C.

Kiersey, A.M.
Kirkpatrick, Hugh
Knott, W.H.
Lane, S.L.
Lawson, H.B.
Lawson, W.A.
Lee, Byrd
Leister, J.K.
Lewis, W.H.
Lincoln, W.B.
McGarrah, George
McRae, W.C.
Mack, Clay Jr.
Mack, R.P.
Maddox, M.B.
Malone, J.W.
Melton, Arthur
Meroney, Albert
Meyers, J.H.
Moore, Locke
Moore, M.L.
Murley, B.R.H.
Murphey, Wm.

Negbour, R.A.
Ogilvie, J.W.
Pafford, Lawrence
Palmer, F.H.
Perkins, F.D.
Powell, A.N.
Powell, Lee
Powell, W.F.
Quisenberry, George
Rambo, E.A.
Reynolds, J.L.
Rickerson, J.M.
Riggers, V.B.
Roach, E.B.
Rogers, James
Rogers, S.P.
Ross, Harry
Rowland, S.E.
Sampson, O.B.
Sapp, W.H.
Sherrill, Richard
Smith, B.F.
Spray, J.H.

Stancell, Mancel
Stephens, S.H.
Stewart, W.T.
Stiff, Ollie
Straus, S.G.
Tarpley, W.A.
Taylor, C.E.
Thompson, W.D.
Thompson, W.F.
Veon, A.
Ward, C.C.
Wyatt, Harris
Welbonds, J.L.
Williams, John
Williams, Samuel
Williams, W.H.
Wilson, J.B.
Wilson, Walter B.
Wolam, J.H.
Wooten, L.B.
Worthy, A.V.

The following paid their own way and joined the company on July 10.

Brown, C.E.R.
Brumley, R.H.
Cecil, Samuel

Dilbeck, J.L.
Flanagan, E.E.
Jackson, E.A.

Love, O.M.

The company remained at Camp Ball until Spain surrendered, July 17, then were transferred to Camp Mosby in San Antonio to await discharge. Peace was made with Spain on December 10 and the men expected to be sent home at once, however the term of enlistment was for one year and they were asked to volunteer for duty in the Philippines where troops were needed in the 33rd Volunteer Infantry. They voted not to go and were discharged.

GREAT MEN OF COLLIN COUNTY . . .
By Capt. Roy F. Hall

Naturally, the names of Collin McKinney and James W. Throckmorton come to mind at once. But were they the greatest, or were they great because at the time they served the people there were very few inhabitants of the county and almost anyone who displayed any leadership whatever stood out? We must take that fact into consideration, along with the other attributes of the two men. Let us see.

In order to qualify for greatness a man must attain to leadership; not merely occupy an office or such due to accidents of the times, and mostly, he must not have attained leadership because of pure luck; like being on hand when needed and the like. We have always had plenty of such leaders. Plainly, man who attains greatness must arrive at a high office because he can fill that office better than anyone else in the community, whether it be mayor of a small town or the President of the United States. In order to be great he must not have attained leadership due to a political ring, a clique or as the chosen candidate of a political party. Did Collin McKinney and James Throckmorton become leaders of men due to chance or to party adherance or were they great men due to their own conduct? Let's look further into this.

As early as 1832 Collin McKinney was chosen by the people of the Red River District in northeast Texas as a delegate to represent them in the legislature of Coahuila and Texas at Coahuila, and later that same year, he was named a delegate from the Red River District to the First Convention at San Felipe. He was also a delegate to the Second Convention at San Felipe the following year, and to the Consultation in 1834, and of course, he was a member of the Convention at San Felipe in March, 1836, that declared for Texas independence, and helped draft that declaration.

Collin McKinney was already an old man, having been born in New Jersey in 1766, and his help in drafting the Texas Declaration of Independence was his last public service. His signature on that historic document is the last he ever wrote for his country. He returned to his home near present Texarkana, and came to present Collin County in 1845, settling seven miles southeast of present Van Alstyne. He never sought public office again, but lived in peace on his farm until his death in 1861, at the age of 95. His remains rest in the cemetery at Van Alstyne.

James W. Throckmorton had been in present Collin County three years when Collin McKinney came to the present county. With his father and three others, James Throckmorton settled seven miles north of present McKinney in 1842. He was then 18 years of age, and on the death of his father the following year, assumed the leadership in the new settlement. He alone was responsible for the continuance of the settlement, holding the pioneers together and encouraging others to join them from the settlements in northeast Texas.

He was one of the first to locate in the new county seat of McKinney where he entered upon the practice of law, his office being where the law firm of Moses & Truett was located on West Virginia Street. Throckmorton had studied medicine in Kentucky and at first practiced medicine in McKinney. The Mexican War of 1846 however, in which he served, influenced him to believe that his life work lay elsewhere. He entered politics and was elected to the Texas Legislature where he served both as a senator and as a representative for almost 11 years.

On the outbreak of the Civil War, 1861, he led eight counties in north Texas in voting not to leave the union. The Secession Convention though voted to secede and Throckmorton came back to Collin County and organized a company for the Confederate Army. Other than his service with this company, he was appointed commander of the Third Military District of Texas and as a brigadier-general in command of the Frontier District.

After the war he was president of the Constitutional Convention at Austin. This was in early 1866, and later that year he was elected Governor of Texas. Afterward, he served almost 20 years as Congressman, and was nominated for Governor by the Democrat Party in 1890. Ill health forced him into retirement, and he died in April, 1894, and rests in Pecan Grove cemetery. His monument stands on the courthouse lawn in McKinney.

Now, records show that Throckmorton did far more for this county than did Collin McKinney, but that is not the point of the question. Mrs. I.R.S. wants to know who was Collin County's greatest man, irrespective of his service to the county. Apparently she wants to know who was the greatest man who ever lived in the county; not alone the one who served us best.

This county has produced many great men, but in the popular mind of all the people, Collin McKinney and James Throckmorton stand first. Which was the greater? I wonder who is in position to say. The accomplishments of Throckmorton far outweighed those of Collin McKinney, but the popularity of Collin McKinney far outweigh those of Throckmorton. This writer gets ten letters inquiring about Collin McKinney to one, asking of James Throckmorton. In naming this county and its county seat for Collin McKinney, he was assured of a place in history. When James Webb Throckmorton became the first settler in this area, the future Collin County was assured.

There is no reason to believe that either of the two men were anything but great, but in totally unrelated characteristics. Collin McKinney was a quiet, unassuming man. He could not make even a short speech, but he was a doer when Texas needed doers. Throckmorton, on the other hand, was a gifted orator, some of his speeches have became classics. He also was a soldier, serving the Republic of Texas as a ranger and the Confederacy as a general officer, and in the Mexican War, as a surgeon. Collin McKinney had no military record.

The answer to Mr. G.I.M.'s question as to the county's greatest soldier, is contingent, like reputations of Throckmorton and Collin McKinney, on popular opinion to an extent. General W. S. Scott of Melissa, served as Chief of Staff of the U.S. Army, while Admiral Henry Wiley of McKinney was in command of the battleship division of the U.S. Navy. Farmersville furnished our greatest hero, well-known to all—Audie Murphy.

This writer could name over a hundred men who attained to commissioned rank and served in the armed forces from Collin County. To name the greatest however, is totally beyond his scope. All were great. All served to the fullest degree in the capacity in which they occupied. This writer is compiling material for a book on the military history of Collin County, and I wish to tell you this: no county in the United States has furnished more soldiers per capita than has Collin County. And too, none has paid a higher price for patriotism. Over 2,000 of our men have died on the field of honor.

There is no way to compare them. In greatness they stepped forward when their country needed them. All were great.

Capt. William Fitzhugh came to Collin County in the 1840's and was involved in the early life here, served in the Civil War. When his daughter, Sarah Elizabeth, married Henry C. Herndon at Melissa in 1871 he invited the Indians to attend the wedding, the first and perhaps the last time Indians attends a wedding. (Biography *Daily Courier Gazette,* Aug. 23, 1923)

Henry Wetsel, who started the first grist mill in McKinney and was a fine cabinet maker, came to Collin in February of 1848, lived to be 89 years of age.

William Warden was born in Missouri January 1833, and came with his parents to Texas in 1844, crossing Red River at Bonham which at that time had one log cabin and one log cabin store. The family settled at Climax in 1857, the first settlers. Warden served in Alf Johnson's Spy Company, surrendered at Appomattox.

A.J. Taylor came to Collin from Tennessee in 1853. He was one of the first cabinet makers and coffin makers in the area. He married Tabitha Jane Scott, daughter of an early pioneer who served in the Legislature. His son, Wash Taylor, worked on early newspapers, the *Messenger,* also *The Democrat,* and the *Examiner.*

Lewis Shirley settled one half mile west of Melissa in 1852, coming there from Kentucky. His daughter Anna married Good Graves who was a Capt. in the Civil War.

Joseph R. Rhea came to Collin in 1855 and settled at Rhea Mills where he died in Jan 7, 1863. His son, W.A., was in mercantile business with Larkin Adams at Weston. He started the mill that took the family name. He served in Co. D, 7th Texas Cavalry and was Capt. in 1862. He lost a foot at Corinth, Miss. He served as Adjutant General under Governor Murrah. (Biog. Daily CG, March 29, 1906)

James Sandford Muse was born in Virginia Oct. 31, 1804, one of 17 children. Joined with the Christian Church movement in Kentucky in the early 1840's and was a friend of Alexander Campbell, founder of the movement. Came to Collin in 1857 and built his big house on present Waddill Street with the intention of opening a school in it. His school was one of the finest to be found in North Texas. (Biog. Daily CG, July 9, 1936)

George S. Morris came to Collin in 1853 with his stepfather, Robert L. Waddill. In 1855 he erected a big house on Benge Street. He served two terms as District Judge. (Biog. Daily CG, June 2, 1910)

I.D. Newsome came to McKinney from Mississippi in 1852 with his bride, the former Lucy Willingham. He opened a small mercantile store. He served in the Confederate Army. (Biog. Daily CG, Sept. 20, 1900.)

Abe Enloe came to Collin with his parents at age 5, in 1850 and camped on Wilson Creek near Fitzhugh Mills. He later said that in 1850 McKinney had few houses other than log cabins. (Biog. Oct. 11, 1900, Daily CG)

Wiley Dugger settled four miles east of McKinney in 1851, pioneer farmer and community builder. He had 13 children and has many descendents in Collin Co. (Biog. Daily CG, April 19, 1928)

Isaac Talkington, born in Kentucky in 1795 came to Collin in 1856. His son, Leonidas, came with his father, served in the Civil War in Capt. Haynes Company K. He served as County Treasurer in 1888.

Dr. Reuben A. Taylor came to Texas in 1853 and located at Weston later moved to Millwood and practiced medicine there. He married Sue, daughter of Capt. James Naylor, early settler. He served as First Lieutenant in Capt. Naylor's company in the Civil War.

William H. Perkins came to Collin in March 1855. He was an architect and builder and built many homes in McKinney, including the old Tucker Hotel that stood on the northeast corner of the square. (Biog. Daily CG June 2, 1904 and April 30, 1936)

G.H. Fields came to Collin in 1853 and settled at Sedalia, six miles northeast of Anna. His son, D.L., was a freighter from Jefferson using ox wagons and five or six yoke of oxen per wagon, buying for I.D. Newsome and Jack Tucker's stores. He used huge wagons made of Bois d' Arc wood. He served in the Civil War under Capt. Bush. (D.C. June 9, 1904)

Frank M. Hunn, born in Kentucky in 1838, came to Collin in the early days, and served during the Civil War in Johnson's Spy Company. He married Cynthia Ann Dunn, daughter of Tola Dunn, one of the very first of the settlers. She was the first white child born in Collin Co.

Capt. W.P. Wiygle, a close friend of Alexander Campbell, founder of the Christian Church, came to Collin Co. from Mississippi by boat to Jefferson and by stagecoach on to McKinney in 1866. He purchased the farm where Ft. Buckner had stood, later settling in McKinney. (Biog. DCG, Nov. 13, 1919)

D.W. Fulton came to Van Alstyne in 1849, later married Margaret E., granddaughter of Collin McKinney. He served in the 6th Texas Cavalry in the Civil War and was in 85 battles.

C.B. Moore settled near Chambersville in 1856 and kept a diary for 60 years.

Dr. B.M.E. Smith came to McKinney in 1853 from Kentucky. He was a partner of Dr. Fitzgerald. He was one of the founders of the drug store that still operates under his name. He served in Col. J.B. Wilmeth's regiment in the Civil War. (Biog. Daily CG, March 17, 1904)

John Bowman, his wife and children, came to two miles south of Blue Ridge from Virginia in ox wagons in 1849 and settled there.

Samuel Bogart came to Collin County in 1845 from Tennessee where he had served in the Blackhawk War. He later moved to Missouri and took part in expelling the Mormons. In 1839 he commanded a company in the Meir Expedition. He was an important figure in the early development of the county, elected to the Legislature from 1847 through 1859, and held positions of honor in the Democratic Party from 1848 to 1857.

John B. Martin came to Dallas in 1842 and stayed with John Neely Bryan for a while then back to Fannin Co. In Feb. 1843 a report went out that Dr. Colder had been killed near present McKinney. He and 25 men under Hack McGarrah were in the saddle in a matter of hours and trailing the Indians. He later served in Col. Wm. Young's regiment from Bonham. He secured a headright in 1852. He was elected County Commissioner in Collin and had 11 children.

Josiah Nichols came to Collin Co. in 1846 and shortly enlisted in Capt. Stapp's Co. at Ft. Buckner. He served with Capt. Fitzhugh's Company in the Civil War. He settled four miles east of Melissa and held a number of county offices: Sheriff, tax assessor, and collector. (Biog. DCG, May 14, 1914)

James M. Graves came to Collin in 1845 and married Martha, the daughter of pioneer settler John Coffman. He served with Bell's Regiment in the Mexican War and stayed several years on the frontier. He came to Collin Co. with 50 cents, a flintlock, a pony and saddle and soon lost his pony to the Indians. He became a big landowner.

C.A. McMillen (Comfort Allen) came to Murphy in Collin County in 1845, camping first at Buckner, to graze the sheep he had brought with him. The first night they camped near McGarrah's, Indians raided nearby and wiped out a whole family. Few people were here. Charlie Wysong was the sheriff. He and his family and friends who came with him settled at Murphy Jan. 1, 1846 and found land selling for 25 cents per acre. (Biog. DCG, Feb. 20, 1908)

Capt. Thomas Morton Scott served in the Mexican War and later commanded troops against the Indians on the fronteir, coming to Texas in 1852. He served in the 9th Texas Cavalry during the Civil War and was made Capt. after the Battle of Shiloh, and later was assistant adjutant General under President Jefferson Davis. One of his ancestors, Thomas Scott, was an officer in Cromwell's army, served in Parliament and signed the death warrant for King Charles Stuart. (Biog. Confederate Vet. Mag.)

J.R. Gough who was born in west Collin County was a Justice of the Peace, served six years in the Legislature, and was Senator for Collin and Hunt Counties. He was a "free silver" advocate.

George M. Watts came to Collin County from Kentucky in 1855, coming down the Mississippi to Shreveport and getting outfitted with wagons, made the long trip overland. Once owned the Tucker Hotel, after a year bought a home just east of McKinney and opened a flour mill, said to have been the fore-runner of the Bur--rus Mill. Later operated a gin. (Biog. July 14, 1904, Dem.)

Dr. Anderson Gullett, a surgeon in the Confederate Army came to McKinney in 1867, making the trip from Missouri in an ox wagon. His wife and son Joe came with him and made their home on South Church Street. (Biog. Dem. June 16, 1938)

Johnnie Faires and family came to McKinney in 1857 to join his son John who came in 1852. He built a home in the 400 block of South Tennessee St. in McKinney. He and his son were both skilled wood workers. (Biog. DCG June 23, 1932)

Joel F. Stewart came to Collin County from Missouri in 1845 and settled 1 mile north of McKinney. Later headrighted land seven miles northwest of McKinney, rearing nine children.

Salathial Coffey came to McKinney in 1855 and settled on a farm near Wetsel, had seven children, reared six stepchildren and several orphans.

Preston Witt settled six miles east of Plano in 1849. He was in the Battle of San Jacinto and also served in the Mexican War. He built the first mill in Dallas Co. at Carrolton, hauling the machinery from Illinois when he came. At first it was a tread mill but later converted it into the first steam mill. (Biog. Dem. Aug. 7, 1924)

John Parker and family came to Old Decatur, later Murphy, in 1856 and opened a general store. One of his sons, Samuel L., was with Frank Weldon when he captured Bell Starr and put her in jail at Paris. He was a ranger also.

So far as is known there are five graves in Collin of veterans who served in the American Revolution. In 1913 the Richard Royal Chapter of The Daughters of The American Revolution marked the grave of one of them who lived in Collin Co. He was John Abston who lies in a small cemetery between Millwood and Lavon.

E.W. Kirkpatrick came from Jefferson County, Tennessee to Collin Co. with his family in 1856. He entered the Confederate Army at age 18 and was with Martin's Regiment, wounded at Cabin Creek, Indian Territory. He came home, taught a free school in 1872, afterward was County Supt. of Schools in Collin. Also a surveyor. He entered the nursery business and developed many varieties of new fruits and nuts. At one time he shipped several ship loads of Mustang Grape cuttings to France and used them as grafts to save France's many vineyards that were dying. He organized the Throckmorton Camp of the Confederate Veterans and his home was the headquarters for the annual picnic and reunion of all veterans, and Daughters of the Confederacy. (Biog. and Photo in Confed. Vet. Mag. May 1924)

Joseph W. Baines married Ruth Huffman at McKinney Sept. 12, 1869 and began to practice law and also dealt in real estate. He was Secretary of State from 1883 to 1887. He owned and edited the McKinney *Advocate* in McKinney in 1877, later called it the *Black Waxy;* later consolidated with the Collin Co. *Citizen*. He was an ancestor of Lyndon B. Johnson, past President of the United States.

Thomas W. Wiley, a physician, served in the Civil War in Alabama with the 6th Alabama Infantry, was badly wounded and walked home after the war on crutches. He came to McKinney after the war. One of his sons, Henery A., was later to become an Admiral.

Jesse Shain came to Collin in 1851 with his parents, Tom Shain. Tom ran a blacksmith shop at his farm east of McKinney. Later he became a deputy sheriff and was killed by a horse thief in 1860. His wife died the same year and the four children lived with the Burrell Stiff family during the Civil War. At 18 Jesse started his own livery stable, later a merchant, also he dealt in real estate. He started a private bank on the west side of the square in 1902. At the time of his death he owned 23 brick buildings in McKinney, much land, and many houses. (Biog. Will. Photo. Dem. May 3, 1906)

Henry C. Miller, son of Judge and Mrs. L.L. Miller of Farmersville, came to Texas when a few months old in 1889. They settled at Climax, later moved to Farmersville. He joined the law firm of Merritt and Merritt in McKinney on July 1, 1913. He was elected mayor of McKinney in 1921, the youngest mayor in the state. (Biog. Dem. Sept. 22, 1921)

Andrew J. Atkinson came to Rowlett with his family in 1852. He helped Oliver Hedgecoxe survey Collin County and married Hedgecoxe's sister. He served in Co. E in Stephen's Regiment during the Civil War. (Biog. Dem. April 23, 1908)

Grafton Williams headrighted land in Mt. Olive community in 1848 and married Lizzie Standifer. She was the first person buried in the Mt. Olive Cemetery. (Biog. DCG Nov. 3, 1921)

Ben T. Estes came to Texas from Kentucky in 1856. He was a guard on the mail stage coach that ran from San Antonio and El Paso and in that year settled in McKinney, and married Nannie Powell in Jan., 1967. He started a mercantile store. (Biog. DCG Jan. 3, 1918)

James McKinney, cousin of Collin McKinney, came to McKinney in 1868 and built a hotel. Later he ran the Foote House and the Heard House. Charles, his son, built the first telephone line in Collin Co. It ran from the Foote House to the H. and T.C. Railroad depot. (Biog. DCG Feb. 11, 1926)

William and Mart Kindle came to the Higgins community before the Civil War and were early settlers and farmers.

Reddic C. White came to McKinney in 1858 and was in business until the Civil War. He was in Co. K, 6th Texas Cavalry under Capt. Throckmorton. After the war he was admitted to the Bar and practiced law in McKinney. He married Virginia Plummer and served as Mayor.

Dr. Bere S. Shelburne came to Lebanon from Kentucky in 1857. He served as brigade surgeon with Gen. Albert Pike during the Civil War. He went to the Texas Legislature in 1869 from Collin and served four years.

John D. Brown, his wife and children, came to Collin from Virginia in 1845 and settled at Cottage Hill on Honey Creek. His children married and settled around him. Joseph Russell and family started to Texas with them but took separate routes. It was a coincidence that both ox wagons arrived at Buckner the same day. Russell headrighted between Plano and Allen on Russell's Branch. Wallace Hughston was his grandson.

Jake Chamberlain, born July 10, 1897, was a slave of J.B. Wilmeth. He married five times and had several children. He did some preaching and owned a farm on Millwood Road. (Biog. Photo, CDG Jan. 28, 1904 at age 105 years.)

Henry H. Tucker got one section of land as a grant, north of Buckner.

Henry Stiff came to the Stiff Chapel ahead of his brother Lewis who arrived in the area in 1849. For ten years Henry freighted from San Antonio, Jefferson, Houston, Galveston, and Ft. Smith, Ark. He also freighted for the Confederacy, bringing them supplies. (Biog. D. June 12, 1913)

Capt. John (Rutabaga) Johnson came to Collin from Missouri in August 1861. He had 13 children and served in the Texas Legislature and later in the Constitutional Convention in 1875. He also served in the State Senate. He is buried in the Johnson Cemetery four miles east of McKinney under the largest monument in the County.

Tom and Mary Bradley settled in McKinney in 1848 and were active in helping form the new town. He gave the land for the first High School. Bradley Street was named for him.

Captain Robert Milton Board came to McKinney from Virginia in 1856. When Capt. Dixon was killed in battle at Shiloh, Lt. Board was made Capt. of the company, one of the youngest in the war. He became the partner of I.D. Newsome and they were the first cotton buyers, shipping it to Jefferson. (Biography Dem. Oct. 29, 1930)

Mansel Wilmeth came to Texas with his father's wagon train in 1845. He and James Reed moved the first store in McKinney from Ft. Buckner and hauled logs to build the first house in McKinney. He had the first nursery in the area and was noted for his fine fruit. (Biog. Dem. June 23, 1904. Photo)

Major John A. Buck and his son A.C. were widely known for the fine horses they raised and trained. The most famous of the horses was Reno Clipper.

John L. Lovejoy came first to Texas in 1845 and lived at Old Wilson's Mill on Sister Grove. He opened a dry goods store at Ft. Buckner in 1846. His was the first business in the new county seat of McKinney and opened for business May 6, 1848. His eldest son, George, died in 1856 and was buried in the old McKinney Cemetery where the Trinity Presbyterian Church now stands. (Biog. Dem. May 6, 1920.)

W.C. Burrus came to Texas in 1861 and joined Company E of the 15th Texas. In 1875 he started milling on the branch in northeast McKinney, and from this beginning came the famed Burrus Mills.

G.W. (Wash) Ford located at Buckner in 1843, later headrighted land near Allen in 1846. He was the first man married in Collin. He married Parmelia Langston in 1844 to which union 11 children were born. In 1850 he, Tola Dunn, John McGarrah, Tom McDonald joined about 150 others at Ft. Worth and went to California by way of the El Paso route. The trip took seven months and they suffered many hardships, going as long as six days without food, and finally ate one of their horses. He returned in 1853 and later served in Capt. Chambers' Company in the Civil War. (Biog. Dem. Mar. 10, 1904)

John M. McKinney came to McKinney in the early 1850's and for seven years freighted supplies from Wright's Landing on Red River to I.D. Newsome and Frank Daugherty, partners in business in McKinney. (Biog. Dem. May 4, 1905.)

Major W.M. Bush came to Texas in the spring of 1855 along with A.E. Quesenberry and family. Bush served in the Mexican War at age 17 and in the Civil War with Jordon O. Straughan's Company. When Straughan came home on account of age, Bush became captain in his place and was mustered out at Hempstead in June of 1865. (Biog. Dem. Nov. 15, 1900.)

Mrs. Ann S. Hurt came to Collin as a widow, age 30, and headrighted land in 1846. She later married Joe M. Bounds, merchant, and opened McKinney's first hotel. (Biog. Dem. Nov. 2, 1922)

Oliver P. Mallow came to Collin with his parents, Michael and Charlotte. He was the youngest of 19 children. (Biog. DCG May 8, 1930)

Capt. John K. Bumpass came to Collin in 1857 and settled at Prairie Grove with his family. His children went to school at Bear Creek school, south of Copeville. (Biog. DCG Mar. 4, 1926)

George Nipp came to Fitzhugh Mills in 1857 and worked for Bob Fitzhugh in the mill. Later he drove ox wagons between Jefferson and McKinney, freighting in goods for the settlers.

William Hampton came to Collin from Missouri in 1846 and settled at Weston. Later he ran the Squeezepenny gin and custom mill.

Ludsen Lewis and family came to Collin in the fall of 1845, stopping for a while at John Fitzhugh's where there was a sort of fort. All the young men made up a ranger company to watch the frontier and Lewis joined with them. He settled where the old Hatler home was in 1848. The Hatlers built a log cabin near in 1849. (Biog. Dem. Dec. 13, 1934)

Moses Moore of Lebanon came from Arkansas during the Civil War and brought 110 slaves with him and 85 mules to keep the Federal forces under Gen. Curtis from capturing them. Many of his neighbors in Arkansas, hearing that he was moving to Texas, sent their slaves and mules in his keeping until the war should end. After the war, Collin County people prevailed upon him to take them all back to Arkansas.

Dr. R.C. Buckner suggested the idea of a home for orphans at a convention of Deacons in Paris on July 18, 1877. He later presented his idea to a convention at which time J.R. Rogers of Melissa offered a resolution that the home be undertaken. The first charter for the home was written by Dr. Buckner at a meeting in the First Baptist Church of McKinney. Deacon F.H. Ogilvie came up with the idea of each one planting an acre of wheat each year to help finance the home.

Dr. Holmes was an early doctor in the Westminister area, living one mile northeast. He drove a horse named Bill to his rig and people named the little community Graybill as a token of their esteem. (Dem. Aug. 13, 1925)

Captain J.L. Greer. Came to Collin 1867. Taught school at Mantua. Founded Anna. In Texas Legislature. Lived No. Ky. St.

J.W. (Woot) Hill. Came to Collin 1865. Married Eugenia Hill. Lived in west McKinney.

E.W. Kirkpatrick. Came to Collin with parents and settled in White's Grove. Father died and he took over family at age 13. Great civic leader. Nurseryman. Lived S.W. McKinney.

James W. Throckmorton. One of first five settlers in Collin. Governor of Texas. Lawyer. Lived W. La. St. opposite present library.

I.D. Newsome. Came to McKinney with bride, 1853. One of first businessmen. Great leader in civic development. The Newsomes here are descendants.

Captain W.L. Boyd. Civic leader. Developer of early McKinney. Business man.

Henry Wetsel. Came to Collin 1848. One of first businessmen and a builder of early grist and flour mills in and near McKinney.

William H. Burger. Gin man. Had one of the finest cotton gins in Texas on N. Tenn. St. Civic leader. Started the first real flour mill in Collin, on the Woodlawn road.

Charley Wysong. Came to Collin 1846 and founded old Highland, north of present Melissa. With Sam H. Parris started a gin, grist and flour mill at Highland. The Drs. Wysong of McKinney are descendants.

G.M. Watts. Early miller and gin operator. Bought the Wetsel mills and became a leading ginner and miller in McKinney. Mrs. Bob Tucker, E. Greenville, descendant.

J. Westley Kirby. Came to Collin 1845, to Forest Grove. Texas ranger and soldier.

J.B. (Burl) Stiff. Came to Collin 1854. Related to Shains. Gentleman saloon keeper.

Alfred Johnson. Came to McKinney, 1846. Confederate soldier. Was Justice of the Peace and other offices. Lived S. Chestnut.

J.L. Doggett. Came to McKinney early. Lawyer. County offices and Judge.

John L. Lovejoy. First merchant in McKinney, 1848. Settled first at old Buckner. Lovejoys and Comegys are descendants.

Dr. B.M.E. Smith. Came to McKinney 1853. Druggist and Dr. Founded Smith Bros. Drug Co.

Jesse Shain. Came to Collin 1849. Great business man. Civic leader and builder; McKinney's biggest. Howells are descendants.

Jeremiah Horn. Pioneer settler in Walnut Grove area, 1845. Soldier. Stockmen. Church leader.

Captain E.R. Stiff. Merchant. Soldier. Married daughter of Jack McGarrah, founder of Buckner. Judd Stuff, Dallas, descendant. Others here.

Captain W.A. Rhea. Pioneer. Founded Rheas' Mill. Soldier. Civic leader. Brought the first shorthorn cattle to Collin.

George White. Came to Collin, 1847. Surveyor. Surveyed Collin Co. Surveyed the first roads, and Pecan Cemetery. Gave the ground for the High School. Mrs. W.T. Hoard.

Dr. W.T. Moore. Came to Collin, 1869. Leading Dr.

Thomas Rattan. Came to Collin 1844. Pioneer settler near Anna. His children married some of the most important people in the county, as Mrs. Governor Throckmorton and Mrs. William Fitzhugh.

William Rice. Came to Collin 1844. East edge of McKinney. Indian fighter, Ranger.

Dr. T.E. Wiley. Early Dr. Founded sanitarium. Civic leader.

Henry O. Hedgecoxe. Came to Collin 1844. Manager for Peters Colony.

T.B. Wilson. Came to McKinney, 1849. Surveyor. Great land owner. Ad Wilson, descendant.

Dr. James A. Caldwell. Dr. at Climax, 1889. Located at McKinney, 1891, and built big sanitarium on So. Tenn. St. Father of Gibson and Roy.

G.A. Wilson. Came to Collin, 1845. Pioneer land owner. Sheriff. John A. Wilson, descendant.

J.C. Largent. Early implement dealers in McKinney. He and W.B. Civic leaders, Harness, etc.

T.C. Goodner. Came to Collin, 1868. Business man. Civic worker.

H.L. Davis. Lawyer, Judge.

R.L. Parker. Pioneer shoe and boot maker.

J.G. Barnes, Cotton and Grain merchant. Mule dealer.

Dr. T.W. Wiley. Doctor

Dr. E. Lee Burton. Pioneer eye, nose and throat specialist.

B.F. Houston. Dry goods merchants. Land owner.

E.M. McAuley. Early druggist.

M.H. Garnett. Lawyer. Judge.

J.P. Dowell. Early merchant, hardware. On N. Ky. St. Later on E. La. St. Clifton, Ed and Jim P. Dowell, descendants.

Hugo E. Smith. Gin man. Business man. Postmaster, 1890. Oscar E. Smith, descendant.

Walter B. Wilson, postmaster. Newspaperman.

L.A. Scott. Business man. Banker. Civic leader.

W.C. and J. Perry Burrus. W.C. Burrus founded the Collin County Mill and Elevator Co. J. Perry developed it into one of greatest mills in state. W.C. came to Collin, 1875. Was captain in Confederate army.

J.C. Moore. The leader in securing and introducing the latest farm machinery to farmers in Collin Co. Civic leader.

Tom W. Perkins. Newspaper man. Founded several newspapers in Collin. State Senator. Mayor of McKinney several times. Editor. Came to Collin, Mrs. Tom Perkins, Sr., wife.

Dr. G.A. Foote. Pioneer Dr. Surveyor. Office holder in early Collin. (Mrs. W.E. Ditto) Banker. Merchant.

John M. McKinney. Pioneer preacher. Confederate soldier. Mrs. Arbie Sparlin, descendant.

J.M. Wilcox. Came to Collin, 1845. Miller. Merchant. Lumberman. Joe E. Wilcox, descendant.

Capt. Tuck Hill. Confederate soldier. Civic leader. Developer. Clarence Hill, descendant.

A.L. Darnall. Educator. Operated the Muse College in 1860. Darnall's are descendants.

James H. Jenkins. Lawyer. Civic worker. Church leader.

Robert Fitzhugh. Great land owner. Soldier. Ranger. Newsomes are descendants.

B.C. Whisenant. Pioneer. Large land owner. Civic worker.

Captain J.H. Bingham. Confederate officer. Newspaper man. Editor. Owned the Enquirer, now the Examiner. Mrs. Good Bingham, So. Chestnut.

W.H. Andrews. Leader in developing agriculture in Co. District Judge. Mrs. J.E. Hunter, Dallas, descendant.

W.T. Beverly. Pioneer. District Judge. Civic leader. Hon. Wallace Hughston, descendant.

George Herndon. Came to Collin and to old Buckner, 1847. Pioneer. George and Henry Herndon married daughters of Jack McGarrah, the founder of Buckner.

Isaac and Albert Graves. Came to Collin in 1857 with the Muse families. Pioneer farmer. Built the big house in which Geo. Cameron lives. N.W. McKinney. Geo. Cameron.

Jesse H. Gough. Came to Collin, 1847. Pioneer settler. Land owner. Lawyer. Judge.

Lite T. Morris. Came to Collin, 1855. First settler at Roland. Had 13 children, Mrs. T.L. Webb, last one. She died, 1931.

Joe Russell. Came to Collin, 1845. Settled at Cottage Hill.

Langdon C. Searcy. Came to Collin, 1846. Three miles west McKinney. In Mexican War, 1846. Texas Ranger.

Coleman White. Came to Collin 1845. Settled at Lebanon. Established a mill there.

Thomas T. Bradley. Came to Collin, 1846. Home just west of present high school. Soldier. Civic builder.

Alfred Chandler. Came to Collin 1843. Ranger. Soldier. Settled at old Hackberry.

S.H. Fox. Came to Collin, 1850. Soldier. Rancher. Civic builder and church man. Mrs. Richard Bass, descendant.

J.L. Moulden. Came to Collin, 1853. Sheriff of county four times. Ranger. Confederate soldier.

Isaac Talkington. Came to Collin, 1856. Settled at Cottage Hill.

A.E. Quisenberry. Came to Collin, 1850. Settled at Rowlett.

James Snider. Came to Collin, 1845. Settled at Forest Grove.

Capt. Thomas M. Scott. Served in Mexican War. In Civil War, and against Indians. Scotts of McKinney, descendants.

Lindsey L. Lewis. Came to Collin, 1845. Ranger. Soldier.

R.C. White. Came to Collin early. In Civil War, Confederate. County Judge. Mayor of McKinney several times.

Dr. Joseph E. Dulaney. Came to Collin, 1867. Confederate surgeon in Civil War. Family all Drs. Joe Dulaney, So. Chestnut, was descendant.

James M. Graves. Came to Collin, 1850. Settled near present Melissa. The Melissa Graves are descendants.

J. Henry Faulkner. Born near McKinney, 1861. Educator. County Judge. Mrs. Tom Perkins, Sr., descendant.

William B. Benge. Came to McKinney, 1850. Civic builder. Soldier. Mrs. Ella Quesenbury a descendant.

Salthial Coffey. Came to Collin, 1855. Coffeys here are descendants. Salathial settled near Wetsel.

John Campbell. Came to Collin, 1854, with Jack Faires, and with Jake Kirkpatrick, father of E.W. Campbell ran the Fitzhugh Mills during the Civil War.

Capt. John Johnson. Came to Collin, 1861. 13 children. Home on South Chestnut. Served in State Legislature, Constitutional Convention and in Texas Senate.

Maj. Green Kerr. Came to Collin, 1859, to Vineland. All Kerrs related.

A.J. Tucker. Came to Collin, 1856. Tucker Street named for him. Operated the old Tucker hotel and stage stop.

Col. Russell de Armond. Came to McKinney, 1859. Confederate veteran. Lawyer. Married Sarah, daughter of Isaac Graves.

Alexander Berry. Came to Collin, 1850. Lived where A & P was on Va. St., now Sears. Confederate veteran. In State Legislature. Helped survey the town lots of McKinney. Great church worker.

Collin McKinney. Came to Collin, 1845, southeast Van Alstyne. Signer of Texas Declaration of Independence. In Legislature. County and county seat named for him. His old home stands in the city park.

J.B. Wilmeth. Came to Collin, 1846, two miles north McKinney. Helped lay off the city of McKinney and the first county Judge.

Charles T. Fox. Came to Collin, 1850, seven miles west McKinney. Married a Herndon, sister to George and James.

Col. Joe M. Bounds. 1846. Had the first hotel in McKinn_,. Mexican War veteran. Confederate veteran. Married Eliza Hurt, who had come to Collin with her mother, Mrs. Ann Hurt.

John Kincaid. Came to Collin, 1844. Seven miles northeast McKinney. Mexican War veteran. Married a daughter of Thomas Rattan.

John D. Brown. Came to Collin, 1845. Honey Creek. Later moved to Plano. Related to Beverlys.

Samuel Bogart. Came to Collin, 1845. In Indian wars. Texas-Mexican war. In State Legislature. Many state offices. Lived six miles northeast McKinney. Related to Moores.

A.C. (Armp) Mallow. Came to Collin, 1850. Came with his parents, Michael Mallow and wife. Married Dade Johnson, daughter of Captain John Johnson.

Rev. Jeremiah Horn. Came to Collin, and to Walnut Grove, 1845. Mrs. Thomas McNeil of McKinney, a descendant.

Joseph R. Rhea. Came to Collin, 1855. His sons, Will and J.C., founded Rheas' Mill.

J.M. Kendall. Came to Collin, 1854. Woodlawn. Mrs. T.E Hardeway, West Virginia Street, a descendant.

Col. Lee M. Martin. Came to Collin, 1855. Lived four miles south of McKinney. Raised a regiment for the Confederate army.

R.L. Waddill. Came to Collin 1853. Educator, started first schools. Lawyer. District Judge.

Isaac Crouch. Came to Collin 1848. One of first business men. In hardware and general merchandise. Crouches are descendants.

A. Craus. Came to McKinney, 1891. Built the first bottling works in county, S. Ky. St.

Dr. Anderson Gullett. Came to McKinney 1867. Confederate surgeon. Drove all way from Missouri in wagon. A leading physician in McKinney for 30 years.

John Church. Came to McKinney early. Civic leader and Judge. Son, Marion, lived in Dallas.

M.H. Garnett. Came to McKinney early. Lawyer. District Judge.

Captain J.S. Dowell. Early Collin ranger. In Confederate army. Dowells of McKinney.

Francis Emerson. Came to McKinney, 1854. Established first bank in McKinney, which became the First National in 1873.

Dr. J.E. Gibson. Came to McKinney, 1880. A leading Dr. for 47 years.

Captain W.H. Bristol. Came to Collin, 1872. Confederate soldier and business man. Founded several post offices in county. Mrs. C.C. Cobb, Foote St., descendant.

Mrs. Frances J. Abernathy. Came to Texas 1882. Father was once governor of North Carolina. An uncle commanded Americans at King's Mountain. Her sons were: W.M., J.F., G.E., M.G., and H.E. Daughter was Mrs. W.T. Brooke.

William H. Perkins. Came to Collin, 1855. Great builder. Built many of the finer homes in McKinney, and also business houses. Dudley Perkins a descendant.

Dr. T.F. Keith. Came to Collin 1873. Moved from Rock Hill to McKinney, 1890. Married Dr. J.A. Moore's daughter. The Moore's—McCarty family—and others are descendants.

Tom Muse. Came to Collin 1857. Was a Confederate soldier. Married Mary B. Beaty, a teacher in J.S. Muse's college. Muses are descendants.

Dr. M.S. Metz. Came to McKinney early, and was for years an outstanding physician. Mrs. Metz, N. Benge.

J.S. and S.D. Heard. Great builders. Built most of west side of the square. Merchants. Civic leaders.

David Stiff. Came to McKinney 1847. Blacksmith. Office holder. Was postmaster, 1856.

Captain R.M. Board. Came to McKinney before Civil War. Merchant. Confederate officer.

David Melton. Came to Collin, 1849. Confederate veteran. Home in west part of county. Meltons and Findleys, descendants.

A.C. Weeks. Came to Collin, 1853. Home near old Vineland. Horns are descendants.

R.C. Whisenant. Came to Collin, 1846. Near Allen. Confederate veteran.

Malichi Allen. Came to Collin, Confederate veteran. Came to five miles north McKinney, 1866. State Senator. L.A. Scott's family, descendants.

Dr. William D. Lair. Came to Collin, 1857, to old Mantua. State Senator. Parris family are descendants.

F.H. Ogilvie. Came to Collin, 1872, and laid out the town of Melissa, and was first merchant. Graves are other descendants.

Captain W.N. Taylor. Came to Collin, to old Mantua, 1860. Ran a store there. County officer. Confederate veteran.

William P. Honaker. Came to Collin, and to Farmersville, 1853. Bains, Phillips and Howards, descendants.

Capt. John K. Bumpass. Came to Collin, 1857, and settled at Farmersville. Civil War veteran.

Robert H. Brown. Came to Collin, 1845. First settler at Plano. Beverleys, Browns and Russells, descendants.

Dr. W.F. Wolford. Came to Collin, 1871. Helped lay out the town of Allen. Wolfords of McKinney, descendants.

Silas Harrington. Came to Collin, 1848. Settled near Plano.

William Foreman. Came to Collin, 1849, to Plano. He established the town, had its first store and was first postmaster.

W.B. Largent. Came to Collin before the Civil War. Home was on present Bradley, opposite high school.

Jordon O. Straughan. Came to Collin, 1846. Held many early county offices. All present Straughans are related to him.

Elijah Chambers. Came to Collin, 1847. Big land owner near Chambersville. His father was Elisha.

Sanford Beck. Came to Collin, near Rowlett, 1847. Moved to Plano. Daughter, Matilda, first child born there.

Jacob Moore. Came to Collin, Farmersville, 1850. Big land owner.

Jesse Stiff. Came to Collin, Stiff Chapel, 1850.

EARLY COLLIN COUNTY DOCTORS

James Madison Feland. Born Ky. 1822. Came to Collin 1844. Four miles west of McKinney. Did not practice much. Died Dec. 24, 1894.

James W. Throckmorton.

Benj. M.E. Smith. Born Tenn. 1816. Came to McK. 1855. Retired 1882.

Henry Dye. Born Ky. 1830. Came to Plano 1848. Died Aug. 10, 1878.

Harvey Marshall Markham. Born Va. Came to Farmersville 1854. 1876 to McK. and went in mercantile business. Helped organize the banks. Born Va., 1829. Died

March 25, 1891.

Reuben A. Taylor. Born Ky. 1833. Came to Weston 1853. To Millwood 1856. Went to Nevada 1889. Died July 15, 1891.

Wm. Dixon Lair. Born Ky. 1814. Came to Anna 1858. Farmed and practiced. Died June 3, 1887.

Alvan Charles Lacy. Born N.Y. City 1805. Came to near Melissa 1859. On a farm. And practiced. Died April 14, 1883.

Bereman S. Shelburn. Born Ky. 1817. Came to Lebanon and practiced till 1885. Had large farms. Served in C. War as surgeon in Albert Pike's brigade.

James Wilson. 1857. Practiced. Died, 1904. Born Tenn. 1821. High Mason. Grandson of James Wilson, signer Amer. Dec. of Independence.

Jacob Stogsdale. Born Ind., 1825. Came to Weston 1855. Practiced till death 1872. Large and portly.

James L. Leslie. Born Ala., 1825. Came two miles south Van A. 1853. Praticed. 4 children. Master Mason. Church worker. Temperance advocate. Died 1891.

George W. Patterson. Born about 1820, and came to Collin before C. War. In Med. Depart. in C. War. Came back then to Pilot Grove. Moved to McK., 1866. A gentleman. Practiced till his death, 1884.

Allen H. Neatherly. Born A.K. 1833. Came to Farmersville Jan. 26, 1856. Started in a shanty. Also went in mercantile business there. Retd. 1886. One of the organizers of the 1st Ntl. Bank at Farmersville, 1887, and its first president.

Duncan T. Pardue. Born Miss. 1842. Came to two miles north McK. Oct., 1865. and rented a farm and practiced. Next July went to Miss. and got his mother. Also got his widowed sister with her three children and settled 7 miles NE McK. Practiced and farmed till 1884 when he came to McK. and engaged in lumber business. Retired in a few years. (Moved NE McK Oct, 1866)

Moses Hubbard. Born Va. 1827. Came to NW Rheas Mill 1859. Died 1906.

Wm. H. Pierce. Born Tenn. 1833. Came to Weston 1857. Practiced till 1859 and went to I.T. Came back to Pilot Grove 1861. Joined Capt. Baker's Co. in Hardeman's regt. as 2nd Lt. and acted as asst. surgeon. Came home 1864 and was assasinated in the Lee-Peacock feud, Feb. 27, 1867. He was the first one killed in that feud.

W.C. Holmes. Born S.C. 1840. Capt. in C. War. Came to Blue Ridge from Pilot Grove, 1867. Moved back to Pilot Grove 1868. He was the first Dr. at Blue Ridge. Later he edited a paper.

Joseph E. Dulaney. Born Tenn. 1830. In C. War as Pvt. Soon surgeon of 19th Tenn. Came to Rowlett Cr. June, 1867. Went to Lebanon 1868. There with Dr. Shelburne till late 1872, then settled at McK. Went back to Tenn. 1874. His family all Drs. Died Tenn. 1877.

John F. Butler. Born Tenn. 1836. Capt. Co. F., 26th Tenn. Inf. Came to Wylie 1871, and practiced.

Edward N. McAuley. Born N.C. 1838. In C. War as asst. surgeon. Came to McK. 1873, and in 1875 estab. drug business with Dr. Alonzo Sims. Retd. from practice 1879. Sold out 1895. One of organizers of Collin Co. Ntl. Bank V.P. and Pres. Died 1903.

Andrew Gullett. Born Del. 1820. In Med. Dept. in C. War. Came to McK. from Ark. 1869. Retd. 1875 and went in drug business. Died 1893.

Dewitt C. Pardue. Born Miss. In C. War. Came to Tex., taught school and practiced, 1866. 1871 settled at Wylie. 1905 moved to Hopkins Co.

John McCarty. Born Ky. 1836. Came to McK. 1871. Went to Williamson Co. and came back to McK. 1875. Moved about, and finally went to Burnet Co., 1892.

Gerald Alexander Foote. Born Va., 1826, and came to Buckner, 1845 and practiced there. He was first Dr. in Co. 1846 was contract surgeon for Capt. Wm. Fitzhugh's rangers. Got $5 a day. Got $1,200 and put it all in land at 25 cents an acre. In C. War was surgeon in Col. Wm. C. Young's 11th Tex. Cav. Mercantile business after war, no medicine. Died McK., July 16, 1902.

BRIEF HISTORY OF SETTLEMENT OF COMMUNITIES AND TOWNS OF COLLIN COUNTY

In pioneer days the neighborhoods of Collin County were designated in two ways: they were either "settlements" or "communities." A settlement was just what the name implies, an original settlement in the virgin country of the county. Usually it started by some first settler in the vicinity building up the area around him with his "kin" and his friends from the "Old Country," meaning they were from such states as Tennessee, Missouri, Mississippi, and Alabama.

As this settlement expanded and acquired more population, a school and church would be built and the settlement usually took the name of the first man there. As these settlements were miles apart, in the course of time, the land lying between settlements was taken up by later pioneers who lived so far from the settlements that it was too far to attend church or send children to school there so they established their own right at home. These later ones were called "communities" and seldom took the name of the first one there. Instead they were given such names as New Hope, Mount Olive, Walnut Grove, and Trinity. In rare cases the settlements took such names but it was most unusual.

ALLEN

Allen was founded in 1871 by Oglesby, a purchasing agent for the Houston and Central Railroad, then building through Collin County. Many people lived in the vicinity long before this, as the locality was settled in the 1850's. Here the Wetsels lived and had the first grist mill in the county. Dr. W.F. Wolford came to Allen in 1871 and helped organize the town. Some of these pioneer families have been prominent in the growth of our county a hundred years. Some of the early settlers were W.N. Bush, W.O. Matthews, J.M. Gibson, Geo. Mountcastle, James Spradling, G.W. Ford and W.P. Yeary. The first school taught in Allen was with Prof. J.B. McMurray in 1876 who had come there from Georgia. The Allen Christian Church was organized in 1886 with the Rev. J. Ben Faulkner the first pastor. The Allen Baptist Church was a consolidation of the Wilson Creek and the Faulkner Prairie Churches, in May of 1878 with E.S. Haynes the first pastor. George Mountcastle established a store in 1876 and W.P. Yeary a barber shop the same year. Sam Bass robbed the H and T.C. train here in 1878. A number of shots were exchanged between the passengers and the robbers but no one was hurt. Allen today is one of the fastest growing towns in the county.

ARDATH (GHOST TOWN)

Ardath, once a thriving little town northeast of McKinney, is now completely gone. Alma Wilson built the first house there in 1878 on land adjoining her father-

89

in-law, Jordon O. Straughan. H.C. Rutledge opened a store in an old house. They organized an Odd Fellows Lodge in 1900 with John R. Wilson, W.A. Straughan, M. George, D.W. Bagwell, and Dr. T.G. Boorman. Ardath had a well known string band in 1902. Burl Odell opened a barber shop in 1902.

ANNA

Anna, located 11 miles northeast of the county seat, is a fast growing little town, led by progressive business men. Capt. J.L. Greer is the founder of Anna, coming there from Alabama in 1867. He had the first home and first store there, and was also Justice of the Peace. Dr. W.D. Lair came to the vicinity in 1857 and for many years was the only doctor. By 1884 Anna had a population of 200 persons, a steam grist mill, a Baptist Church, Wm. Barnett's General Store, E.H. Guinon's store, and Greer and Barnett's store. Andrew Sherley was the first H. and T.C. Agent and the second post master.

There is some question as to how Anna got its name. Reports of C.P. Huntington, who built the railroad, made to his stockholders says that he had two daughters, Melissa and Anna, and they begged their father to name a little town on the railroad for them, which he did. Other sources say Anna was named for a daughter of Capt. Greer, and another says for Anna Quinlan, but Huntington's report to his company seems conclusive.

ALTOGA

Altoga, an agricultural town, grew up to meet the needs of this rich agricultural area. It is northeast of McKinney and today is still an active town. It was at its heyday in 1910 and at this time had a brass band that played all over the county and was much in demand. They had at this time 7 big stores—Moreland, Masse Mantooth, and Henry had General Merchandise. W.T. Dunn, drugs, Carson, blacksmith shop, Noah Hale, a barber shop, two doctors, Mantooth and Dobbs., a Baptist Church, a gin, and fine school.

SHORT HISTORY OF OLD BUCKNER MANY YEARS A GHOST TOWN— RECENTLY A GROWING COMMUNITY

John (Jack) McGarrah came from Washington County, Arkansas, in early 1843 and headrighted 640 acres of the Peters Colony land three miles west of present McKinney. In April of that year he built a small log cabin to use as a trading post in trading the Indians tobacco, liquor, calico and a few other articles for hides and furs. The cabin was about 20 feet in length and 10 feet wide, with a door at one end. Late that year McGarrah went back to Arkansas and brought out his family, consisting of his wife and seven children, one of whom had already married James Herndon.

McGarrah was born in 1805 and married Polly Graham, a half-blood Cherokee Indian. In late summer of 1846 Buckner was made a post office, the first in the county, with John McGarrah as postmaster. By that time two other businesses had opened at Buckner; John L. Lovejoy built a small general merchandise store, and a blacksmith shop of sorts was started.

Indians attacked the cabin at Buckner in the summer of 1843 while McGarrah and six other men were in it. They fought the Indians off all day, and then the seven men escaped at night by going down a ravine to the southward. As a trading post for the Indians it was never successful, but after the white settlers began to arrive, McGarrah did fairly well by trading with them.

In 1849, when the Gold Rush took place, McGarrah and several others joined the general rush and went overland to California. He died on the way back, as did his son-in-law, Tola Dunn. Mrs. McGarrah was left with the six children to support. Descendants still live in the east part of McKinney, by the name of McGarrah.

In 1846, Collin County was organized by the Texas Legislature and an election was held at Buckner to decide where the new county seat was to be. Two places were up to vote on; one, the present site of McKinney, and the other was across Sloan's Branch two miles south. Only twelve votes were cast: 11 for the present site of McKinney and one for the Sloan's Grove site.

In May, 1848, the Lovejoy small store was moved from old Buckner by oxen and placed on the northwest corner of the present McKinney square, which was, at the time, a great thicket of small and large trees, vines and briars. From this store the town of McKinney was laid out.

Efforts were made to make Buckner a town. In 1846 the town site was laid off, streets were named and lots sold. Several bought lots there but no building was ever erected. Buckner was finished.

BLUE RIDGE

Blue Ridge, named for the blue-flowering grass that covered the area, is situated on a high point of land on the Matthiss Mowry survey granted to him by the Republic of Texas for service in the Texas Revolution. The first settlers were I.D. Sellars and Henry Eakle who farmed where the town was to grow up. 1873. The first store was operated by William and James Moyers in a one room log cabin. In 1874 another one room cabin was built for a school and Sam McKinney was the teacher, holding class twice a week. In 1876 Julius Conner and William Moyers bought the townsite from Abernathy and had it surveyed into lots. The town grew rapidly. Some of the pioneer names were J.S. Sinclair, Gabe Warden, Jesse Short, Jack Smith, Geo. Hart, William Pruitt, Robert McCarley, J.A. Barnett, James and John Griffith, William Christian, Ike Dodson, and William Warden. The first gin was built in 1877 by J.A. Barnett, and ran until 1934. The Methodist Church began in 1880 with the Rev. M. Gentry pastor. In 1898 the town was moved two blocks to its present site. In 1909 the first brick structure was built. The first good road leading out was to Melissa in 1920. 1928 Blue Ridge got electric lights. Some pioneer names of the vicinity are Isadore Brown who came in the late 1840's, John Bowman in 1849, Wilson McDonald, and Dr. W.C. Holmes 1867, who was the first doctor in the area. The town was incorporated in 1936 and is now experiencing a new growth.

CHAMBERSVILLE

Chambersville, 7 miles northwest of McKinney is a lovely spot. Visitors are struck by its simple dignity, its pretty church, and well kept cemetery. It was named for a pioneer settler, Elisha Chambers, who came here before 1850. He gave land for the school, church, and cemetery. The Chambersville community has always had a progressive school and is a beautifully kept community, ideally located on a hill overlooking rich black farmland.

CLIMAX, TEXAS AS IT looked in 1952. Like all Collin County towns it is growing and changing. Climax was first settled in 1848 by William War-den, and later by Lott Bruton, I.J. Rudge, D. Van Winkle, and Abe Recer who built the first toll bridge between McKinney and Farmersville.

ONCE JUST A STOP on the railroad, Clear Lake is a fast growing community, popular because of its close proximity to beautiful Lake Lavon.

HART HOME NEAR Cottage Hill (1956). These were the farm houses that came after log cabins.

THE OLD CULLEOKA STORE that long served Culleoka as a social gathering place, the center of community life. A bustling, growing community has taken its place. Mrs. Belle Jones was prop. in 50's.

COPEVILLE

Copeville in the southeast part of the county was named for Miles Cope who lived west of Copeville. At one time mail came by Star Route from Farmersville to the area and was delivered to his home. He delivered it to the people. Several stores sprang up and a little town grew to serve the area. J. Goodwin built a gin in 1880. J.E. Jones gave the right of way and the depot for the Santa Fe Railroad and he later became one of the biggest merchants in the county. The area abounded in Bois d'Arc and when the value of this toughest of all wood became generally known, Copeville shipped out trainloads of the wood.

CLEAR LAKE

Clear Lake became a town about 1890 when the Santa Fe Railroad came through and made Clear Lake one of its regular stops. A post office was established there, Robert Palmer built its first store in 1897 and the next year he and his brother Joe built a gin near the store. In 1884 the U.S. Government built and opened a distiller on the banks of the lake. P.Q. Russell was the revenue agent in charge of the still. Houses grew up around the businesses and by 1890 Clear Lake was a well known shipping point. For years Clear Lake furnished the City of Dallas the Bois d'Arc blocks they used to pave the streets of Dallas. In 1890 Dallas discontinued the use of this kind of paving and Clear Lake went into a slump but the building of Lake Lavon has made it a popular spot for outings.

CLIMAX

William Warden who brought his family by covered wagon from Missouri to Texas in 1844 was the first settler in Climax. Soon others came—Lott Burton, I.J. Rude, and D. Van Winkle. Abe Recer came also and built a toll bridge across Sister Grove Creek. Climax reached its greatest population around 1910 when A.M. Anglin and W.K. Long operated stores there. More than 100 persons lived in Climax. The old Van Winkle Cemetery lies south of the town and many of the earliest settlers are buried here.

CELINA

Celina began October 20, 1879 when W.C. Burrus and T.J. Mulkey built a little box house store 16' by 18' at the cost of $65. and opened for business in general merchandising. They decided to name the place for their home town of Celina in Tennessee. They asked Throckmorton, a member of the Texas Congress, to get them a post office and when they presented a petition with 12 names requesting one, it was done. John T. Mulkey was the first postmaster. In 1885 a gin was moved there from Rheas Mill. Other pioneer merchants were Geo. Pigg, William Hays, Tom Eaton, the doctors were Hubbard, Wade, and Varns Kirkpatrick. The Church of Christ was the first church built in 1886, in 1901 Celina had a bank (Collin County National Bank) with Ben Smith as Cashier. The town incorporated in 1906 with A.M. Marsh the first mayor. 1908 the Celina State Bank was opened for business with B.F. Geer, Pres.

CULLEOKA

Culleoka lies three miles south of Princeton and was once a busy place with several stores, and at one time had the first rural high school in the county, started by J.L. Hickshaw. Culleoka once had a post office, later closed by the government when good roads drained away the business, and some of its population. It is still one of the most active of our rual communities with good churches drawing people from a wide area.

FAYBURG

In 1877 Captain W.H. Bristol located at present Fayburg and set about getting a post office for the place he called Fayburg. The post office was in his home and he was the postmaster. Later Mose McDonald opened a store. Bristol operated a gin and later a mill. Fayburg lies on the high plains between Pilot and Indian Creek and dairying is now the coming thing for the area. The land here is Wilson Clay which produces grass of highest quality.

FARMERSVILLE

Farmersville is built on the grant given W.B. Williams for service in the War between Texas and Mexico, 1836. In the fall of 1849 Moses Jones, Walter Yeary, John Haven, and Hugh Gotcher were already living in the area, and by 1853 others had moved there too, Sugar Hill was the only semblence of a town (2½ miles north of the present site of Farmersville), it had one small store built in 1852. On Dec. 25, 1853 a fight took place in which three were killed. The others left the country and the settlement abandoned. Farmersville began in 1854 and was located on a fine spring, George Dollarhid built the first cabin and Mack Henslee built a log cabin grocery store. In 1855 Dr. S.G. Parson built a cabin on the north side of the square then Peter Chisholm put up one. Up until the end of the Civil War all the houses were of log. The John Yeary family came to the area in 1845 and opened a general merchandise store, said to be the oldest in Collin County. On Christmas Day of 1854 Indians staged a massacre and three settlers were killed. The town was named Farmersville because the area was a rich farming section of the county, the name suggested by John I. Hendrix, and the land for the public square donated by William Gotcher. The town grew rapidly and was incorporated in 1873. In 1883 the first railroad came through Farmersville, the Missouri, Kansas, and Texas. In 1887 the Santa Fe arrived and with the two means of shipping out their farm goods, Farmersville prospered. By 1885 it was a flourishing town with over 100 businesses, six gins to take care of the cotton grown locally.

Farmersville was the hometown of World War II's most decorated hero, the late Audie Murphy.

Dec. 24, 1854, at a saloon brawl at Sugar Hill, Captain John Yeary was killed when acting as peace maker at what time John H. Glass and Samuel Glass were killed in the ensuing brawl. The Glass boys are buried in the Chapman Cemetery west of Farmersville, in a double grave.

FRISCO

Frisco in West Collin was first known as Emerson because the land on which it was built was then owned by Francis Emerson. It took the name of Frisco from the railroad that came through the area in 1902, the St. Louis and San Francisco. The land was bought and developed by the Blackland Townsite Company, one of the few in this area to be developed by outsiders. Frisco was incorporated in 1907 when Dr. I.S. Rogers became the first mayor.

JOSEPHINE

Josephine, in southeast Collin, had its beginning, like so many others in that area in 1888 when the St. Louis and Southwestern Railroad came through the vicinity. J.C. Hubbard donated land for a town and it was decided to name it for his daughter, Josephine. Some of the pioneers of the area were Sam Farris, P.R. Jordon, J.C. Copeland, A.J. May, E.A. Jordon, Joseph M. Stubblefield (who served as the first postmaster) and W.E. Swanson who is credited with erecting the first dwelling in Josephine.

LAVON

Lavon was started when the St. Louis and Southwestern Railroad came through the county in 1886. There were many very early settlers in the area who became a part of the new town. E.C. Thompson was in the area in 1854 and others came not long after 1854. John McMinn, Capt. J.D. Naylor, John Smith, who was the first settler in Millwood. Lavon was named for Lavon Thompson, son of E.C., who was the postmaster and operated the store. By 1910 Lavon had a population of 300. The coming of Lake Lavon to the area has made Lavon a popular resort spot, since the huge lake brings fishermen, boating enthusiasts, and swimmers from many states.

LEBANON

Lebanon is a very old town. John Huffman, Silas Harrington, Z.T. Rainey, Alfred Harrington, John Crosier, and Phillip Huffman settled in the area before the Civil War. Phillip Huffman operated the first post office in his store in 1858. The town grew rapidly and in the 1890's they were selling millions of dollars in goods. Their gins were turning out a thousand bales of cotton annually. By then they had three churches, a high school, seven stores, three blacksmith shops, two doctors, and two barber shops. How the town got its beautiful name is obscure. The area was originally known as Shahan's Prairie. A man by the name of Shahan came in 1849 and was the county's first rancher, not cows, but horses.

LOWRY CROSSING

Lowry Crossing was named when the Millwood Road crossed East Fork at that spot in 1853. William Lowry lived there at the time so his name was used. Wade Biggers had the first store in 1901. In 1905 Biggers secured a post office for the town. The old Higgins Cemetery is the final resting place for many of this section's early pioneers.

LUCAS

The town of Lucas took its name from Gabe Lucas (son of Peter F.) who opened a store there in 1870. Joe McKinney, another early settler, wanted to name the town St. Jo, but the post office department over-ruled him and gave the name Lucas to the new post office. At one time it had four stores, a gin, and was a busy little town. Descendants of the pioneers from this area are scattered all over the county and have contributed to the County's history.

MANTUA

Mantua is truly a ghost town, a town that grew and flourished for only 25 years, but was an important one during that time. It was situated five miles northwest of Anna. It was conceived and founded as a site for a college, the Mantua Seminary, and the founders were Wm. C. McKinney, James W. Throckmorton (later Governor of Texas), and Joe H. Wilcox. They purchased 200 acres of land from Wm. C. McKinney and donated the tract to the trustees of the new Seminary. Some of the land was divided into lots and sold to help finance the Seminary, with certain restrictions—no liquor was to be sold, no gambling, no horse races staged, and anyone who violated these laws would lose his lot and improvements back to the trustees. The first lot was sold to Horation Walcott for $60, who became the owner of the first store. In 1857 Dr. W.D. Lair bought a lot and began his practice of medicine in the new town, others went to James B. McBride, H.N. Walcott, William C. and Y.S. McKinney, Jas. L. Leslie, and James Enloe. The seminary was for both male and female students, classes being taught for 10 to 20 dollars per class each session. The subjects taught were about like the modern high school would teach. In 1846 the McKinney family and J.B. Wilmeth organized a Christian Church that met in the home of Carroll McKinney near Van Alstyne and in 1854 the church was moved to Mantua. Drs. James Leslie and Rollins put in a drug store soon afterward, and J.M. Douthitt a dry good store. The Civil War brought all growth to a standstill here as everywhere in the county and it was not until after the war that it began to grow and thrive. The Masons agreed to build a big building for the Seminary and work got under way. A post office was established in 1856 with E.B. Rollins as postmaster. A Methodist Church began in 1866 and Oscar Riddle opened a saloon just outside the town boundry. It is interesting to note that a member of the Texas legislature came to Mantua on a visit and heard a woman praying that the saloon be removed from their midst. When he went back to Austin he helped frame a bill that eventually closed all saloons in Texas. The population of Mantua reached 300 right after the war.

MELISSA

Melissa, north of McKinney, was named for Melissa Huntington, whose father was a builder of the Houston and Texas Central Railroad when it was built through Collin County in 1872. Some of the first settlers of the area were John Coffman, Marshall Pulliam, and others. The town was laid out by F.H. Ogilvie and he became its first merchant. Later Hogue Coffman and L.A. Scott opened a general store and in 1876 a flour mill was opened for business and at that time the population was 300. By 1910 the town had electric lights, a telephone exchange, two cotton gins, shipping 3,000 bales of cotton annually. They also had a grain elevator, five grocery stores and a baseball team that drew great crowds wherever they played. A tornado on April 23, 1921 virtually destroyed the entire town, killing or wounding more than 100 persons.

MILLWOOD

Millwood in Southeast Collin is one of the most interesting towns in the county, as well as one of the oldest. Back in 1849 when the Gold Rush was on to California, it was a wild scramble for people bent upon getting to the gold. They went anyway they could, and many of them poured across Texas. At that time there were no roads so the gold rushers established their own roads as they went. One such path led past the newly built cabin and grist mill of Drury Anglin, on whose survey Millwood was later established. The travelers bought any kind of food offered and Anglin had soon sold off all he had at great prices—mules, a cow, hogs, they bought everything except two oxen he kept for his own use. Anglin and James made a trip to Jefferson in the summer of 1849 and brought back a wagon load of boots, flour, coffee and other supplies. They opened a small store in the cabin and one minded the store while the other took the oxen and wagon and went to Jefferson for more supplies. The trail they took through the wilderness later became the well traveled road the big freight wagons took to Jefferson for lumber and other necessities. Two years later the gold rush was over, but the little town was well established and Jim Smith was appointed the first postmaster. A mill was soon established. It was run by a large inclined wheel 40 feet across. Eight head of heavy oxen were placed on the wheel to give it power by walking all day up the inclined wheel. Later lumbering was a lucrative business.

MURPHY

Comfort McMillan started the town of Murphy in 1846 when he erected a big pen west of his cabin and began selling sheep. These were the same strain of sheep the McMillan family drove overland when they came to Texas. Everyone wanted sheep in the frontier settlements because they were easily herded and the wool was in great demand for clothing. He sold only his male sheep and bred new sheep until he was furnishing the entire area. He called the town Old Decatur after his original home and some settlers called it Maxwell's Branch until the railroad came in 1888. Later the town was named for the beautiful daughter of William Murphy, a very early settler. Murphy got its post office in 1891 with James Murphy its first postmaster.

NEVADA

Nevada in southeast Collin County, was named by Granville Stinebaugh for his hometown of Nevada, Missouri. Later he moved to California and named another town Nevada. Among the first settlers were Emmitt Mack, Granville Stinebaugh and Nick White. Mack and his son established the first livery stable in 1884 and about this time Frank Yayne and Sinclair Brammett put in a general store, a man named Warren put in a blacksmith shop, R.N. Jones a gin, and Sam Stinebaugh a hardware store. By 1890 Nevada had a population of 400, a Justice of the Peace court, and several new businesses. It was a flourishing town. The last of the great virgin forests stood in the area and the last of the big game was in them. A tornado struck the town May 8, 1927 killing almost a score of people and wounding over 100.

PARKER

The Parker settlement nine miles south of McKinney is very old. It is situated in some of the richest black land in the county. Maxwell Creek that runs close by used to be spring-fed and here were to be caught the only trout in the county. In the 1880's the St. Louis and Southwestern Railroad went through the site and the town was laid off in lots. Though the railroad was surveyed through town it was later built through Wylie and Parker's dream faded.

PLANO

In the fall of 1850 William Foreman, his wife, four sons, and one daughter came from Nelson Co. Kentucky and bought the headright of Sanford Beck, and on this land the city of Plano was built. In 1851 Foreman got John C. Easton to write a petition for a post office at Foreman's home, to be named Filmore for the President of the U.S. The other settlements objected to the name. Foreman's little house stood on the highest point on the Beck survey with vast prairies all around it. They decided to put a Spanish sound to the name plains, and called it Plano. The Post Office Dept. approved and Foreman was named Postmaster. Among the first settlers of the area were the Klepper family, Sam and Joe, Sanford Beck, Jake Routh, Dr. Henry Nye, who suggested the name Plano, Bill Foreman, Bill Beverley, the Harrington family, Alf and Silas, W.B. Blalack, Robert Brown, J.K. Aldridge, and the Russells. When the H. and T.C. Railroad came through Plano in 1872 the town grew up along it.

Plano is the fastest growing town in Collin County today.

PIKE

The town of Pike started in the 1860's. Among its pioneers were Asa Blankenship, T.W. Norman, J.J. Bradley, T. Slover, C.L. McGowan, John Boren, and the Mannings. A Baptist Church organized in 1866 with 48 members, with the Rev. Wm. Cummings the pastor. The Rev. W.L. Fagg built the first store in 1887. A post office was established in 1886 with Charles McGowan the postmaster. By 1900 it had six stores, a blacksmith shop, two churches, and a gin.

PRINCETON

The real beginning of Princeton was when the old East Line Railroad came through the area. One small store was built near the railway track. Next year another small store was put in and the Railroad Company put in a switch and for a while it was called Wilson's Switch, since the Wilson family owned a large section of land nearby. Timber was cut away and a town laid out, and a post office was given the new town. Wilson was suggested as a name but Texas had a town by that name already so it was decided to call it Princeton for another land owner, Princeton Dowlen. W.A. Harrelson was the first postmaster and it was he who built the first dwelling here. The town was incorporated in May of 1912 and John K. Wilson was the first Mayor. The town grew for it is located strategically in a rich farming area. Trainloads of Bois d'arc were shipped from the area and later Princeton became the Onion Center of North Texas. In 1938 Princeton had an Onion Festival and crowned Miss Ethelene Gamble of McKinney, "Queen Onion." A Prisoner of War camp was established by the government near Princeton and the park and other improvements were made in Princeton by the prisoners. Later the camp was used as a Migrant Camp for the workers needed in season to harvest the vast fields of Onions. Princeton in 1970 is again a fast growing town.

PROSPER

Prosper lies in the eastern edge of one of the richest agricultural areas in Texas—The Flats, or Little Elm Valley. The entire area was once covered with gama grass and wild flowers until 1880 when it was discovered that the prairie was valuable farming land. The town began when the old Richland school in Rock Hill was moved to Prosper to be near the Frisco Railroad that had just come through. Sam Sproles moved most of the buildings from Rock Hill to Prosper behind a big steam thresher. Prosper reached its peak about 1920 when it had 500 persons living there. Prosper was incorporated in 1914 with U.N. Clary its first mayor.

RHEAS MILLS

Rheas Mills began when Capt. James C. Rhea and his brother, W.A. purchased land in 1855 there as soon as they arrived from Tennessee. Both entered the Civil War and left their business in the hands of their father, Joseph R. They operated one of the finest carding machines to be found. After the war they operated a corn and flour mill, along with a general store. They bought their supplies in St. Louis and hauled it here by stage and ox wagons. In 1876 James Rhea applied for a post office.

RENNER

Renner located in the far southwest corner of Collin County is today the location of the Texas Research Foundation that has done much to improve farming in this county. The town was built on the St. Louis and Southwestern Railroad when it came through in 1888.

ROLAND

Lite T. Morris settled seven miles north of McKinney in the 1850's and built a cabin near the present site of Roland. Morris was a great admirer of the old romantic stories and his favorite story was about the brave young Roland who served under Charlemagne, and it was for him that the town was named. It had been called Liberty Springs. The town prospered until about the time of World War I when the advent of the automobile started most small towns on the downgrade. Liberty Springs nearby was the site of the biggest Camp Meetings in the section. These Camp Meetings were always held in July or August when the crops were "laid by" and all the people were free to attend. The actual preaching was at night and the days were spent in visiting and renewing old acquaintances, a rare treat for the settler who lived far apart and seldom had the opportunity to rest and visit free of the work of the farm.

ROWLETT

The old settlement of Rowlett sat for a hundred years eight miles southwest of McKinney on the headwaters of Rowlett Creek, cut off from traveled roads. The building of highway 121 gave it a new life and importance. The Rowlett Baptist Church was organized in 1848 at the home of Jonathan Phillips and was called the Wilson Creek Baptist Church. It was changed to Rowlett Church in 1852. From it sprang most of the other Baptist Churches of Texas. Many of the earliest pioneers lie in the well kept cemetery, such as George R. Yantis who came here in 1852, Jacob, Godfrey, and Benjamin Baccus, who came in 1845, Dr. Bereman Shelburnee, Daniel Melton, 1849, Silas Harrington, 1848, Hogan Witt and his wife Lousia, who came in 1844 to the area, and many other pioneers.

SNOW HILL

Nobody knows exactly how Snow Hill got its pretty name, but some say that when the original survey was made for Benjamin Bland and Joseph Matthews that snow lay on the ground on the ridge and the surveyors used this snow covered hill as a base. It is situated on the high land between Pilot and Indian Creek, five miles south of Blue Ridge. Snow Hill once had one of the best rural school systems in the county. Much of the land in the area has been turned back to pasture for the cows that have become a good business. The soil is Sumpter and Catalpa Clay and is ideally suited to native grasses.

THROCKMORTON

The old settlement lies seven miles north of McKinney. It goes back to its beginning when Dr. William E. Throckmorton and eight other men came to the vicinity from Fannin County and selected a site for a stockade, intending to take up land and make it their home. Dr. Throckmorton died a year after the settlement and his tombstone gives this information: born 1795, died 1843. The State of Texas put a marker over his grave that is located on a point of land overlooking the settlement. Here also lies the oldest person who lived in Collin County. Sally Foster, born 1777, died 1858.

SQUEEZEPENNY

Squeezepenny began in 1855 when William Hampton and family came to the vicinity and started a mill. This mill ground corn and also carded wool. During the Civil War this mill made woolen cloth for the Confederates. The mill was sold after the war to Tom Craft, who turned it into a grist mill and cotton gin and installed a big boiler to replace the power formerly supplied by the oxen. On the old Neal homeplace was the only stagecoach robbery or attempt on record for Collin County, This too is the vicinity of the famed Haunted Crossing on Indian Creek. Here it was during the Civil War that a traveler and his small son were killed by a patrol from McKinney one moonlight night. Legend has it that on certain moonlit nights the rider on the big horse has dashed across the rocky creek with a child's screams growing fainter. No one knows how Squeezepenny got its name. Many theories have been advanced but it is still a good point to discuss when old timers get together.

VERONA

Verona started in the fall of 1882 when A.R. Womble built a store beside his grist mill. In 1883 he became Verona's first postmaster, with the post office in his home. A fine school was already in operation there in 1880, using the name of Mississippi School and later Womble. Verona lies five miles northeast of Princeton. From the Methodist Church here came Miss Nettie Stroup, one of the great missionaries of Texas. On August 8, 1912 a straight hard wind with velocity of up to 150 miles an hour raked this area along with other communities in the area. The storm wrecked all Verona church buildings, many people were injured but none killed here.

VINELAND

One hundred or more years ago Vineland was one of the leading settlements in the county. In 1845 Henry H. Tucket secured a grant of land, a mile or so north of Buckner and built a log cabin, the first in the section. Settlement was slow because the settlers were uncertain about the Indian situation. But in 1853 a caravan of people seeking land arrived by wagons from Tennessee and decided to stay. This caravan was headed by Jabes P. Scott and W.P. Foster. The people wrote back glowing accounts of this new land and in 1856 another band of settlers arrived. Some of the pioneer families were Major G.W. Kerr, Doc Franklin, J.M. Feland, R.C. Horn, Alf

Chandler, E.R. Stiff, Thomas J. McDonald, Tola Dunn, Frank Dowell, Matthew Williams, Col. Ed Chambers, J.I. Chastain, John and Enos Scott, J.S. Carruth, and Luke George. In the Dowell community to the south were Wood Elkins, Charley Fox, Meredith Ashlock, David Melton, J.R. Spradley, and J.W. Wilcox. The prime movers for a school were Stewart and Leonidas Talkington, and school began in 1858, but it was not very successful. People were still too afraid of Indians to risk their children taking long walks through the woods. It was abandoned during the Civil War but was started again in 1866 with 90 pupils. In 1866 also the Christian Church was organized. Some of the early preachers were J.B. Wilmeth, W.B. Stinson, B.A. O'Brien, T.J. Hunsaker, and R.C. Horn. Although the church and school used the same building, the school was called Hackberry and the Church Vineland. Nothing remains today of Vineland. It stood five miles northwest of McKinney.

WESTON

Larkin Adams was the first business man in Weston when he started a small trading store in 1884. He named it for his home town in Missouri. In a few years other settlers came to live on the high prairie until it reached its highest population with 2,000 people living there in 1910. Some of the pioneer settlers were F.M. Douglas who opened a gin in 1873, Dr. J.S. Wade who had an office in 1878, J.M. Wilcox had a mercantile store (married Nancy Throckmorton, sister of the Governor Throckmorton), G.W. Curtis, W.S. Maxwell, T.C. Bounds the Constable, and many others.

VALDASTA

T.W. Smith laid off the town of Valdasta in 1886 and called it Vandersville but as there proved to be another with that name he gave it the French name of Valdasta. Smith ran the post office in his home. The first business was a gingercake stand run by David Herron in 1886. G.W. Airhart opened a store and the post office was moved there. J.W. Combest operated a gin for forty years. A.D. Patterson operated his blacksmith shop for 50 years, with a grist mill and a saw mill at the same site. Valdasta had a Holiness Church, a Baptist Church, a Methodist, and the Church of Christ. The first schoolhouse was built in 1889 by John Airhart who donated lumber and work to build it.

WETSEL

Wetsel is small but has been there a very long time. It began when Henry Wetsel sold his grist mill in McKinney and headrighted a square mile of land four miles south of McKinney. He built his cabin on the stage line that ran from Austin through McKinney. On one of his freighting trips to East Texas he brought back Bermuda Grass sod and soon had the first lawn of its kind in the area.

WYLIE

The coming of the Santa Fe Railway to the area was the beginning of the town of Wylie in 1886. The Cotton Belt Line came through the following year. Among the first settlers were Dr. J.F. Butler, J.V. Russell (he walked overland to the '49 gold rush in Calif.), Ed Neilson, R. Housewright, C.D. Colson, Dr. T.O. Staples, W.A. Rippey, G.W. Housewright, J.B. Baskette, and J.W. Russell. Howard Pickett was the first mayor. Town W. Perking published the first newspaper "Wylie Rustler" beginning in 1891. A three-story school building housed 350 pupils in 1902. Wylie had four churches. The first post office was called Nickelville with Frank McCarty the first postmaster. When the Santa Fe came through Col. Wylie was the right-of-

WYLIE, TEXAS, 1899. This is a photograph of the children who attended Wylie Common School. Out of this group came many of the leaders of Collin Co.

THE OLD METHODIST CHURCH and General Store at Verona, Texas (picture made in 1955). Verona began in 1882 when A.R. Womble built a store, a gin, and a grist mill just south of the church shown.

WYLIE, TEXAS STREET SCENE of 1890 is in sharp contrast to the fast-growing town of the present. Wylie, in extreme southern Collin County is one of the most rapidly growing communities in the county.

way agent and the town was named for him. In the very early days Wylie had four saloons.

WESTMINISTER

Westminister is part of the old John Roland survey given him for service in the Mexican War. It was first known by the name of Seven Points. A stagecoach stand was located three miles west of Westminister, just east of Rosamond. One half mile away was a camp ground for soldiers during the Civil War. In 1860 the Martin family gave land for a school and one was erected, made of logs with a puncheon floor, they called it Prospect, also called Martin's Box. Two miles northeast another was built and used as a Baptist Church and also a school. It was the Butler District No. 5 but was called Harmony by some people and Monkey Run by others. C.H. Wysong organized a Mason Lodge in 1888 and served as Grand Master. Westminister was at its best in the years before World War I, they had voted $10,000 for a new school, $100,000 for good roads and sank two deep wells.

WILMETH

The first settler in the Wilmeth settlement was J.B. Wilmeth in early 1846. The next permanent settler was Abe Hall and family in 1852. Others were Tola Dunn who headrighted land in what later became The Wilmeth School District, 1843, T.J. McDonald in 1844. Later settlers were Bob McLarry, and around 1880 the Newt Stagner family arrived, J.S.M. Brock, Bob Mullins, W.B. Pope, and James Jones. This community had the first schoolhouse in the county, taught by J.B. Wilmeth in a log cabin in 1848.

6

Collin County Churches

CHAPTER VI

Collin County Churches
The Oldest Church Record Found

The oldest church records found are some of the session books of the Parker Presbyterian Church. The old books were started in 1873 but state that a church was founded there August 2, 1846. In September, 1873, the name of the church was changed to White Rock Presbyterian Church and its organization started on September 14 of that year.

The First Baptist Church of McKinney—according to an early account, on August 11, 1872, Elder A.C. Stanton of the Rowlett Church preached in the old court house and at the end of his sermon organized the First Baptist Church of McKinney. According to another account, the First Baptist meeting in McKinney was in August, 1859, when Charles Breedlove preached and started a Sunday School in the Christian Church building on North Lenge Street in which Thomas J. Brown was named Sunday School superintendent.

The Rowlett Baptist Church, one of the first in north Texas, was founded on February 12, 1848 in the home of Jonathan Phillips with seven members. It was called the Wilson Creek Church of United Baptists. This name was changed in 1857 to Rowlett Creek Baptist Church and the first building was erected there in 1865-66 on land donated by George White. In 1872 J.H. Gough was appointed as a deacon or "second elder" and Joab Butler was named clerk.

The First Christian Church of McKinney has been confused with the Liberty Church established by Collin McKinney in his home southeast of Van Alstyne in 1847. The elder J.B. Wilmeth, founder of the McKinney Church, aided in the founding of the Liberty Church, which was attended by the McKinney family and their slaves but Liberty became a part of the Manua Church when it was established in 1854.

After the railroads arrived, the church was moved to Van Alstyne, the last service being at Mantua in 1921.

A letter written to the old *McKinney Enquirer* by the Elder John M. McKinney told of his experiences in early Collin County.

The letter, now in the George P. Brown files in the Texas State Library in Austin, is quoted in part:

"The most important experience I ever had was when I joined Brother Wilmeth's Restoration Movement on April 1 (1848). We had a meeting in the briars where we thought the new county capitol was going to be and I went along because I had been at the Wilmeth home helping the boys bust some wild horses. Just for devilment I asked if I could be the first to join the movement. Brother Wilmeth said I could right after they had the meeting. We had prayers and some voting was done. Brother Wilmeth was elected as elder of the new movement and Jim Wilmeth was appointed by him as clerk and second elder. (This title of "elder" was carried by J.B. Wilmeth until his death in 1892, being known by everyone as the "Elder Wilmeth." "Jim," as named by Johnny McKinney, was James R. Wilmeth, son of J.B. and later a minister in the Christian Church. James had studied under Alexander Campbell and was always a prime mover in the Christian Church. I go on with more of John McKinney's letter:

"After I offered my hand I asked to be baptized that day, so as to be the first in the church. We went down to Pleasant Wilson's Creek and I was baptized by Jim at the sand crossing." McKinney says he joined the Movement—as the Christian Church was then called here—but he changed later, as witnessed further along in his letter. It reads:

"The more I thought of what I had done the more scared I got. Soon I was getting down on my knees at night and asking the Lord to forgive me. Soon I got a Bible from Brother Wilmeth and was reading it. Soon I saw that I had to help carry the Message, and that I have done for 22 years, and will do till I die." John M. McKinney died in 1918.

For actual organization, it seems that the First Christian Church stands first in the county, but as for the founding of various churches, it is outdated by the church at Rowlett and the one J.B. Wilmeth founded at Forest Grove in 1846, and the church in Andrew Culwell's home on Honey Creek in 1845. The latter was a Methodist Church, and the church at Weston was a later outgrowth of this Culwell Church.

OLD ALEO BAPTIST CHURCH and Cemetery five miles north of Nevada. J.K. Bumpass settled here in 1857. Aleo had a post office, gin, small store and gin run by Coke Prater. Other settlers at Aleo were Lim Smith and relatives from Person Co., North Carolina.

THE BETHLEHEM BAPTIST CHURCH northeast of Farmersville about 6 miles. (Photo by Paul Russell.)

CHAMBERSVILLE BAPTIST CHURCH (present bldg.) (Photo by Paul Russell.)

THE EAST FORK BAPTIST CHURCH southeast of McKinney about 7 miles. (Photo by Paul Russell.)

LEBANON BAPTIST CHURCH still holds services. (Photo by Paul Russell.)

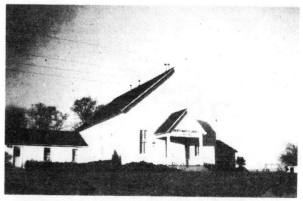

LIBERTY BAPTIST CHURCH organized 1850. Eight miles west of Plano. (Photo by Paul Russell.)

PRAIRIE MOUND CHURCH. Baptist Church north of Nevada, 5 mi. (Photo by Paul Russell.)

THE LITTLE FLOCK Primitive Baptist Church. Organized in 1855 at Farmersville. It is the oldest organized church and is still being used. (Photo by Paul Russell.)

PROVIDENCE PRIMITIVE Baptist Church near Blue Ridge. The church was organized at the Arnold Creek School house.

THE OLDEST CATHOLIC CHURCH in North Texas at Wylie-St. Anthony's. (Photo by Paul Russell.)

FIRST CHRISTIAN CHURCH—Celina, Texas. (Photo by Paul Russell).

EPSICOPAL CHURCH at the Frankford Cemetery in southern Collin County. (Photo by Paul Russell.)

THE METHODIST CHURCH, Anna, Texas. (Photo by Paul Russell.)

COTTAGE HILL METHODIST CHURCH northwest of McKinney, organized in 1848. (Photo by Paul Russell.)

THE METHODIST CHURCH at Weston, Texas. Present Bldg. (Photo by Paul Russell.)

THIS WAS THE OLD First Persbyterian Church in McKinney and its tall spire was a well known landmark. (Photo by Paul Russell.)

PARKER PRESBYTERIAN CHURCH organized in 1847, still in use. (Photo by Paul Russell.)

WALNUT GROVE CUMBERLAND Presbyterian Church near Phea Mills, northwest of McKinney. The Church is being considered for a historical marker. The picture was given my grandmother in 1920.

7

Collin County Miscellania

CHAPTER VII

Miscellaneous

McKinney, Texas, Thursday, March 22, 1956
Ex Miser

WHEN COMPLETION OF THE NEW COURTHOUSE WAS CELEBRATED BACK IN 1876
By Capt. Roy Hall

Dusk was falling in the little town of McKinney on that Saturday, January 1, 1876, and what a dismal dusk. It had been raining all the morning, but had stopped about the middle of the afternoon, leaving the village under gloomy, threatening clouds. It remained rather warm though, with temperatures in the 70s, and everywhere was mud and water.

Out in the center of the Court Square, as our public square was called then, stood the magnificent courthouse, recently completed, and towering far above any other building in town. The courthouse was ablaze with lights, as much as coal-oil lamps could make it blaze, and inside it hummed with activity. Tonight was to be held the public ball, celebrating the completion of the finest courthouse in Texas.

And it was to take place within the courthouse itself; upstairs in the present District Court room. That room was larger than it is now, with none of the offices completed on the north and south sides, and the floor was level. Downstairs, only the present Sheriff's office and part of the present office of District Clerk had been started, with only a partial wall up around them. Eight long tables, donated for the purpose by the Henry Hotel and the Thomas Hotel, occupied the entire west part of the lower floor. Table cloths for these tables had been supplied by R.M. Board and Abe Rhine. They were of unbleached domestic, unrolled from bolts the entire length of the tables, which reached from the south to the north wall of the huge room. The tables were loaded with everything under the sun that was good to eat.

This food had been cooked and baked by the ladies of the town, and a lot of it had been collected by Charles Hedrick and T. Bement, who were among the leading grocers of the village. Presiding over the spread in person was Capt. Ben Johnson, of the Johnson Hotel, and scattered among the tables were some fifteen or more colored boys, dressed in white, who were the waiters. Everything here was ready. Everything was ready to serve the guests, but would anybody come? Foul weather!

Up in the dance hall above, Rudolph'a Silver Cornet band was tuning up. They were seated where the District Judge's bench is now, and on the new Excelsior desks furnished by the McKinney Academy. Six of them, led by that old master musician, Lige Rudolph. From the ceiling hung long festoons of Chinese lanterns donated by I.D. Newsome, Jesse Shain and the Heard Brothers. Long planks had been placed on nail and beer kegs around the room and the floor had been covered with wheat bran, on which the children of the town had been skating all afternoon. The floor was now swept clean, and fairly glistened under the lights. All was ready here, but what of the guests? It was dark and dismal outside.

On the square, two lights flickered, throwing a circle of light at the southeast and at the northwest corner. There were lights took near the north entrance to the courthouse; lights and much yelling and shouting back and forth. Bill Merritt, the Sheriff, had mustered a score or more men and was laying a plank walk from the middle of the north side to the courthouse. Merritt and his men were wading through the ankle-deep water and mud, placing the bridge planks on layed-down fence posts, so that people could get to the ball from the plank sidewalk from the north side. There was no other way. All the other sides were blocked by knee-deep mud that a horse-drawn rig could not get through. Four men stood in the slop and held lanterns for the others to work by.

By the time the walk reached the north side several people were waiting. They started across; the gentlemen carefully guiding the lady ahead of him while the workers held lanterns so that they could see where to walk. Several stepped off the single plank walk, and others lost balance and fell into the mud, mostly though only getting their feet soiled.

The crowd grew on the north side, and soon the

walk was full of young people crossing over; screeching and laughing, with now and then a full-blown curse from some swain who had got his dancing slippers full of watery mud. From the northeast corner of the square came the rattle of harness and the plop of hooves being pulled from the mud. Out of the darkness came the road of S.J.B. Plemmons' voice, roaring as only Mr. Plemmons could roar, ''Where you want 'em, Bill?''

The sheriff told him to pull his omnibus up to the stones left after finishing the courthouse, about where the Throckmorton monument is now, and unload his passengers on them. The young ladies and their escorts got out on the big rocks, paid Mr. Plemmons fifty cents for each couple, and went giggling and chattering into the courthouse.

Hacks from Snapp's stable, from Stiff's, Short's, and Jesse Shain's, were also out, hauling people from various parts of town. Plemmons' route was along Chestnut Street, then the fashionable part of the city, and he would start at the north end of the street, north of Rich Rambo's, and continue south until his omnibus was loaded with about ten couples. The others took care of the rest of town; Snapp's hack going out North Kentucky to the Stiff home, and Shain's west and north as far as the present Central Ward School. Short took care of those living down South Tennessee. All hacks and the omnibus had four horses hitched to them, save Short's which had four little mules. There were no telephones, and the people had to wait along the streets until a hack or bus picked them up. Many, of course, had their own saddle horses and rigs, and they were the ones who had congregated on the sidewalks on the north side, after hitching around town and at the livery stables.

The planks laid down from the courthouse soon went under the sloppy mud, and Shain's hack was diverted to carrying people from the sidewalks fifty yards to the stones at the courthouse. At first the driver, a colored man called Mose, charged a nickel, but business got into such a rushing state that he finally left this off, and the rest rode free.

Upstairs Rudolph's little band swung into Strauss' ''Blue Danube,'' that waltz that was taking the world by storm, and the ball was on. Young ladies, gay and laughing in their tarletom mesh, and young gentlemen in evening dress, glided under the Chinese lanterns, some uncertain of their steps, as the waltz was new to McKinney. The schottiche they knew, and of course, the square dance, but the slow swing of the waltz was difficult to learn.

The small orchestra played many pieces, but over

and over again they had to return to ''The Blue Danube'' by popular acclaim. By ten o'clock the big upstairs hall was becoming crowded. Not only were the elite from McKinney and the surrounding country present, but there were socialites present from as far as Austin, from whence came the Secretary of State and his retinue in a special car on the new railroad, the Houstin & Texas Central.

At eleven o'clock Captain J.H. Bingham and Captain B.F. Houston called a halt to the dancing, and announced that dinner was ready down stairs. The thousand or so guests filed down the north stairway—the south one not yet completed—and to any place they could find around the long tables. There were no chairs, everybody ate standing. And there was plenty. My aunt, who attended this function, said the guests hardly made a dent in the food loaded on the tables.

''Ball-room'' dancing was resumed upstairs shortly after midnight and continued until about three in the morning, when the guests began leaving. Dawn was showing in the east when the last of them had departed. Word ws sent to various parts of town for those who wished to repair to the courthouse to eat, but few came. The streets were too bad and a cold norther had blown in at daybreak, keeping the people who had not been present at the ball, at home. In the afternoon G.A. Foote and others had the left-over food collected, placed in drays and hauled to different parts of town to be delivered to the poor.

No social event held in the county since that gay night eighty years ago has approached that New Year's ball in gayety and beauty. The best of North Texas were there. It was a stately occasion, as were most of the social affairs in those days, and it was glamorous. It was the county's greatest effort along social lines, and espite unfavorable weather conditions, it is not known that anyone remained at home who had planned to attend.

FARMING OVER 50 YEARS AGO IN COLLIN COUNTY

By Capt. Roy F. Hall

The biggest events ever held in Collin County, so far as actual attendance was concerned, were the old Confederate and Old Settlers picnics. They reached their height about 1904 and 1905, when they were staged down on Wilson Creek in what was known as Benge's Park, on land now owned by Mr. B.P. Klein. People from all over this section of the state attended, and almost everybody from Collin County. This article will attempt to describe one held August 16-17 and 18th, 1905.

The officials of the Picnic Association for that year were Mr. Walter B. Wilson as president, E.W. Kirkpatrick as vice-president, Tom W. Perkins as secretary, and F.M. (Tuck) Hill as grand marshal. Several days before the opening day the barbecue pits had been going under old Major's direction. 30 beeves were to be barbecued and given away to those wishing it at the picnic. Gangs of laborers had cleared all the underbrush out of the woods and placed water barrels and seats on the ground. Major started his fires two days before the first day of the picnic so that he would have a two-foot bed of glowing coals in the pits on the morning of the first day.

To get to the grounds one had to go down the old road leading from the extreme southwest part of McKinney, or else come in on the same road from across Wilson Creek. The picnic ground consisted of about 20 acres, part trees and part bermuda-grass prairie, and started right at the creek bank. The old road is still there; the ground is too, but overflows have filled it in to a depth of ten feet or more above the original site.

By nine o'clock on the 16th a solid line of wagons buggies and horses were going down the old road from McKinney. This road then was almost exactly in the same shape as it is now—almost a one-way road, and some means had to be taken to allow those returning to town to get back. This was done by turning the traffic off the road at the edge of the bottom, and directing the conveyances out into the woods east of the picnic grounds. Johnny McKinney was stationed here on the morning named—one of his first jobs as a traffic policeman. From here wagons and buggies went into the woods where the drivers found a place to hitch and feed them. Usually this was the headquarters for the particular family during the three-day picnic. They slept here, ate, and returned to the wagon occasionally to rest.

Most people living within driving distance—up to ten miles—went home at night, but thousands remained to camp for the duration on the ground. And "thousands" is right. 20,000 or more attended those picnics in a single day. The only trouble experienced was in getting somebody to attend to the stock at home. Everybody wanted to go.

There were not so many attractions. The "Flying Jenny" of course was there, as were several small concessions like Esaw the Snake eater, the colored boy on a scaffold to be dumped into the water when you hit his head with a baseball, and the doll racks. Very little more. But, it was a get-together; the

biggest in the whole state of Texas, a place where you were sure to meet old acquaintence if they lived within a hundred miles or so. The governor of Texas was there, and made a speech. Joseph Weldon Bailey was there, the famous silver-tongued Senator, who was the only man living that had the power to hold small children spell-bound by the hour. This writer has seen children of all ages sit on the hard bridge planks and listen to Senator Bailey with mouths agape and staring eyes till he had finished speaking. A golden tongue if there ever was one.

Just before noon a crier went about the ground calling "Come and get your barbecue. Bring your dishpans or a tub." This was not a joke. Beef was rather common then, and there was always too much barbecue for those wanting it. This writer saw great chunks—ten pounds or more—thrown out on the ground by some family who had more than they wished. By two o'clock the grounds were filling up with people, and the big picnic was well under way.

Over all there was the picnic noises; the McKinney band and the Altoga band playing alternately, the hum of human voices and the occasional bray of a mule, and the rattle of harness. The cry of the side-show barker, and the blare of mechanical music was totally absent. As a matter of fact, the bandstand was the center of attraction, especially when they were playing, and nothing was quite so pleasant to a young girl as to have one of the band boys speak to her from the band stand. Those bands were the "hot stuff" in those days.

A company of militia from Dallas was there, and drilled on the prairie late in the afternoon. At six o'clock they went through the formality of closing the day by a drill and climaxed it all by firing the muzzle-loading cannon. Long before the time for this exercise people gathered around the edge of the prairie to see the big gun let loose its tremendous blast.

At night the flares were lit, and the picnic went on till about midnight. Those lights were a sputtering kerosene affair hung on the sides of trees. It was a naked light, but wind could not extinguish it. Water was served from barrels set about on the ground and filled often by the street-sprinkler wagon of McKinney. Ice was coming into use then at picnics and a whole cake was dumped in a barrel occasionally. A member of the McKinney Fire Department went about from barrel to barrel during the afternoon calling, "Don't throw the water on the ground. What you can't drink put back in the barrel." This was not to save water, but to prevent the muddy mess that formed around the barrels. It did no good. They formed anyway.

In the afternoon Oscar Brannon rode people around a half-mile track on the prairie in his small steam automobile for fifteen cents. In the oval formed by this track various horse exercises were going on; spearing an overhead ring with a lance at a dead run, picking handkerchiefs from the ground at a run and other of like nature. There usually was some speaking in the afternoon also, but mostly it was given over to wandering around the grounds looking for relatives and friends. All animals were watered at the creek, and there was steady stream of them going and coming all day long.

By modern standards those old picnics were rather crude affairs, riding a hundred miles in a wagon through the August heat is no fun anywhere. Camping out among hundreds of horses and mules is not fun either—not to us nowadays. But those people were used to hardship. To them, getting to see and talk with an old friend was worth all the trials and troubles incidental to the occasion. They seemed to have liked to be with each other in those more than we do now, and to share hardships sort of brought them into the same brotherhood.

BRIEF HISTORY OF THE DALLAS—SHERMAN—INTERURBAN

The idea of the interurban originated in April, 1903, and on September 1, 1906, J.S. Heard and J.F. Strickland signed papers in Boston for the building of the line. McKinney was to get the powerhouse and at least four miles of street railways.

Contracts awarded, September 16, 1906, and the Texas Traction company was chartered on the 25th. The first dirt was broken at Choctaw Bayou, south of Sherman on October 31, but actual construction started on November 6, 1906.

T.E. Craig, of the General Electric company, was named supervisor in laying the track, constructing the powerhouse and drilling a deep well. Equipment, powerhouse machinery, five sub-stations and 15 cars were purchased in November, 1906, for $250,000., and in January, 1907, 20 acres were purchased from the Berry homestead for a powerhouse site.

Grading the roadbeds from the powerhouse site to East Fork started February 7, 1907.

The first car over the line under power was June 30, 1908. The next day, July 1, 1908, the Texas Traction Company went into regular operation.

August 20, 1910, R.L. Waddill executed a contract with the Texas Traction company for street cars in McKinney.

In April, 1911, the Texas Traction company purchased the Sherman-Denison interurban line. This was the oldest electric in the southwest, having been in operation since May 1, 1901.

The Dallas-Waxahachie, the Waxahachie-Waco and the Dallas-Corsicana interurban lines were built by the Dallas Southern Traction Comapny during 1911-12-13, and were consolidated, January 1, 1914, as the Texas Electric Railway. January 1, 1917, the Texas Electric acquired all the property of the Texas Traction Company and the whole system became the Texas Electric.

Normal operating equipment for the line was 22 passenger cars, 10 express cars (The Electric Express & Baggage company was a subsidiary of the Texas Electric and operated separate express and baggage trains); 10 work and freight cars, 19 express trail cars, five box cars, five flat cars, three locomotives and two welding and materials cars.

There were nine sub-stations on the Dallas-Denison division eight miles apart, using 600 volts, D.C., and on the Waco division there were six sub-stations using 1200 volts, 15 miles apart. The company owned and operated freight and passenger depots from Waco to Denison.

Rail was 70 to 80 pounds ASCE section. All ties were creosoted and all ballast was gravel. There were 4,884 lineal feet of steel bridges on the line and 7,959 of wooden trestles.

Trolley wire was 4-0 grooved, and the feeder wire was 350 M circular mill capacity. Overhead was mostly caternary construction.

Normal operation consisted of 56 cars in and out of Dallas daily, with a basic passenger rate of 2 cents a mile.

M.J. Loftice was the first superintendent of the Texas Traction company with offices at Woodlake, between Sherman and Denison. The company shops were located at the powerhouse, McKinney. On consolidation the general offices were located in the Interurban Building in Dallas. The shops were removed to 2110 Denley Drive, Dallas, and the freight terminal was located at 601 Young Street, Dallas, covering an entire block.

Officials, after consoslidation: some before:
James P. Griffin .President
C.F. McAuliff . . . . .Vice-President
James B. Griffin .Secretary
D.W. Milam . . . . .Treasurer and Auditor
H.G. Floyd . . . . .General Superintendent

A.P. Smith . . . . Freight Traffic manager
H.C. McIntosh . . . . Passenger Traffic manager
Sam P. Burford . . . . General Attorney
E.H. Sieberg . . . . General Claim Agent
G.H. Peters . . . . Superintendent of Power
T.L. Stubblefield . . . . Purchasing Agent

The Dallas-Corsicana branch line was abandoned February 4, 1941.

The rest of the Texas Electric Company ceased operation at midnight December 31, 1948, after 40 years and six months of the finest kind of service to the people of north Texas.

By Roy F. Hall
Former sub-station operator.

"FIRSTS IN COLLIN COUNTY"

The first building in the newly formed town of McKinney was a small frame building hauled from the former county seat of Buckner to the Northwest corner of the Square—May 3, 1848.

The Houston and Texas Central Railroad came through McKinney in 1872 and started the town on its way.

The telephone came to Collin County in 1878.

The first telephone in McKinney was installed between the Foote House and the H. and T.C. Railroad station for the use of the hotel guests.

The first telephone out of McKinney was in 1883, connecting Dallas and Sherman, Denison and McKinney. Three years later the company was allowed to attach lines to the electric light poles. In 1913 The McKinney Telephone Company was organized with S.O. Scott, Pres.

Coldest weather to hit Collin County was January 13, 1877 when the temperature dropped to 18 degrees below zero.

The hottest weather was August 10, 1936 with 118 degrees registered.

The First Confederate and Old Settler Picnic was held August 11, 1883 at the old fair grounds on Wilson Creek. 20,000 attended.

The First Fire Company was organized in McKinney in 1887. Equipment was a small pumper pulled by hand, a hose cart, with 500 feet of hose. There was no fire station so the equipment was stored in the Bingham Building.

King Custer was Collin's first Sheriff and was paid $100 for the period between July, 1846 and July 1848.

1911 was Collin County's driest year.

The first airplane flight in Collin County was in 1912. Prof. C.F. Walsh flew a Curtiss airplane at the Fair Grounds.

The first bottled cold drinks were made by A. Craus at his plant on South Kentucky Street. He bottled two kinds—strawberry and lemon.

The first Rural Free Delivery of mail was started at McKinney on December 2, 1901.

The first taxes collected in Collin County was the year 1848 and amounted to a total of $718.83.

The first commercial nursery was started in Collin in 1883 by the Kerr brothers.

Ex-Governor Throckmorton, McKinney's only man to head Texas government, died at his home April 26, 1894.

A statue of Gov. Throckmorton was presented to the city by the Federated Women's Clubs on July 4, 1911.

The Celina Pike was the first good road built in the county. It was completed in Feb., 1915.

The first automobile race in Collin County was staged at the picnic, August 24, 1905. The winner went a mile in a minute and a half!

Stock law elections were held all over the county in June of 1903.

1884 bridges were being built over the creeks of Collin County for the first time by the County.

The Cotton Oil Mill was built in McKinney in the fall of 1892. Up to that time farmers had no way to dispose of the cotton seed.

The first train robbery in Collin was at Allen in 1878. An out-bound train was robbed by Sam Bass and his accomplices.

Electric lights came into use in Collin County in 1886.

Heard's Opera House was completed in January of 1885, and on its stage appeared all the great entertainers of the era—John Phillip Sousa's Band, Maxine Elliot, and etc.

100 mile bicycle race between Dallas and Van Alstyne and return. J.B. Cave proclaimed the winner.

The opening of Highway 75 coincided with the Centennial celebration in 1936. A two-lane highway!

Street cars came to McKinney through the efforts of R.L. Waddill August 20, 1910.

Collin County Bank was established in 1869.

the Union Depot was completed here March 1906.

A monument to pure bred swine was erected at the McKinney Coliseum Oct. 11, 1923, declaring Collin County was free of scrub bores.

Automobiles did not replace horse-drawn vehicles on a big scale until 1915.

The Electric Interurban between Sherman and Waco came through the county in 1907 and was abandoned in 1948.

A Good Roads Election was passed in Feb., 1914 and Collin finally began to get out of the mud.

January 1, 1929, stoves taken out of the Courthouse and replaced by a heating system.

William blazed the first road in the county from McKinney to Greenville.

April 1, 1873 S.J.B. Plemmons started a bus line and in point of service could be called the oldest in the state.

Site for Finch Park presented to the City by the McKinney Federation Women's Club, June 11, 1914.

The first automobile to come through Collin County belonged to the railroad man, H.E.R. Green of Terrell.

The first auto in McKinney belonged to T.T. Emerson, July 17, 1903.

First mail carriers in McKinney were Will Cloyd and Eugene Rabun, with December 1, 1902 the first day.

Complete list of marks and brands of Collin County may be found in the Microfilmed *Daily Courier Gazette*, April 13, 1917.

Fire Company organized in McKinney in 1887, with a small pumper pulled by hand, and a hose cart with 500 feet of hose. There was no fire station so it was stored in the Bingham Building.

A contract that would supply McKinney with electric lights was signed May 1, 1889.

Heard's Opera House was completed in December, 1884.

Marketing on the square was first prohibited on the 5th of August, 1926.

F.B. Pope gave $75,000 to build a Nurse's Home in connection with the hospital in 1924.

McKinney was incorporated May 28, 1859. 60 votes for and one against.

First child born in Plano was W.S. Forman, Feb. 25, 1852.

First bank in McKinney was Emerson's private bank, a good one, for it withstood the crash of 1873.

First airmail letter received in McKinney was May 13, 1926 and was brought from Dallas to McKinney by the Interurban.

First Collin County election was July 13, 1846 at Buckner with Z. Roberts elected ounty Judge, Moses Wilson the District Clerk, and Tola Dunn the County Clerk and King Solomon Custer the Sheriff.

First Collin County boy killed in World War I was Jimmy Geigas, Sept. 20, 1918.

Present Preston Road was called the Washita-Dallas Road in 1848.

ALEO, PO est. April 13, 1895, Lemuel C. Smith, 1st PM, Disc. 1-10-1901.

ALLEN, PO est. 1-10-1876, J.W. Franklin, 1st PM. Settled about 1870 and named for Ebenezer Allen who promoted the Houston & Texas Central Railroad through the area in 1872. On February 23, 1878 Allen was the scene of a bank robbery by Sam Bass and three members of his gang.

ALTOGA, PO est. 1-4-1889, James A. Moreland, 1st PM, Disc.

ANNA, PO est. May 29, 1883, William Y. Barnett, 1st PM. Settled about 1846 when Collin McKinney built a cabin three miles southeast of the present townsite. No village developed until 1883 when a town was laid out on the newly constructed Houston & Texas Central Railroad and named for Anna Greer, daughter of John L. Greer. Another source says the place was named for Anna Quinlan, daughter of G.A. Quinlan, former superintendent of the H&TC at the time the place was founded.

ARDATH, PO est. October 11, 1899, John T. Williams, 1st PM, Disc. 11-18-1901.

ARNOLD, PO est. 12-6-1899, John R. Self, 1st PM., Disc. 11-30-1902.

BETH, PO est. 6-4-1884, Wm. G. Matthews, 1st PM, Disc. 4-15-1886.

BETHANY, settled about 1876 and named after an early church.

BIGGERS, PO est. October 24, 1899, Wade Biggers, 1st PM., Disc. 12-31-1903. Located on Wilson Creek in central Collin County. Named from the Bigger's Allen mill which was established at the site in the late 1880's.

BISHOP, PO est. 6-30-1893, Geo. E. Allen, 1st PM, Disc. Dec. 28, 1893.

BLACK HILL, PO est. 2-24-1879, Benj. H. Bounds, 1st PM., Disc. April 29, 1883.

BLUE RIDGE, PO est. 9-27-1876, Wm. Worden, 1st PM. Town situated on a hill and from a distance one can see a blue looking ridge with a little town on top; hence the name.

BRANCH, PO est. 1-14-1901, John T. Branch, 1st PM, Disc. 12-31-1903. Located in southwestern Collin County 11 miles from McKinney. Named for J.T. Branch who operated a store here and was first postmaster. 1940 population was 25.

BUCKNER, PO est. 5-22-1846 (CH), John McGarrah, 1st PM. Name changed to McKinney 5-31-1848. Buckner was County Seat from 1846 to 1848.

CALLIS, PO est. 2-25-1891, Wm. C. Satterwhite, 1st PM, Disc. 3-31-1904. Located in northeastern Collin County. 1940 population was 25.

CELINA, PO est. Feb. 28, 1881, John T. Mulkey, 1st PM. Named after Celina, Tennessee by John T. Mulkey. Town moved to a new site on the St. Louis and San Francisco Railroad in 1902. Incorporated 1906. 1915 population was 724.

CHAMBERSVILLE, PO est. 3-6-1894, Jacob M. Bryan, 1st PM, Disc. Dec. 31, 1903. Settled in 1847 when Elisha Chambers, of Indiana, located on the East Fork Creek. Jacob M. Bryan established a store here in 1892 and became first postmaster. 1947 population as 75.

CHAMBLISS, PO est. 11-17-1898, James L. Davis, 1st PM Disc. 9-15-1903. Located in northern section of the county four miles from Melissa. Named in honor of Charles Chambliss who settled in the community in the 1880's.

CLEARLAKE, PO est. December 10, 1898, Robert L. Palmer, 1st PM, Disc. ——. Founded near a large clear lake and named from that lake.

CLIMAX, PO est. May 25, 1895, John G. Osborne, 1st PM, Disc. 11-30-1901. Located about five miles from Princeton. Settled by William Warden in 1857.

COPEVILLE, PO est. 6-5-1878, John M. Cope, 1st PM. Named for Miles Cope who settled here in 1859.

CULLEOKA, PO est. 5-29-1883, John P. Morros, 1st PM, Disc. in 1910. Settled in 1846. 1940 population was 150.

DESERT, PO est. January 7, 1893, Miss A. Webster, 1st PM. Disc. in 1910. Settled about 1890. 1940 population was 25.

DONNA, PO est. October 9, 1897, James A. McClure, 1st PM. Disc. 8-31-1903.

DUMP, PO est. 3-2-1899, Edward Bellingre, 1st PM, Disc. 11-30-1901.

EMERSON, name changed to Frisco—see that place.

EMPIRE, PO est. 1-28-1885, John T. Grimes, 1st PM, Disc. 4-25-188? (fold).

ENGLEMAN, PO est. 1-21-1886, Robt. S. Sneed, 1st PM, Disc. 8-6-1897.

ERUDIA, PO est. 6-17-1895, Wm. H. Bristol, 1st PM, Name of PO changed to Frisco, April 24, 1902.

EUREKA, merged with Wylie—see that place.

FARMERSVILLE, PO est. 5-4-1857, Thos. E. Sherwood, 1st PM, Confederate PM Samuel Lansford appt. October 12, 1861. Founded in 1845 by John Yeary and located 2 miles southwest of the present town. It was originaly called Sugar Hill. The name was changed to Farmersville in 1857. The name was suggested by the large number of farmers residing here at the time. Another source says the name was suggested because of the fertile black land surrounding the area.

FAY, PO est. 6-8-1882, Knud M. Peterson, 1st PM, Name changed to Royce City, Rockwall County, October 25, 1886.

FAYBURGH, PO est. 3-4-1884 as Fayburgh, Jas. G. Griffith, 1st PM. Name changed to Fayburg 11-6-1893, Disc. 11-18-1901.

FILLMORE, Named in honor of Millard Fillmore, 13th President of the United States. Name changed to Plano—see that place.

FONCINE, PO est. February 18, 1895, Rupert F. Reese, 1st PM, Disc. 11-30-1901. Named for Foncine Fisher, daughter of R.C. Fisher who established a gristmill, store, gin and grain elevator at the site about 1890. 1940 population was 15.

FOOT, PO est. 1-16-1901, John W. Cox, 1st PM, Disc. 11-14-1903. Named for a pioneer family who settled here in the early 1880's. 1947 population was 50.

FOREST GROVE, a farming and school community on White Rock Creek which was settled about 1858. 1940 population was 50.

FRANKFORD, PO est. 5-11-1880, Samuel T. Hammond, 1st PM, Disc. May 14, 1904.

FRISCO, PO est. April 24, 1902—late Erudia, Thomas Duncan, 1st PM. First called Emerson for Francis Emerson but with the arrival of the St. Louis and San Francisco Railroad the name was changed to Frisco (the nickname of the Saint Louis, Santa Fe and Texas Railroad). Incorporated 1907.

GRAYBILL, PO est. 6-14-1881, Garland P. Jones, 1st PM. Disc. Graybill merged with Westminster.

GRICE, PO est. 5-29-1893, Alexander Daniels, 1st PM., Disc. 5-14-1894.

GROVE, PO est. 5-27-1899, John P. Snider, 1st PM, Disc. 11-30-1901.

HACKBERRY BLUFF, PO est. 1-29-1847, Wm. H. Pulliam, 1st PM, Disc. 3-16-1848.

HANCOCK, PO est. 7-21-1880, Henry M. Rollins, 1st PM, Disc. Sept. 29, 1881.

HICKMAN, PO est. 3-29-1894, Thomas A. Bailey, 1st PM, Disc. 3-1-1899.

HIGHLAND, PO est. 9-9-1853, Isaac N. Foster, 1st PM, Disc. 5-16-1873.

JOSEPHINE, PO est. 7-29-1888, Joseph M. Stubblefield, 1st PM. Established in 1888 when the St. Louis,

Southwestern Railroad crossed the county. Named for Josephine Hubbard, daughter of J.C. Hubbard who donated land for the townsite.

KNOX, PO est. 5-17-1892, John B. O'Neal, 1st PM, Disc. June 30, 1902.

LAKE MILLS, PO est. 10-16-1878, Ransom P. Bills, 1st PM, Disc. 2-1-1887.

LAVON, PO est. 5-1-1888, Elbert C. Thomson, 1st PM. Settled in 1854. Became a flag stop on the St. Louis, Southwestern Railroad in 1888. Named for Lavon Thomson, son of E.C. Thomson who operated the post office in his general store.

LEBANON, PO est. 3-1-1806—late Denton County, Philip A. Huffman, 1st PM, Disc. Settled in 1845 by Danson Clark who built a sawmill south of the townsite. By 1885 the village had a population of 500 but when the railroad missed the town it declined and in 1949 had a population of 50. Named after Lebanon, Tennessee.

LIEU, PO est. 12-20-1887, Moses S. Howell, 1st PM. Disc. 2-8-1890.

LINT, PO est. 7-7-1886, Jas. D. Coleman, 1st PM, Disc. 8-27-1887.

LONE ELM, name changed to Wylie—see that place.

LONE TREE, PO est. 3-4-1859, John Seabourn, 1st PM. Disc. 7-20-1875.

LUCAS, PO est. 5-11-1888, Gabriel H. Lucas, 1st PM, Disc. 9-30-1903. First settled by Peter F. Lucas who came to the area in 1844 and became County Commissioner in 1846. The town was named for Gabriel H. Lucas, owner of the general store and first postmaster.

McKINNEY, PO est. 5-31-1848—late Buckner, Joel F. Stewart, 1st PM. Named for Collin McKinney, born in New Jersey, April 17, 1766; came to Texas in 1823 locating near Texarkana. In 1836 was elected a member of the Constitutional Convention. Signer of the Texas Declaration of Independence. Member of Congress, Representative from Texas. Member of the Texas Legislature. McKinney has been county seat since 1848. Incorporated in 1859.

ASHBURN GENERAL, PO Branch of McKinney, Collin County, Texas.

MANTUA, PO est. June 29, 1858, Elizabeth B. Rollins 1st PM. Disc. 1-23-1867. Re-est. July 22, 1870, Eliphalet B. Rollins, PM (sic), Disc. July 11, 1873. Mantua was established in 1854 in connection with the projected Mantua Seminary. A townsite was developed and proceeds were to pay for building the school. Town was described, in 1867, as a "flourishing village" in the northern part of the county; however when Van Alstyne, 2 miles to the east, was established on the Texas Central Railroad in 1872, most businesses moved to the new town.

MAPLE, PO est. 3-4-1890, Wm. F. Loyd, 1st PM.

MARILEE, located in northwestern Collin County. This was a farming community with a station on the St. Louis & San Francisco Railroad. 1940 population was 20.

MAXWELL, PO est. March 21, 1884, Ben P. McPherson, 1st PM. Disc. 1-20-188? (fold).

MAXWELL'S BRANCH, name changed to Murphy—see that place.

MURPHY, PO est. 1-30-1891, James T. Murphy, 1st PM. Located in southern Collin County. Settled by C.A. McMillen in 1846. First called Old Decatur, then Maxwell's Branch. When the St. Louis & Santa Fe of Texas Railroad established a station here in 1888 it was named Murphy for William Murphy, an early settler. Another source says the place was named for James T. Murphy, early settler and first postmaster.

MELISSA, PO est. 5-16-1873, James R. Rogers, 1st PM. Settled in 1851 when Charley Wysong built a cabin on Honey Creek. With the construction of the Houston & Texas Central Railroad, in 1872, the settlement was named Melissa for Melissa Hunington. Another source says named for Melissa Shirley, daughter of Tom Shirley, pioneer citizen.

MERIT, PO est. 6-15-1885—late Hunt County, Newton H. McCallon, 1st PM., Trans to Hunt County after 6-15-1885.

MERITT, PO est. 3-10-1884, Newton H. McCallon, 1st PM, Trans to Hunt County after 3-10-1884.

MILLWOOD, PO est. 5-21-1851, Jas. Smith, 1st PM. Disc. after 1885. Located in southeastern section of the county. Established about 1850 and named after a lumber mill on the Trinity River. 1947 population was 10.

MIMS, A station on the Southern Pacific Railroad named for A.D. Mims, a former Vice President and General Manager of that line.

MORELAND, PO est. 11-13-1894, Appleton A. Bellows, 1st PM, Disc. 4-13-1904.

NEVADA, PO est. 8-3-1880, Samuel Stinebaugh, 1st PM. The first post office at Nevada was located on the west side of Bear Creek Cemetery in the home of Ben Bounds who was a Methodist preacher. By 1903 the PO was moved to the townsite of Nevada; so named by settlers who came here from Nevada, Missouri. Incorporated in 1891 and "voted off" in 1927. Another source says place named by Samuel Stinebaugh after his former home at Nevada, Missouri.

NEW HOPE, A rural school and church community which was settled about 1850.

NICKLEVILLE, PO est. 8-20-1883, Francis L. McCarty, 1st PM. Name changed to Wylie June 10, 1886. Located in southern Collin County and was one of a group of settlements made by Irish, Scotch and English settlers in the early 1850's. It is reportedly named for a "nickel store" established before the Civil War. The community joined Eureka, Lone Elm and St. Paul in 1886 to form the new town of Wylie.

OLD DECATUR, name changed to Murphy—see that place.

OLD HIGHLAND, name changed to Parris—see that place.

PARKER, PO est. 4-12-1888, Geo. T. Kennedy, 1st PM., Disc. 11-30-1900. Settled about 1880 by T.L. Johnson who had a gristmill and general store here. 1940 population was 86.

PARRISS, A rural community south of Melissa in central Collin County. Named for Thaddeus Parris, a Mexican War veteran who built an ox-drawn gristmill on Trinity Creek in 1859. Place was also called Old Highland.

PAULINE, PO est. 4-17-1886—late Frankford, Sam'l. T. Hammond, 1st PM, Name changed to Frankford June 21, 1886.

PIKE, PO est. 11-11-1885, Chas. S. McGowan, 1st PM, Disc. in early 1900's. Located in northeastern section of the county on the Hunt County Line. Settled in the early 1870's. Fate Fagg established a store here in 1887. 1947 population was 100.

PLANO, PO est. October 9, 1852, William Forman, 1st PM. Place was settled in 1845-1846 by William Forman and other members of Peters' Colony and called Fillmore in honor of Millard Fillmore, 13th President of the U.S. When the court house was established here it was decided a new name should be given the town as a majority of the citizens were Democrats and President Fillmore was a Republican. It was named "Plano" from its location on a plain in south central Collin County, an area which was relatively plain with no major rivers or mountains.

PRINCETON, PO est. 11-24-1888, W.A. Harrelson, 1st PM. Princeton was first known as "Wilson Switch" when the railroad built through here in 1882. Name changed when the PO was established and the name "Wilson" refused as there was already a PO of that name in the State. Princeton was chosen in honor of Prince Dowling who owned a large acreage nearby. Another source says named for Princeton Dowlin, one of the promoters of the townsite.

PROSPECT, Merged with Westminster—see that place.

PROSPER, PO est. May 22, 1893, Larkin A. Adamson, 1st PM. Established in 1902 as a stop on the Saint Louis and San Francisco Railroad. Incorporated in 1904. Town was named by sanguine railroad officials. Another source says the school district was called Richland and that name was desired for the town but due to duplication in names it was rejected by the POD. The name of Prosper was then chosen as being most appropriate because of the prosperous condition of the people living there.

RENNER, PO est. July 13, 1888, Geo. F. Hudson, 1st PM. Named in 1887 for John A. Renner, Civil Engineer who surveyed the townsite. The new town on the Cotton Belt Railroad was begun when F.W. Jackson opened a store there.

RHEA MILLS, PO est. January 27, 1876 as Rhea's Mills, James C. Rhea 1st PM Name changed to Rhea Mills March 10, 1892, Disc. after 1900. Established in 1857 when W.A. and J.C. Rhea built a mill at the site.

RHYMER, PO est. June 17, 1895, Martha G. Tunstall, 1st PM. Disc. Sept. 15, 1903.

ROCK HILL, PO est. Dec. 15, 1854, John L. Moore, 1st PM. Disc. 1867, Re-est. 1873, Disc. Rock Hill was an early settlement in Peters' Colony, J.J. Thompson established an early gristmill and cotton gin here. 1947 population was 25.

ROLAND, PO est. Dec. 4, 1887, Thomas S. Webb, 1st PM, Disc. 12-31-1903. Located in northwestern Collin County on Honey Creek. W.T. Manard operated a general store which housed the post office. 1940 population was 25.

ROSELAND, PO est. 9-23-1852, Wm. H. Herren, 1st PM. Disc.

SAINT PAUL, PO est. 4-12-1876, W.E. Marriott, 1st PM, Disc. 3-20-1894. Merged with Wylie.

SEDALIA, PO est. Jan. 15, 1889—late Yakima, Grayson County, David S. Martin, 1st PM, Disc. Dec. 31, 1902. Settled about 1870. 1940 population was 25.

SELLERS, PO est. May 17, 1890, Daniel B. Nelson, 1st PM, Disc. Dec. 23, 1890.

SEVEN POINTS, Name changed to Westminster—see that place.

SHEPTON, PO est. 12-27-1894, John L. Huffman, 1st PM, Disc. 11-14-1903. Shepton was a crossroads community in southwestern Collin County. Named for J.W. Shephard who operated a general store here in 1890.

SISTER GROVE, PO est. 12-27-1875, CC Frost, 1st PM. Disc. 6-3-1878.

SNOW HILL, A rural church and school community on a mail route from Farmersville. 1940 population was 20.

SPRING CREEK, PO est. 6-10-1850, James G. Vanos, 1st PM, Disc. May 8, 1851.

STIFF, PO est. May 14, 1886, Wm. A. Smart, 1st PM. Disc. Dec. 30, 188? (fold).

SUGAR HILL, Name changed to Farmersville—see that place.

TIB, PO est. 4-22-1899, James B. Wallace, 1st PM., Disc. March 31, 1904.

TICKEY, PO est. 5-29-1888, James C. Payne, 1st PM, Name changed to Viney 3-8-1890.

VALDASTA, PO est. 6-2-1886, Tandy W. Smith, 1st PM, Disc. in 1910. Located in northeastern Collin County six miles east of Melissa. Place was first called Vandersville by Tandy W. Smith who settled here in 1882 and later built a grist mill and cotton gin at the site. Smith chose the new name when Vandersville was rejected by the POD.

VANDERSVILLE, Name changed to Valdasta—see that place.

VERONA, PO est. Sept. 27, 1876, Malcomb N. Stroup, 1st PM, Disc. 11-30-1901. Located on Pilot Grove Creek in northeastern Collin County. A.R. Womble operated a gristmill and cotton gin here.

VINELAND, PO est. 6-30-1888, Mrs. Laura Bass, 1st PM., Disc. Dec. 31, 1903.

VINEY, PO est. March 8, 1890—late Tickey, James C. Payne, 1st PM Disc. 5-12-1891.

WESTMINSTER, PO est. June 15, 1899, Geo. H. Ullinger, 1st PM. Founded in 1860 and named Seven Points. By 1885 the community included the nearby communities of Prospect and Graybill. Seven Points college was established here but in 1886 the name of the school was changed, and the name of the town, to Westminster. The school was named after Westminster, Maryland, a stronghold of the Methodists. The school was a preparatory school for ministers and one source attributes the name to that fact.

WESTON, PO est. January 16, 1854, Larkin Adamson, 1st PM. Founded by Larkin Adamson who settled here in 1850 and named the place for his former home at Weston, Missouri.

WETSEL, A rural community five miles south of McKinney named for James Wetsel, an early settler.

WILSON, A rural community near Princeton which was named for George A. and T.B. Wilson who owned land in the area in 1884.

WILSON SWITCH, Name changed to Princeton—see that place.

WYLIE, PO est. June 10, 1886—late Nickleville, John T. Butler, 1st PM. Established in 1870 when Gus Davis built a store which he called Nickelville. When the Gulf Colorado and Santa Fe Railroad was built through about 1886 Nickelville, Eureka, Lone Elm and St. Paul merged to form the new town of Wylie. Named for W.D. Wylie, right-of-way agent for the railroad.

A TYPICAL COUNTRY SCHOOL

WILMETH SCHOOL, 1903.

122

SCHOOL FACULTY OF McKINNEY SCHOOL IN 1898.

THE OLD McKINNEY PUBLIC SCHOOL

SPANISH AMERICAN WAR COMPANY ORGANIZED IN McKINNEY, 1898.

R.H. SCOTT (Uncle Bob) in 1910. Uncle Bob was a true Confederate. His belief was "Forget, Hell."

MISS AMY BISHOP, the telephone operator in Nevada, Texas, 1911.

ELDER R.C. HORN, pioneer Christian preacher.

THE STATE OF TEXAS awarded a Historical Building Medallion to the old home of Isaac F. Graves in Northwest McKinney. The Graves family came to McKinney in 1857 from Virginia. The house is built of heart pine and oak hauled by ox wagon from Jefferson. The inside walls are plastered with hog-hair plaster still intact. The original pine floors are still beautiful after generations of use. The house is still occupied by descendents, the George Cameron family.

BAPTISM ON East Fork near Wylie, Texas, July 29, 1915.

WHEN "COTTON WAS KING" in Collin County in the 1890s and early 1900s, these cotton buyers and cotton brokers were busy men for the rich black soil ideally suited to the growth of cotton and many fortunes were made in cotton. Some of the men in the photograph are Jesse Shain, Bob Warwick, W.M. Hynds, Henry Lewis, Edgar Board, W.B. Harrison, Charles Heard, and Jack Woodson.

THIS SHOWS THE last season the great steam threshers worked in Collin County harvesting the wheat that grew with such abundance in the "Flats" of west Collin County. But steam gave way to more modern inventions and soon the combine took over the job; however, older people who experienced the thrill of the great threshing machines, enjoy looking back to the days when boys "went with the thresher." (1937)

THE HEYDAY OF THE INTERURBAN, 1907.

TEARING UP THE TRACKS, 1948.

THE HORSE DRAWN fire wagon replaces the old hand drawn pumper.

McKINNEY FINALLY gets out of the mud, 1908.

ONE OF THE last pioneer log cabins in Collin County, built when this was Peter's Colony, 1845. (Picture made in 1955—cabin no longer stands.)

April 10th 1847

Bill of the sale of the personal property of J.C.W.
Hodges &c of the County of Collin and State Texas

Pleasant Wilson	1 Yoke of Oxen	Old York		$22.00
do do	1 do do	do 6 years old		41.0
Nathan Hampton	1 pr Young Steers			17.50
do do	1 pr do do			16.00
ant Wilson	1 pr do Do			17.00
s Rattan	1 Young Steer			13.00
D. G. Franklin	1 Yr Young Ster			26
Nathan Hampton	3 Young Steers 3.75			11.25
Pleasant Wilson	1 Young Bull			11.25
Ezra Shelby	1 Yoke 7 year Old Oxen			34.00
Peter Lucas	3 Stands Bees $2.50			7.50
Thos Stallcup	4 Do Do 2.37½			9.50
Thos Rattan	4 do Do 2.50			10.00
Thos do	9 Do Do 2.00			18.00
Thos Stallcup	5 Do do 2.12½			10.62½
Pleasant Wilson	2 Do Do 2.00			4.00
George Pegues	20 Bushels Corn lot No 1 $1.02½			20.50
do do	20 do do do No 2 $1.13½			22.70
Santa Darby	20 do do do " 3 $1.13			22.60
Saml H. Brown	20 do Do " " 4 $1.13			22.60
do do	20 do do " " 5 $ 1.13			22.60
s. Stallcup	20 Do Do " " 6 $ 1.00			20.00
do	20 do do " 7 $ 1.00			20.00
Ezra Shelby	do Do do " 8 $ .93¾			18.75
			$ 438.37½

RECORDS OF AN estate sale, dated April 10, 1847. Looking at the buyers' names is like calling the roll of the first settlers. Pleasant Wilson, who came with Throckmorton on the first exploring party, Peter Lucas, Thomas Rattan, G.A. Foote, pioneer physician, James Herndon, William Rice, and Tola Dunn.

ONCE A BOOMING operation in Collin County, now idle. The Collin County Mill and Elevator.

MRS. B.L. DEMPSEY of Wylie, Texas sends this picture of the Morris School in the St. Paul Com-munity. The teacher, Wallace Dunn, was also a Methodist preacher. The year was 1895.

OLD BLOOMDALE SCHOOL and Teacherage. Photographed in 1915.

ABOUT 1900 IT WAS the custom in Collin County to have "Singing Schools." In summer when the crops were laid by, some singing teacher usually showed up at each community and offered to teach a two week singing school to be held at the little school house. For a very small fee all the young people could enjoy not only the pleasure of each other's company, but also learned to sing by learning "shaped notes." This little picture, while unidentified, was typical of scenes repeated many summers in every rural community in the county.

JOHNSON SCHOOL GROUP, Johnson School, near Altoga in 1898. Ed Magee's picture.

OUR FIRE BOYS
THE PRIDE OF McKINNEY.

THE FIREMEN OF McKINNEY.

1907

IT WAS A GALA day for all of North Texas, as well as Collin County, when the Interurban cars made their first run from Sherman to Ennis. From 1907 until 1948 citizens had the assurance that there would be a car by every hour on the hour and at a nominal fee. A trip to Dallas became a favorite pastime with young and old for now it was a matter of minutes where once it took half a day with a horse drawn vehicle.

THE LITTLE COFFMAN SCHOOL was established about 1890. It was located north of McKinney. The picture was sent by Clara Allison of Texarkana, Texas who as a student at the school until she married the teacher, Mr. Scoggins about 1900.

THE HONORABLE SAM RAYBURN, many years Speaker of the House making a talk at Legion Hall, McKinney, Texas in 1950.

THE LAST CAR TO run over the Interurban tracks in 1948. All day the cars were crowded.

LEBANON STORE, 1952.

McKINNEY BEFORE THE days of the automobile. Note the raised court house grounds!

WILMETH SCHOOL, 1899. From left to right: top row, Roy Hall, Clyde Dunn, Emma Reed, Ivy Cave, Prof. T.D. Simpson, Mary Hall, Nellie Cave, Mrs. Simpson, Charley Elmore, Babe Hall, Luey Hall, Dolly Straughn; second row, Elmore, Barney Hunn, Sue Pendergrass, Hattie Hall, Artie Hall, Carrie Elmore, Watus Pendergrass, Joe Hunn, Wade Jordan, Everitt Cave, Sol Skidmore; third row, Jim Mullins, Jack Hall, A.B. Cave, Etta Simpson, Autie Hall, Linnie Straughn, Katie Crutcher, Bettie Hall, Ora Hall, Lizzie Reed, Jennie Cline, Elmore, Unidentified; fourth row, Dollie Pope, Elma Hunn, Emmie Pendergrass, Maudie Pope, John Pendergrass, Gault Simpson, Reed, Mack Dunn, Tommy Lane, Mae Skidmore, Jess Dunn, Unidentified, Mae Jordan, — Elmore.

READY FOR A HAPPY FOURTH is this group of McKinneyites gathered on the west side of the square. All are ready for the Old Settlers Picnic, an affair which dominated the day in Collin County just after the turn of the century. Sorry we have no date for this photograph, but antique car experts might place the time as being between 1910 and 1915. Henry Ford was just a lad at the time. It must be 1915. My dad kept his old 1914 Ford for many years. It had a brass, octagon shaped radiator, like these.

OIL MILL FIRE

OLD POST OFFICE AT Lavon, Texas. The building of the Lavon Lake has brought thousands of tourists to the area and the towns, like Lavon, are growing rapidly. Lavon Water District furnishes water to most Collin County towns. E.C. Thompson, first settler, named town Lavon for his son.

THE WILMETH SCHOOL STOOD ON Wilmeth Road on land now used for the Golf Course north of the Job Corp.

WILMETH SCHOOL, 1902. Left to right: Roy Hall, Clyde Dunn, Emily Pendergrass, Vona Harrison, Jack Hall, A.B. Cave, Nugent Hall, Jess Dunn and Mack Dunn. A favorite game at recess was drilling, marching, etc.

WHY GRANDDAD CAME TO TEXAS

Composed by Capt. Roy F. Hall for a pioneer program at school for one of his children.

I think some times I would like to know
  Why Granddad dropped his plow and hoe;
Why he made for shelter on a Texas Plain
  And never went back home again.

For Granddad left in the dead of night,
  He swam the river and took to flight.
He wore no shoes, or coat or hat,
  The Sheriff was close and he got that.

He never heard from the folks back home;
  He said they knew why he had to roam,
And if they wanted to contact him
  They would find his name was new to
them.

He came to Texas and he came to stay.
  He fought the Indians and drove 'em
away,
He founded a state and gave it birth
  While chasing buffalo right off the earth.

He couldn't read and he couldn't write,
  But he could cuss and he could fight.
He could ride any old horse alive
  While fanning the hammer of a Forty-
Five!

As I recall the things he did,
  I think it's well that he fled and hid
And I trust in the great long run
  They'll find his traits in his own grand-
son.

But I would like right well to know
  Just why he busted the Ohio;
And what lay back of the words he'd say,
  "I came to Texas and I came to stay."

8

Pioneer Families

THE D.A.R. MARKER at the grave of Collin County's only Revolutionary War veteran located in the Belew Cemetery one mile north of Lavon. He was one of the twelve Revolutionary War veterans buried in Texas.

JOHN ABSTON

John Abston is Collin County's only veteran of the American Revolution. He is buried in the Belew Cemetery one mile north of Lavon.

He was born in Scotland in 1756 and died at his home near Old Millwood in 1856. He had one son, John Abston, who died at Independence, Missouri, and another son, Jesse H., who came to Texas from Missouri before 1850, settling near Melissa. It was here that Jesse H. died and was buried in 1850. Jesse's wife, Sarah E., and father, John Abston, later moved on, settling near Millwood. She was born in 1797 and died in 1879. All this family are buried here except Jesse.

The children of Jesse H. and Sarah Abston are as follows:

Sarah F. was born August 6, 1830, and died Feb. 2, 1879. She married Daniel W. Stimson.

Lucy F. was born June 3, 1839, and died November, 1908. She married Gabriel Fitzhugh who headrighted land near Lucas, Texas.

Mary C. was born Feb., 1842 and died July 25, 1876. She married Miles L. Williams.

Jeriah J. was born 1846 and died in 1870. She was the wife of Ruben A. Williams.

John Abston lived his remaining years with his daughter-in-law, Sarah E. Abston. Dr. R.A. Taylor of Millwood was his physician during his last days and at the time of his death.

He is one of twelve American Revolutionary War soldiers buried on Texas soil. The Richard Royal Chapter of the D.A.R. erected a granite marker at his grave.

Submitted by Paul Russell, Box 1524, Grand Prairie, Texas 75050.

THE ADDINGTON FAMILY

The Addington family originally came from England, the surname being of Anglo-Saxon origin. John Wesley Addington came to Collin County in 1877 from Water Valley, Mississippi. He was the son of Jesse and Elvira Addington, a farmer and rancher as well as a bricklayer. John first lived at Parker in Collin County, but in 1879 he purchased 306 acres where Clear Lake now is located. Later he moved near McKinney. After the death of his wife Martha Jane Price Addington, J.W. Addington married Mrs. Fannie Martin.

Nine children were born to J.W. and Martha J. Price Addington. The eldest was Carrie Eugene (1864-1954) who married George Lee Townsend. Of this marriage, six children were born, William, Eddie Lee, Edna Nora, Lillie Dovie, Horace H., and Eula.

The second child was Pearl (1871-1960) who married Clarence Shuman and became the parents of five children, Laurence, Earnest Clarence, Ora, Annie, and Martin Vincent.

The third child, Rasha Robinson Addington (1873-1963), married Callie Russell and they were the parents of 9 children: Jessie, Alice A., Paul, Mary Chrystal, Hazel, Jewel Edna, Russell Robinson, Morris Sheppard and Lometa Myrtle.

The fourth child was Walter Price Addington who married Sallie Ellen Davis, daughter of Thomas Jefferson Davis and Caroline W.J.P. Rice. Walter P. and his wife donated land for a Methodist Church at Clear Lake now disbanded. They were the parents of 11 children, 2 dying in infancy. First was Claud then Faye who married first Herschell Snider. Of this marriage two children were born. Her second marriage was to Bert R. Hodges and of this marriage three children were born, Don, Betty, and Jimmy. The third of the 11 children of Walter P. was Grace who married Hubert O. Poor and they are the parents of four daughters. Fourth was Ollie who married Emma Marie Locke and to them was born one son, Ralph Wendell. The fifth child was Opal who first married Lester C. Malone and later to James A. Long. She now lives in McKinney. The sixth child was Elsie Mae first married to James

MARTHA JANE (PRICE) Addington. 1849-1900.

J.W. ADDINGTON'S CHILDREN about 1891 or 1892. From left to right: Buddie, Walter, Pearl, Johnnie, Carrie, Willie, Cora and Jewell.

"AUNT" DELIA WILSON, sister of John Wesley Addington (1844-1936).

JOHN WESLEY ADDINGTON'S children at a family reunion. Top, left to right: Buddie, Walter, Johnnie. Bottom, left to right: Carrie, Pearl, Cora, Jewell.

JOHN CLARK & MATTIE ADDINGTON, son J.C. and daughter Lexie Addington.

R.R. (BUDDY) & Callie Addington with children Jesse & Alice about 1900.

MAYNARD FAMILY ABOUT 1904. L-R, Ogle, Dr. Maynard, Cora and Eva.

WILLIE D. & ZELLA M. Addington about 1913.

1948, TENNYSON PARK, Dallas-Addington Reunion.

1948, TENNYSON PARK. Brothers and sisters (children of John W. Addington). Left to right: Walter, Johnny, Willie, and R.R. (Buddy) Addington. Bottom row left to right: Cora Maynard, Carrie Townsend, Pearl Shuman.

ADDINGTON FAMILY REUNION at Finch Park in 1945.

JOHN WESLEY ADDINGTON

Newt Orr, then to Glenn C. Hall and thirdly to Harold O. Heiner. The seventh child died as an infant. The eighth child was Della Kelly who married George Garcourt Bull who was born in London, England. They have two children, Mrs. Brian N. McCarthy and George Harcourt Bull of California. The ninth child was Elmo Dudley, the tenth child was Vince Raford who married Virginia Janell Leake and had one daughter. The eleventh child was Oleta Jane who married Edward W. Arnsen and they are the parents of three daughters.

The fifth child of J.W. and Martha Addington was an infant who died. The sixth child was John Clark Addington who married Mattie Lafon and to them were born three children, Nettie May, Texie Irene and J.C.

The seventh child was Cora Mary who married Dr. George Pembert Maynard of Wylie and to them were born 4 children, Ogle L., Eva Adaline, Ruth Jane, and Esther Gladys.

The 8th child was Willie D. Addington who married Zilla May Marriot and to them was born 5 children, Agnes Pearl, Raymond Lee, Infant son, Lloyd Ernest, and an infant who died. Willie D. married a second time, this time to Jessie Ross Gault and they had five children, Mary Catherine, Willie Ross, Geneva Ruth, Doris Nell, and Zeta Ann.

The 9th child was Annie Adela who died young.

The 10th child was Jewel Bessie who married Oliver Roscoe Cosby and to them were born 5 children, Dorothy Nemo, Orpah Marjorie, Roscor Addington, Earl Bell, and James William.

J.W. and Martha Addington have hundreds of descendents, many still living in Collin County.

Story written by George Harcourt Bull
San Clemente, California

AKERS FAMILY
As reported by Mr. and Mrs. Johnny Akers

Abraham Akers and his family moved to Lucas from Dallas County in 1900. He ran a cotton gin in the early years. He and his wife, Janette, were the parents of six children: Isabel, Pearl, Clifton, Evy,

George and Johnny. Of the group only George, who married Pearl McCormac of St. Paul area of Collin Co. and Johnny, who married Sadie Spears, stayed in Lucas. George died here in 1924. Johnny and his wife now live in the Akers homeplace.

ARMSTRONG
Written By Mrs. John Shipp
Our thanks to Naomi Snider of McKinney
for names and dates of the children.

Dr. Stokley T. Armstrong, a veterinarian, was born in 1873 and died in 1951. He married Miss Missouri Snider, born in 1873 and died in 1963. They were the parents of two daughters: Ruth, born in 1904, died in 1932; Ruby, born in 1908 and died in 1931 and a son, Don, born in 1903 and died in 1927. Dr. and Mrs. Armstrong lived in their home in the heart of Lucas until their deaths. The farm and home was sold. He was a merchant and postmaster for a time in the early days of Lucas. He was also a brother of the aforementioned Dr. John Armstrong.

LUCAS "STOREKEEPERS"

Others who operated the store or stores down through the years were: A Mr. Lee, J.E. Stratton, Ed Knight, Dr. Abbott, and his son, Charley of McKinney, Johnny Snider, and Otis Morrow ran the store for a time, as did two brothers, J.B. and Pat Murphy. Also Tom Spurgin and Leonard Cole, then Buddy Wilmouth, Bob Coffey and Roy (Shortie) Biggs. In this year of 1973 Lucas again has two grocery stores, Strains and The Lucas Food Mart, owned and operated by Mr. and Mrs. W.T. Parchman. Nathan Strain also has a thriving worm and fish bait business. Lucas has a farm and ranch store, Mr. John Moore owner. Mrs. Eddie Payne has a beauty shop and Mrs. Phillip Kapp has a day camp for children.

THE ANDERSON FAMILY

Miss Fletcher Anderson, prominent business woman of McKinney, is the daughter of Mr. and Mrs. Will Anderson who came to Collin County in 1890 and settled first in the Sister Grove Community in northeast Collin County. There were seven children born of this union and only three survive: Cecil Anderson of Dallas, W.F. (Andy) Anderson of McKinney, and Miss Fletcher Anderson, also of

MISS FLETCHER ANDERSON, prominent business-woman and civic leader of McKinney.

McKinney.

Miss Anderson is an example of a woman's becoming a success in business and has achieved success in her professional life as well as a humanitarian. She was born in the Sister Grove Community in 1902. Her father was a farmer and her mother, Ida Leah Gay Anderson, was left a widow early in life, so much responsibility fell to her children, no doubt shaping the tone of later life. The mother died in June of 1963 at the age of 89 years.

The family moved to McKinney from Blue Ridge in 1912 and Fletcher attended what is now South Ward School, later Central Ward School. She graduated from Boyd High School in 1922, took an examination for a teacher's certificate and passed. In 1923 she attended Mary-Hardin Baylor College in Belton, Texas. In 1924 she taught school at Big Viney Grove School and the next year taught at Culleoka. Between terms she worked at J.C. Penney Company in McKinney and became a full time worker there until 1937.

1937 was the year she began her association with the McKinney Dry Goods Company where she worked as a saleslady and assistant buyer. In 1942 she became the manager of the company; continuing her rise in the old established business, she became a substantial stockholder in 1955 and increased her holdings until she became half owner of the McKinney Dry Goods Company. She also has an interest in the Annex, another Department Store.

By faith, Miss Anderson is a Baptist and is an active member of the First Baptist Church in

McKinney, serving in every capacity of church life. She has been president of the Women's Bible Class, chairman of the Hudson Circle, served on the Board of Trustees, and served on the 21 member Building Steering Committee of the Church, as well as working on a district and state level.

She has served as president of the Tyrolese Literary Club, and of the Gas Lighters Book Review Club, was appointed to the Alumni Advisory Board of Mary-Hardin Baylor College, and a member of the Collin Memorial Hospital Auxiliary. She has been active for years in the McKinney Chamber of Commerce, and served on the Board of Directors for four years. Miss Anderson is a member of the Citizens Advisory Committee. She recently sold the McKinney Dry Goods Company store that she had operated successfully for 35 years, and is free to devote her energies to the civic, religious, and social activities in the county where she grew up and made so many friends.

MOSES ANDREWS FAMILY

A man who had a broad acquaintance and many friends around Wylie was Moses Andrews. He married Sarah Elizabeth Edens, daughter of E.E. Edens of Judsonia, Arkansas.

In 1885, Mr. Andrews and his family moved to Wylie along with two of Mrs. Andrews' sisters, Lelia and Susie, and three brothers, Bob, George, and Bill Edens. Mrs. Andrews' father also came with the move to Texas.

Mr. Andrews was born Dec. 8, 1843. He was a farmer owning a farm north of Wylie and was also active in real estate around Wylie.

Mr. and Mrs. Andrews reared two children.

Ben, the first, was married to Ella Holland of Judsonia, Arkansas. He came to Texas with his parents and after completing his education, taught school at the Cotton Belt School for several years before returning to Judsonia. He and his family later moved to Little Rock, Ark. Ben and Ella reared three children: Charley, John, and Frances. They were Baptist people.

The second was a daughter, Della, who married Abner McDonald. He was born in 1870 at Wylie and died in 1943. She was born in 1877 and died in 1966. Mr. McDonald farmed and also engaged in real estate at Wylie. Their children were Weldon, Velma who married Johnny Talley, and Vera who married Raymond Posey.

In addition to their own family, Mr. and Mrs.

THE MOSES ANDREWS family of Wylier, Texas.

Andrews also reared two other children. Mrs. Andrews' sister, Lelia, was taken into the family after Mother Edens passed away in 1875. Lelia was born in 1873 and married Jim Russell, a native of Wylie.

The other was Mrs. Andrews' nephew, Jack Saltzman. He came to the family after the death of his mother, Susie, in Denton County when Jack was but an infant.

Mr. Andrews was a lively and restless business man, prompt in keeping his promises and engagements. His purse, his heart and hand were always open to his friend and to those in trouble. Owing to his failing health, he left the farm in later years and bought a home in Wylie. After a long illness, he passed away on July 11, 1918. He was a lifelong Baptist.

Mrs. Andrews was born in 1851 and was reared by a Baptist family with ten children. She passed away on April 1, 1939, on the same day her sister Lelia Russell died. A double funeral was conducted at the Methodist Church.

Submitted by Paul Russell, grand-nephew of Mrs. Andrews.

WILLIAM CORNELIUS ANDREWS

William was born September 2, 1819 in Tennessee and married in Fayetteville, Tenn. on September 16, 1841. His wife was Martha Ann Darnell, a 15 year old orphan. Both her father and grandfather served in the Revolutionary War, her family dating back to 1688 in America. She was born in Lincoln County, Tennessee June 26, 1825. She became the mother of 14 children, eight sons and four daughters reaching adulthood.

After serving in the Confederate Army, William found life changed in Petersburg, Tennessee. In

THE FIVE ELDEST children of W.C. Andrews, Jr.: Thomas Clayburn (Clabe), Mary E. Andrews Marks, John Cornelious (Neal), Martha Ann Andrews Scott, and Sarah Leona Andrews Smith.

1860 he had listed his pre-war assets as $20,940, and after the war they had shrunk in value to $5,400. Hoping to find a better future for his family they came by wagons to Collin County. It was a very large group that came since the older children now had families of their own. The family prospered in McKinney and they were well established by the time of William's death in 1892. His wife died in 1897. Both are buried in the Horn Cemetery.

William and Mary Ann have hundreds of descendents in Collin County.

WILLIAM CORNELIUS ANDREWS JR.

This early day citizen of McKinney was born August 23, 1842 in Marshall County, Tennessee. He was a Confederate soldier and at the time his first child was born (Mattie Andrews who later married Frank Scott of McKinney) he was away at war. His wife marked around the baby's hand and baked a cookie to send him. He became so homesick that he ran away and came home to see his wife and baby. When he returned to the army his punishment was to hang by his thumbs for a period of time. The story often told is that he was born double jointed and could slip his thumbs loose whenever the guard was not looking.

By the time he moved to Collin County (1877) he had lost his wife and had five children to rear. Two years later he married Tobiathia Scott and nine children were born to them. In 1899 he moved to the Indian Territory with his five younger children, camping out along the way. His fifteenth child was born in a half dug-out near Norman. He was the first Justice of the Peace after Statehood in 1907, served as Supt. of School, and preached.

His five oldest children stayed in McKinney and their descendents are in the seventh generation of the Andrews family of McKinney. Their children are: Judge T.C. (Clabe) Andrews, Mary E. (m. J.A. Marks), John C. (Neal), Martha A. (Mattie) married Frank Scott, and Sarah Leona (Lonie) married J.P. Smith.

Story sent by Kay Steenerson, 3000 NW 11, Oklahoma City 73107.

JOSEPH WILSON BAINES
Grandfather of Lyndon Baines Johnson

Joseph W. Baines was born in Louisiana in 1844. He served in the Confederate Army, taught school, studied law, and in 1867 came to live in McKinney. He set up a small law office upstairs over the Foote Drug Store on the northwest corner of the square. On September 12, 1869 he married Ruth A. Huffman, a descendent of a pioneer family in Collin County. He went into real estate, selling lots in the city of McKinney. In late 1873 the block east of the Trinity Presbyterian Church on Davis Street was placed in his hands to sell. He bought the entire block for $600 and in a few months sold all of its except lots 177 and 178 on which there was a small frame house built by Colonel Ingram. This became his home from 1869 to 1883 when he left McKinney.

In 1876 Thomas E. Bomar came from Sherman and established a weekly newspaper on South Tennessee Street. He called it the McKinney Advocate and it was a good paper. Clint Thompson, later owner of the Examiner, worked there as did several other men later to be associated with Collin County newspapers. In early 1878 Baines bought in with Bomar as part owner of the newspaper and a year later purchased his partner's share, thus becoming the sole owner. Baines moved his paper office in 1880 to the north side of the square over the present North Side Drug Store. Baines ran a good newspaper. No copy of the newspaper has been located but quotes from the paper by other sources seems to show that he was outspoken about local problems and affairs. In 1881 Baines again moved the Advocate. He took over the vacant upper floor over the present Woolworth Store on the west side of the square. In 1882 Bomar consolidated the McKinney Citizen with Baines' Advocate and the name was changed to The Black Waxey, and soon became one of the leading weekly newspapers in North Texas. Baines' editorials were copied all over the state. The Black Waxey prospered but Baines did not confine his activity solely to the paper. He again took up real estate, buying and selling property long after he left here in 1883. He believed in the future of the town and constantly said so in his editorials.

Joseph Baines' father, Robert, was a personal friend of Sam Houston and was aided by Houston in getting his appointment as President of Baylor University at the start of the Civil War. John Ireland, elected Governor of Texas in the fall of 1882 was an admirer of Robert Baines and knew young Baines also. Before Christmas he wrote Baines that he was going to appoint him Texas Secretary of State, providing Baines would accept. Baines accepted and on January 18, 1883, he was appointed. He sold The Black Waxey to Tom Ed Bomar on January 3, 1883 and moved his family to Austin and only came to McKinney now and then to attend a funeral of old friends. Baines served during Gov. Ireland's term of office then moved to Blanco where he practiced law until 1903 when he moved to Fredericksburg. He

died there on November 18, 1906, leaving three children, one of whom was Rebekah who married Samuel E. Johnson and became the mother of Lyndon Baines Johnson, later to be President of the United States.

Weekly Democrat, Aug. 14, 1900
Weekly Democrat, Nov. 22, 1900
Jerome Sneed Jr. A grandson.
Story by Roy F. Hall, McKinney Examiner, Dec. 19, 1963.
Sources: Collin County Clerk's files, Box 24, Marriage records.

BARNES—GRAVES—FOX

Sally Barnes, born August 20, 1839 in Boonville, Missouri, and the grandmother of Mrs. Richard (Vivian Hill) Bass came to Texas in 1852 with her parents, Thomas and Susan Ann Field Barnes. On January 1, 1856 she married Samuel H. Fox (born in 1836 in Missouri). They lived for several years on their farm nine miles west of McKinney, later moving to McKinney. Samuel H. Fox died April 24, 1921 and Sally Barnes died June 6, 1925 at age 85. They are both buried in Pecan Grove Cemetery in McKinney, Texas. They were the parents of 14 children:

Cora Isabelle (December 1, 1856—December 8, 1858).

Charles T. (Tobe) March 6, 1858—December 2, 1937).

Frances (Fanny) Fox September 9, 1860—November 8, 1927. She married Wicliffe Graves who was born December 6, 1848 in Johnson County, Missouri. They had six children, Bertie, Iva, Charles, Wicliffe, Jesse G., Lucretiou Harrison, and Roy Leighton. Charles Wycliffe Graves married Helen Horn, daughter of the Rev. R.C. Horn, pioneer preacher of Collin County. Helen Horn Graves lives on Grave Street in McKinney and has two children, Rebecca Graves (married Francis Taylor) and Charles Wicliffe Graves Jr. who married Frances Taylor and they are the parents of three children, James, Robert, and Helene.

Jesse G. Graves married Mary Ann Duffey September 29, 1909 and settled on his land near Allen, Texas. They had three children, James (1912), Madelina (1914) who married Loren Wilder, and Mary Ann (1921) who married Quinn L. Allen, and live in Dallas and are parents of one son, John Quinn Allen.

Lucretius ''Creash'' Graves (December 22,

1891) married Evelyn Waters and were the parents of two children, Pearl Waters Graves who married Porter Cochran and L.H. Graves Jr. who married Catherine Lee Conroy and had two children, Phyllis Evelyn and Timothy Harrison Graves.

Roy Leighton Graves (September 2, 1894) married Gladys Johnson of McKinney and had three children, Amelia, Gladys Leighton, and Roy Jr.

Mary "Mollie" Fox (September 10, 1862) married Joseph Mahlon Ware on September 22, 1881. They made their home on Tucker Street. Both are buried in Pecan Grove Cemetery. They had four children. Samuel Ernest Ware (July 17, 1882—July 18, 1884), Lura Ware (February 10, 1884) married Albert Brandon Mayhew (1879-1947). They had one child, Martha Brandon. William Franklin Ware (December 22, 1885) was for many years an employee of the City of McKinney. Earl Fox Ware (May 25, 1889) married Josephine Burger.

George Fox died in infancy.

George Fox (March 31, 1867 in Collin County) married Lula Lilliard (1870-1919). They made their home on North College Street in McKinney, and they were the parents of three children, Louise, Grace, and Maude. After the death of his first wife he married Mrs. Annie Taylor. George W. Fox died October 26, 1924. Grace Fox married Edgar McKinney and lived on College Street in McKinney. They had two sons, George Fox and John Edgar. George Fox McKinney married Norma Turner of Dallas and has one daughter, Shonnye. John Edgar McKinney married Martha Nell Baker of Dallas and they have two children, Rebecca and John Edgar Jr. Maude Fox married Titus J. Furr and has two children, Titus James, Jr., and Sarah Jane.

Lura Fox (May 21, 1869-September 19, 1869).

Lillian Fox, born in Collin County, October 19, 1871, married William R. Hill on November 4, 1891, who was born in Collin in January 31, 1868. They made their home in McKinney and Dallas. They were the parents of Vivian Hill who married Richard D. Bass.

Story by Mrs. Richard Bass, McKinney.

THE THOMAS BARNES FAMILY

Thomas Barnes, son of Shadrack Barnes, was born in Madison County, Kentucky in 1804. He married Susan Ann Field of Albemarle County, Virginia and first settled in Cooper County, Missouri. In 1852 he moved to Collin County and homesteaded 640 acres of land near the present town of Prosper. He died in 1866. His wife died in McKinney in 1906 at age 91 years. They had ten children: William G., 1835; Phillip, 1836; Henry C., 1837-1925; Sally, 1839; Mary, 1842; Thomas, 1843; John G.M., 1847; Medora, 1849; Robert, 1854; and Jesse, 1858; the last two born in Texas.

William G. Barnes married Ann Crim (1839, Kentucky) and to this union were born three children, William G., Sue Barnes (married Hormy Dawson), and Clifford Barnes.

Phillip Barnes served in Company I, 9th Texas Infantry during the Civil War, having enlisted in McKinney.

Henry C. Barnes married Frances Jane Field, October 13, 1847, in Missouri and died July 6, 1925 in Collin County. They were the parents of 12 children. Nanie (October 20, 1965) married Robert C. Kimbrough of Tennessee in McKinney May 6, 1890. They were the parents of two children, Robert Cook Kimbrough Jr. and Mary. Mary Kimbrough has always been active in all cultural pursuits of McKinney and Denton where she lived. Robert Jr. married Leona Morris of Denton and lives in Ennis, Texas.

Robert C. Kimbrough III married Edna Gibson of Denton and now lives in Ft. Worth. Virginia Kimbrough, daughter of Robert Jr. married Thomas H. Briscoe of Krum, Texas and lives in Denton.

Edward Barnes, second child of Henry C. and Frances Kimbrough was Edward, born November 17, 1867 and died in Sulphur, Oklahoma in 1950. Joseph Wood Barnes (January 26, 1870) married Florence Largent at McKinney in 1897. He died August 5, 1924. They had two children, Joseph Wood Barnes Jr. and Rosabel Barnes.

The fourth child, Nola Barnes, was born January 16, 1872 and married John R. Chitwood at Ardmore, Oklahoma. They had one child, Ethel, who married Claude Benton and they have one child, Douglas. Douglas married Evelyn Febring and they have two children.

James Barnes (February 25, 1875) married Lucille Ferguson of Sulphur. They have three children, Houston (1911), Rosa Jean (1925), and Herbert (1928).

The sixth child, Josie Barnes (September 2, 1877) married Montague Kingston Brown of London, England.

The seventh child, Lillie Pearl Barnes, (July 10, 1880) married Paul B. Jones and lives in Ardmore, Oklahoma.

The eighth child, Margaret Barnes, married

George Hurt and lived in Ardmore, Oklahoma.

The ninth, Rosa Barnes, (December 1, 1884) married Gene Hurt.

The tenth child, Claudine Barnes, lives in Ardmore, Oklahoma.

The eleventh child, Jeanette Barnes, (March 2, 1889) married Walter Strong.

The twelfth child, Thomas J. Barnes, (May 4, 1892) never married.

THE JONAS DAYTON BASS FAMILY

The Phillips family came from Wales, a rugged province of the British Isles, to America in 1755. Joseph Phillips first settled in the vicinity of West Chester, Penn. near Philadelphia. His Malissa Phillips married Robert C. Bass August 23, 1848 and they migrated to Texas, partly by rail and the last lap of the journey in a covered wagon. Malissa died in 1913.

Jonas Bass was one of Robert and Malissa's sons and in 1881 he was married to Lou Carr. He was a successful farmer in early Collin County then was a cotton merchant in McKinney until his death in 1934. He served as Alderman of the City of McKinney for 12 years, and was a director of the Electric Railways. They lived at 806 Tucker until their death. He was born February 15, 1859 and died October 17, 1934. Malissa was born December 27, 1861 and died in January of 1945.

Mary, their daughter, was born January 11, 1884 and died in July of 1968. December 11, 1907 she was married to Ula A. Saunders. He was born Sept. 12, 1883 and died in 1967. They had one daughter, Virginia Lou, who married Therman Henderson. She was born December 3, 1908 and died in November of 1958. They had three children, Mary Lou, Diana, and Tommy.

The second of Malissa and Jonas Bass' children was Richard Dayton Bass, born February 29, 1892 and died April 7, 1952. On March 28, 1913 he was married to Vivian Hill (born August 2, 1894). To this union, three children were born, William Dayton Bass, Richard Carr Bass, and Vivian Hill (Poppy) Bass. William Dayton was born October 10, 1914 and was a cotton merchant in McKinney. He married Fay Powell of Lone Oak in 1938. Their son, Richard Hill Bass, was born January 3, 1949 and is a graduate of Austin College, a coach and a teacher.

Dr. Richard Carr Bass was born April 25, 1917 and was married to Elizabeth Rhea Vaughan of Russellville, Alabama in 1947. He is a graduate of Texas Christian University and has a medical degree from A&M. He was a veterinarian. He retired from the U.S. Air Corp as a Lt. Col. They have four children, Patricia Ellen, born March 27, 1951, Penelope Ann, born July 31, 1952, Richard Jr., born August 30, 1956, and Betsy, born January 16, 1958.

Vivian Hill (Poppy) was born November 27, 1919. She is a graduate of TCU and married Dr. Charles McKissick in 1939. He too is a graduate of TCU, an optometrist and served as a lieutenant in World War II. They are the parents of four children, Poppy, Charles Bass, Lillian, and Louise. Poppy was born September 16, 1943 and married Jim Airhart of Anna. They have four children.

Charles Bass McKissick was born August 1, 1945 and after graduating from TCU he became a coach and teacher. In November of 1969 he married Judy Wallace. The third child of Vivian Hill and Charles McKissick was born October 21, 1951 and was named Lillian. The fourth child is Louise who was born December 20, 1956.

Each member of this family has always played an important role in the community life and worked for its betterment.

Sent by Mrs. Richard Bass, McKinney.

ELIJAH BAXTER
1840-1900

Elijah "Lige" Baxter was born June 10, 1840, in Cocke County, Tennessee, the youngest son of Aaron Baxter and Leaner Brown. He came to Collin County in 1869 or 1870 after inheriting his share of his father's estate at the top of English Mountain. Elijah died September 24, 1900 at his home on the farm he bought in the Franklin Community soon after coming to Collin County, and is buried in Scott Cemetery.

"Lige" had been captured at Vicksburg, Mississippi during the Civil War but was released in about a week and returned to Cooke County where he married Aron Bryant's daughter, Margaret. "Lige" and Margaret had three children born to them before they came to Texas: George Washington, who married Rebecca F. Mayes on August 25, 1890, she being a half-sister of John William Dowdy; James Lafayette; and Anna Belle Baxter. These children grew up and married in Collin County but took their families to Oklahoma while still young and lived the remainder of their lives in Oklahoma.

148

He probably came to Texas after hearing many stories of Texas while he was at Vicksburg and he also had brothers-in-law here before him. They were James Polk Duncan; Felix Grundy Lewis; and James "Jim" Stuart. These fellows had all married daughters of Aron Bryant. "Lige" Baxter and Aron Bryant came to Texas together.

Aron Bryant's wife was Elizabeth Mantooth and their children were Emiline, who married Jim Stuart and after his death a Benjamin Johnson who was preacher; Jane who married Samuel Baxter—Lige's brother—and stayed in Cocke County, Tennessee; Lavinia, who married Grundy Lewis; Margaret, who married Lige; Elizabeth who married Jim Duncan; James; Lucinda, who married Houston Weaver; William; Harriett, who died of pneumonia when about eighteen; and Aaron. Aron Bryant settled on Gray Branch Road in the Foote Community where some of his descendents still live. A good number of his descendents still live in Collin County.

Elijah first leased land in the Walnut Grove Community and it was here his fourth child, William Jasper, was added to the family—March 27, 1871. Elijah had the misfortune of losing his wife in August, 1872. She is buried in the Scott Cemetery near her parents and younger sister. Elijah then bought a farm and settled in the Franklin Community.

In a couple of years Elijah found himself another very fine and dedicated wife in Eliza Jane Hunter, the daughter of John and Comina Hunter who had moved to Collin County from Tennessee in the 1850's. They were neighbors of "Lige" in the Franklin Community. Eliza Jane had a brother, B.L. "Lef" Hunter who was a prominent Presbyterian preacher, once pastor of the Walnut Grove Church and married many of the pioneer couples of west Collin County.

Elijah and Eliza Jane were the parents of Samuel Houston, who married Dora Belle Profitt; Margaret Jane, who married Robert Cowan; Comina L. who married Sam Stephens, a prominent Collin County educator; Charles L. who married Sarah Cowan, sister to Robert; Ida married Austin Hicks and after his death married Will Costello; Elbert Elijah who married Rhetta Lou Scott; Amanda Lou who married William J. Gilbert; Mary Elizabeth who married William Alonzo Stine; Leota who married Vardry P. Hill and later Roy Priest; Irma who married Ben B. Cooper. Elijah died September 24, 1900 and Eliza Jane on November 26, 1920 and they are buried in the Scott Cemetery southwest of Bloomdale with several of their children and grandchildren. Elijah's life of sixty years was a full one. His father died when he was just a few months old. He lived in Tennessee thirty years, then moved to Collin County where he lived for thirty full years. He was proud of his farm in the Franklin Community, but his fortune was his children—fourteen—all living to be men and women of their own.

Elijah's son William Jasper "Billy" was the first child born to the family in Collin County. Billy's mother passed away when he was only a few months old and his grandmother Bryant took him for the tender years of his life and he always had a warm place in his heart for his grandmother and the old Bryant homeplace down on Gray Branch Road. When he became a man of his own he married Sarah Idella "Della," the youngest daughter of Robert H. Foster and Malinda Caroline Scott. Mr. Foster was a prominent farmer and land owner of the Bloomdale Community. Billy bought a farm from his father-in-law in the west part of Bloomdale Community on the east bank of Stover Creek. Here he and Della reared their ten children:

Robert Elijah, who married Joy E. Ramey and their children are William R. "Hun" and Frances Eugene. Caroline Ophelia "Carrie" who married Henry C. "H" Reeves and their daughter was Marcella M. William Cloyd who married Iva L. Carnell. James Floyd who married Rosalie Griffin and their children are: James Edwin, Meriem Louise, Sarah Alzada, William Andrew, Rebecca Marie, Lillian Elizabeth, Kenneth Lee, David Rhea, and Paul Whitfield. Eugene Edward who married Clyde Rickerson and their sons are Ewing Fitzhugh, Thomas Benjamin, and Eugene Edward. Houston Jasper who married Carrie Mae Nelson. Henry Osborn who married Vivian Francis Freeman and their children are Melba Joyce, June Marie, and Billie Henry. Lula Susan who married Willie Lawrence Jetton and their daughters are Doris Jane and Dorothy Sue. Leona Baxter. Harold Foster who married Vivian Gertrude Renfrow and their children are Wanella Kathryn, Lloyd Wayne, Clifford Weldon and Freida Carolyn.

Billy was born March 27, 1871 which was only about a year after his father arrived in Collin County. He lived to Feb. 10, 1927 and passed away at his home which had also been his birthplace. He was fond of his farm and livestock; but cherished his position as Elder of the Walnut Grove Church. The pride of his life was his children most of whom lived out their lives in Collin County.

Della was the daughter of Robert H. Foster and Malinda Caroline Scott. Malinda Caroline was the daughter of James Preston Scott and Jane C.

Caruth.

The tenth child of Elijah Baxter was Elbert E. who inherited his father's homeplace and lived out his life in the Franklin Community of Collin County. Elbert married Rhetta Lou "Lula" Scott and their children were:

Velma Louise who married Jack Cottle and had a son Jack Jr. Benjamin F. "Benny" who married Ruby Alys Duncan and their children are Frankie Alice, Rhetta Maye, James Andrew, Roy Elbert, and Mary Elizabeth. Wilma Gladys who married John Thomas Jones and their children are Thomas Wayne and Sue Evelyn. Ernest Elijah who married Grace Alline Swatsell. Joseph Lewis who married Beatrice Freeman and their children are Mary Francis, Shirley, and Lewis Ray. James William "J.W." who married Janelle Haggard. Charles Alonzo "Lonnie" who married Neva Jean Hope and their children are Charles Ronald, Donald Ray, Connie Hope, and Bonnie Jean. Tipton Leon "Leachie" who married Evelyn Bradley and their children are Patricia Ann, Tipton Ray, and Christi. Ola Mae who married Hulan Rutledge. Wood Ferguson who married Frances Maurice Vinson. Mary Lee who married Judge Murry Dean and their children are Judge Murry Jr., and Brenda Jo.

Elbert was by trade a farmer. He was also a good mechanic and once built a hay baler that served the family for twenty years. He taught his children to appreciate music and several of them are good musicians and singers. Elbert outlived all of his Baxter Kin when he lived to be eighty-nine years one month old.

Rhetta Lou "Lula" Scott Baxter, Elbert's wife was the daughter of Benjamin Franklin "Frank" Scott and Mattie Andrews of Collin County. Frank was the son of John Scott of Tennessee.

Story by Judge W.C. Dowdy, McKinney (District Judge for many years)

SAMUEL R. BERRY FAMILY

Samuel R. Berry and two of his brothers came to McKinney with their slaves immediately after the Civil War. They gave the slaves their freedom but one remained with the family until all of the children were grown. Sam was born August 28, 1830 and died December 20, 1904. His wife died in 1885. His two brothers never married. The original property owned by Sam Berry includes property now owned by the Pavillion Rest Home, The King's Barbecue and the old location of the power plant.

John W. Berry, sixth child of Sam and Mary Ellen, married Alta Elizabeth Bryan of Chambersville and to this union were born seven children: Marion Bryan Berry who married Mary Inez Ives and to whom were born three children, Sharon, Bryan Kent, and Allan John; Mary Ellen Berry Roberts who had four daughters; Virginia Ruth who married Harold Slaughter of Anna; J.W. Berry who was twice married but no children and is now deceased; Clarence Berry who married Mary Norma Nichols and had no children; Ruby Elsie Berry who married Clovis M. Swanner and to whom were born Clovis Malcolm Jr. who married Elizabeth Hutton of Tulsa, and became parents of three children, Mark Clovis, Michelle Faye, and David Andrew; Gladys Elizabeth Berry who married Charles Kazen and had three children, Gladys Elizabeth, Charles and Geralyn; Buena Vista who married Gerald Skrentner and are parents of Pamela, Robert, and Mary Margaret; and Joseph Ardell who married Bobbie Vaughan of Melissa and had a son, Jeffrey Allen.

CHAMBERS, MUSE, BERRY, BRYAN LINEAGE

Jacob Marion Francis Bryan was born in Lawrence County, Tennessee February 20, 1839, the son of John Bryan (North Carolina) and Millie Pullen Bryan (daughter of Moses Bryan of North Carolina). They were the parents of ten children, Jacob being the fourth child. When Jacob was 21 years of age he came with his family to Texas in 1859. When the Civil War came he enlisted in Company C of the 9th Texas Infantry. He was injured at Shiloh and taken prisoner. Later in the war he was exchanged and returned to his home, then enlisted in Bourland's regiment and did duty on the Texas frontier for the duration of the war.

When he came home he married Elizabeth Chambers in 1866. To them were born 10 children, John A., Lorena, Mary M. Hollie, William T., Charles M., Alta Elizabeth (who married John Berry). and Samuel H., and three unnamed infants died at birth. Besides farming his large acreage, he was a successful businessman in ginning, milling, and merchandising. His store was at a corner on the Chambersville Road.

Children born to Alta Elizabeth Bryan and John W. Berry are Marion Bryan Berry (Sept. 1903) who is married to Mary Inez Ives, an artist of great talent. She was born in Los Angeles, California in February of 1906. The second child was Mary Ellen who married Luther Roberts of Anna; J.W. Berry (born 1909; Clarence, born 1911, and married Mary Norma Nichols who was born in Melissa in June 1915; Ruby Elsie Berry, born December 14, 1913 and married Clovis Malcolm Swanner; Gladys Elizabeth, born 1915 and married Charles Kazen of Doredo; and Buena Vista, born September 1917 and married Gerald Skrentner of Detroit, Michigan.

ELISHA CHAMBERS FAMILY

Elisha Chambers came to Texas in 1847. He was born in North Carolina the son of Elijah and Rebecca Moore Chambers. He was the eighth of their nine children. Elisha's grandparents were James Chambers and Nancy Windsor who were married in England, then settled in Maryland, and reared their family there and in North Carolina. Elisha's great grandparents on his mother's side were Jerry O'Rielly and Margaret Ann Mannon who were married in County Cork, Ireland.

Elisha and Margaret Manning were married in July 1835. They were the parents of 13 children, of which Elijah was the third. The couple bought 320 acres on East Fork Creek near Chambersville. Elisha Chambers and Jacob Bryan gave to the people of Chambersville the school and the church properties. The Cemetery was donated by Elisha Chambers ''to surround the grave of their small baby forever and forever.''

The children of Elisha and Margaret Manning Chambers were William P., James H., Margaret M., Florence J., Elisha M., Robert M., Elizabeth, and Mary W. Elizabeth married Jacob Bryan. Three stories sent by Mrs. Bryan Berry:

CAPTAIN WILLIAM BEVERLY
1806-1882

In January, 1880, William Beverly wrote the following: ''My father John Beverly, was born in Virginia in 1743 and died August 23, 1829. He was a captain in the Revolutionary War . . . My son, John Beverly, was born in Roane County, Tennessee on July 6, 1829, and came to Texas with me.'' William Beverly was born in Virginia, November 28, 1806. His twin sister was named Nancy and married Joseph Klepper, who had a land grant from Peter's Colony. Sometime in 1837 William went to Illinois, and married Nancy DeLozier (b. March 10, 1806). They lived in Tennessee and came to Texas in 1846, receiving a land grant from Peter's Colony of 640 acres west of Plano.

William and Nancy Beverly had nine children,

seven boys and two girls. Five of their boys were killed in 1864 as they fought for the Confederacy in the Civil War. Namely: Tommy (their youngest son) b. April 27, 1845—d. January 23, 1864; Columbus b. August 14, 1836—d. May 14, 1864; Andrew b. March 1, 1840—d. May 20, 1864; Guilford, b. February 12, 1838—d. June 7, 1864; Allen b. March 9, 1842—d. (?). Sorrow and sadness reigned over the Beverly household and community each time a message arrived. Twice word came from returning soldiers who had known two of their sons on the battlefield. The Beverlys had two sons left, John, who became a Methodist minister, and James, who followed his father as a farmer. Each of them had a half section, a land grant from Peter's Colony.

There were two daughters, Mary who married Fountain Vance, and Pernina who married James Vance. Each Vance owned a half section east of the Beverlys. Thus, William Beverly had his sister, Nancy Klepper and his two daughters and a son James each owning one half sections of land near by. His minister son, John, lived about two miles north and within a mile or more of John Russell, his father-in-law. John had a land grant from Peter's Colony.

Captain William Beverly's wife, Nancy DeLozier died June 16, 1851, and was buried on a plot that would later, in November, become the Jacob Routh Cemetery. The grave of a child who belonged to a migrant family, was near by. This cemetery is east and on land adjoining Highway 75, about a mile or more south of Plano. His second wife was Rebecca Crownover, and to this union was born five children, Henry, Benjamin, Ann, Rachel and Lucinda.

Captain Beverly was a county commissioner from Plano precinct in 1852, '54 and '56. He also assisted in the development of the courthouse square.

On April 11, 1849, Reverend John Beverly married Isabel Wilburn Russell, daughter of Joseph and Elizabeth Russell. John was a circuit rider of the Methodist Conference and also served as minister in many North Texas churches in this area. Among them, First Church in Dallas, then located on Allen Street, and McKinney church in 1866-67. The Beverlys had twelve children. The oldest girl was Pernina Ann (b. July 22, 1852). The Plano Methodist Church was organized in 1847 in the Russell home and they met there for nine years, until the school house was built in 1856. This was used for all denominations to hold services at various times. Ann Beverly attended this school and later the Dallas Female College. When she returned home she was asked to be the teacher of Spring

MRS. JOHN BEVERLY and her two oldest children, Joseph and Ann.

Creek School. In 1871, June 29, Ann married Thomas Finley Hughston.

About 1885 word came to the community from John Beverly that a Methodist camp meeting would be held on White Rock Creek, 10 miles north of Dallas, on what is now Alpha road, and west of Hillcrest road. John Bryan gave the land and the community erected a large tabernacle. The Northwood Country Club is located on this land at present. Isabel Russell Beverly was always proud of the fact that she attended the camp meeting in the days when she went in a wagon pulled by oxen and lived to be driven in an automobile. It was a time when families and friends could be together for about a week or more. The Russells, Beverlys, and Browns had inter-married, and sometimes the Methodist relatives from Cottage Hill would be there. Some of the names of families were: Dennis, McCamy, Jackson, Julian, Winn, Smith, Bachman, Barlow, Coxe, Webb, Armstrong, Knight, Bowman, Hughes, Johnson, Cochran, Foard, Taylor and Wells. A detailed account is given by Miss Eva Hughston in the fall issue, 1972 Quarterly of Dallas Genealogical Society, as she began her camping experience in 1889 when she was about ten years old. Camp meeting days ended about 1930, when the pioneer spirit faded and the automobile came into general use—it was more convenient to come and return home for the night.

REFERENCES:

Peter's Colony of Texas, Seymour V. Conner
1850 Federal Census of Collin County, Texas—
Family No. 278, John Beverly
1880 Federal Census of Collin County, Texas.
Precinct 5, Dist. 24. Dwelling No. 186—Family No. 190, John Beverly
Beverly Family Bible Records, Birth Records, Death Records, in possession of Mrs. E.W. Hughston, McKinney
Beverly Family Tombstones, copied from Old City Cemetery, Plano, Texas
Jacob Routh Cemtery, Plano, copied from tombstone.
History of Texas Methodist, 1900-1960, edited by Olin W. Nail
Texas Methodist Centennial Year Book, 1834-1934
The Quarterly, September, 1972, page 143, local History and Genealogical Society.
The Quarterly, December, 1972, page 171, Local History & Genealogical Society.

BIGGS FAMILY
Written by Mrs. John Shipp
As reported by Roy Biggs of Plano.

Benjamin Franklin Biggs served in the Civil War. He married Aisle Jane Starr and he and his wife came to this area from east Texas in 1867. They were the parents of seven children, one of whom was James William Biggs who married Mary Appaloni Burch. To this union were born fourteen children, eleven of whom lived to be grown. One of their sons: Roy Biggs, was a merchant in Lucas for a number of years. (See Coffey History.) Other sons, Fred, farmed in this area for years and Gene Biggs, a landowner and farmer. Both now live in McKinney. Also F.W. Biggs, who married Alma Boyd of Allen, worked the Stratton farm here for years. A daughter, Helen Biggs, married J.T. Lewis of the Parker area.

THE GREEN BISHOP FAMILY

Green Rice Bishop was born February 11, 1866 in Spartanburg, South Carolina. Little is known of his family but he did have a young brother named Elijah and a sister named Betty. He came to Texas in 1884 at age 18 and settled just north of Renner in Collin County and worked for John Dickerson. On February 4, 1890 he married Annie E. Heustis of Lebanon. She was the daughter of Henry Heustis and Elizabeth Cook who had settled in Collin

County in 1858 with ancestors going back to Cumberland County, Pennsylvania in 1755.

Green and Annie Bishop farmed land that is now the site of Texas A&M University, east of Renner. They lived here until 1911 when they moved to the Crawford Lease farm, northwest of Plano. In 1915 they bought a large tract of land west of Marilee on the Collin-Grayson line. They lived at Dalhart for several years before returning to Frisco where Green Bishop died April 3, 1936. Annie died on August 8, 1937, and both are buried in Baccus Cemetery.

The couple had five children: Almedia Bishop married Grady Cothes of Plano and died August 13, 1939; Harry Bishop moved to Waka, Texas and died May 18, 1971; Oscar Bishop died in service, World War I; Fred Bishop moved to Ft. Worth and died February 1, 1960; and Andy Bishop lives in Pilot Point in Denton County.

Two of the Green Bishop grandchildren now live in Collin County, Mrs. J.B. Cannady of McKinney and Grady E. Cothes of Plano. Two great-grandchildren live in Collin County, Johnny Harrington of Frisco and Randy Cothes of Plano.

Sent by the Cothes family, Rt. 1, Plano.

SAMUEL BOGART

Samuel Bogart has been termed by historians as one of the great men in early Texas. He was born in Carter County, Tennessee April 2, 1797. He fought in the Battle of New Orleans in 1815. In 1818 he married and moved to Illinois and while living there he engaged in the Black Hawk War of 1832. The next year he moved to Missouri and helped to expel the Mormons from the state. In 1839 he came to Texas, settled in Washington County. While here he commanded a company of Rangers in the Mier Expedition in Old Mexico.

He came with his family to Collin County in 1845 and settled in what is now the Woodlawn Community. He was a driving force in developing this section. He served in the State Legislature from this county in 1847, 1849, 1851, and 1859. He held various positions of honor in the Democratic Party in Texas. He died March 11, 1861.

The Bogart home stood intact until the 1960s when it gradually fell apart. His home was a stopping place on the road to Jefferson in East Texas.

JOHN WESLEY BOILS

John Wesley Boils came to Texas in 1883 from Burksville, Kentucky in Cumberland County. He was born July 9, 1862 the son of Mary Daniels and Sevier (Bur) Boils in Albany, Kentucky in Clinton County. He was one of nine children. He came to Texas by himself but in later years brought two sisters Vian Boils and Anne Boils Pennycuff to Princeton, Texas to make their home.

John came to Bonham, Texas where he taught school in Bonham and the surrounding area. In nobility, he lived with Bent and Lula Webb.

In 1894 he came to Collin County. He married Lizzie Bell. John and Lizzie taught school in Allen, Culleoka, Back Bone, and Bonham. Bailey Jerome, their first child, was born June 23, 1898 in Allen and a daughter Orelean was born Oct. 1, 1899. She died in Princeton on August 12, 1900. In 1903 Lizzie Boils became ill. Knowing she would die, she wanted to be buried in Kentucky so John, Lizzie, and Bailey went back to Burksville and lived there until her death in 1904.

After her death he returned to Princeton with Vian Boils and Ann Boils Pennycuff and Anne's four children. Anne's husband Elam Pennycuff had died in Kentucky.

John returned to Burksville and married Mary Cash in Byrdstown, Tennessee on Sept. 6, 1904. Mary was the daughter of James Matthew and Jemima Cash. She was born Dec. 15, 1885 in Burksville, Ky.

They returned to Princeton to make their home. They had seven children. Bertha Alice, James Matthew, Bonnie (Stanfield), Grady Nathanul, infant died at birth, Leo and Emmett Leon (Twins).

After their first two children were born they returned to Burksville, while they were there their daughter Alice died on Aug. 6, 1911. They buried

OLD BOILS STORE, Princeton, Texas.

her on their farm. The farm was sold to Mary's brother and they returned to Princeton.

Members of the Boils family still living in Collin County include; Grady N. Boils, Bonnie Stanfield and daughter, Janice B., Leo Boils and his wife Peggy Penland Boils, and their children; Charles Leo, Mary Ann, Kimberly Jean, also Leon Boils and children; John Wesley, Betty Jane, and Jimmy D. and Bailey Jerome and Jean Boils.
Story sent by Bonnie Stanfield.

FAMILY HISTORY OF THE BOMARS

In the mid-1850's the family of David Elisha Bomar came to Texas to settle in that part of Collin County which became known as the Bomar's Chapel community . David and his wife, Melinda Wallace, had three sons: Newt (1842), Pete (1845), and Bill (1848), and one daughter, Sallie (1854). Born in Collin County were two more boys, Jim (1851) and George Franklin (1857). The journey from Bellbuckle, Tennessee to Collin County was made in an oxen wagon and lasted some 60 days. David homesteaded some 700 acres of land northeast of McKinney, paying 25 cents an acre for the land. He later gave each of his six children 100 acres of that same homestead. David Bomar built and operated the first cotton gin in Collin County. The gin was constructed around 1867 and was powered by oxen. David and his two oldest sons were participants in the American Civil War.

Jim Bomar, one of the two sons of David Bomar born in Texas, was born at Bomar's Chapel in 1851 and was reared on the Bomar farm some six miles

THE DAVE BOMARS

northeast of McKinney. He married Missouri Milligan and had two sons by her, Pascal H. and Willie D. Pascal married the former Cora Bales, and the couple had one child, Mack Bomar. Willie was married to the former Collie Neal, and three children were born into their family: Walter, Jimmy and Martha Ann.

George Franklin Bomar, the youngest of David Bomar's six children, married the former Minerva Jane Dunn and had four children by her: Wallace (1883), Lawrence (1885), Tom (1889), and Elmer (1892). G.F. and his wife lived their entire lives on their farm at Bomar's Chapel. George died at age 90, and three years later, in 1951, Minerva succumbed.

Wallace Bomar, grandson of David Elisha Bomar and the eldest of the four boys, was married to Leona Ashford in 1908 and had one child by her, Verta Lou. Wallace passed away, at age 49, in the McKinney Hospital in June of 1932. His wife and daughter live together today in Dallas.

PIONEER HOME of David Bomar, more than 100 years old when the photograph was taken in 1957. Beside it, the barn of the same age.

OLD HOME of Dave Bomar. The house is now gone.

Lawrence Bomar lived the duration of his life at Bomar's Chapel and died in McKinney on October 18, 1970.

Tom Bomar, as did his three brothers, lived as a youth on the farm. He was married to Virgie Neal in 1914. Tom was employed at a McKinney department store and later his business moved him to Port Lavaca on the Texas coast. Tom and his wife had two children, Pat and Thomas D. Tom passed away in Port Lavaca in May of 1968. His wife and son, Thomas D., were survivors.

The youngest of George Franklin's four sons, Elmer, was born at Bomar's Chapel on May 9, 1892. Elmer married the former Daisy Henry on October 19, 1912, and the couple lived and farmed on their homeplace northeast of town. Three sons were born into the family: Winston, Avery, and Forrest. Elmer today resides on his farm northeast of McKinney; his wife Daisy passed away on September 21, 1969.

The three sons of Elmer Bomar—Winston, Avery, and Forrest—all attended school as boys at Viney Grove near their farm home. Winston married and had one daughter, Billie June, by his first wife, Wanda Myrick. Winston was married again in 1940 to Marie Streigel, and the two live today in Dallas. Winston is an employee for The Dallas Morning News. Billie June married Choyce Watkins in 1962, and the couple, with their two daughters, Renee and Cynthia, live in Dodd City, Texas.

Avery D. Bomar was born in Melissa on May 4, 1918. He served in the U.S. Army during World War II and married Hilda Marie Cox on September 7, 1944 in North Carolina. Avery had one son by his wife while living in Portsmouth, Virginia. The couple, with their son, Forrest D., moved to Texas by train in 1948 and lived in McKinney. A second son, George Wayne, was born into the family on October 3, 1950. Avery worked at the Veteran's Hospital in McKinney for 18 years. A third son, Byron Lee, was added to the family on September 6, 1961. Today Avery is employed by the U.S. Treasury Department in Dallas.

Forrest Dowell and George Wayne Bomar attended school in McKinney, graduating in 1965 and 1969, respectively. Forrest, a 1970 physical education graduate from North Texas State University, teaches school today in Dallas. George, a 1973 graduate in meteorology from Texas A&M University, married the former Judy Lynn O'Dell of McKinney on August 16, 1971. He and his wife live today in Bryan; George is a graduate student at Texas A&M. Byron lives with his parents and at-

tends school in McKinney.

Forrest Rodgers Bomar, the youngest of Elmer's three sons, was reared on the Bomar farm and graduated from McKinney High School in 1946, later attending Southern Methodist University. In 1954 he married the former Thelma Main and had two daughters by her, Susan Charlene, born on September 17, 1954, and Julia Anna, born on August 25, 1958. Forrest, a Korean War veteran, and his family live today in Denver, Colorado, with Forrest being employed at American Telephone and Telegraph. Susan is a student at Colorado State University in Fort Collins; Julia is a high school student in Denver.

RALPH C. BOYER

Ralph C. Boyer, banker of Prosper, is descended of pioneers reaching back to the early 1700s when the family fled England because of the persecution the French Huguenots were undergoing in all England at that time. After reaching America, they ran into more trouble. In migrating from eastern Pennsylvania westward, one ancestor was killed by hostile Indians and his children were taken captive. One daughter became the wife of a Chief in Ontario, Canada during the French and Indian War. The first of the family to come was Andrea Beyer and his family. (The spelling of the name changed to Boyer later.) Their names appear in the Pennsylvania Archives and on the ship's register. He prospered in the new land and at his death left each of his six children 80 acres of rich land that he had cleared of the forests it once was.

Ralph C. Boyer was born in Shelby County, Ohio February 27, 1921, the son of Clyde L. Boyer and the grandson of John A. Boyer. George W. Boyer was his great-grandfather and a veteran of the Civil War. He enlisted with the Ohio Volunteer Infantry in 1861 at age 14 years and served until 1865. Ralph Boyer is married to Mary Lynn Boyer (Nesbitt) and has a daughter, Julie Ann Boyer Vest and a son, John P. Boyer. Ralph Boyer was in the automotive industry from 1938 to 1941, then joined the Air Force in December of that year. He served as a pilot, navigator, and bombadier until October 1945.

After being discharged from the Air Force, he married and went to work in the Prosper State Bank in February 1947 and has been in the bank since then. He is a Methodist and a member of the Masonic Lodge.

CAPT. JOHN HENRY BINGHAM, commander of "Bingham's Battery" in the Civil War.

JOHN HENRY BINGHAM

John Henry Bingham born September 13, 1839 at Harrow Gate Springs, Alabama was the son of John Gaines Bingham and his second wife, Catherine Mariah nee Fisher.

After the death of his father in 1854 John came to Texas along with his widowed mother and two younger sisters, Sallie and Mattie. They settled in Dallas and John went to work as a typesetter (Printer's devil) for the Dallas Herald a predecessor of the Dallas Morning News. He worked for this newspaper until the outbreak of the War Between the States at which time, the entire staff of the newspaper signed up for military duty with the Confederacy. He served over four years.

After the end of the war he returned to Dallas and again worked for this same newspaper. During this time he set a speed record for setting type which was never broken or even matched until mechanical typesetting was introduced. In 1867 he purchased a newspaper in McKinney and continued to work in Dallas to earn the money to pay off his indebtedness for the purchase of the paper. Isaac Finks Graves and Judge Muse had signed his note with him when he purchased the paper.

He began publishing the ENQUIRER in February 1869 and continued to publish same until 1898 at which time he retired.

On September 30, 1869 he married Eliza Virginia Graves the eldest daughter of Isaac Finks Graves and his wife Margaret Ann nee Stevens.

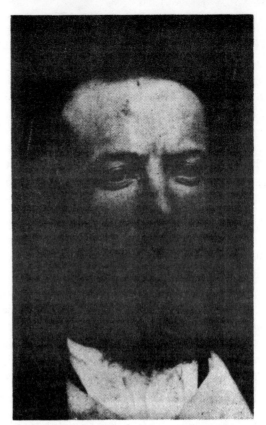

CAPT. JOHN HENRY BINGHAM

The Graves couple came originally from Orange County Virginia but moved soon after their marriage to Columbia, Missouri. Eliza Virginia was born there on Christmas day 1841. The family came to Texas in 1856 and settled in McKinney, Collin County, Texas.

The family of John H. Bingham lived in a house on Louisiana Street which was next door to the printing office of the Enquirer until 1883. In 1882 John began to build the home located at 804 Chestnut Street. All the lumber used in the construction of the home was hauled overland from Jefferson, Texas by ox-cart. The residence was under construction for a period of two years. The lower floor of the home was sufficiently completed in the early spring of 1883 for the family to move in and occupy the lower floor. The house plan was drawn from memory of a home in Georgia which John Bingham had admired while serving in the war.

The children of John and Eliza Bingham were Margaret Gaines born August 18, 1870 (died young), Sallie Mills born February 3, 1873 (married James T. Couch, Sr.), Isaac Graves born November 21, 1874, Nathaniel Stevens born June 9, 1877, Stephen Goodwin born May 4, 1880 and Eliza Virginia born January 18, 1883 (married Watt Eli Morelock).

NANCY SHELTON BRADLEY

EDWARD BRADLEY
1787-1855

Edward Bradley was born in North Carolina on January 21, 1787. Little is known of his early years but it is assumed that he came with his family when they went out of North Carolina into Kentucky through the Cumberland Gap. Edward was married in Warren County, Kentucky January 27, 1814 to Nancy Shelton (1792-1883), the daughter of Nelson Shelton. Nancy was attended at the wedding by her sister, Sarah. She and her husband John Fitzhugh later migrated with the Bradleys into Peter's Colony.

Edward and his bride were among the first to settle at the present site of Russellville, Kentucky, just north of the Tennessee State line. Before 1820 the young couple moved westward into Missouri, stopping to settle where Booneville now stands. Here were born the five children: Mary Ann (1820-1873), Thomas (1824-1881), Sarah W. (1828), James S. (1829-1866), and Daniel S. (1833-1862).

Edward Bradley settled in Texas about 1842 and received his land certificate (Fannin Third Class No. 1039) in the colony from Thomas William Ward in 1850 and patented 640 acres in Collin County in two 320 acre tracts. These tracts were about two miles apart along the Old Denton and McKinney Road. At that time the Edward Bradley Survey ad-

joined the town of McKinney, now it lies inside the town, including Finch Park.

Edward Bradley's house no longer stands but older members of the family recall it as a log house which stood on the east side of the Hill well.

The family cemetery was on a hill adjoining the Samuel McFarland 640 survey to the south. This cemetery tract was included in a portion of the Edward Bradley Survey that was willed to his daughter, Mary Ann Howell, and later was sold to E.W. Kirkpatrick.

Edward Bradley served in the Mexican War, enlisting at Buckney on July 24, 1846. He served in Captain Andrew Stapp's Company in the Regiment of Mounted Volunteers under Col. Bell. This was the only company from Collin County to serve in the Mexican War. They served on the frontier protecting settlements against Indians who were causing great misery to both settlers and travellers. For this service Bradley was given a bounty land grant of 40 acres in 1850.

Bradley died September 24, 1855 and was buried in Bradley Cemetery, his grave is the oldest on record there and is marked by two large stones.

GEORGE ROBERT (BOB) BRINLEE

George Robert (Bob) Brinlee was born July 28, 1838, at Stony Point, Collin Co., Texas, the third child of Hiram and Elizabeth (Betsy) Ann McKinney Brinlee. He has been described as a quite, and gentle fellow as going about minding his own business. He grew up in the Stony Point area on the old Brinlee homestead.

He was Pvt. G.R. Brinlee. Commanding Officer William A. Rhea's Co. D. 6th Regt. T.C. Col. L.S. Ross commanding C.S.A.

He enlisted March 13, 1962 in Arkansas for 12 months.

April 16, 1861 he was married to Miss Molinda J. Horton. To this union were born eleven children: George Mason Brinlee, William Carroll Brinlee, John Harm Brinlee, James (Jim) Lafayette Brinlee, the girls, Sarah, who died in infancy, Mattie J. who married Matt Swafford, Missouri Ann, married Levi Akin, Orella Lizzie, married Wardlow Hendricks, Flora, who married Will Bunch.

Molinda J. Horton Brinlee died June 3, 1926. She is buried in Elm Grove Cemetery, Westminster, Collin, Tex.

George Robert Brinlee died Dec. 23, 1927, and

GEORGE ROBERT BRINLEE and wife, Molinda J. Horton Brinlee.

is buried in Elm Grove Cemetery Westminster, Collin, Tex.

Many descendants are scattered throughout the world.

LEFT, HIRAM CARROLL BRINLEE and nephew William Carroll Brinlee.

HIRAM CARROLL (DINK) BRINLEE

Hiram Carroll (Dink) Brinlee was born in Red River Co., Tex. in 1844. His parents were Hiram and Elizabeth (Betsy) Ann McKinney Brinlee, who had come from Lincoln Co., Kentucky.

Hiram Carroll Brinlee grew up in the wilds of Collin Co., Texas. He is recorded on the 1860 Census, Collin Co. Texas, Precinct 2. He was the fifth child of a family of seven children.

He was a daring and colorful man. He became an accomplished fiddle player, and an expert dancer. He could dance all night, then work all day. Riding horses, fancy roping and riding tricks were favorite sports. He was also an expert marksman. He was happy when sitting in his saddle with his lariat and six-gun.

As time went by, he became a cattle drover, driving cattle to Abilene, Kansas, passing through Bonham, crossing Red River en route to market.

Hiram Carroll's first discharge from the Confederate Army, Capt. William Rhea's Company D, 6th Regiment of the Texas Cavalry was the 13th of June, 1862, for being under age (17), after having served 10 months.

He re-enlisted under Gen. Gano's Regiment, and served out the rest of the war. He was five feet and 10 inches tall, with black eyes, dark complexion, black hair and dashing physique. He was popular with the fair sex.

After the war he met and married Dicie Caroline Boone, a relative of Daniel Boone; they were married April 15, 1863. She was three-quarters Comanche Indian.

To this union were born the following children: James Edward, William Leon (Hoss), John Ervin, Laura Lee, Elizabeth Anne (Doll), Geneva H. (Sis), Ambert Hatler (Bert), and Lewis Boone.

An honorable discharge was given at Camp Maxey, the 13th day of June, 1862.

Hiram Carroll Brinlee was a farmer by trade. Cotton was raised and hauled by wagon, horse, mule or oxen drawn to shipping points in New Orleans. Hiram and his brother, Richard, would take the crop to market. At one time the cotton was burned while waiting transportation to England. They expected the U.S. Government to reimburse them for the loss. The North burned the cotton.

Later, Hiram Carroll took over his father's general merchandise store at Stony Point. The remains of the store's foundation can still be seen. Daily necessities were sold here. Also blacksmith tools, farming tools, wagon parts, and buggy repairs, whips, etc.

Hiram Carroll's life was terminated with Dicie Caroline Boone after eight children.

Loneliness and longing for compansionship, he ventured into the Indian Territory, Chickasaw

Nation, at the age of 47 years, he met and married Susan L. Smith Bonner December 1, 1891, at White Bead Hill, of The Chickasaw Nation, Indian Territory. Susan Smith Bonner was aged 23 years. To this union were born: ? Brinlee, Lawrence Carroll, Cordie, Austin, Cecil O'Dell.

Susan Lizzie Smith Bonner Brinlee was three-fourths Choctaw Indian.

Hiram Carroll Brinlee got sick and died Jan. 20, 1920, he died at his sister's house in Van Alstyne, Collin, Tex. He is buried in the Brinlee Cemetery, on the Original farmstead, and burying ground. A casket was bought at the Shirley Store, and he was taken by wagon to the cemetery. A long rain had set in. The roads were muddy, sticky and almost impassable at that time.

Susan Lizzie Bonner Brinlee is buried in Restland Memorial Cemetery north of Dallas, near Plano, Texas.

THE BURTON FAMILY

In the far northwest corner of Tennessee four families were caught up in the maelstrom of Reconstruction days. The Civil War had closed and residents of the defeated South were preparing for mass migration to the West where farm land was waiting to be claimed. Weakley County had been the home of these families for decades. The four families were Edward Burton, who married Malinda Harvey about 1830; Thomas Harvey, who married Rachel Harvey about 1809; Reuben Ross, who married Polly Ann Henderson first, then Minerva Vincent; and Thomas Kendall who married Clementine Cordelia Burton.

Edward Burton's father was Samuel H. Burton, a native of Virginia; however, records show that in Tennessee in 1835 he hosted a meeting in his frontier home when Benton County, Tennessee was organized. He married Martha Jane Ross (born in 1839) in 1858, the daughter of Elder Reuben Ross, a fiery preacher of Irish extraction.

The children of Edward and Malinda Harvey Burton were: Samuel Harvey Burton (1832) who first came to Limestone County, and, about 1870, came to Collin County. Clementine Cordelia Burton (1834) married Thomas Kendall in 1860 and had four children, Callie, Lois, Jimpy, and Elizabeth.

Callie married J.B. Randels at McKinney in 1881, Lois married Arthur Lawrence at McKinney in 1895, Jimpy never married and Elizabeth died in infancy. All are buried in McKinney. Solomon

Ethridge Burton, second son of Edward and Malinda, was born in 1838 and came to Texas as part of a wagon train in 1865. He was married in 1860 to Christine Gutherie. He and his wife reared a large family, Thomas David (September 17, 1861-December 7, 1949) married Corena Williams, John (September 7, 1863), James William (December 14, 1868 died in April of 1942).

Lafayette (Tobe) was born June 15, 1870 and died in 1954, Callie Louzetta (August 15, 1872 and died January 17, 1923

Lafayette (Tobe) was born June 15, 1870 and died in 1954, Callie Louzetta (August 15, 1872) died January 17, 1923. George, Anne, Evie and Solomon Etheridge Jr. (March 3, 1879 and died in July of 1947). Alfonso and Rachel Burton had these children: Sina Evelyn (1864), Laura Bell (1866), Hazel C. (1868), James Luther (1874), Beecher (1877), and Hallie C. (1880), all born in Texas.

The family lived in McKinney for a number of years before moving to Gainsville where they operated the Chickasaw Hotel. The mother died in 1925 (1912) and the father in 1912 (1925).

Descendants of the Burton, Harvey, Kendall, and Ross families still living in Collin County are: Mrs. Jack Lanier of Frisco, Woody Rains of McKinney, Mrs. Charles Melotte of McKinney, Miss Faye Randels of Sherman, J.F. Drake of Denton, Mrs. Dick Miller of Ft. Worth, Homer, Douglas, Alma, and Charles Tarin, all of McKinney. There are scores of others.
Submitted by Nora T. Lanier, 101 Bison Trail, Frisco, Texas.
Written by: J.F. Drake, Denton, Texas.

J. PERRY BURRUS

J. Perry Burrus was born near Clarksville, Missouri, the son of a school teacher, W.C., in March 10, 1872. The family moved to Texas in 1875 and his father bought Shirley Mill, a buhr grist mill. He operated this mill until 1888, then sold it and went to work for the Collin County Mill and Elevator Company that had been erected by the Farmer's Alliance. At that time this company was operating at a loss and were looking for a buyer. Burrus bought stock in the company and later added more, until he and E.W. Kirkpatrick became sole owners of the mill. Under new management it became a thriving business since wheat growing was at its peak in Collin County at that time. There was a setback in 1900 when the mill suffered severe fire damage but that was repaired, and completely rebuilt.

As the operation grew, they added other mills until they had the Collin County Mill and Elevator Company, Burrus Mill and Elevator Company of Ft. Worth, Morten Milling Company of Dallas, and the Fant Milling Company of Sherman.

The Burrus family moved to Dallas, where they are still successful in the same business.

Story from the files of the McKinney Democrat.

BURRUS FAMILY

William C. Burrus started a store in Weston in 1854. Later he came to McKinney to settle and bought a small flour mill that George M. Watts had established on a small branch in the northeast part of town in 1856. In a few years he helped to establish the first real flour mill in McKinney where the old ice plant stands.

During the Texas Centennial in 1936, the old hewn logs of the original Burrus Mill were taken apart and hauled to the Fair Grounds in Dallas. The mill was reconstructed and is still a part of the yearly exhibits at the State Fair.

William Carrol Burrus was born in Missouri, in December of 1831 and died in McKinney June 29, 1911. He served in the Civil War in Company B., 15th Texas. This company later consolidated with the 10th Texas Cavalry. He was made first Lt., and when his captain was killed at Atlanta, he was made Captain. He was badly wounded at the battle at Franklin and was hospitalized at Columbia, Tennessee as a prisoner. After the war he farmed and milled, and in June of 1869 married Mary A. Covert of Collin County, the daughter of Luke B. Covert who had settled in Collin . They became the parents of the following children, Mrs. Edgar Averett of Claude, Texas, J. Perry, and Mrs. Richard W. Burrage of McKinney.

William Burrus opened the mill northeast of town in McKinney and closed it in 1888. Soon he became interested in the Alliance Mill. William Burrus was first married to Mary C. Guyer of Missouri in 1869 and had three children by her. Complete biography: Microfilmed newspaper of July 6, 1911, McKinney Library.

THE BUSH FAMILY

The Bush family, originally from England, was living in Orange County, Virginia prior to 1746. They are said to be descended from John and

MAJOR WILLIAM MARTIN BUSH, veteran of both the Mexican War and of the Civil War.

Elizabeth Bush who came from England on the "Neptune" and settled in Kiccoughtan, Virginia in 1618.

John and Margaret Bush lived in Orange County in 1746 and were the parents of 8 children. The youngest son, Phillip, was born October 19, 1736, married Mary Bryan of Culpepper County and they had 12 children. Their son, Captain Billy Bush, was one of the most colorful members of the family. He married Frances Tandy Burris and became the father of nine children. He was an Indian fighter and close friend of Daniel Boone, whom he accompanied on his second trip to Kentucky about 1780. He also took part in the Lewis and Clark Expedition to the Northwest Territory. Capt. Bush secured vast tracts of land near Boonesborough, Kentucky and persuaded friends and relatives to move to Kentucky. His five younger brothers and a sister, Liza Mary, joined him in forming the famous Bush Settlement in Clark County, Kentucky in 1784. Indian trouble kept them in Virginia for three more years. A log church was built in 1787 with loop holes through which they could fire on the Indians who frequently disrupted religious services. This building was replaced with the "Old Stone Meeting House" with the Bush families surrounding it.

Ambrose Bush, brother of Capt Billy, and son of Phillip Bush was born April 8, 1748. He married Lucy Gholson and they had six children. His brick house with its projecting gables and stile block gate was the first brick house in Kentucky.

Jeremiah Bush, son of Ambrose and Lucy

ELIZABETH BUSH

Gholson Bush, was born January 20, 1789 and died in 1842. He married Nancy Gentry in 1811 and they became parents of ten children.

Major William Martin Bush, son of Jeremiah, was born June 20, 1827 near Boonesborough, Kentucky and died November 3, 1900 at Greenville, Texas. He married Nancy Gholson Elkin on September 6, 1848. Their three children were Leslie Walker Bush, Walter Hamilton Bush, and Nancy who died in infancy. When Major Bush was 18 years of age he joined the Volunteers for the Mexican War and took part in the battles of Vera Cruz and Cerro Gordo. In 1858 he moved his family to Collin County where he settled near Rowlett Creek, about 6 miles southwest of McKinney. Major Bush helped organize a company of Collin County volunteers and had an illustrious career as an officer from 1861 to 1865. When General Polignack was wounded, he assumed command of his brigade in fierce fighting at the battles of Pleasant Hill and Yellow Bayou in Lousiana. After the war he returned to his home in Collin County and enjoyed a career of farming and as a stockman.

Leslie Walker Bush, son of Major William and Nancy Elkin Bush, was born September 8, 1850 and died January 23, 1913. He was only 8 years old when he rode horseback to Texas with his parents. He married Lula Jane Franklin on December 30, 1873. They were the parents of six children, Mary Ella, Lillian, Will, Walter, Edgar, Howard and Leslie. He lived near Allen and was a successful landowner and stockman.

Ella Bush, daughter to Leslie Bush, married Professor Franklin G. Jones. Their two children were Louise Elizabeth, who married Morrow H.

Boynton and Bush Jones who married Charlotte Smith.

Lillian Bush married The Reverand Richard D. Shults and had three sons. They were Richard Bush Shults who married Mary Frances Flannery, Leslie Shults who married Mable Hamilton and Edgar Shults who married Jean Sisson. Edgar served in the Navy in the Pacific War Zone in World War II.

Will Bush married Marguerite Stollings and they were the parents of four children. Maurine who married Jack Castles, William S. married Dorothy Harris, Bill who served as a navigator on a fighter plane in World War II was shot down over Germany and was held prisoner of war. Dorothy Louise married Capt. James Drake, World War II Naval Commander. Betsy Jane married Sam Young, Air Force Officer in World War II.

Walter Bush married Elizabeth May Holloway and their three children were Dr. Holloway Bush who married Jean MacDonnell. Dr. Bush served in India during World War II. Janelle Bush, the daughter of Walter and Elizabeth, married Glenn Coleman and their children are Glenn and Linda. Capt. Glenn Coleman served in the U.S.A.F. as a helicopter pilot in Vietnam and as instructor at the Air Force Academy.

Joyce Bush married Frank Benton and they are the parents of 4 sons. Frank Benton served in the Navy in World War II.

Edgar Bush married Elizabeth Bishop and they are the parents of Nancy who married Tucker Frazer Morian. Frazer Morain served in the Air Force in World War II. They are the parents of two children, Barbara and Rick and live in Houston.

Leslie Bush married Moran Hill and they have one son, Dr. Mack Moran Hill who married Anne Wilks. They are the parents of Martha Leslie and Ben Hill. Dr. Hill was on active duty in the Pacific War Zone with the U.S. Navy in World War II.

Walter Bush son of Major and Nancy Elkin Bush, was born in 1852 and died in January of 1928. He married Nancy Brooks and they were the parents of Katherine, Walter, and Dr. Leslie Bush. Walter Bush was a pharmacist and operated his drug store in Greenville, Texas. Later he became President of a Greenville Bank and was a successful businessman there.

Members of the Bush family living in Collin County now are Walter Bush and his daughter, Janelle Bush Coleman, Edgar Bush, and Leslie Bush Hill and her son, Dr. Mack Hill and his family.

Dreams of this pioneer family have come true for

the numerous descendents who have found the good life in God's Country, Collin County, USA.

Written by Mrs. Edgar Bush.
101 Westwood Circle
McKinney, Texas

THE JOHN F. BUTLER FAMILY

John F. Butler, M.D., pioneer physician of Wylie, Texas was born in Roane County, Tennessee October 16, 1836. His father, Jacob M. Butler, a native of Tennessee was a man of considerable prominence, serving as sheriff of Knox County, justice of the peace and county judge. His wife was Sarah G. Hardin, the mother of nine children. John F. Butler was the seventh child. He was educated in Tennessee and was teaching there when the Civil War broke out. In 1861 he joined the Confederate Army as a second lieutenant of Company F, 26th Tennessee Infantry and in 1862 was promoted to Captain in which capacity he served until the war ended. He surrendered at Fort Donelson with the rest of the Confederate Army and was held prisoner for six months at Camp Chase in Ohio. He was twice wounded during the war.

After the war he went to Bristow County, Georgia and began teaching and reading medicine with Dr. J.C.C. Blackburn and in 1871 graduated from the University of Louisiana. He located in Collin County practicing medicine, operating a drug business and serving as postmaster at Wylie. In 1875 he married Mollie S. Latham and to this union were born three children, Mattie Stella, Mary Z., and Sarah V. Mrs.Butler died in 1881 and in 1887 the Doctor married Miss Fannie J. Martin of McKinney.

Dr. Butler was a Democrat politically and was always active in political campaigns.

Source: Biographical Sketches, Old News Clippings.

THE CALDWELL FAMILY

Dr. James A. Caldwell, pioneer physician of Collin County, came from Conway, Arkansas in the year of 1885. The family lived for the first two years on the Dangerfield Dunn farm and it was here that Gibson Caldwell was born and was named for the attending physician, Dr. J.E. Gibson. In 1889 Dr. Caldwell built a home for his family on South Wilcox Street. In this home Roy Caldwell was born.

DR. JAMES A. CALDWELL'S Sanitorium about 1890.

In 1889 the family moved into a new home on South Tennessee Street and on this block of land Dr. Caldwell built a large two-story hospital that attracted patients from all over the country. Dr. Caldwell died April 6, 1937 and his wife on March 3, 1933.

In 1909 Gibson Caldwell was married to Goldie Warden, daughter of another pioneer family. Three children were born of this marriage, James A. Caldwell, Mrs. Paul C. Young, and Mrs. George C. Webb.

Gibson Caldwell has been a civic leader and successful businessman in McKinney for over 60 years. He was first associated with J.W. Webb Grain Company and for 30 years was head of the Collin County Mill. For the last 17 years he has been president of The First Savings and Loan Company of McKinney. He served as President of the McKinney School Board for 14 years and under his leadership several new school buildings were erected. He is a Mason of 65 years membership, and for 53 years has been a member of the Rotary Club. He was a moving force in the organization of the Chamber of Commerce as well as of the Industrial Foundation. There is no area of community life that has not benefitted by Gibson Caldwell's public spirited leadership. He has 7 grandchildren and 8 great-grandchildren.

Story given by Gibson Caldwell.

THE CAMPBELL FAMILY

John Campbell was born June 21, 1828 in Green County, Tennessee, the son of Mr. and Mrs. Arch Campbell who lived and died in Tennessee. John married Margaret Grantham, who was born July 21, 1827 in Green County. They were members of the Cumberland Presbyterian Church. Three children were born to them before they left Tennessee. Archibald Alexander Campbell (June 13, 1847), Sarah Margaret (September 16, 1849), and Andrew J. Campbell (July 10, 1853).

In 1854 John and Margaret Campbell came to Collin County with Jack Faires and Jacob Kirkpatrick, whose wife, Sarah Jane Campbell was the sister of John Campbell. The son of Jacob and Sarah Kirkpatrick, E.W., was a well known citizen of McKinney in later years. The lovely old Kirkpatrick home near Finch Park in McKinney is one of the most treasured landmarks today.

After arriving in Collin County, other children were born to John and Margaret Campbell, Martha Jane (August 27, 1856), William Alvis (Dec. 19, 1858), Robert Allen (February 17, 1861), John Elbert (February 17, 1864), Mary Eliza (January 10, 1866), Demmie Ellen (November 11, 1869), and Alice (January 4, 1875).

In 1861 John Campbell bought a tract of land 10 miles southeast of McKinney in the Blythe's Chapel community—Winningkoff School District. This home was where they reared their children.

At the outbreak of the Civil War, John joined the Confederate Army, but as he was a miller by trade, it was considered that he would be of more value to the Confederacy following his trade than in the ranks. He was sent back to operate the Fitzhugh Mill while the men of that family were away at war. Gabriel Fitzhugh had bought extensive acreage in the Calvin Boles Survey and gave 160 acres to his nephew, Bob Fitzhugh to build a mill in 1853. Gabriel Fitzhugh was the grandfather of Fitzhugh Newsome of McKinney. This was the first flour mill in this area and people came from Louisiana, Jefferson and other towns in east Texas. With the aid of his teenage son, Archibald Campbell, John Campbell ground flour for many years. After the war he moved to McKinney where he lived in the family home at 64 South Wilcon Street. He died here September 9, 1906.

In 1888 Archibald Alexander Campbell bought the homeplace and built a home there. He married Dorinda Pettus Scott, daughter of another pioneer couple, Adam and Mariah Scott who had come from Missouri to settle in Collin County. The children of this couple, A.A. and Dorinda Campbell were, John Adam (June 19, 1870), Etha B. (June 17, 1872), Tom H. (September 4, 1873), Samuel Oscar (September 6, 1875), James Robert (December 24, 1877), Margaret Frances (August 9, 1880), Ida Mae (February 21, 1883), Susie Elberta (March 29, 1888), and Oda (July 2, 1894).

John Adam Campbell married Eady Arminta

Graham, daughter of William L. and Sarah Simmons Graham who settled at Old Willow Springs-Lucas from Rusk County in 1867. In 1907 John and Minnie Campbell bought the homeplace at Blythe's Chapel and reared their children there. Mr. Fred Petway now owns the homeplace.

James Robert Campbell married Sue B. Vance in 1899 and lived in Collin County for many years before moving to Bonham, with three children, Leta, Lester, and Inez.

Margaret Frances Campbell married Euram B. Moore in 1903 and they lived on a farm near Forest Grove until their death, leaving two children, Horace and Genie May Moore.

Ida Mae Campbell married Dr. Rufus E. Morrow in 1906 and in 1924 they bought the old Campbell home and lived there until her death. They were the parents of two children, Venita Morrow who taught in McKinney Junior High School before marrying Clinch O. McMillan, and a son, Dallas C. Morrow, prominent oil field wildcatter.

Susie Elberta Campbell married George W. Crittenden in 1910 and had three children, Gene, Pauline, and Ray Crittenden. Oda Campbell taught for many years in Collin County schools and her last school was a Methodist Mission school in Collegio, Saltillo, Mexico. The John Adam Campbells were the parents of five children, all born and reared in Collin County, Stokley Elbert married Pearl Biggers and lives near McKinney. The second child, Ruth, married Leland Horn and taught in McKinney schools for many years. After his death she married Jasper L. (Jack) Weeks and still lives in McKinney.

Lois Campbell married J.G. Smith and they live south of McKinney where their children grew up. Their daughter Bobby June married Joseph Hollman and lives in Arlington, and Euram Campbell Smith lives in Dallas. Cora Campbell taught in Collin County schools for several years before marrying Noble Spurgin, and they became the parents of Noble David and Stephen Paul Spurgin.

Gladys Campbell married Jim Lawrence Ferguson and she too taught in Collin for many years. They were the parents of one daughter, Carol Ann Ferguson. Gladys is deceased but Jim still lives in McKinney.

THE CAVE FAMILY

George Washington Cave, son of John Talbot Cave, was born in Missouri. On December 5, 1866 in Springfield he was married to Eliza Frances Fulton and the couple lived there until they decided to come to Texas to live in 1876. They settled north of McKinney where they reared five boys and two girls, all deceased except the youngest son, Abb Cave, who lives on the Uncle Jimmy Cave place on Telephone Road, five miles north of McKinney. They were the parents of six boys and three girls: James Talbot, William Thomas, John (called Tanner), Everett, and Abb. One son died in infancy. The girls were Iva and Nellie.

James Talbot Cave married Lillian Darland in January of 1891 and they lived all their lives in Collin County around Melissa, Plano, and Princeton. They were the parents of 13 children, eight boys and five girls. Olan died at age seven and was a twin to Mrs. Clyde Crouch of Melissa.

Bertha Cave Wilson, eldest of the 13 children, lives in Princeton and is the last charter member of the Princeton Church of Christ. She married Walker Wilson August 15, 1909 and their children now living are Mrs. Orbrey Rhea Braswell and Mrs. Zelma Pinckney.

W.T. Cave married Qillie Laverne Shelton in 1894. They were the parents of the following children: Walter, Clarence, Clifton, and Royce. Clarence lives in Princeton and Clifton in Farmersville.

Everett Cave married Effie McBee and have seven living children. One son, Provine, lives in Princeton. Abb Cave, the youngest son of G.W. Cave, married Ida Clark and reared two sons, Roy and Doyle. He lives on Telephone Road north of McKinney.

Story sent by Bertha Cave Wilson, Princeton, Texas.

THE CHAMBERS OF CHAMBERSVILLE

Elisha Chambers, one of Collin County's early settlers, was the son of Elisha Chambers, a Primitive Baptist preacher, and Rebecca Moore Chambers of Burke County, North Carolina.

In 1835 the younger Elisha Chambers was married to Margaret Ann Mannon in Owen County, Indiana. In 1847 he and his wife and six children came to Collin County, settling in what is now known as the Chambersville Community. He bought the headright (640 acres) of John Larrimore and later bought 320 acres from William Lindsey. Some of this first headright is still owned by Chambers' descendents.

A son, Lewis Cass, died in 1853 and his was the first grave in the Chambersville Cemetery, the land being given by Elisha Chambers. He and his wife are both buried here.

Elizabeth Chambers, who came with her parents, Elisha Chambers, to Collin County in 1847, was married to Jacob Francis Marion Bryon who was born in Lawrence County, Tennessee in 1839. He was the son of John and Millie Pullan Bryan. The family came to live in Collin in 1859. At the outbreak of the Civil War, Jacob enlisted in Company C of the 9th Texas Infantry and served east of the Mississippi River. At the Battle of Shiloh he was wounded and taken prisoner. He was taken to St. Louis and held for five months, then exchanged and was allowed to return home. As soon as he recovered from his wounds, he enlisted in Col. Bourland's Regiment and served on the frontier of Texas until the end of the war. He married Elizabeth Chambers in 1866 and they made their home in the Chambersville Community. Ten children were born to them, three dying in infancy.

Story sent by Mrs. Hubert White.

THE ALFRED CHANDLER FAMILY

Alfred Chandler was born in Arkansas July 13, 1821, where he grew to manhood. Learning about the Throckmorton Settlement, seven miles north of present McKinney, he decided to see what the new country looked like. Texas had opened up the land for free settlement and the Three Forks of the Trinity had been praised highly by the McGarrahs who had already settled there. He and several other young men rode horseback, aiming to settle at Cedar Springs, now Dallas. They rode through the Indian Territory to Coffee's Station where a man named Reece Murray operated a ferry across Red River, charging 25 cents (two-bits). They decided the charge was too much, so they hired an Indian on the Territory side to bring them across in a canoe, with the horses swimming behind them. His charge was a drink of whiskey.

They found Coffee's Station run by Major Coffee and his lovely wife and a man named John Ribern. This was in 1843. They were advised not to go to Cedar Springs since there had been Indian trouble at the Buckner Settlement. They waited until a wagon train of 10 wagons came by on the way to Cedar Springs and they joined the train. They arrived at the home of John Neely Bryan in late January. They were so impressed by the beautiful prairies west of the Trinity River that they built a log bridge across the river and built the cabins there, in spite of Bryan's warning about Indians. One night they were awakened by yelling and noise of dry buffalo hides being drug on the dry ground. They rushed out with their firearms but the Indians already had all their horses except two old mares. This was enough. Chandler went with Bryan to Pinhook (now Paris) for supplies Bryan needed for his little store he operated from his cabin. With Bryan's help he opened a store of his own in Pinhook.

In 1846, hearing that a company was being organized at Buckner to go to the Mexican War he went to join them. He came too late, the company had already departed, but Andrew Stapp, who organized the company, had been sent back due to illness. He set about organizing a company of rangers to serve against the Indians on the frontier. Alf volunteered and was made a 2nd Lt. The ranger company went to Denton County and served all the way to Red River. Chandler said they would have starved after they lost their gun powder swimming across the False Wichita River, if it had not been for an Indian guide who went with them, Frank House. He showed them how to live on wild fruits, bark, and how to snare fish. Frank House was well known in McKinney in later years and was always a friend to the settlers. The ranger company was led by William Fitzhugh. After the company was disorganized in 1849, Alf lived with James Herndon of Buckner, and married Mary Ellen Magner, a daughter of another pioneer. (1849) They were married by Alfred Johnson, who lived one half mile west of the present Whisenant home on Rock Hill Road. (Johnson in 1854 killed Jo Peak in a pistol fight at a saloon where the Ritz Theatre now stands. This was the first killing in the new town of McKinney.)

In the spring of 1850 Chandler returned to a beautiful spot he had selected for a home while with the rangers. He bought 275 acres of land, also bought a lot in McKinney where Penny's Store stands. Chandler fenced his land with rails, placing 10 buffalo skulls under each corner post, just as a whim, he said. He and Frank House kept the settlement in meat by killing buffalo that fed on the lush prairie grass on the flats west of McKinney. It was then known as "Mustang Flats" because of the many wild mustang ponies that lived there.

During the Civil War Chandler served in J.B. Wilmeth's regiment on the Texas coast. After the war he returned to his home and lived there until his death in 1911. In 1904 he and Josiah Nichols were the only ones left of the ranger company.

There are many descendents of Alfred Chandler still living in Collin County, all leading citizens and all proud of this staunch old pioneer who helped carve a civilization from the wilderness.

CHRISTIAN FAMILY

Written by Mrs. John Shipp

John W. Christian, born in 1844 in Tennessee, came to Collin County at age 18. He lived for three years with Indians. He married Missouri Warden of Blue Ridge and settled on the farm in the Lucas community now owned by his grandson, Wallace Christian. The John W. Christians had three sons, Gabe Williams, Fred and Ernest and one daughter, Pearl. G.W. (Gabe William) who continued to live on the homeplace here, married Carrie E. Actkinson. They were the parents of four daughters and a son. As stated above, the son, Wallace Christian, who married Gloria Staton of Farmersville, owns and lives on the place. They have two daughters: Suzanne (Mrs. David Calton) and Charlotte (Mrs. Kenneth) Dean. Both of whom have homes on this farm.

The daughters of Mr. and Mrs. G.W. Christian: Ethlyn (deceased) married Leon Snavely; Lucille, whose first husband was the late Gobel Riffe. A son, Jerry Riffe, was born to this union and lives in California. Later Lucille married Ed Coffey, son of Mr. and Mrs. Robert Coffey, of Lucas. Ed Coffey and his parents are deceased. The other daughters are Hazel and Willie Pearl. Hazel married the late Roy Miller and Willie Pearl Christian married Forest Gaines. They have two daughters and live in south Texas. Both Lucille and Hazel live in McKinney.

John William Christian owned three farms, two of which are still in the family, owned by grandsons.

Suzanne and David Calton's two children, Bryan and Deidra, and Charlotte and Kenneth Dean's daughter, Melanie, are the fifth generation to live on the land settled by their great, great grandfather, John W. Christian.

HISTORY OF THE COFFEY FAMILY

The Coffey family came from an ancient Irish family which is said to be descended from Milesius, King of Spain. The first emigrant by the name of Coffey came to this country from Ireland about 1637 and lived in Surry Co., Va. One of John Coffey's descendants became a Baptist missionary and moved to Wilkes Co., N.C. Some of the family later moved to Kentucky.

One of the descendants of this family was Salathiel Coffey who married Nancy Dunbar. To them were born seven children. When Salathiel's first wife died, he married a widow, Mary Ann Ballew, who had six children. The following year which was

1855 the family came to Texas and settled in Collin County where three other children were born to them, Margaret, Josie, and Sterling Coffey. From the ten Coffey children were descended over 1100 direct descendants, many of whom were prominent in affairs in church, business, and political life in Collin County and the State of Texas.

One son, Will Coffey, a confederate veteran, served as Sheriff, as did a grandson, Will Kerby. One grandson, Homer Coffey, served as county commsisioner, as did two other grandsons, Frank Kerby and Lee Cook. One great grandson, Orlia J. Moss, served as county tax assessor-collector. Another great grandson, William T. Dungan, served Collin County as State Representative for several years.

Many of his descendants were prominent in other fields of business, as one son, Sterling Coffey, banker and business man, and his son Fred Coffey, long time in business in McKinney. Others were grandson Joe McKinney and brother Giles McKinney, business men and bankers and another brother John McKinney who served as Police Chief of McKinney for many years. Their father was Rev. John McKinney who married Salathiel Coffey's daughter, Polly Ann. Another great grandson, Clarence Kerby, was divisional manager of J.C. Penney Co. until his retirement.

Another great grandson, Dr. Walter McKinney, was a well known business man and philanthropist in Philadelphia.

The children of Salathiel Coffey were: Letitia, married Thos. J. Reagan and Mat Wason (second marriage); Polly Ann, married John Meyers McKinney; William Stanton, married Sarah Elizabeth Lucas; Harriet, married R.B. Whisenant; Milton W., married Amanda Virginia Lewis; Zachary Taylor, married Mary Snider; Nancy Jane, married Joe Liggett; Margaret, married John Kerby; Josie C., married Geo. D. Kerby; and Sterling, married Ida E. Rountree.

Story by Mrs. Bill Dungan of McKinney.

THE EBER COMPTON FAMILY

A handwritten deed which I now have in my possession, shows that in the year 1860 Mr. Eber Compton and his wife, Angie Frye Compton, purchased one hundred sixty acres of land approximately eight miles south of McKinney in what later became known as the Forest Grove community. The deed bears the signature of William Snider and the official stamps. The Comptons had come from Springfield, Missouri, traveling by ox-drawn wagons. Four very young daughters accompanied the parents to Texas. Their only son, John, was serving in the Civil War, where he was killed in battle.

One daughter, Jennie, was later married to Mr. Will Merritt, an early sheriff of Collin County. The Merritt family contributed much to Collin County history. Three of the sons: Will, Clarence, and Eber were lawyers. The youngest son, James H. Merritt, was a merchant whose store was located on the south side of the square. The Merritts' only daughter, Minnie, was married to Mr. Clarence Smith of the well-known Smith Brothers Drug Company of McKinney.

Eber and Angie Compton are buried in Fitzhugh Cemetery, south of McKinney. Another daughter of the Comptons was Mary Frances, who was later married to John Wilson Hunter. The story of the Hunter family is included in this history.

(Written by Eula F. Hunter, granddaughter of the Comptons)

JOHNATHON H. COOK

Johnathon H. Cook, who was born in January of 1828 in Missouri and died in November of 1917 in Collin County, married Miss Julia Ann Lanham. To this union were born six children: James William (J.W.), born in October, 1849, died in 1934; Sylvester, born in October of 1852, died in November, 1935; Margaret Jane Cook; Laura Cook; Mack; and Van Cook.

Later J.H. Cook married Margaret (Peggy) Winder, born in July, 1842, died in October, 1911. She was a widow with two children, John and Alice Winder. Johnathon H. Cook came to Collin County with his family in 1859 and lived north of McKinney for a time. He bought more than a hundred acres of land in the Lucas area. He remarked he would sell a plot of land only to a doctor and a blacksmith. In time a doctor and a blacksmith bought enough land from Mr. Cook for a home and office and a shop.

Mr. and Mrs. J.H. Cook's first child, J.W., married Elizabeth Bowman of Lucas; Sylvester Cook married Mary Ellen McKinney, daughter of John Myers McKinney (a minister) and Mollie Ann Coffee McKinney; Margaret Jane Cook married Elkanah Spurgin; Laura Cook married George Bradley. Their daughters were: Lola, married Ed Dutton of Allen and Hattie married Hervey

Walker. Van Cook married Bill Campbell. Peggy Winder (Mr. Cook's step-daughter) married John Doyle, a teacher in the Lucas School. All of Mr. and Mrs. J.H. Cook's children grew up in Lucas, but the one that stayed longest, reared his family here was J.W. Cook. In February of 1883 Mr. and Mrs. J.W. Cook bought 62 acres of land one-half mile from the Lucas store from George White, and built a home. It was here that most of their children were born and all lived to be grown as follows: Otelia, Willie, Allye, Ruth, Dean and Earl.

Otelia Cook married Tom Burch of Wylie, where they reared their family. Willie Cook married R.P. (Bud) Spurgin of Lucas, where they lived all their lives. (See Spurgin family history.) Allye Cook married W.M. Anderson of Lucas. They were landowners and continued to live here. They had no children. He died in 1940 and she died in 1972. Ruth Cook married J.L. Graham of Lucas. They continued to live here until his death. They were the parents of four children: Leo, Eustace, Willie and Eunice, all grew up in Lucas. Leo married Jessie Armstrong of Forest Grove; Eustace (Buddy) married Louise Anderhub of Wylie; Willie married Joyce Ballew of Allen. Eunice married Virgil Richards of Allen, and now lives in McKinney. Dean Cook married Carey Pharr of Lucas. They are the parents of three children. (See Pharr family history.)

Earl Cook married Musa Gray of Lucas. They have a daughter, Erin, who married Joe Henry Leach of Allen. They live in McKinney.

Sylvester F. Cook and Mary Ellen McKinney Cook lived in Lucas many years. They were the parents of six children: Charles Monroe Cook married Cora Pharr. Alvona Cook married Bob Bowman. Lawrence Cook is deceased. Myrtle Cook married Dick Falkner. Joe Lee Cook married Lennie Pharr, daughter of Mr. and Mrs. D.N. Pharr of Lucas. To this union were born three children: Manley A. Cook, now of Big Spring, Texas, Bernice, who married Hugh Straughan of McKinney and Agnis who married Armer Mitchell and lives in Big Spring. Eva Florence Cook married Carl Berry. All of this family at one time or another lived in Lucas.

Tom Spurgin, the oldest child of Elkanah Spurgin and Margaret Jane Cook Spurgin, married Lizzie McKinney. He and his family lived in Lucas many years. One of their sons, Ernest, died here and another son, Milford, is a Lucas city councilman.

Written by Mrs. John Shipp
Our thanks to Earl Cook, Mrs. Dean Cook Pharr and Mrs. Hugh Straughan.

COTHES FAMILY

Herman Cothes who was born in Bardwell, Kentucky in 1849, came to Collin County and settled just east of Plano in 1871. He stayed for a while with the William Forman II family and worked until 1876, then returned to Kentucky where he married George Anna Brown, the daughter of George and Caroline Mercer Brown. They returned to the Forman farm and lived in a cabin just south of Plano Mutual Cemetery. In 1878 they bought a farm southwest of Allen in the Bethany Community. Seven children were born to them:

Frank Cothes (June 16, 1877) lived on the homeplace near Allen until 1929. He never married. He is buried in Rowlette Cemetery. Mattie Belle Cothes (January 26, 1879) married Sam Moulden of Murphy on January 30, 1900. They later moved to Houston where she died in 1968. Abbie D. Cothes (February 26, 1881) married Bert Carpenter in 1907 and died in 1915. She is buried at Rowlette. Chester Cothes (April 14, 1883) moved to Seminole in 1909 and was married to Gertrude Anderson in 1911. She died in 1912 and in 1915 he married Done Giddings of Allen. He died in 1937 in Seminole. Fred Cothes (November 6, 1887) married Vivian Gates of Allen in 1913. He died May 25, 1933 and is buried in Rowlette. Mary Ethel Cothes (January 17, 1889) married Dennis Knight of Allen March 2, 1924 and moved to Gaines County in 1926. She died July 8, 1972 and is buried in Seminole. Grady Cothes (August 22, 1891) married Alonedia Bishop of Celina on September 24, 1919. She died August 13, 1939. Grady is the only surviving child of the Herman Cothes family and still lives in Collin County. Chester Reeves Cothes of Seminole and Randy Cothes of Plano are the only great-grandsons of Herman Cothes.

Herman Cothes was a farmer and stockman, raising Poland China hogs and Short-horn cows. Being a firm advocate of improving seed of wheat and oats he spent many hours each year selecting his seeds as well as his livestock for improvement. His hobby was grafting and he developed a peach tree bearing five different kinds of peaches, and plum trees bearing three kinds of plums. He died February 2, 1917 at his home near Allen and is buried in Rowlette Cemetery. His wife, George Anna, died August 16, 1905.

Sent by Cothes family, Rt. 1, Plano.

THE NORTH HALF of the Nevada, Texas square, 1911.

GABRIEL JONES DAVIE

Born in Montgomery County, Tennessee March 9, 1836, Gabriel Jones Davie was the grandson of William R. Davie, General in the American Revolution, Governor of North Carolina and founder of the University of North Carolina. G.J. Davie moved to Arkansas in 1860, enlisted in Company C of the Confederate Army Second Arkansas Mounted Infantry in 1861 under McCullough, and went to Corinth in 1862. He was at the Reorganization after Second Corinth and was Captain of Company B Second Kentucky. He was wounded with two sabre strokes at Elkhorn, received a shotgun wound at Oak Hill on Wilson Creek, and surrendered under Taylor in Louisiana. He was graduated from the University of North Carolina with a degree in Civil Engineering, moved to Nevada, Texas and followed his chosen profession of Engineer. Davie laid off the town of Nevada and was paid for his work with the gift of a choice lot which he gave to the Methodist congregation to build a church on. (He was a Baptist.) He was appointed Post Master of Nevada, Texas on December 18, 1893. He taught school at Prairie Grove. He was survived by nine children at his death January 8, 1907: James Mack Davie, Thomas Marion

UNCLE BOB SCOTT'S HOUSE. It was on the south edge of Cotton Belt right of way. The part of the house with the flag painted on the side faced the railroad so everyone on the train could see it.

1911—LOOKING EAST ACROSS the square at Nevada.

JESS H. HUFFMAN, RFD mail carrier, in his mail cart with "Old Gyp" as horse power. This was on the square in 1911.

THE HOTEL LOVE built in 1898 in Nevada, Texas. It was on the southeast corner of the square and faced the depot.

Davie, Monett Davie, Sallie Fannie Davie, Roland Gooch Davie, Mary B. Davie, Edna Belle Davie, Hallie Manson Davie and Gabe Jones Davie, Jr. and was buried beside his wife who died November 19, 1893 at Pleasant Hill Cemetery (South Church) two miles south of Nevada, Texas.

169

NORTH SIDE OF NEVADA, TEXAS SQUARE, 1916.

FIRST GRADE of the Nevada, Texas School, 1914, Mrs. Davis, teacher.

JUDGE H.L. DAVIS FAMILY

After recieving his law degree from the University of Texas Judge Davis and his wife, Emma Umphress Davis, moved from Van Alstyne to McKinney where he opened a law office in 1887. He later was appointed Assistant District Attorney. In 1910 he was elected to the office of County Judge. While serving, the first all weather roads were built in Collin County with the County's First Bond issue. (The Celina Pike was the first surfaced road built in 1914.) He was the first County Judge to serve three two year terms.

No other Collin County family has been in public service on the Commissioner's Court as long as the Davis family. Judge Davis' son, Don O. Davis served as Commissioner for 11 years in precinct 1. Judge Davis' grandson, Don Weaver Davis, served as County Judge for 12 years and after leaving this office has gone into private practice.

Judge Davis was active in all phases of community life. He and his descendants are all active in the Church life of the First Christian Church of McKinney, where he taught a class for 35 years.

Three of his grandchildren are still living in McKinney: Carrie Jean Davis, Mrs. Richard Carr, and Judge Don Weaver Davis.

Story sent by Carrie Jean Davis

WILLIAM DAVIS

Governor P.H. Bell, for the State of Texas, granted William Davis and wife, Margaret, two-thirds of a league and one labor of land where the town of McKinney now stands, totaling 3,130 acres. This was in support of a decree from the District Court of 1841, but was registered and patented at the Land Office in Austin August 1, 1856.

William Davis and his family had a little log cabin on the land in 1848 when the new County seat was moved to present McKinney. He and his wife gave 120 acres to the new town of McKinney to be used as the townsite. Commissioners receiving the donation were J.B. Wilmeth, James McReynolds, John Fitzhugh, and William McKinney. William Davis asked that lots 13-27 and 65 in Blocks 2-4 be reserved for his use. Neither he nor his wife could write so signed the document with the "Mark," as many other pioneers had to do. Schools were non-existent in the very early days and few could read unless they were educated before coming to Texas. Joel Stewart was then the county clerk.

Several descendents of Willaim Davis lived in Collin County and some are still here. Ida Lee married Conley Hockett, a Virginian. Her inheritance from her grandfather was a farm northwest of McKinney and here she reared her family. One of the Hockett children was Dewey Hockett.

DEAL—PETWAY—STRATTON

These three families were landowners, one a merchant and all influential citizens of this part of Collin County. The history of these families goes back to Michael Koiner, born in Germany in 1720.

"Near the flow of the Danube River not far from the noble Rhine

"Where the golden harvests quiver came a son of the Koiner line."

That son was Michael Koiner who followed the lead of William Penn and came to the town of Philadelphia in the "New World" about 1740. He married Margaret Diller of New Holland, Pa. in 1749. The subject of this narrative, an ancester of the late Mrs. J.N. Deal and her daughters, the late Mrs. W.P. Petway and the late Mrs. J.E. Stratton and their children, grandchildren and great grandchildren in Collin County, lived at a time when America was still in its primitive wilderness save on parts of its eastern border. Rebecca Koiner, born in May, 1815, married Capt. George W. Deal of Missouri. The second of Capt. and Mrs. Deal's children was John Newton Deal, who married Maggie Engleman, daughter of John Engleman and Elizabeth Koiner Engleman. Mr. and Mrs. John Engleman were great grandparents of the Petway men, Leroy and Fred, of this area.

The history says "the John Englemans greatly prospered" in Collin County, and at one time owned a thousand or more acres of land, much of which is within the city limits of Lucas. They gave each child a good farm. After Mr. and Mrs. J.N. Deal came to the Lucas area they sent their daughters, Virginia and Annie, back to Missouri to college. There Annie met James E. Stratton. He followed her back to Texas and they were married. He was the son of Mr. and Mrs. Robert Stratton of Missouri. Mr. and Mrs. J.E. Stratton's home, a large two-story building in the heart of Lucas, still stands. For years he had a general merchandise store on the same lot, and had other business interests. They were the parents of three children: Elmer, Robert and Margaret. Elmer married Zelma Housewright of Wylie. They have one son, Elmer Jr.

(Mann) who now lives in New York state. Margaret married Gene Biggs of Lucas. They had no children. Robert married Laverne Roper of Anna. To this union were born three sons and two daughters. Two of the sons, Bill and Wayne, live in Allen.

W.D. Petway married Virginia Deal. They were the parents of four sons: Leo J., born March, 1889, died Jan., 1969; Fred I.; Eber G. and Leroy. Eber G. married Pauline Kerby. They had one child, Malcolm Leo. Dr. Malcolm Petway lives in California. Later Eber Petway married Bernice Boren. They had no children and now live in Farmersville. Fred I. Petway married Essie Lee Barry (deceased) of Winningkoff. They had one daughter, Mary Louise, who married Billy Miller of Allen. They live in Lufkin, Texas. Later Fred Petway married Edna Moore of Garland. They had no children. Leroy Petway married Delia Moore of Lucas and have no children and live in Allen.

Mr. and Mrs. John N. Deal were the parents of six children: Annie, Virginia, Ed, Will, John N. Jr. and Roy Deal. All grew up on the Deal farm in the Lucas area. Will Deal married Serilda Snider, daughter of Uncle Bud and Aunt Kate Snider of Lucas. John N. Deal Jr. married Annie Ruble of the Parker area. Ed Deal married Minnie Fitzhugh of Forest Grove. The Fitzhugh family came to this area before the Civil War and one member of the family donated 10 acres of land—the original part of Fitzhugh Cemetery. Roy Deal married Myrtle Walker of this area. The Roy Deals lived on the homeplace here following his father's death and continued to live here for a time after his mother's death. They were the parents of two daughters and a son: Juanita, Dorothy and Walker Eugene. None of the family has lived in this area for years. The Deal farm passed into other hands years ago and the Startton and Petway farms in recent years.

Written by Mrs. John Shipp

Taken from the family history belonging to the Petway family.

JUDGE W.C. DOWDY

W.C. Dowdy was born September 16, 1891 in the Franklin-Bloomdale Community about eight miles northwest of McKinney. His parents moved to McKinney in 1909 to educate their seven children.

W.C. Dowdy graduated from the high school in McKinney, then went to The University of Texas where he earned his LLB Degree in 1916. He was admitted to the Texas State Bar that same year. He

JUDGE W.C. DOWDY, District Court Judge from 1944 to 1964.

attended the historical Inns of Court in London, England in 1919. He practiced law in McKinney from 1916 to 1944.

In 1911-12 he worked in the District Clerk's office and from January 1923 to December 1934 he was assistant and County Attorney for Collin County. He was elected County Chairman of the Democratic Party in 1940-42 and has served as precinct chairman for many years.

On June 1, 1944 he was appointed Judge of the District Court of the 59th district by Governor Coke Stevenson and was re-elected to this office until he retired on December 31, 1964. Since his retirement he has been called upon to hold District Court in many parts of Texas. He is a member of, and past-president of, the Collin County Bar Association, The American Bar, The Texas Bar Association, served as president of the Lion's Club, past post commander of the American Legion, V.F.W., is a Mason, a Shriner, Scottish Rite, and KCCH. He is a veteran of World War I, having served in the Meuse-Argonne Offensive and in the Army of Occupation after the war ended.

He is a member of the Trinity United Presbyterian Church, U.S.A., is on the session, was clerk of the church and session for 32 years, teaches a Sunday School class, and has a perfect attendance record at Sunday School for more than 50 years.

The Paternal grandparents of Judge W.C. Dowdy.

John William Dowdy, born May 24, 1868 in Tennessee, was the son of John Wesley Dowdy, a school teacher in Tennessee. John William Dowdy was a farmer and stockman and in 1880 he and his mother came to Texas to live, settling at Nicholsville (later called Wylie). With him and his mother came his sister, Elizabeth F. Dowdy, who married W.F. Russell of Wylie in 1883. The mother, Sarah G. (Wells) Dowdy, was married three times, first to Mr. Mayes by whom she had three children, Jim, Margaret (married Jim Hall), and Rebecca F. (married George Baxter in 1890). Her second marriage was to Dowdy and from this marriage two children were born. Her third marriage was to Joe Thomason and they had no children. She died February 12, 1897 and is buried in Scott Cemetery.

The maternal grandparents of W.C. Dowdy were: Lucy Jane Foster, his mother, born November 28, 1886 and died February 26, 1940 and lies in the Scott Cemetery. Her father was Robert Henry Foster, who was born in Tennessee on June 3, 1829 and died April 20, 1911 and is also buried in the Scott Cemetery. He was the son of James Foster and Malinda Caroline Scott Foster.

The Foster family came to Texas in 1853 with the James Preston Scott family and the A.J. Taylor family. They all settled six miles northwest of McKinney in the Vineland Community. All were large land owners and farmers, and strong Presbyterians.

Malinda Caroline Scott's father was James Preston Scott, who was born October 23, 1809 in Wilson County, Tennessee and died in McKinney March 13, 1858. Her mother was Jennie Craighead Caruth, born October 6, 1806, and died October 12, 1885. They were farmers and land owners. He was serving in the Texas Legislature at the time of his death.

W.C. Dowdy married Elimy Harrett Gilson on July 5, 1918. She was born in Calvert, Texas and was the daughter of Harry Wilson Gilson, a banker. Her mother was Blanche Clark Gilson, a teacher, (born Oct. 14, 1870 and died April 30, 1944).

Harry Wilson Gilson's mother was Emily Elizabeth Jennings. Her father was Artemus Gumpton Jennings, a native of South Carolina and her mother was Rebecca Pou. William Pou was Rebecca's father and her mother was Elizabeth Glessesdanner of Swiss descent.

Blanche Clark Gilson's father was John N. Clark (1850-1920) of Mariposa, California and her mother was Louisa Jane Riley of Mississippi. His father was John Riley also, an Irishman from Georgia who fought in the Revolutionary War. Her mother was Drusilla Pitts from Pendleton District, South Carolina and her father was Charles Pitts, a Methodist minister.

W.C. and Emily Dowdy had three children,

Eugenia, married to C.E. Graves, Jr., William C. Dowdy, a Dallas attorney, and James R. Dowdy, a Dallas physician.

CAPTAIN JONATHAN STEWART DOWELL

Jonathon Stewart Dowell was born in Smith County, Tennessee on August 22, 1841. He was the son of Willis and Martha Doss Dowell. While still a young boy his parents died and he was reared by his uncle, Frank Dowell, the father of J.P. Dowell a pioneer merchant in hardware in McKinney. The family lived in Wilson County, Tennessee until 1856 when he came to live with Frank Dowell who settled 10 miles southwest of McKinney.

Two years later he went back to Tennessee to be educated and was a student there when the Civil War began. On May 1861 he enlisted at Nashville and served in the Confederate Army until 1865, as a soldier and a prisoner for a time. He was wounded three times, once at the Battle of Seven Pines when he was shot in the arm and the arm was stiff the remainder of his life. The second time he was wounded at the Battle of Fredricksburg, Virginia, and the third time was at the Battle of Gettysburg, Pa. He was wounded and taken prisoner and taken to Johnson Island where he was held for 20 months. At that time he was paroled and started back to join his outfit, but Lee surrendered before he made it back.

The United States government required all soldiers to return to the place of enlistment in order to get transportation home. He made his way to Nashville on foot.

In March of 1866 he returned to Collin County and spent his remaining years as a successful businessman, farmer and stockman. He owned many acres of fine land between McKinney and Lebanon.

In 1869 Capt. Dowell married Ruth Kerr. At the birth of their first child, Ruth died. Later he married Miss E. Williams of Dallas County. Ten children were born to this union; three sons and seven daughters. The children were; John, Tom, Horace, Mrs. W.E. Ditto, Mrs. C.T. Provine, Mrs. Tilman Bryant, Mrs. Conant King, and Ruth Dowell.

The story may be read on microfilmed newspaper at the McKinney Public Library, under the date, August 11, 1924 also: November 26, 1929, April 28, 1927.

THE DOWELL FAMILY

Nehemiah Dowell, (1767-1842), was one of the very early settlers of Virginia who made their way over the mountains to Tennessee when the state was very young. The exact date of the trip is not recorded, but a study of the early settlement of Alexanderia and Liberty in DeKalb County shows that they were settled in 1795 and 1797. There was also a settlement at Brush Creek, Tennessee early enough for Cantrell Bethel of Liberty to constitute a Baptist Church May 2, 1802.

The descendents of Nehemiah Dowell and his wife, Elizabeth Deering Anderson were John, William, James, Elias, Mary, Elisha, Willis, Presley, and Robert. Francis·Dowell married Caroline Doss and they were the parents of J.P. Dowell.

Francis Dowell, father of James P. Dowell, came to Texas in 1865 from Lebanon, Tennessee. He migrated at an early age to Tennessee from Virginia, Forquer County and originally settled close to the city of Dallas, later moving to McKinney. On March 20, 1868 he was married to Ida Sparks and to this union were born the following children, Cora, Francis, Lina, James Wallace, Allie, William Avery, Edward S., Clare, James P., Ida, and Clifton Dowell.

James and his wife spent the first two years of their married life in the big farm house of his parents, Mr. and Mrs. Francis Dowell. When they moved to McKinney Mr. Dowell entered the farm implement business on North Kentucky Street about 1875 and built the J.P. Dowell Hardware Building.

When J.P. Dowell died his four sons, Avery, Ed, Jim, and Clifton carried on the business until 1945 when it sold to Luther Cadenhead.
Story sent by Mrs. Clifton Dowell

THE DUNCAN FAMILY

James Polk Duncan was born November 1, 1844 in Cook County, Newport, Tennessee in what was known as the Borgart Community, on the English Mountains. He was the son of William Duncan and Elizabeth Bates Duncan. He married Elizabeth Mantooth Bryant in Newport, Tennessee May 25, 1865.

At age 17 he enlisted in the Union Army and served throughout the Civil War in Company E., 2nd Tennessee Cavalry in General Grant's army. He served under his brother, 1st Lt. Daniel B. Dun-

can, and was in several battles in Tennessee, as well as the Battle of Vicksburg, Mississippi. He received his discharge at Nashville, Tennessee on July 14, 1865 and returned to Newport.

When he was 22 years old he and his family moved to Texas to live. The family and five other families made the trip in a boat made by William Duncan. The boat was 56 feet long and 16 feet wide. Besides the six families, the boat contained all their household goods, the provisions, and F. Grundy brought a span of mules and others their milk cows and chickens. The six families were Martin N. Lewis and family, F.G. Grundy Lewis family, G. Tucker family, Will Clevenger family, J.P. Duncan family, and the Phil Roberts family.

They started on the French Broad River at Hay's Ferry, then into the Tennessee River, then hay the Ohio River and at last into the Mississippi. They left the Mississippi to go down Red River to Jefferson, Texas where they sold their boat and came overland to Collin County. They joined his father-in-law and family who were already living in the vicinity of Walnut Grove Community. They arrived March 27, 1868. All of these people were neighbors on old Tennessee and they all located six to eight miles west of McKinney. They were Presbyterians and united with the Walnut Grove Presbyterian Church.

J.P. Duncan later bought a farm in the Bowlby Community where his family grew to adulthood and prospered. He was an Odd Fellow and a leader in community life.

The following children were born to this couple: Mary Etta, who married Calvin Hutcherson; Landon Duncan, married Rachel Shelton; R.L. (Bob), married Ellen Hardin (Bob had a twin who died in infancy); Edward Duncan, married Monnie Elmore; Aaron, married Zula Elliot (Aaron had a twin, Will, who died as a young man); James A. Duncan, married Bulah McGarrah; Ray Duncan, married Ethel Lemons; Clay Duncan married Atta McCandless; and Betty married Owen Matthews.

J.P. Duncan and his father-in-law, Aaron Bryant, sat on the first legal murder trial that was held in McKinney, the Belew trial, 1872.

J.P. Duncan and his wife are buried at Pecan Grove Cemetery at McKinney. Both passed away in 1932.

Some of the Collin County members of the family are Mrs. Smith Roberts, S.H. Lemons, Betty Darland, Dan Hutcherson (Plano), and Lucille Ford of McKinney.

THE DUNGAN FAMILY

Martha Jane Beverley was born in 1854 in what was then a small settlement named Dallas. Here her father operated a mill on the Trinity River and served as a peace officer. He had several brothers and sisters who settled in or near Dallas and whose descendents figured prominently in the history of Dallas and Collin Counties. One of them well known in Collin County was Wallace Hughston, longtime resident of Plano and McKinney, an attorney of distinction who also served as State Senator and head of the Masonic Lodge of Texas.

After the death of her parents, Martha Beverley went to live with an aunt in Mississippi and here she married Moses Bill Dungan, a Confederate veteran. They settled in Collin County and became parents of the following children: Robert L., James M., Will A., Mrs. Annie Gibson, Mrs. Stella Drain, and Mrs. Mattie McKinney.

Many of their descendants still live in Collin County. William T. Dungan, Eustace Dungan, C.R. Dungan and Ruth Atterburt are children of Will A. Dungan and live in McKinney. Fred Mc-Kinney, son of Mattie Dungan and George McKinney lives in McKinney. Mrs. Bessie Mae Hatfield is the daughter of Annie Dungan Gibson and lives in McKinney. Joe Dungan lives in Allen.

Submitted by Mrs. W.T. Dungan, McKinney.

THE DYSART FAMILY

The origin of the Dysart Family goes as far back as 874 at the time of the Danish Invasion. Samuel and Frances Anderson Dysart had a home near Londonderry, Ireland which he called Brook Hall. The children were James, Elizabeth, Margaret, Nancy, Fanny, Sarah and Jane. James later came to America working his way to the Holston Valley in Virginia. In 1770 he joined James Knox in the exploration of Tennessee and Kentucky and the two are called by historians "Long Hunters." He was married in 1775 to Nancy Beattie. He served in the Revolutionary War and was badly wounded at the Battle of King's Mountain. After the war he served Virginia in the Legislature. He had three sons and three daughters. His home is still standing in Glade Springs, Virginia and he called it Brook Hall.

Johnston Dysart, fifth generation Dysart, the son of Samuel Dysart, was taken by his family to Missouri when he was 12 years old. He served in both the Kansas War and the Civil War. He was married February 16, 1853 to Mary E. Simmons, daughter of Humphery Simmons an early settler of Kentucky. Thirteen children were born to them, Samuel H., Frances T., Emma, William C., Louis F., Florence, Lulu M. James L., Lallah R., Jack, Maggie, Verna, and Thornton. At the close of the war he found himself deprived of all his property, except one team and with this he went to work rebuilding his life, farming, and teaching. After a number of years of hard work he owned 800 acres of land and a cotton gin.

William Christopher Dysart was born on Old Telephone Road in a house built in 1853 on one of the highest points in Co' n County. The home was always one of much activity since the household consisted of the parents, thirteen children, several slaves, a dairy maid, and always one or two visitors. W.C. and the other children attended school at Mantua, and attending church services at the Christian Church there was a must for the family, who up until that time had been Presbyterians. When William Christopher was older he was sent to school in Bonham and later attended A&M where he was a member of the first graduating class but did not stay to graduate. He married Kitty Miller Renfro at Claude, Texas. Their first son was named Blan Powell for Dr. B.P. Powell, an uncle who was head of the Oklahoma Medical Society. Later twin sons were named Leland Thornton and Lester.

William C. went into business in Bowie and later in Sherman selling farm implements. He returned to his land on Telephone Road and in 1906 built Brook Hall, a beautiful home overlooking the valleys and hills. The home is still occupied by the Dysart Family, Leland and Alice. William was for many years a progressive farmer, delving to find better and more productive ways of farming for Collin County. He died in 1953 and his wife, Kitty, in 1944. Both are buried in the Melissa Cemetery.

Sent by Mrs. Leland Dysart, Brook Hall, Telephone Road, McKinney.

Taken from the McKinney Courier-Gazette, Sunday, November 19, 1972.

THE GOOD LIFE
By Ginny Beverly
Women's News Editor

Within the county there is an enclave that embodies the Jeffersonian ideal, his vision of what the young country he helped to shape sould be. An agrarian society, small shops, local industries, and the independence of land owners who could direct their own destinies as well as those of a decentralized government were superseded in his own day, but the spirit and the dream of building a home, growing food and flowers, sheltering family and friends is still given a few. What else could have brought a successful businessman and his wife, a former debutante, to the country but the tug of that inchoate mixture of blood and bone and soil latent in the human race.

The tug was tentative at first. On the death of Leland Dysart's parents, he and Alice found it easier to live at Brook Hall in order to maintain the place, yet kept their Dallas home for two years before embracing eighteen years ago a way of life that was their common heritage.

They became country squire and his lady in the best sense, engaged in perpetual remodeling of the house, raising sheep, chickens, horses, and entertaining family, friends, and organizations. What woman has a kitchen exactly the way she wants it, everything built by her husband? Converting old dry goods store cases into kitchen cabinets and using scrap lumber, he made a herring bone patterned ceiling, shelving, built a fireplace, laid counter tile, and put down a terrazzo floor. Having left no plan of his plumbing system however, its intricacies provide intermittant surprises.

Entertaining went on apace with the building and gardening. A children's paradise of swimming pool, playground equipment and a climbing tree not only entices nine grandchildren and their friends, but each year provides a unique experience for the kindergarten children of Church of the Incarnation in Dallas, who come to watch the sheep shearing. Last year the Richardson YWCA held their day camp in June, and in appreciation each child signed a bright piece of glass, constructing a brilliant mobile that now hangs in a kitchen window.

Probably the most famous and fitting party occurs on the 4th of July. Starting with family and four couples in their gun club, the celebration of the nation's independence has burgeoned beyond estimation, as friends brought other friends, who in turn invited others. It was this pebble-in-the-pool effect that brought a member of the Channel 13 staff to the extravaganza, and struck by the sheer enjoyment of the host calling the square dance figures, of some 400 people bringing food to add to the barbecue, lemonade, and iced tea prepared at the farm, of visiting, playing, riding, of fireworks on the dam at night, created a program for the station.

The paradox of a message of bucolic independence on the latest medium of mass communication underlines the technological age which is our mixed blessing, covering the earth in concrete and construction. What it underlines even more is that those who are part of the fast-paced modern world recognize their roots and appreciate the actual embodiment of that early American dream.

That the dream works, that the land is not a tax dodge, the house an anachronistic escape, can be illustrated briefly. Last Saturday, one of the grandchildren from Dallas had her birthday party at Brook Hall. The past Monday, after fixing tea for the photographers, Mrs. Dysart prepared for 60-70 Highland Park Junior High School students. They had been studying Washington Irving's THE LEGEND OF SLEEPY HOLLOW, and there would be a trip to an old cemetery nearby, a big bonfire and weiner roast, and acceding to a request, a fortune teller, for which role she donned a ruffled black dress and strings of gypsy beads.

Having studied architecture in college, Mrs. Dysart has had the opportunity to see those carefully drafted plans turn into reality. Deciding to move the location of the front door to another side of the house in order to have a sweeping circular driveway she heard her husband, toiling away on a tractor as he carved out the drive, answer a questioning friend with, ''I'm building a whim.''

What they really built was a world.

ABE ENLOE FAMILY

The Rev. Abe Enloe (a Baptist minister), was the son of Abraham and Sarah Pate Enloe, his father being a native of North Carolina and his mother of Kentucky. Abraham and Sarah were married in Kentucky, moved to Tennessee then to Missouri. When Abe was five years old his parents moved to Texas, arriving in 1850, by ox wagon. They first lived east of McKinney on Pete Fisher's farm then to the Strode homeplace between Ardath and Altoga. Everything was a wilderness when they came in 1850 with nothing but Indians and wild animals. Only 5 families lived east of McKinney at that time. They stayed here 3 years, clearing some ground for a garden to supplement the diet of wild game. In 1857 they moved to what is now the Milligan Community and located on what was known as the Uncle Bill Anderson place. Abe grew to manhood here. Their only neighbors were the J.J. Massies, Burl Massies, and Wiley Druggers. His mother died in 1871 and his father in 1875, both are buried at the old Stiff Chapel graveyard. The couple had 10 children who were Benjamin L.,

ABRAHAM (ABE) ENLOE, pioneer settler of Collin County, 1850, Milligan Community.

who died during the Civil War serving under Jim Reed's Command, J.S., John, Abe, William, Enoch, Mrs. Elizabeth Feagley, Mrs. Jane Anderson, Mrs. Polly Estepp, and Mrs. Sallie Kindle.

Abe was still living at home when the Civil War broke out. His brothers, Benjamin and Joe enlisted, so Abe ran away and rode horseback to the Indian Territory where he enlisted even though he was only 16 years old. When his age was discovered he was sent back home, where he stayed until he was 18, then enlisted in 1863 and served in Co. D. of the 28th Texas Dismounted Cavalry in 1863 under Baxter. At the end of the conflict he was discharged at Hempstead and walked the many miles home in the company of 15 or 20 other soldiers. On November 23, 1865 Abe married Mattie Kindle and to this union were born 8 children, two of whom died in infancy. The children were W.A., J.M., John C., Dove, G.B., and T.B.

When Abe came to Collin County, McKinney was only two years old and he described the houses as being constructed of posts driven into the ground and logs fastened to them for walls. In later years he freighted from McKinney to Jefferson and brought back lumber for the growing town. These were long hard trips with the heavy freight wagons being pulled by oxen. He told of the first cotton gin built in Collin County by Collin McKinney's brother near Van Alstyne. It was built with an inclined wheel with oxen walking up the incline.
Story by Mrs. Wylie Griffin. Complete biography in McKinney paper of June 11, 1921.

DR. JOHN CALEB ERWIN, JR.

Dr. J.C. Erwin Jr., one of McKinney's well known physicians, is the son of Dr. J.C. Erwin Sr. The elder Dr. Erwin came to Collin County from North Carolina in 1884, after graduating from Louisville Medical School. His wife, Evelyn Wilson, came to Texas from Pickens, Mississippi and was married to J.C. Erwin February 17, 1886 by the father of J.C., The Rev. T.W. Erwin, pastor of the Ennis Presbyterian Church. The elder Dr. Erwin served the people of Collin County with untiring devotion all his life and retired late in life. He was followed in medical practice by his son, J.C. Erwin Jr., who, with his partner, Dr. L.J. Hines, have offices on West Virginia Street.

Dr. Erwin was married June 14, 1927 to Annie Malone Barbee of Ripley, Tennessee. They have two daughters, Annie Malone Erwin Christie and Betty Erwin Dunham of Ft. Worth. Each daughter has three children.

Dr. Erwin is a graduate of Washington and Lee University (1918), Lexington, Virginia, and the Texas Medical School at Galveston (1922); he interned at Cleveland City Hospital, Cleveland, Ohio, and had a three year residence at Dallas Medical and Surgical Clinic, Dallas, Texas. He resumed practice of medicine and surgery in McKinney in 1928. He is a Fellow of American College of Surgery (1935) and a member and Elder of the Presbyterian Church.

JACK C. FAUBION
SUPERINTENDENT OF SCHOOLS

The present superintendent of schools, Jack C. Faubion, has served since June of 1968. He has been in the system since 1959 as a teacher, and jun-

JACK C. FAUBIAN, Superintendent of the McKinney Schools.

ior and senior high principal. The Faubions came from Groesbeck, Texas in Limestone County.

Mrs. Faubion, or Eddie, teaches Language Arts in the McKinney Junior High School. There are three children, Jack, Rasie Lynn, and Joe, who have received all or nearly all of their public education in the McKinney schools. Jack is a graduate of Rice University and an accountant in Houston. Rasie Lynn is a senior at Texas University and Joe is a freshman at East Texas State.

The family belongs to the First United Methodist Church and Mr. Faubion is a member of the Lion's Club as well as several professional educational organizations at the state and national level.

THE FINCH FAMILY

Dr. William J. Finch lived in Smith County, Mississippi and graduated from Tulane University in the early 1860s. He fought in the Civil War for the South. Although he was a doctor, he fought side by side with the other soldiers. He was wounded and did not completely recover from the bullet wound he received in his leg. He and his wife and son, H.A. (Henry Arthur) came to Texas after the war. He lived on Bannes Street and I understand often buried money on the premises. He practiced medicine in McKinney and did a great deal of dental work along with his general practice. My father, H.A. Finch, was born in Smith County in 1853 and died in 1934. He attended Swanee University (think that is the way to spell it) from which he graduated in law. Although he never really practiced law, he officed with Judge Dan Garnett and Wallace Hughston in a building where Abernathy Abstract now occupies. He represented this area in the Texas Legislature and was a Senator for two sessions. He was Mayor of McKinney from 1917 to 1925. He was interested in McKinney: he gave the land for Finch Park along with a zoo. He gave ten acres for the Methodist College on Waddill, a junior college which folded up after two years. He served on the school board for a number of years resigning in 1925. His wife, Fanny Finch, was elected to take his place on the school board. Throughout his life he was interested in politics and was a great friend of Joseph Weldon Bailey.

Mrs. H.A. Finch (Fanny Shipe Finch) was born in 1866 in Woodstock, Virginia and was educated in Cleburne, Texas public schools and Irwin College. Prior to her marriage in 1891 to H.A. Finch she taught school in McKinney. She joined her husband in philanthropies such as the Park and College.

She had seven children. In 1917 she became the first woman in McKinney and one of the first in Texas to serve on a school board.. As a member of the board, she not only advocated the advancement of education but she also became involved with the physical well-being of the students. During the depression she prepared and served sandwiches to the unprivileged children at the South Ward School. Because of her love for humanity and her achievements in education the South Ward School PTA and the Southward School were named "Fanny Finch." She died in 1941.

Both my father and mother supported all cultural projects in the community and I can remember years and years ago the active part they took in bringing the Chautauquas to McKinney.
Submitted by Betty Finch Hill

THE FITZHUGH FAMILY

Solomon, Gabriel, and George Fitzhugh were among the first settlers in the vicinity now known as Forest Grove, coming there in 1854. The family had come to Texas in 1844. In 1857 a brother, William, came to join them and he and George started a grist mill on East Fork of the Trinity and called it Fitzhugh Mills. The home later was occupied by J. Ed McGee.

Sol Fitzhugh built a log cabin under a big pecan tree in 1854 and later, when the cabin burned, had lumber hauled overland from Jefferson in East Texas to build a frame house.

In 1846 William Fitzhugh organized a ranger company in Collin County and engaged in campaigns along Red River against the Indians. The following year he organized another company of Rangers.

In 1861 William was commissioned by Jefferson Davis to raise a regiment in Collin County for the Confederacy. He held meetings at his home under the big pecan tree and recruited many men from the county. He moved his headquarters later to McKinney and served the Confederacy as a colonel in the 16th Texas Cavalry.

Fitzhughs who served the Confederacy from that locality were John, George, G.H., and Sol.

Capt. William Fitzhugh had a daughter, Sarah Elizabeth, who married Henry C. Herndon at Melissa in 1871. Indians were invited to the wedding, the first time Indians were invited to a Collin County wedding. A full acount of the wedding is in the microfilmed McKinney Democrat of August

23, 1934 at the McKinney Library. William died at his home near Melissa in 1883.

George Fitzhugh's daughter Frances married Gabe Beck. George married Voltaire Roundtree in 1866.

Many descendents of the Fitzhughs still live in Collin County.

THE FLESHER FAMILY

George Adam Flesher and his two brothers, John and Henry, came to Texas in the year 1880 from Terre-Haute, Indiana. The three brothers bought a farm together in the Mantua area. Later John and Henry sold their interest in the land to George.

George Adam Flesher was married January 18, 1887 to Mary Ellen Portman. They reared a family of five boys and three girls as follows, Mabel Clair, Virgil Ray, Preston Roy, Mamie Ethel, Montrose, Ralph Dewey, Pearl Irene, and Clyde Spenser.

Mabel Clair was first married to Allen Bryant and after his death married Leslie Baker. Virgil Ray was married to Vera Spearman, Preston Roy married Margaret Baker, Mamie Ethel married Leonard Gregory, Ralph Dewey married Linnie Cribs, Pearl Irene married Otho Murphy, Clyde Spenser married Ruby George.

George Adam Flesher and his wife were members of the Methodist Church and both are buried in the Van Alstyne Cemetery as is their son, Virgil Ray Flesher.

Story sent by Clyde Flesher

THE GEORGE WASHINGTON FORD FAMILY

Wash Ford was born January 15, 1821 in Missouri and moved with his parents to Fayette Arkansas in 1837. In 1843 he came to Peter's Colony and settled at Buckner. On August 29, 1844, he was married to Parmelia Langston, step-daughter of George McGarrah, another pioneer settler of Buckner. That same year he headrighted his land one mile southeast of Allen. At the time of his marriage Collin County had not been formed so he had to go back to Bonham for his marriage license. Their marriage was one of the first recorded in Collin County records. The couple farmed their headright on Mustang Branch, near where Allen was later to be. They built their log cabin near a spring of water. Among those coming to Texas with him were William Rice, George McGarrah, John

Graham, Joe Stover. Wash Ford took his turn with other settlers who formed groups to stand guard against any surprise Indian Raid, for there had been several at that time and all settlers kept guns ready. He helped bury the Muncey family who were all killed near Rowlett Bridge on Old Highway 5 between McKinney and Dallas.

Ford made the long trip to California during the gold rush of 1849. He went with Jack McGarrah, Tola Dunn, and Tom McDonald who joined a party of 150 men at Ft. Worth. He returned to McKinney by steamer from San Francisco. Cholera broke out on shipboard and about 200 men died and were buried at sea. When the ship reached Panama the remaining men walked across to the other side and took another ship to New Orleans, then by stage coach back to McKinney. He served with the Confederate forces, a member of Captain Ned Chambers Company.

Eleven children were born to the Ford family, Wilburn, Tobe, George, Jim and Stanley. Their daughters were Jane Groeman, Irene Chapman, Caroline Green, Mary Warrengton, Harriett Gulledge, and Ida Thomason. Mr. Ford died in March of 1904 at the age of 83 years and Mrs. Ford died in 1885 at age 54. The family of Jim Ford have owned the old headrighted place until 1966 when they sold all but a few acres to W.E. (Pete) Ford, the youngest son of Jim and Marzie Berry Ford. Other Jim Ford's children are Augusta Angel, Mindie Strain, Shelley Ford, Berry Ford, Irene Boren, and Ruby Ruyle.

Sources:
Capt. Hall's notes taken from old McKinney papers.
A letter from Augusta Ford
Angel of Plano.
(A descendent)

THE GANTT FAMILY

About fifty miles north of Liverpool, located in what has been said to be the most beautiful area of all England is Lancaster. Extending eastward from Lancaster is the wild moorland sweeps of the Pennine Range of mountains at the foot of which is the boundary between Lancaster and Yorkshire.

John O'Gaunt, Duke of Lancaster lived in the John O'Gaunt Castle which has to this day a portion of its most important feature still intact and is used by Law Courts. It has a very wide gate leading into the castle ground and was called John

O'Gaunt's Castle Gateway.

Near the castle is St. Mary's Church which possesses remarkable 14th Century Oak Stalls said to be the finest example of English woodwork of that period.

John O'Gaunt (1310-1399) was the fourth son of Edward III and father of Henry IV. Thomas Gaunt, Edward Gaunt, and Richard Gaunt of England were descendants of Henry IV.

Thomas Gaunt Jr., son of Thomas Gaunt Sr., landed at White Landing, Prince George County, Maryland in 1654. He was followd by his father in 1660. Other relatives came to America also about this time.

Different spellings of the same original surname are a common occurrence. On arriving in America the name Gaunt was changed to Gantt, Gant, Gauntt or Gantte.

Reverend Edward Gantt, a descendant of Thomas, married Ann Sloss and moved to Louisville, Kentucky. His son, Dr. Edward Sloss Gantt, married Sarah Smith and moved to Molten, Alabama where his son, Dr. John Clement Gantt, was born. Dr. John Clement Gantt married Jennie Hardin at Jackson, Arkansas and practiced medicine at Arkadelphia, Arkansas for a while before moving to Texas near the town of Kaufman, a few miles southeast of Dallas.

Dr. John C. Gantt had ten children. Of these, three moved to Collin County. They were Laura Jennie Gantt, Susan Gantt and Mort Couts Gantt. Frank Wheeler, a Methodist minister and a son of Sally Gantt, married Thirza Lovell from Farmersville, Texas who is now ninety years old and living in Blanton Gardens, Dallas, Texas.

Laura Jennie Gantt and Susan Gantt, daughters of Dr. J.C. (John) Gantt met and married two brothers from Collin County, Henry and Elmer Wallis, who lived northeast of McKinney. They settled on adjoining farms and lived there until their death. The area is known as Wallis Chapel, located between Melissa and Stiff Chapel.

Laura Jennie Gantt Wallis and Henry Orman Wallis had five children. They were Oma, Mortie, Effie, Willie and Alta Wallis. Two surviving daughters are: Effie Wallis Roberts and Alta Wallis Estes, who still live in the Wallis Chapel community.

Susan Gantt married Elmer Wallis. At the death of her mother, Susan took her young brother, Mort Couts Gantt, to live with her. Her father, Dr. J.C. Gantt, also spent part of his last years with her. Mort Couts was about five years of age when his mother died and nine when his father died. Susan and Elmer were always looked on as grandparents by Mort Couts' children. Susan Gantt Wallis was an excellent cook. Elmer usually raised ten to fifteen hogs a year to slaughter. He always had an orchard and an excellent garden. It was always fun to visit them as Elmer was a great talker, constantly joking and full of life.

Elmer and Susan Wallis had two children, Ora and Randolph. Randolph fell in love with a cousin, Jennie Gantt, who died suddenly. Randolph was never interested in anyone else. He died a bachelor in 1965. Ora Wallis married Laurence Martin and they had one daughter, Ora Anise, who married Millard Lacy and moved to Lubbock, Texas. She died in 1972 leaving two daughters.

While Mort Couts was living with Susan and Elmer Wallis, he met and married Lillie Florence Wilson who lived with her brother, Thomas M. Wilson. She was teaching school with her brother Thomas at that time just a mile or so south of Wallis Chapel at Wilson or Big Viney School.

When one thinks of the Gantts of Collin County, you cannot get away from the Wilson family. Henry and Elmer Wallis' mother was a Wilson, the sister of Uncle Gus Wilson, the well known eccentric bachelor of Collin County who gave away many cars, etc. He offered to send Couts Gantt through school but he married Lillie Wilson instead. Lillie Wilson Gantt's father was Adam Teel Wilson. Adam Teel lived in Murphysboro, Illinois. He was married three times. In the first marriage there were three children: only one, Thomas M. Wilson, survived. He was the father of Paul K. Wilson who lives in McKinney, Texas.

In his second marriage there were three children and only one survived, John Wilson. His daughter, Leona Waters, and step-daughter, Pearl Furr, presently live in McKinney, Texas.

In the third marriage there were three children and again only one child survived, Lillie Florence Wilson, who married Mort Couts Gantt.

Thomas M. Wilson, who had graduated from Prairie View Normal School near Cairo, Illinois; Charlie Thompson (the first editor of McKinney Examiner) and a Mr. Pierce who settled at Pilot Point, Texas, walked to Texas to seek their fortune. One evening they came to a farmhouse about six miles northeast of McKinney and after knocking asked a lady at the door if three tramps could ask for food and shelter for the night. "No, I have no room for tramps, but three nice young men can find a wash basin, water, soap, and towel behind the house on a shelf. Wash up, and be ready. Supper's almost ready to put on the table." This they gladly did and eight years later Thomas M. Wilson came back to the community and married her daughter, Jennie Wilson who was only nine years old when he had stopped there originally.

After Tom and Jenny were settled, his brother, John, some cousins, Walter B. and Alfred Wilson, came to Texas. Another cousin, Matilda (Cousin Mattie), sister of Walter B. and Alfred, and husband Webb Bagwell also came to Collin County.

After Adam Teel Wilson's third wife was buried he brought his young daughter to join his sons, Thomas and John. He started a restaurant and hotel business on the southeast corner of the square in McKinney, Texas.

Lillie Wilson lived with her brother, Tom, and wife, Jennie, until she met and married the quiet dignified well-read young, Couts Gantt. Tom and Jennie were also looked upon as grandparents by Couts and Lillie Gantt's children.

Written by E.L. Gantt, a teacher in Collin Co. for many years.

JIMMIE GEIGAS

Jimmie Geigas, first young man from Collin County to be killed in World War I, was born and grew up in the Noyes Community northeast of McKinney. Before the war he worked for Giles McKinney. At the outbreak of the war, he trained at Camp Travis in San Antonio and served overseas in the 259th Infantry of the 90th Division. On September the 12th, 1918 American soldiers began their first offensive and were involved in the Battle of St. Mihiel. During a lull in the fighting the men were all wishing for water to drink. Jimmie Geigas and Jack Campbell took canteens from the men of the company and went back to a spring they had seen in a small town. Coming back, on a public road, a German plane came over dropping bombs. As it swooped down over them, Campbell dived into a ditch and was saved, but Jimmie Geigas was killed, the first casualty from Collin County. His body was returned to McKinney and services were held in his memory. He left one sister, Miss Edna Geigas. He died September 15, 1918.

The American Legion in McKinney took his name and it is called the Jimmie Geigas Post of the American Legion.

Source: Microfilmed Daily Courier-Gazette. June 24, 1921.

THE GEORGE FAMILY

Lucas George, born in Virginia in 1805, was orphaned when both his father and mother died on their way to Tennessee to settle. He grew up in Wilson County, Tennessee near Lebanon and there met and married Nancy Forbess, the daughter of Tennessee pioneers, Arthur and Rachel (Carruth) Forbess. The young couple farmed until 1856 when they decided to move to Texas in a covered wagon. Other families came at the same time, Frank Dowell, Col. Ed Chambers, and others. In 1858 Lucas George bought a tract of land from Paschal H. and Martha H. Rice. The land lay northwest of McKinney in what was later called the Vineland Community. They were members of the Vineland Christian Church. With them on the trip from Tennessee were their seven children. Later an eighth child was born in Collin County. Their children were Elizabeth Jane (1842), Jeremiah W. (1845), Permelia (1847), Arthur (1850), Thomas Alexander (1851), Mary Rachel (1855), and Cantrell Francis (1861).

Elizabeth Jane married James E. Carruth and were the parents of three children, Charles Carlton, Theodosia, and Nola.

Charles C. Carruth married Minnie Ann Helms and they were the parents of eight children, Jessie, Levi, Lela, Georgia, Nova Howell and Creek Carruth, both living in Weston.

Theodosia Carruth married B.A. Comer, a Weston Druggist and they were the parents of four children, Ella B., Stella Comer Taylor, William, and Agnes Comer Snelson.

Jeremiah George was a Confederate soldier, and drowned in East Fork Creek as he returned from a mission to Bonham.

John H. George married Sarah Ann Reed and made their home northwest of Weston. They were the parents of two children, neither of whom lived past youth. They reared a nephew, James A. Reed, who married Susie McNew and were the parents of three children, Leland, Royce, and J.W.

Parmelia George married R.W. Weaver and had ten children, Annie E. Weaver Welch, Mary Jaje Weaver Babb, William R., Ida Weaver Jenkins, George W., Eva Weaver Roark, Houston A., John, Jesse, and Margie May.

Arthur Forbes George married Mrs. America Hightower Carruth and they had two children, Vernor who married Ella Speck, and Callie who married Milton A. Wells.

Thomas Alexander George married Frances Jane Reed and made his home northeast of Weston. They were the parents of three children, Viola George, William Dennie George who married Rhonda H. Baker, of Weston. They were the parents of two daughters, Mrs. Frank May Hix, and Mrs. Ruby George Flesher who lives in Howe, Texas.

Mary Rachel George married Jo Abb Alexander and made their home in Brown County.

Cantrell Francis George married Jennie Nixon and they were the parents of six children, Lula, Walter, Mary Nancy Pane, Allie F. Rucker, Roy Lucas George, Oscar George. After his wife's death Cantrell Francis George married Martha Minerva Driver and they were the parents of eight children, Eva Ethel Miller who lives in Van Alstyne, Abbie Crosswhite of Celina, Iva J. Miller of Van Alstyne, Tom R. George, Lawrence George now living in Dallas, Infant, Hattie May Cunningham living in Gunter, and Edgar George living near Celina.

Lucas George has hundreds of descendents in Collin County and Texas.

GRAHAM—SIMMONS FAMILY

James H. Graham, born in South Carolina, came to Texas in 1845, settling first in Rusk County where he operated a grist mill and tannery. James H. and Mary Jane Graham were the parents of the following children, William Lafayette (Feb. 16, 1833), Prudence Ann (April 26, 1842), Matilda (1845), Lucinda (1847), James H. Jr. (1850), and E.A. (1850). James H. Graham was a good businessman and amassed a sizable fortune before his death in 1869, when he fell from the mill wheel and was fatally injured.

William L. worked with his father in the grist mill and tannery until the Civil War, when he and his brother-in-law, Sharp R. Whitley, joined a group known as the New Salem Invincibles which became Company F. of the 7th Regular Texas Cavalry. Whitley had married Prudence Ann in 1860. The two young men later served in Sibley's Brigade. After the war W.L. returned home and married Sarah Simmons, daughter of James Simmons who had come to Texas from North Carolina and his wife, Edith Arminda Sparks Simmons.

The family of Edith Sparks came to Texas from Mississippi with Austin's Colony, settling near Palestine. This family gave land for the first Baptist Church built in Texas. The church was actually organized in Illinois because Mexico, which claimed Texas, prohibited Protestants from organizing churches in Texas. It was organized in July of 1833 by Elder Daniel Parker, then the entire flock moved to Austin's Colony where they arrived November 12, 1833. The first recorded meeting was January 20, 1834.

James and Edith Arminda Sparks Simmons moved to Collin County in 1859 settling near Forest Grove where they helped to organize the Old Orchard Gap Primitive Baptist Church and James Simmons was its first minister.

William L. Graham, following his marriage, worked in the grist mill until moving to Collin County in 1867 where he settled near Luca, then called Old Willow Springs. They were the parents of Martha Graham (August 8, 1866), Elvira Pettus (Nov. 6, 1868), Cleopatra (August 24, 1870), George William (Nov. 22, 1872), James Lafayette (October 1, 1974), Eady Arminta (May 10, 1877), Martha married J. Allen Biddy and moved to Oklahoma, Elmira married William Thomas Newsome, a well known Baptist minister of Collin County. The Newsomes were the parents of seven children, William, Clyde, Dr. Asa, Cecil, Alta, who taught music in Collin County for years, Georgia and Amy, both teachers, in Ft. Worth. Cleopatra married William P. Biddy. James L. married Ruth Cook. James L. lived in the homeplace until his death in 1947. He was the father of three sons, James Leo, who married Jessie Armstrong, Eustace Earl married Louise Anderhub, Eunice married Virgil Richards, and Willie who married Joyce Ballew.

James Simmons died April 16, 1879 and his wife March 2, 1897. William L. Graham died Nov. 3, 1882 and his wife, Sarah Simmons Graham, on Nov. 26, 1903. All are buried in Fitzhugh Cemetery at Forest Grove about ten miles southeast of McKinney.

THE CHARLEY GRAVES FAMILY OF CULLEOKA

Charley Graves (November 10, 1884-1961) was born in Graveston, Knox County, Tennessee, the son of William H. Graves, and came to Princeton with his parents and one sister, Bertha, in 1890. The family settled on a farm just east of Culleoka. His mother died in 1892 and lies in the Higgins Cemetery. Later his father married a widow (formerly Emma Renfro) who had two children. Six more children were born to them, including twin girls. In 1900 when Charley was only 16 his father died and he took on the responsibility of rearing the large family. He was active as a member and officer of the Culeoka Lodge of the Woodmen of the World, served on the County Road Committee, and the Culleoka School Board for a number of years.

In 1915 he married Lectie Campbell, daughter of the late Charles T. Campbell, whose family came to Princeton from Woodbury, Tennessee. Their marriage ceremony was a double ceremony along with Mr. and Mrs. Dick Young of Culleoka, with the Rev. Abe Enloe. They lived on their farm a mile southwest of Culleoka. They were the parents of three children: Wayne, 1917; Charles Cliffird, 1919; and Strelsa (Pat), 1921. The couple retired in Princeton in 1933.

They are buried in the Princeton Cemetery. Wayne and Charles now live in Garland, while Strelsa, married to Joe McGraw, lives in Colorado Springs, Colorado. Joe is the son of Lawrence and Kate long time residents of Princeton and Culleoka.
Written by:
Wayne E. Graves

THE GRAY FAMILY
Written by Mrs. John Shipp
As reported by
Earl and Musa Gray Cook

Joe B. Gray came to Collin County from Alabama as a young man in 1887. His father, William S. Gray followed him in 1890. Other members of the family came in 1893. All settled in South Collin Co. Joe B. Gray married Miss Tennie Eldridge of near Plano. He and his family came to Lucas area in 1907. Mr. and Mrs. Joe B. Gray were the parents of seven children: J.B. Jr., Clarence, Roy E. Foyd K., Musa, Mable and Bernice. All the children attended the Lucas school.

J.B. Jr. married Lilly Anderson of Wylie; Clarence married America Snider and they continued to live in Lucas for a time. Roy E. married Miss Tillie Williams of Allen; Floyd K. married Annis Boyd of Allen. (He is a member of a quartet in Dallas and is a radio and TV personality.) Musa married Earl Cook, son of Mr. and Mrs. J.W. Cook of Lucas. Mr. and Mrs. Earl Cook own and live on part of the farm which belonged to his grandfather, Johnathon H. Cook, early-day settler of the Lucas area. The Earl Cooks have a daughter, Erin, who lived in Lucas until her marriage to Joe Henry Leach of Allen. They now live in McKinney. They have one son, Larry, who lives in Houston. Mable Cook married Joe Knight (deceased) of this area. They have one daughter , LaVerne. Mrs. Knight lives in Garland. Bernice Cook married Clyde Biggs of Lucas. Most of

their married life was spent in Denton Co. After Clyde's death Bernice returned to Lucas and established a home near her sister, Mrs. Earl Cook, where she lived until her death in April, 1963. They were the parents of four children, none of whom lived in Lucas.

Mrs. Earl Cook died Dec. 11, 1973.

THE GRAY FAMILY

The Gray family were very early settlers in Collin County. Joseph Ross Gray and his wife Olivia Allison Gray filed on land in 1853. The land survey still carries his name and is the Joseph R. Gray Survey. Adjoining that is the survey filed on by his brother, James A. Gray.

There is a family tradition or story that when the Grays were first living on their land west of McKinney the Indians were very troublesome in the early 50s. Once an alarm was sent out to run to the fort for the Indians were on the warpath. Olivia Gray was busy making her soap, doing the boiling in the fireplace inside the house. She sent the family on and insisted on staying behind to finish the soap. The Indians came and began attacking the house. Olivia grabbed an old dipper and began throwing boiling soap at the Indians, driving them away and so saved herself and her house.

The Grays were one of the 31 families who settled near the present community of Foote, in the Grays Branch Community. Joseph Ross Gray was one of the earliest surveyors of the county.

Dr. J.B. Wright and his family moved to the community from Hardinsville, Illinois in 1876. Dr. Wright, who had been a surgeon in the Civil War, bought 1,000 acres of land just north of where Culleoka now stands. His daughter, Lillian, married R.L. Gray. In 1887 Dr. Wright was elected to the Texas Legislature to represent Collin County. His sons were Dr. E.F. Wright of Royce City, Dr. James B. Wright of Weatherford, L.N. and W.W. Wright also of Royce City.

Mrs. Lillian Wright Gray was a 1871 graduate of Sam Houston Normal Institute of Huntsville and taught her first school at the Hobbins School house in 1891, receiving a salary of $35. per month, out of which she paid $10. a month for room and board. She later taught at Longneck School.

The Wright family moved from the Culleoka Community in 1887 to the "Illinois Community" which later became Climax. They are buried in the old Van Winkle Cemetery near Climax. Elizabeth Higgins, wife of Dr. James B. Wright was also a school teacher, having taught in Illinois during the Civil War. She was the daughter of John Arnold Higgins and wife, Ruthie Ann Martin Higgins of Crawford County, Illinois.

This biography written by Mrs. Anna Gray Davis of Royce City, Texas

THE JOHN F. GREER FAMILY

John F. Greer, founder of the town of Anna, was born March 17, 1850 in Waverly, Alabama. John was one of the eight children of Joseph Greer, a planter. In 1870 John settled at Old Mantua and operated a farm there for several years. In 1878 he went back to Alabama and married Laura Ellis. With the coming of the railroad Mantua was moved from its location to a more convenient one on the railroad. John F. had the first house in the new town of Anna and was always a leader in helping to develop the town. He operated the first store in Anna, served as its mayor, postmaster, and in his private life was a member of the Presbyterian Church and a Mason. John F. and Laura Greer reared eleven children, six sons and five daughters—Thomas E., Baxter D., James H., William Bryan, and his daughters were Mrs. James McMahan, Mrs. Herman Rutherford, Mrs. Lee Mitchell, Laura Mae, and Anna Lou who was the first child born in the new town of Anna and she was given its name.

Complete biography, McKinney Daily Courier-Gazette, Aug. 19, 1924. Microfilmed at the McKinney Public Library.

JOHN FLETCHER GRIFFITH FAMILY

John Fletcher Griffith was born about 1811 in Tennessee and was married to Edith Elvira Morrill who was born in Tennessee in 1814. Both died in Collin County and are believed to be buried in the Snow Hill Cemetery near Blue Ridge. The family came to live in Collin County in 1861 with their daughter's family, the Sam McKinneys. Their children were: William W. Griffith who married Crissy, the widow of Henry Echols, Clarisy E. married Dixon, Addiver died unmarried, and Virginia who married Samuel McKinney.

HAGGARD

The Haggard family originated in Denmark, migrated to England, then came to America. James Haggard who had been educated for the ministry came to America in 1698, landing at Norfolk, Virginia. Here he married and had 4 sons. Nathaniel (November 21, 1723) married Elizabeth Gentry and settled in Kentucky in the Bush Settlement. They had seven sons and three daughters.

John Haggard, third son of Nathaniel and Elizabeth Gentry Haggard (April 7, 1754—February 9, 1832) was born in Virginia and married Mary Shepard. They moved to Kentucky and were the parents of 8.

John Haggard, the 3rd son of John and Mary Shepard Haggard, (March 17, 1794 - December 11, 1858) married Mouring Quisenberry and they became parents of 5 sons and 4 daughters. He was a planter and prominent in church affairs, being a member of the Unity Church.

Clinton Shepard Haggard, youngest son of John and Mourning Quisenberry Haggard (November 12, 1838-June 30, 1930) was born in Winchester, Kentucky. His mother died when he was eight years old and when he was 18, he and his father came to Texas and settled on a section of land near Plano. September 1, 1859 he married Nannie Kate Lunsford and they became the parents of 9 children. When the Civil War began Clint Haggard joined Confederate forces and served in Alexander's Regiment and later in Martin's Regiment. After the war he returned to his home and became a successful landowner and stockman. In 1904 he gave each of his children 320 acres of land and retained farms in Collin and Denton County. Both he and his wife were members of the Christian Church and contributed liberally to the Church and church related universities and homes. Both are buried in Restland Cemetery after having been moved from the old Bethany Cemetery.

Mary Catherine, eldest child of Clint and Nannie Kate Haggard (May 30, 1861-March 26, 1943), married J.W. Shepard December 30, 1880 and they became parents of three sons and three daughters.

Bessie Shepard (March 31, 1884) married Leslie Shelton June 7, 1906. They had one son, Robert Leslie Shepard. Theodore Shepard (August 5, 1884-November 7, 1973) married Bernice Gale March 4, 1909. Two of their three children died young. Rogene was married to Dr. Gerlad Wagner August 13, 1915.

Nannie Elizabeth, daughter of Clint and Nannie Kate Haggard, (February 24, 1863-November 15, 1954) married James Baxton Newsome of McKinney, November 2, 1882. They had one daughter, Lottie Kate (1885-1915). After Mr. Newsom's death, Nannie Haggard married Thomas Conner Bishop December 31, 1891. He was formerly mayor of Paris, Texas. To this union three children were born, Clinton Conner, Gladys, and Mary Elizabeth. Connie Bishop (January 29, 1896-December 27, 1972) married first Dora Witherspoon then Dorothy Greer, whose son, William he adopted. Later he married Norma Hess.

Gladys Bishop (May 29, 1901)—second child of Nannie and Tom Bishop, married Frederick Harrington October 8, 1919. Their two sons were Joseph Hunter and Frederick Conner, who was elected Mayor of Plano in 1970. Gladys had the distinction of having the City of Plano name their new library the Gladys Harrington Library because of her many years of dedicated work in establishing a library for Plano.

Mary Elizabeth Bishop was born May 3, 1903 and on January 16, 1923 was married to Edgar Howard Bush. Their daughter, Nancy Lou Bush, is married to Tucker Frazer Morian.

John William Haggard (December 23, 1865-August 30, 1937) married Hallie Fletcher November 18, 1885. Their six children were: Clyde (January 20, 1890-October 2, 1958) married Beatrice Daffron November 28, 1909. They are the parents of three daughters, Marguerite, Hallie Maude, and Quincy Pearl. Clint (January 20, 1890-September 5, 1967) married Quincy Scott December 1, 1915. Their son, Dr. Scott Haggard was born July 17, 1925.

Ray Haggard (July 10, 1893)-married Jessie Dean November 11, 1920. Their son, John Yates is the fourth John Haggard in direct line from Nathaniel Haggard.

Jennie Jackson Haggard (December 17, 1896-October 12, 1912). Walter Dewey Haggard (September 14, 1898-March 28, 1967) married Florrie Bowman September 21, 1921 and became the parents of two daughters, Mae Lott and Florrie Kate.

Martha Kate Haggard (July 2, 1907) married Edward Cullen Allen September 6, 1927. Their children are Annette and Mary Kate. Jennie Lee Haggard, daughter of Clint and Nannie Kate Haggard, (July 19, 1868-September 9, 1958) married George Albert Ray June 22, 1892 and became the parents of Haggard, Mary Katherine, Romayne, George Jr. and Dorothy.

Clint Haggard Ray (August 4, 1895) married Monna Bates, June 28, 1922.

Mary Katherine Ray (November 29, 1896) married Dr. S.F. Harrington May 10, 1921. Their children are Dr. Ray Harrington and Mary Katherine (Kay) Harrington.

Romayne born September 12, 1900, died Sep-

MR. AND MRS. C.S. HAGGARD.

tember 12, 1941. George Albert Ray (August 27, 1903—September 1972) married Paulyn Gardner and they adopted a son, Trace.

Dorothy Ray (September 17, 1909) married Lillard Lewis of Washington, D.C. November 14, 1931. Their children are Millard Lewis Jr., George Ray, and Dorothy Lewis.

Annie Belle Haggard, daughter of Clint and Nannie Kate Haggard, (June 6, 1873-September 5, 1969) married James Shelton Aldridge November 15, 1893. Their children are Minnie Lee, Katherine, James Clinton, and Emma Ruth.

Emma Frances Haggard, daughter of Clint and Nannie Kate Haggard, was born September 15, 1870. She married William Preston Bishop August 11, 1896 and after his death in 1901 she returned to her parents' home to live.

Walter Owen Haggard, youngest son of Clint and Nannie Kate Haggard (March 9, 1880-May 8, 1956) married Rosa Rice March 8, 1905. Their children are Clifton, Irene, Clint Shepard, Emajean, and Walter Owen Jr.

THE FAMILY OF
GOV. DAVID HALL OF OKLAHOMA

The first of this Hall family arrived in Copeville in 1880. The Rev. G.M. Hall was born in Maury County, Tennessee, April 29, 1846 and died at Copeville March 30, 1931. He married to Nancy Bishop at Enterprise, Tennessee February 1, 1870 by the Rev. J.W. Howard. After settling in Copeville community, the family farmed and the father, a Presbyterian minister, rode the circuit of the community churches in a radius of 15 miles from Copeville.

Ten children were born to this union: Mary E.

DAVID HALL, former Governor of Oklahoma, a descendant of pioneers of the Copeville Community.

Hall (1870), W.A. Hall (January 18, 1872), J.W. Hall (September 6, 1873), Susie M. Hall (November 29, 1875), N.L. Hall (March 7, 1877), M.D. Hall (December 28, 1879), G.M. Hall Jr. (December 31, 1882), A.F. Hall (January 5, 1886), J.M. Hall (March 1, 1887), B.B. Hall (May 1, 1890). All of these children are now deceased.

David Hall, now serving as Governor of Oklahoma, is a great grandson of George M. Hall Sr., the grandson of William A. Hall and the son of William A. Hall Jr.

Information sent by:

Mrs. Nell Hall Beggs, daughter of George M. Hall Jr.

William A. (Rad) Hall
3715 N. Chicago Street
Oklahoma City 73112

HALL

Another early family in this area was the Gabrial Hall family. Mrs. Hall was the former Susan Wright of this area. They were the parents of six children: Homer, married Myrtle Wyall of Royce City; Iza, married Dick Snider of Lucas; Annie, married George Kerr of Forest Grove; Cassie, married Robert Parr of Lucas; Myrtle, married Drew Enloe; Mable Hall deceased. Of the children Cassie, Mrs. Bob Parr, is still in Lucas.

STUART HOLLAND HALL

Stuart Holland Hall (Steve) was born January 15, 1855, the son of John Wesley and Elizabeth Holland Hall. He was born on one of his father's steamships that plied up and down the Tennessee River and his mother died at his birth. He survived by being nursed and cared for by "Aunt Nancy Hall," one of his father's slaves. He was one of the thirteen children his father had by two marriages. When the Civil War came, life was hard for those left at home. He recalled that the only diet the people of the Cumberland Mountains of his area had for more than a year was dried black-eyed peas obtained when a Yankee boat loaded with the peas was captured on the river.

Rumors of the plenty that existed in the new land of Texas interested most of the young people of Tennessee and like many others, young Steve set out for the new frontier on December 19, 1874. He stayed with an uncle for a while in Little Rock, Arkansas, then came to Texarkana where he worked for a while in a big saw mill. When a big explosion in the mill killed some of the workers, he moved on and came to his Uncle Abe Hall's home near McKinney. He went to work for Isaac Graves and in 1880 married the granddaughter of J.B. Wilmeth, Princess Annie Thompson, and the young couple went to live on the Graves ranch west of town. The next year J.B. Wilmeth gave them land joining his so they could be near him and his aging wife. While their home was being built, their first child, Roy F. Hall, was born in the Wilmeth home. Steve and "Sannie," as she was called, were the parents of five children, Roy Franklin Hall, Artie, Ora, (now Mrs. J.D. Craft Sr. of 110 Bradley Street in McKinney), Sue Hall Walker, now living in California, and Nugent who died following World War I of injuries sustained in the war.

The family cleared the land of its great forest trees and farmed it until 1907 when the newly built interurban track cut through the middle of the farm. No longer happy with the cut up farm, they sold and moved to the newly established town of Crystal City, the winter garden region of South Texas. Once more the family lived in pioneer conditions, helping a new town to get started.

Princess Annie Hall died in San Antonio on her 56th birthday, Dec. 9, 1916 and is buried there. After her death, Steve came back to McKinney to live.

Stuart Hall died in 1944 at the age of 89 years. He is buried in Pecan Grove Cemetery beside his son, Roy F. Hall.

SAM HARRIS

SAM HARRIS WON FAME AS ONE OF BIGGEST MEN IN THE WORLD

From The *Farmersville (Collin Co.), Texas, Times*
Thursday, May 24, 1973

(EDITOR'S NOTE: The following story about Sam Harris ran in the Nov. 10, 1966 issue of The Times. All of the copies of that issue were sold to readers who wanted to keep the story and pictures among their souvenirs. The Times has had numerous requests since then for copies of the story and picture, and so they are being repeated in this Centennial and Progress edition. The story was taken from the Dallas Times Herald of March 30, 1924.)

Texas has always been proud of her big men. And that is why Texas is proud of Sam Harris of this county. Sam has the distinction of being, not only the biggest man in the state, but the largest in the nation. He tips the beams at 692 pounds and swears that he is "still gainin'." But his avoirdupois is not all fat as might be supposed. Sam is solid as a rock, according to those who know him intimately, and is as powerful as a team of oxen. He admits that he "can lift anything that is loose at both ends," and has come pretty near demonstrating that he is right on more than one occasion. Years ago when he was city marshal of Farmersville, the town was visited by a disastrous fire. Entering one of the threatened buildings he pushed a safe, weighing a ton, out onto the sidewalk without assistance. The next day it took two of the largest horses in town to return the safe to the spot from which he had moved it. Passing the scene of the fire the next day, Sam saw another safe, which was no small one, lying in the wreckage and debris. "Wisht I had of seen that one yesterday," he drawled. "I'd a put her in my vest pocket and toted her out."

Has Jolly Disposition

Sam Harris, according to his friends, is just a big, happy-go-lucky boy, always jolly and full of fun. He refuses to take anything seriously and enjoys a more or less indolent existence as he says "work don't agree with me no how." He owns a beautiful farm, two miles south of Farmersville, and spends his winters there. In the summer he packs his grip, which is in reality a steamer trunk, and tours the country with a carnival company.

He has his special attendant, a regular "man Friday," who caters to his every need, and spends the day "jollying" the more fragile and unfortunate mortals who clink silver into the coffers of his

SAM HARRIS at 692 pounds.

manager to enter the tent and take a peep at him.

But Sam admits that life has its little inconveniences. He is getting so heavy on his feet he finds it difficult to "get about" much. Most of his traveling is done in a specially built buggy drawn by a team of white mules. He has a Ford car but he had to abandon it because he said it was too much trouble to put the top down every time he wanted to get in or out. Then, too, he found the going rather rough as the springs would sag until the body rested on the axles when he was aboard and every bump in the road was transmitted directly to him. "It is kind of cramped riding in the back seat alone, too," he says. At home Sam has his furniture made to order, but when he goes visiting he has many difficulties to overcome.

Has To Sleep On Floor

"I can get pretty comfortable," he says, "by placing two chairs together and sitting in them, but I haven't yet found a bed that will bear my weight. Usually I put a mattress on the floor and place a chair under my head so I won't lie down flat. It chokes me to lie flat of my back."

On the road Sam has to overcome all kinds of difficulties. "I can manage to get about in a chair car pretty well," he says, "but these dern smoking rooms with their narrow passages and dining cars, where you have to crawl through a narrow alley alongside the kitchen, have about banned me from these kind of coaches. Sometimes I have a pretty tight squeeze getting in through the vestibules in the chair cars, too."

Climactic changes have very little effect on Sam and he explains it in a novel way. "I guess I am so big it takes all summer to get hot through and all winter to cool off, so I don't bother much," he says.

Sam eats as much at one sitting as the average man would eat at six and friends declare that in the pre-Volstead days an attempt to fill him up on beer was like pouring it into a hole in the ground. He never did get full, they say.

Has Coffin Built

Although in perfect health and a true optimist, Sam stepped into the Stringer Undertaking company's establishment in Greenville recently and ordered a coffin for himself. "Just want to play safety first," he explained. It is the largest casket ever built and will easily accommodate four average men. It is 6 feet 6 inches long, 36 inches deep, 38 inches wide and weighs 576 pounds. Sam weighs 692, the coffin 576 and the box in which it is placed 250 pounds, a total of 1,518 pounds.

"There isn't a hearse big enough for that coffin," the undertaker told him after the casket was completed, "and I don't know how we are going to handle you when you die," he concluded jokingly.

"You needn't worry," Sam replied. "I ain't ready to turn in yet."

As mascot of the Farmersville Woodmen of the World degree team, Sam created quite a sensation in New York City recently. Outfitted in a specially made uniform, he carried an ax made for him by an eastern hardware manufacturer, that was too heavy for the average man to lift.

During his service as city marshal of Farmersville, "Big Boy," as he is known to the natives, carried neither gun nor club. He also saved the city the expense of purchasing a patrol car as he never found a man too big to pick up and carry to jail, provided the offender wanted to resist arrest. Sam also says he never hit a man with his fist in his life. "I'm afraid I might kill 'em," he says. He has slapped several of them unconscious, however, with his open hand.

Has Visited Dallas

Sam used to visit Dallas on occasions at the request of the chief of police. One day he was rambling

SAM HARRIS' MEASUREMENTS

Weight, 692 pounds.	Thigh, 52 inches.
Height, 6 ft. 2 ins.	Calf, 30 inches.
Waist, 78 inches.	Shoe, No. 11.
Chest, 70 inches.	Collar, 24 inches.
Hips, 84 inches.	

down Elm Street when he happened to spy a man weighing about 400 pounds waddling along in front of him.

Sam put on some extra speed, overtook the man and bumped into him with the exclamation, "Get out of my way, kid, or I'll run over you." The man looked up in surprise and answered, "Say, I thought I was the biggest thing afloat, but, boy, I'll take my hat off to you." They shook hands and waddled off up the street together.

While in New York an afternoon paper carried a picture of Sam and a brief account of his life. An enterprising merchant wrote Sam some time later that he had a suit of clothes of enormous dimensions made for a customer who refused to accept it and that he would let Sam have it for a greatly reduced price. Sam looked at the dimensions as listed in the letter and wrote the merchant that "his youngest son might be able to wear the suit, but that he wore men's size clothes."

Just at the present Sam is enjoying a new vehicle that he has designed himself. It is a Ford truck with a platform on the body, a canopy over the top and a specially built settee in the center. "It is the only conveyance I have found yet that I can ride in in perfect comfort," he says.

Sam is married and has four sons and four daughters. The total weight of the girls is 686 lbs., his "baby daughter" weighing 186 pounds. The boys weigh 720 pounds and Mrs. Harris weighs 190 pounds. As Sam weighs 692, the combined weight of the family is 2,288 pounds. He has two sisters and two brothers, but none so large as he, although all are of considerable size.

(Seven months after this story appeared, Sam Harris died Oct. 19, 1914, of pneumonia.)

SEBRON D. HATLER

Sebron D. Hatler (Sebe) was a native of Kentucky, born February 15, 1836. He was reared on a farm, and although he received only nine months' schooling, he became one of the wealthiest men in North Texas. His father, Michael Hatler, was of Irish descent and married Lavinia Brackins, whose father, Henry Brackins, was a soldier in the Revolutionary War. Sebron was the fourth of five children and at age two his father died.

In 1856 he went to St. Louis, Missouri and worked on a railroad that was being built, then in 1857 he came to Texas. When he arrived in Collin County he had only five gold pieces, but he had an abundance of energy and ambition. He bought a team and went to work breaking the prairie and hauling from Jefferson.

In 1860 he joined the Texas Rangers and after a year of service, he joined the Company K, 6th Texas Cavalry, served in Missouri and the Indian Territory, and later in Mississippi. At Corinth, he became ill and received a discharge, returning to farm his land. In 1862 he married Segeous Polk Lewis. In that same year in December, he joined Captain Johnson's Spy Company and the following January he was captured but managed to escape before they reached Camp Chase where he would have been held. He rejoined his company and served the rest of the war with them.

On his return home he was penniless but his wife's father, an extensive land owner, was killed in a railroad accident while serving in the militia. Mrs. Hatler inherited 2000 acres of land and 1000 head of stock. With this start and careful management he increased the value of his holdings year by year. The large two-story house still stands set back from the roads east of Melissa.

Mrs. Hatler's father, Lindsey L. Lewis, was from a pioneer Missouri family. He came to Texas in 1845 and was a large landowner.

Sources: Old newspaper accounts.
Biographical Souveneers of Texas, published in 1889.

HEDRICH FAMILY

John F. Hedrich was born in Rockwood, Tennessee, in 1877 and moved to Blue Ridge, Texas, in 1895, where he engaged in farming. He married Iris Barnett, daughter of James A. and Mary Cantrell Barnett. To this union one son was born, Clarence Clyde Hedrich, June 10, 1900.

Katie Buchanan moved with her parents to Melissa, Texas, from Arkansas in 1870. James Henry Fisher also moved to Melissa from Tennessee in 1870. They were married in 1875 and to this union several children were born including Flossie B. Fisher, February 19, 1903.

Clarence C. Hedrich and Flossie B. Fisher were

married May 19, 1920 in Farmersville, Texas. They engaged in farming. Two children were born, James Burt (September 12, 1923), and Lena Victoria (December 30, 1936).

Lena V. Hedrich married Early B. Milstead in McKinney, July 25, 1964. They have one daughter Holly Beth, born December 28, 1965. Mrs. Milstead is a graduate of the Southwestern Graduate School of Banking at Southern Methodist University, Dallas. She was employed by the Collin County National Bank in 1956, named director of women's personal services in 1969, and was elected assistant vice president in January 1971 and served in that capacity until June 1973.

She served as a director of the McKinney Chamber of Commerce, 1970-73, president of Hurricane Creek Country Club Ladies Association, member of Willa Largent Garden Club, McKinney Business and Professional Women's Club, active member of Westside Church of Christ, where she teaches a high school girls class.

Sent by Early and Lena Milstead
McKinney

HEIFNER FAMILY
Sent by Mrs. John Shipp
As reported by Mr. and Mrs.
Jim Heifner of Lucas

Joe Heifner and Levonia Russell Heifner were both natives of Alabama. After Mr. Heifner died, his widow and children moved from Alabama to Collin County, Texas. They first settled east of Wylie, coming to the Lucas area in 1905.

Joe Heifner and Levonia Russell Heifner were the parents of seven children, four sons and three daughters, all of whom lived in the Lucas area and attended local schools. Their names: Clinnie, who married Maud Moore of near Wylie (both deceased); Mary, married Nealy Binkley of this area; Beuliah married John Jones of near Wylie; Irby, married Pearl Jones of Winningkoff; Jim, married Allie Sanders of this area; Martin, married Nona Tomberlin of Lucas; and Jodie, married L.T. Proffitt of Higgins community.

Of these Clinnie, Irby and Jim continued to live and reared their families in the Lucas area, and Mr. and Mrs. Martin Heifner lived in Winningkoff many years, later moving to McKinney.

Clinnie Heifner and Maud Moore Heifner had one son, Earl, who married Elsie Fultz. They made their home in McKinney. (Earl Heifner is deceased.)

Irby Heifner (deceased) and Pearl Jones Heifner were the parents of seven children, four boys and three girls, as follows: Lynas, Etherd, Weldon, Charles Ray, Mable Lois, Margie Nell, Dorothy. Most or all the children attended Lucas School, later the family moved to Allen.

Jim Heifner and Allie Sanders Heifner were the parents of two children: Estelle and Jimmie. Estelle married Orval (Cotton) Spurgin of Lucas. They are the parents of two daughters: Janet and Mary Helen, both students at North Texas State University. Janet now (1973) teaches in Plano.

Jimmy Heifner is not married and lives with his parents in Lucas.

Martin Heifner (deceased) and Nona Tomberlin Heifner are the parents of two children: Maurell, who married Iola Rolf of Winningkoff and Fay, who married Gene Dobbs of McKinney and continues to live there.

Maurell Heifner and Iola Rolf Heifner are the parents of two children: Bobby, who lives with his parents in Winningkoff (North Lucas) and Janelle. Janelle married Willis Joe King of Irving and the Kings live in that city.

THE HENDRICKS FAMILY OF VALDASTA COMMUNITY

The descendents of James Asbury and Malinda Catherine Hendricks number 516. The couple lived out their life on their many acres in the Valdasta area and their youngest child, Hester Hendricks, still owns a portion of the original acreage.

Their children follow. William Larkin Hendricks married Clifford Pauline Lee. He was known as "Friday." He and his wife bought his mother's old homestead, the Derrick farm, and lived there the rest of their lives. The old home, over 100 years old is still occupied by members of the family. Friday and his wife have 110 descendents.

Annie Laurie Hendricks married Thomas Morgan Airhart and they were the parents of 8 children. The old Airhart home near Valdasta, with its 600 acres of rich land is still retained by members of the Airhart family. There are 110 descendents of this couple living.

John Wesley Hendricks married Louella Astin and they became the parents of 8 children. Dow, the eldest child was once Superintendent of Collin County Schools. This couple have 97 descendents living.

Hannah Catherine Hendricks married Rufus A.

Long and they were the parents of 4 sons, all engineers, who built roads and bridges all over Collin County. James Long was Collin County Engineer for several years. Johnny Mae, the eldest daughter, began teaching school at age 15 and helped her brothers and sister through college. Their paternal grandfather, Dr. J.R.D. Long lived near and sold his country estate to J. Wesley Hendricks and moved to McKinney where he lived until his death.

George Hendricks married Amanda Perkins. He was a Spanish American War Veteran. He died young leaving his wife and 7 small children, living in his grandfather's old log cabin that stood on the first 110 acres the family had cleared. His wife went ahead with their plans and built a new home, where the youngest child lives now. George has 13 living descendents.

Lula Mae Hendricks married Burl Erwin Roper and they became the parents of 10 children. Their children still retain the land owned by their forefathers and are adding to it. This couple have 88 living descendents.

Mary Elizabeth Hendricks married Leeford W. Nichols and they were the parents of a daughter, Mrs. Katherin Caldwell, and three sons. The couple has 18 living descendents.

Cleveland Hendricks married Quincy Carwell and they had seven children. Charley and Douglas, the older sons, are grain dealers and land owners. Own, another son, operates a grocery store and the youngest son is in oil. The couple have 45 living descendents.

Henry Washington Hendricks married Goldie Tillett. He was known as Doc. A daughter, Alma, married Garnet Howell and teaches in Algeria. Betty Anderson, a daughter, is employed in the Collin County Court House. Paul, a son, recently formed a non-profit organization to train and employ handicapped workers at Renner, Texas. Virginia married a great grandson of Collin McKinney, Bill Bryant and settled on his grandmother's old homestead north of Anna, known as the Kelley place. The couple have 21 living descendents.

Hester Hendricks, the youngest child of the original family, and the only one living lives in McKinney, where she was a teacher until retirement. She is active in literary circles of the town and is soon to enroll at SMU in Dallas to study writing.

Uncle Jim and Aunt Sis Hendricks, as the old pioneer couple who settled in Valdasta in 1850, are known leave a total of 516 descendents, many of them still prominent in the life of Collin County today.

Story sent by Hester Hendricks, McKinney

THE HENDRICKS FAMILY

James Asbury Hendricks, son of Larkin and Nancy M. Gilbreath (an English woman) was born in South Carolina. About 1850 the couple, with their nine children, moved to Collin County settling four miles east of present Anna. James Asbury, 10 years old at the time of the move, drove one of the covered wagons all the way to Texas. They brought with them a few slaves and money to buy up the rich farm land.

Near the Hendrick new home lived the Derrick family. Henry Derrick was born in Virginia in 1788 and married Catherine Brammer who spoke only German. They moved to Woodville, Alabama in 1815, where he was the first Judge. Henry's son, William M., married Cynthia Joplin and moved to Collin County in 1846, settling two miles east of Annam where they reared several children. The youngest, Malinda Catherine (called Sissy) was born in 1854.

In September of 1861 James Asbury Hendricks enlisted in Co. D, 2nd Cav. at Dallas, Texas at age 21. After the war he went back to school for a while and at age 30 married Sissy Derrick who was then 16 years of age. The couple bought 100 acres of land at $5. per acre and settled on the land. Just before their 11th child was born, his brother left eight orphaned children at his death, and they too came to live, making 18 children in the home. In the next year the family built a large two-story home to house the big family.

THE HERNDON FAMILY

George Herndon went from Madison County, Kentucky in an early day to Cooper County, Missouri, having been born February 2, 1818. The family moved to Arkansas and on April 6, 1841 he married Cynthia A. McGarrah, daughter of John (Jack) McGarrah, one of the first settlers of old Buckner. In 1842 he visited present Collin County while on a trading trip to Mexico and was so impressed with the fine land he saw that in 1847 he and his wife came to Buckner and lived for a year with her parents. The next year he settled on 640 acres six miles west of McKinney. One account

gives that he received the grant for a year's service in the Rangers who protected the frontier from Indians and family records show that he recieved the grant for his payment for a year's work as a surveyor with Peter's Colony. He later traded it for three sections three miles further west. In 1886 he moved three miles southwest of town on what is now known as the Singleton Place. George Herndon died in McKinney September 22, 1902 and Cynthia March 8, 1913 and both were buried in a family plot near Foncine but later moved to Rowlett Creek Cemetery.

James R. Herndon, son of George and Cynthia McGarrah Herndon was born December 15, 1847 at the home of his grandparents at Buckner. (Jack and Polly McGarrah.) He lived with his parents in the Upper Rowlette Community until he married Susan Ellis Bush, October 7, 1869. They lived for a short time in Cooke County and grazed their sheep on the open land, then returned to Collin County and lived one half mile east of the old homeplace. They were the parents of 12 children. Eula (Mrs. Will Lucas). May E. (Mrs. W.R. Moore), Sallie B. (Mrs. H.H Stephens), C. Harriett (Mrs. D.B. Fritts), Dora F. (Mrs. Ed.F. Sharpe), Annie (died young). Bish, Ed, Glenn, Jerry, James and Henry (died young). James R. Herndon moved to McKinney in the early 1900s and died there March 27, 1942 at the age of 95 years. Susan, his wife, died December 26, 1918. Both are buried in Rowlette Cemetery.

Oliver E. Bush, father of Susan, was born February 7, 1825 in Clark County, Kentucky and married Dorinda M. Crim (born January 16, 1828) on May 22, 1845. To this union were born nine children, Mary Belle (Mrs. Commodore Fewell), Sarah Frances (Mrs. Wick Graves), Susan Ellis (Mrs. J.R. Herndon), William Rhodes (married Ellie Graves), Henry Lewis (married Mittie Walker), Porter and Edward never married, Jerry and Fletcher died young. Dorinda Bush died January 27, 1861 and is buried in Rowlette Cemetery. Oliver married Harriett F. Griffing, daughter of Henry Oliver Hedgecoxe. They had one son, Oliver Hedgecoxe Bush. Most of the families lie in Rowlette Cemetery.

FRANCIS (TUCK) MARION HILL

Francis Marion Hill was the fifth child in a family of thirteen. He was born February 13, 1843 in Lexington, Kentucky. His parents were Robert M. Hill (12-9-1815 to 5-27-1895) and Susan E. Poor (7-

20-1818 to 12-29-1896) and they married in Logan County, Kentucky July 15, 1835. After marriage they moved to Todd County, Kentucky and remained in Kentucky until 1846 when they moved to Pleasant Hill, Missouri. In 1890 they moved to McKinney, Texas where they lived until their death. They are buried in Pecan Grove Cemetery, McKinney, Texas. The Hill family consisted of the following children: Mary E.E. (1836), John W.W. (1836), James W.W. (1839), Robert E. (1841), Francis Marion (1843), Thomas Jefferson (1846), George E. Taylor (1848), Doctor Colman (1850), Susan Melinda (1853), Benjamin B.L. (1855), Sally Cornelius (1857), Armstead M.M. (1859), and Heneritta Pricy (1863). Of this family the following came to McKinney, Texas to live: Marion Francis, James W., Doctor Colman, Susan Melinda, Armstead M.M., and Heneritta Pricy.

When a mere lad of seventeen, he made three trips across the continent as far as Salt Lake City. He enlisted for Civil War duty in 1861 at Lexington, Missouri under General Sterling Price's command, Colonel Gorden's regiment, Captain Scott Bullard's Company A. He became a Captain and his brothers, James Woot and Thomas were Lieutenants under him. His brother, John, was killed during this Civil War. Captain Hill served only three months and was given an honorable discharge in order that he might join with Colonel Charles William Quantrell. In 1863 and again in 1864 Quantrell brought his men to Texas spending considerable time in and around Sherman and McKinney, Texas. Captain Hill was an expert marksman. He carried important dispatches through the Union lines from one General to another, and he led his own company, which he recruited, into many successful battles. He was captured several times but each time managed to escape. He was wounded twelve times and had seven horses shot out from under him.

Captain Hill had the distinction of having been the last Confederate officer to surrender his company, which he did at Lexington, Missouri May 2, 1865. Jesse and Frank James, cousins of Tuck Hill, Alan Palmer, Woot Hill, George Todd, Bill Anderson, Dick Maddox, Peyton Lang, Bill Gow, Dave Pool, Jim and Cole Younger, John Ross, Bill Hulsey, Lee McMurtry, Jim Hinds, and Bud Spence were under Captain Hill's command.

Captain Hill returned to Texas from Missouri after having surrendered at Lexington, Missouri and took up his residence at McKinney, Texas. He married Mary Quintillia Graves, daughter of Albert Gallatin and Frances Harrison Graves, January

CAPT. FRANCIS MARION HILL

1866. To this union nine children were born. They were W.R., Lucy F., Doctor Wootson, Annie, Jesse, Effie, Ollie, Marion L., and Clarence O. Grandchildren that are living are Mrs. Vivian Bass, Mrs. Marian Truitt, Mrs. Maybelle Hilliard, and Ralph H. Hill.

Captain Hill organized the Ex-Confederate and Old Settlers Picnic Ass'n. He served as Grand Marshall for over twenty years, heading the parade each year. He served the city, McKinney, as an alderman, was ever active in city and county affairs, and in the promotion of every interest calculated to promote the welfare of McKinney and Collin County that would add to the happiness of his home people.

Captain Hill was a member of the First Christian Church, a former Deacon, and a member of the Odd Fellow Lodge.

Captain Hill passed away at his home February 3, 1920 at the age of 77 years. He was buried in the Pecan Grove Cemetery, McKinney, Texas.
Story by Maybelle Hilliards, a granddaughter.

MRS. MARY QUINTILLIA GRAVES HILL

Mary Quintillia Graves was born April 11, 1843 in Pleasant Hill, Missouri.

She was a descendent of Captain Thomas Graves

who was born about 1580 in England and came to Orange County, Virginia in 1608. The lines of descent from Captain Thomas Graves is John Graves, Isaac Graves, Claiborn Graves, Albert Gallatin Graves, Mary Quintillia Graves.

The Graves family came from Virginia to Kentucky, then to Missouri and on to Texas in 1856.

Albert Gallatin Graves married Francis J. Harrison, a first cousin of William Henry Harrison the ninth President of the United States.

Children born to Albert and Francis Graves were: Lucretius Harrison (1840), Aurelius (1841), Mary Quintillia (1843), Eugenia Eveline (1844), Francis Cornelia (1846); James Wycliffe (1848), Lucy Ann (1851), Isaac (1852), William Franklin (1855), Sarah Pamelia (1857), Elizabeth Ellen (1859), and Margaret (1860).

Mrs. Hill passed away December 6, 1926 in the family home in McKinney, Texas and was buried in the Pecan Grove Cemetery at McKinney, Texas.

Source: Maybelle Hilliard, McKinney, Texas.

JEREMIAH HORN FAMILY

Jeremiah Horn was born January 23, 1794 in Tennessee, the son of Jeremiah and Judith Horn. The Horns were originally from North Carolina coming by way of Tennessee, Mississippi, and finally to Texas. The Horns came to Collin County with the Peter's Colony settlers.

Jeremiah Horn married Aley Hicks in June of 1818 and they were the parents of seven children, all born in Tennessee. They were: William Thornbrough Horn (March 13, 1819), Robert Sinclair Horn (February 18, 1821), John Hon (August 2, 1823), George Horn (February 14, 1826), Mary Nealy Horn (July 25, 1828), James Trott Horn (October 17, 1830), and Jeremiah Clark Horn (January 16, 1833).

Jeremiah's second marriage was to Sintha Daugherty Leadbetter on July 6, 1845 and to this union were born the following children, Ruth Ellen Horn (April 15, 1846), Sintha Caroline Horn (November 22, 1849), Charles Wesley Horn (October 23, 1852). Jeremiah Horn was a Methodist minister and he and his family settled on the land just south of the Walnut Grove Cemetery in 1846 and it was said that his family lived farther west than anyone in Collin County at that time.

William Thornbrough Horn was married to Margaret Ledbetter (July 14, 1830), and they settled southwest of Rheas Mill. Their children include John Horn, a Methodist minister who moved to California; Wm. George Clark Horn and Lawrence Horn who were land owners near Rheas Mill; Cynthia Horn Taylor and Fanny Horn Curtsinger who lived in Oklahoma; Florence Horn Barrett; Alicia Horn Grace; Mrs. Neighnors and Mrs. Collins passed away early leaving young children who were reared by their grandmother Horn.

William George Clark Horn was born October 9, 1863. He served as Deputy Sheriff of Collin County for several years and while serving in that capacity, married Mary Catherine Keen, daughter of the Rev. and Betty Orr Keen. Rev. Keen was a Presbyterian minister. The young couple lived in McKinney on Benge Street until they decided to settle on a farm west of Rheas Mill. Their children were Leona, and twins, Leta and Leland. Leona Horn married Walter Snider and they were the parents of Mary Snider McCollum and Dr. L.W. Snider. Leona Horn Snider taught school for many years, then worked with McKinney Dry Goods Company. She is now retired and lives in McKinney. Leta Horn married Ammon Smith and they were the parents of Denna Smith Davis and Marion Smith Story. Leta Horn Smith taught in the Princeton School until retiring a few years ago. She now lives in Princeton.

Leland Horn married Ruth Campbell and taught school for a short time, before he met his death in a boating accident, while on a senior outing, at age 29 years. After his death, his parents moved from the farm to a home in McKinney. She died January 4, 1958 and he died January 22, 1952. They are buried in Forest Grove Cemetery beside their son.

Lawrence Horn was born September 21, 1871 and married Hortense. The couple made their home on their land at Rheas Mill, and ran a grocery store in McKinney. The couple had no children.

Alicia Horn married R.C. Grace, a Presbyterian minister, who at the time was the pastor of the Walnut Grove Presbyterian Church about 1890. The couple later lived in Richardson, then California, where both are buried.

The first child born to Jeremiah and Sintha Horn was Ruth Ellenb, who married Jeremiah Martin, a Methodist minister. They were the parents of eight children, two of them living out their lives in Collin County. Cass Martin Horn was a landowner and farmer of the Bloomdale Community, now deceased, but his wife lives in McKinney with her daughter, Mrs. Eustace Dungan. Mary Catherine Martin married David R. Stubblefield, a landowner of Rheas Mill, and they reared their family there.

The last child of Jeremiah and Sintha Horn was Charles Wesley Horn who lived in the Walnut Grove Community until his death. The younger of his two sons, Ernest Wesley, lived on the homeplace and farmed it until about two years ago when he retired and moved his family to Denton, Texas. Mr. E.W. Horn passed away in 1973.

Jeremiah and Sintha Horn are buried in the private Horn Cemetery about a half mile south of Walnut Grove Cemetery with other members of the early family. Wm. T. and Margaret Horn, Jerry and Ruth Martin, Mary C. and David R. Stubblefield, Mr. and Mrs. Charles Wesley Horn and Ernest Wesley Horn are all buried in the Ware Cemetery about a half mile west of the Walnut Grove Cemetery.

Story compiled by Mr. and Mrs. James Baxter.

THE R.C. HORN FAMILY

Robert Cameron Horn, son of William and Martha Carruth Horn, was born in Wilson County, Tennessee, one of 12 children, on April 26, 1844. His father was one of ten children born to Richard Horn. William, the oldest child, married Martha Carruth in 1836 and to them were born the following children: Gano Horn, James, William H., Nicholas, Mrs. John Douglas, Mrs. A.C. Weeks, Mrs. Henry Andrews, Mrs. Ben O'Brien, and Robert Cameron.

The Horn family came to Texas in 1858 and settled in what became the Hackberry Community and still later, the Vineland Community. They bought 400 acres from the William Rice Survey. Robert Cameron attended private schools since they were the only schools in Collin County at that time. A.L. Darnall was his teacher.

When the Civil War came he enlisted, July 5, 1862, in Company K, Martin's Regiment of the 5th Texas Partisans and Rangers, in which he served for three years. When the war was over he came home to find money worthless and all he had left was a horse and saddle. He turned to farming, but at the same time attending a school taught by Elder J.S. Muse. In 1867 he decided to study for the ministry and drove cattle and horses to Kentucky to help pay his first tuition. He entered the University of Kentucky and studied for three years. Although he did not complete the last year of college, he entered the ministry and preached the gospel for 56 years.

On September 7, 1870 he married Mildred E. Franklin in Tennessee. They were the parents of six children, Mrs. John W. Thomas, Mrs. Ben Oates, Mrs. Eugene Holmes, William F., Mrs. Charles Graves, and Flora who died as a child.

In 1871 he brought his family to Collin County and settled in the Vineland Community. His was a busy life, farming, preaching, teaching, and helping build a community. Not only he, but his wife and daughters taught school in Collin County. He kept a diary from 1868 until his death. His life was spent in preaching in small churches and in helping organize new ones. He was a leader in every fight for Prohibition from 1887 on.

His diary was published in 1930 by J.H. Boyer and C.H. Thurman and is called The Annals of Elder Horn, Life in the Southwest. This book is a valuable resource for historians.

Elder Horn died March 7, 1936 at age 92.

Sources:
Autobiography in McKinney Daily Courier Gazette. August 2, 1924
Roy F. Hall's notes
Stambaugh's Collin Co. History

JONATHAN AND JOANNA HOUSTON

Jonathan Houston and Joanna Houston were living in Lincoln County, Tennessee in 1830 according to the 1830 Census. She was born in North Carolina about 1800. Jonathan Houston died at Salem, Franklin County, Tenn. in 1849, for his will was dated Feb. 13, 1849, attested by William S. Smith and W.S. Murphy, and probated May 7, 1849 (signed) Wm. E. Taylor, Clerk.

According to the 1850 Census for Franklin Co., Tenn., Family No. 350 included: Thomas Houston, age 31; Malinda, age 29; William, age 6; Mary Ann, age 4; and George, age 1.

Family No. 351, of the same Census, shows: Joanna Houston, age 50; Ann S., age 21; John T., age 19; Mary F., age 17; Elizabeth Jane, age 14; Susan B., age 12; James M., ages 10; and Joanna K., age 5.

After the death of Jonathan Houston, Joanna Houston, with these children still at home—John T., Susan B., Elizabeth Jane, James M., and Joanna K. with a married son, I. Thomas S. Houston and wife, Malinda, and three children, moved to Texas about 1852 and settled in the Dump and Wylie area (formerly Rawhide) on a part of the Calvin Boles Survey—"on the waters of the East Fork" 7 miles southeast of McKinney, Texas.

Joanna divided the land with the children on Jan. 5, 1869 which was vested to her by her son, John T. It is presumed she died soon thereafter. She is buried in the old Fitzhugh part of the Forest Grove Cemetery and Christian Church where she and her children were members. As late as 1875, Elizabeth Jane and Jesse Hall and Susan B. Turnbow were members there.

Six generations and about 121 years have passed and still part of their family is located in Collin Co., Texas.

Houston children married in Collin Co., Texas: Thomas S. Houston married Sarah J. Mullins, March 20, 1860; and Catherine Bateman on June 5, 1870. John T. Houston married Jane Wallace on July 23, 1870. Susan B. Houston married E.R. Southwood, then T. Alex Thompson, July 29, 1866, and James Turnbow, Sept. 4, 1871. Elizabeth Jane Houston married Jesse F. Hall, Aug. 23, 1865. James M. Houston married Teressa H. Baugh, Oct. 24, 1867. Joanna K. married William Jasper Chappell, Sept. 6, 1863, and later J. Henry Colvin in Wise Co., Texas.

Four boys served in the Civil War from Collin Co., Texas: John T. Houston enlisted in March, 1862 and served in McKinney's Co., Fitzhugh's Regiment, Johnson's Brigade; William Houston served in Gabriel H. Fitzhugh's Co., in the 16th Regiment; Thomas S. Houston served in the same Company as William; and James M. Houston served in Co. C., Martin's Regiment, Ganos Brigade. He carried mail into Oklahoma taking tobacco with him to help make Indian friends. He received 1280 acres of land from the State of Texas because of permanent disabilities from the War.

Two girls married in Franklin Co., Tenn. Anna S. married William Simpson Nov. 5, 1851 and Mary F. married Green B. Simpson, Dec. 24, 1850.

HOUSTON—HALL

Elizabeth Jane Houston, daughter of Jonathan and Joanna Houston, born Feb. 14, 1837 in Tennessee, married Jesse F. Hall in Collin Co., Texas on Aug. 24, 1865 by W.S. Fisher, minister. Elizabeth Jane Hall died Aug. 22, 1896 with measles and Jesse F. Hall, born Feb. 5, 1832, died of pneumonia on March 20, 1884. They are buried in Forest Grove Cemetery. They were parents of five children: John Andrew Hall, born 1866 (never married) died in 1934 and was buried at Forest Grove; Tom Hall; Fidelia N. "Della" Hall;

Katherine Joanna Hall; and Robert "Bob" Hall.

John Andrew Hall was born 1866 and never married. He died in 1934 and was buried at Forest Grove.

Tom Hall married Susie Gallagher. Their children were: Ruby, Beulah, and Roy. Ruby Hall married Nathan Eldridge.

Fidelia N. "Della" Hall was born Aug. 14, 1873 in Collin Co., Texas, and married Fountain Lee Myrick, who was born Jan. 1, 1868 in Tenn. and died Feb. 13, 1923. "Della" Hall died June 10, 1962 and both are buried at Forest Grove Cemetery. Their children were: Ethel, Ernest, Leonard, and Fred. Ethel, born Sept. 11, 1893 in Collin Co., Texas, married Robert Stinson (1895-1946). Ethel Stinson died Aug. 28, 1970, and both are buried at Forest Grove Cemetery. Their children were James Stinson, Velma Stinson Spurgin, and Jana B. Stinson who married George H. Hennig.

Ernest Myrick married Gladys Fonder. Their children were: John Henry and Betty. John Henry, born July 12, 1921, married and had the following children: Diana Lynn Myrick, born Jan. 22, 1950 in Dallas, and Sandra Jean Myrick, born May 14, 1953 in Dallas. Betty Myrick, born Aug. 3, 1928, married John Blackwell. Two children born to them at McKinney: Paul Ray born May 21, 1954, and Donna Kay born April 2, 1958.

Leonard Houston Myrick, born Oct. 5, 1899 in Collin Co., married Winnie Spence who was born Aug. 6, 1904. Their children were: Foy Deward, Billy Ray, Betty Sue, and Wanda Gene.

Foy Deward Myrick, born Oct. 18, 1926, married Darlene Askew on April 24, ——. The children are Samuel Leonard Myrick, born Dec. 1, 1947, Jerry Don Myrick born May 17, 1950, Sandra Kay Myrick born Sept. 5, 1951, and Mary Lynn Myrick was adopted born Oct. 18, 1951.

Billy Ray Myrick, born Jan. 10, 1931, married Virginia Johnson, born Nov. 18, 1930; children are: Phyllis Ann Myrick born Mach 16, 1961, and John Raymond Myrick born Sept. 5, 1965.

Betty Sue Myrick, born April 25, 1932, married Luther Joe Coomer, born Sept. 5, 1928. Children are: Jimmy Dale Coomer born Nov. 8, 1950, Vickie Lynn Commer born Aug. 7, 1954, and Wanda LeAnn born Nov. 15, 1966.

Wanda Gene Myrick, born Nov. 19, 1935, married Junior Ray Hatfield. Their children are: Deborah Dianne born July 4, 1958, Todd Glenn born May 2, 1962 and died Dec. 25, 1969, and Jennie LaRay born Oct. 25, 1970.

Fred Lee Myrick was born June 11, 1911 in Collin Co., Texas and married Kate Younger; children: Donald Morgan Myrick, Larry Myrick, Kattie Ruth, Charles Wayne, and Freddie Lee. Other marriages unknown.

Katherine Joanna "Kate" Hall was born June 9, 1876 and died Oct. 12, 1961. She married Thomas Lee Johnson who was born May 4, 1871 and died Nov. 9, 1959. They are buried in Forest Grove; children: Ester, Naomi, Johnnie, Zelma, and Ora.

Robert "Bob" Hall was born Feb. 16, 1879 and died Aug. 23, 1943. He married Elizabeth Walker who was born in 1880 and died in 1962. They are buried in Forest Grove. Their children were: Lennie, Mozelle, Myrtle, and Hazel.

HOUSTON—THOMPSON—TURNBOW

Susan Bird Houston, daughter of Jonathan and Joanna Houston, born about 1840 in Tenn. (Age 20 in the 1860 Collin Co., Texas Census.) She died of measles after taking care of someone with the measles sometime after 1875 as her name is on the Christian Church roll at Forest Grove. Lillie Donnelson and Linda Katherine Turnbow said that Susan Bird was buried in the old Fitzhugh part of Forest Grove Cemetery.

Susan B. married E.R. "Lidge" Southwood and they had three daughters: Joanna F. born in Ky., died young. She was two years old in 1860 Collin Co. Census. Florence Southwood, born 1858 in Kansas, married Frank Maddox and they had two children, Iva and Frank Maddox, Jr. Laura J. Southwood, born 1860 in Texas, married (1) James M. "Mitt" Miller in Collin Co., Texas on Aug. 12, 1875; (2) Sammy Berry, buried in Dallas at Grove Hill Cemetery. They had one child, Ida, who died in infancy. Laura Berry died in 1937 in Dallas and is buried at Forest Grove Cemetery in Collin Co. Her marker was placed at the grave by Juanita Mierzwik, Ruby May Matthews, and Mrs. Price Strickland.

Susan B. married (2) T. Alex Thompson in Collin Co., Texas on July 29, 1866 by Jas. R. Wilmeth, minister. They had two children: Mary Alice Thompson was born about 1867 in Texas. Dovie Frances was born in April, 1869 in Texas. Susan Bird Thompson was a widow in the 1870 Collin Co. Census, living next door to her brother, James M. Houston and family, with four little girls.

Mary Alice Thompson married Will T. Humes in Collin Co., July 27, 1887 by J.W. Waddill, Clerk. Children unknown. Mary Alice and Will T. Humes are buried at Grove Hill Cemetery, Dallas.

Dovie Frances Thompson married Henry Land-

ers on Oct. 15, 1886 by William H. Price in Collin Co. Children: Sam, Bill, Dick, and Annie Mae. Dovie and Henry Landers are buried at Lewisville, Texas.

Susan B. Houston (Southwood) Thompson married James Turnbow in Collin Co. on Sept. 4, 1871. James Turnbow born about 1827 in Missouri. They had two boys: John Wesley Turnbow and Jim Thomas Turnbow.

John Wesley Turnbow, born Sept. 5, 1872 in Rockwall Co., Texas and died Oct. 14, 1951, is buried at Wilson Chapel Cemetery. John W. Turnbow married Linda Katherine Rutledge, born July 2, 1881 in Cumberland Co., Ky., the daughter of Charley and Spicy Rutledge. Mr. Rutledge moved to Collin Co. about 1900 and Linda Katherine (Rutledge) Turnbow said she could not remember her mother (Spicy) because she died when she was a baby at Allen Shade, Ky. Sarah Jane Rutledge, a double cousin, married Jim Thomas Turnbow, brother of John.

John Wesley Turnbow and wife, Linda Katherine, lived in Princeton for 25 years where Mrs. Turnbow continued to live after his death until she moved to Dallas to be near her daughters. She still keeps the home fires burning, plus making a garden at the age of 93. John and "Darling," as she was affectionately called, had three children: Juanita, Ruby Maye; and Charlie Erwin Turnbow. The children went to school at Culleoka, Weston, Alla Hubbard, Celina and Princeton.

Juanita Turnbow married Paul Mierzwik but had no children. Ruby Mae Turnbow, born Oct. 3, 1905, married Ted Matthews; they had no children. Ruby Maye Matthews died Jan. 1, 1970 and is buried at Wilson Chapel Cemetery. Charlie Erwin Turnbow married Emma D. Caves and they had three children: Charlsie Katherine, Hettie Sue, and Bettie Joe Turnbow.

Jim Thomas Turnbow, born in 1876 in Texas, died Dec. 23, 1959. He married Sarah Jane Rutledge, Aug. 10, 1897 in Collin Co., daughter of Mr. and Mrs. Jack Rutledge, born Sept. 12, 1877 in Cumberland Co., Ky. and died May 5, 1973. At one time, the Turnbow family lived near Altoga, then east of Culleoka on the Roy Akin farm, then moved to Lowrey Crossing before buying their home east of Culleoka around 1900 where they lived until their death. both are buried at Wilson Chapel Cemetery. They had three children: Onie Frances, Essie and Floyd E.

Onie Frances Turnbow, born near Altoga on Oct. 10, 1900, married Cecil Puett, born July 14, 1899. They had two daughters: Dorothy Faye and

Francille Ann. Dorothy Faye, born May 12, 1926, married (1) Mr. Milstead and they had two boys: James Roland "Jimmie" Milstead, born 1947, and Robert Preston Milstead, born 1950. Dorothy Faye Milstead married (2) Hiram C. Byers and they had two children: Michael Byers and Karen Byers, born Aug. 19, 1964. Francille Puett, born Dec. 4, 1936, married Charles Clifford Martin, II. They had three children: Charles Clifford Martin, III; Crystal Martin, born May 10, 1965; and, Scott Martin, born Jan. 19, 1969.

Essie Turnbow, born Jan. 7, 1906, married Earl Staples, born Aug. 12, 1905 and had two children: Kenneth Earl Staples and Stanley Norman Staples. Kenneth Earl Staples, born March 24, 1928, married Mildred Hightower. They had two children: Steven Earl, born Sept. 12, 1955, and Rhonda Lea, born Oct. 29, 1951. Stanley Norman Staples, born July 2, 1931, married Mary Ellen Hall. Their children are: Susan Lynn Staples and Sandra Staples.

Floyd E. Turnbow married Edith Yaw.

JAMES M. HOUSTON

James M. Houston, youngest son of Jonathan and Joanna Houston, was born in Tennessee in 1841. Around 1852, he came with his mother and her family to Texas where they settled around the Dump and Wylie (formerly Rawhide) area. On Oct. 24, 1867, James M. married Teressa H. Baugh. They were married by James D. Naylor, J.P. They raised six daughters: Jo Adeline "Jodie" Houston born Aug. 29, 1868 in McKinney, Texas and died July 7, 1948. Mary Jane "Janie" Houston born May 30, 1872 in Collin Co., Texas and died July 27, 1941. She was buried at Sweetwater, Wise Co., Texas. Fannie Houston born Dec. 28, 1873, died Nov. 24, 1944, and was buried at Farmersville, Texas. Nancy Ruth "Ruthie" Houston born Aug. 13, 1875, died June 10, 1952, and was buried at Forest Grove Cemetery. Minnie Houston born Aug. 7, 1878, died Oct. 7, 1946, and was buried at Forest Grove Cemetery. Annie Houston born in 1883, died June 14, 1967, and was buried at Forest Grove Cemetery.

Teressa H. Houston died in 1885, two years after Annie was born. She is buried at Forest Grove Cemetery.

James M. Houston served in the Civil War from Collin Co. in Company C., Martin's Regiment, Ganos Brigade. He carried mail into Oklahoma taking tobacco with him to help make Indian friends. He received 1280 acres of land from the State of Texas because of permanent disabilities from the War. James M. Houston died about 1888-1889 and was buried at Forest Grove Cemetery.

HOUSTON—EDWARDS

Jo Adeline "Jodie" Houston, daughter of James M. and Teressa H. Baugh, was born Aug. 29, 1868 in McKinney, Texas and died July 7, 1948. "Jodie" married William Malcom Edwards on Jan. 9, 1888 at Blythe Chapel.

They had six children: Edgar Edwards born Jan. 30, 1890, died Feb. 27, 1890+; Bessie Alma Edwards born June 1, 1891, at Winningkoff; William Hershel Edwards born Jan. 24, 1894, died March 25, 1960+; Baby Edwards born Oct. 5, 1896, died Jan. 27, 1897+; Ernest Edwards, born March 24, 1898, died May 9, 1899+; and Ruth Lee Edwards born Sept. 4, 1904. (+All the above are buried at Forest Grove Cemetery.)

Bessie Alma Edwards married Wallace Arthur Dale (born Oct. 6, 1890 at Copeville, died with flu on Nov. 28, 1918) in June, 1910 at Branch. Geneva Lee Dale born Dec. 1, 1912 at Branch. Beatrice Marie Dale born Dec. 29, 1918 at Wylie. On Dec. 27, 1924 Bessie Alma married Joe Monroe O'Neal in Plano. Sue Joe O'Neal was born July 14, 1929 in Garland.

Geneva Lee married Cecil Ormand Cathey (born Aug. 18, 1907) on April 8, 1934. One daughter was born to the union, Linda Ann Cathey born Aug. 19, 1936 at Kilgore, Texas. Linda Ann married Roy Milton Ivie on April 5, 1958 in Dallas. They have two children: Craig Milton Ivie born Aug. 2, 1959 in McKinney and Cathey LeeAnn Ivie born Aug. 7, 1964 in Dallas.

Beatrice Marie Dale married John Madison Lane (born July 30, 1908 at McAllister, Ok., died March 15, 1972) at Greenville, Texas on Dec. 11, 1938. They had four children: Sandra Dale Lane born Sept. 14, 1940 at Odessa and died Sept. 14, 1940; Nancy Kay Land born May 27, 1947 at Odessa; Delores Elaine and Donald Madison Land born Feb. 27, 1943 at Greenville. Donald Madison Land married Peggy Sue Dubose on Feb. 25, 1966 in Garland, Texas. They have three children: John Ray Land born April 4, 1967; Jerry Don Land born May 24, 1968; Tommy Dale Land born May 21, 1972. Delores Elaine Land married Michael Bruce Blanton on June 3, 1967 at Garland, Texas. Their two children are: Deborah Kay Blanton born July 30, 1968 and Danny Bruce Blanton born Dec. 7, 1972. Nancy Kay land married Charles Everett Comer on Sept. 9, 1972 in Garland and has one child, Jimmy Everett Comer, born Sept. 18, 1973.

Beatrice Marie Dale Land graduated from Princeton High School with honors. She has been active in church, receiving life membership for WSCS service in New Mexico Conference of United Methodist Women. Member and contributor in several poetry groups, Beatrice M. Land will be included in the ''International Who's Who in Poetry'' Cambridge, England, 1974. Her poetry has won numerous awards including Critic's Award (PST), Harry Kovner Award (PST), Citizenship Prize, and Naylor Award.

Sue Jo O'Neal, born July 14, 1929 in Garland, married Denny Ray McGee on Oct. 27, 1950 in Dallas. They have one child: Kathy Lynn McGee, born Oct. 19, 1953 who married Kenrad Darling on May 12, 1973 at Irving, Texas.

William Hershel Edwards, born Jan. 24, 1894 at Winningkoff, married Lillian Dees. William Edwards died March 25, 1960. They had seven children: Pauline, Bernice, Vera, Billy, Jo Ann, Jean and James.

Ruth Lee Edwards, born Sept. 4, 1904 at Blythe Chapel, married J.P. Thomas on July, 1931. He died Jan. 2, 1969. Their children are: Wallace Edwards Thomas, born Aug. 10, 1932 at Winnsboro; and Pansy Ruth Thomas, born June 19, 1940 at Odessa. She married Holiday Haley of Tyler, Texas and they have three children: David, Debra and Lindy.

HOUSTON—LEAKE

Mary Jane ''Janie'' Houston, born May 30, 1872 in Collin Co. and daughter of James M. and Teressa Houston, married in 1891 to William Wesley ''Wes'' Leake who was born Jan. 27, 1869. Mary Jane's cousin, Mary Elizabeth ''Mollie'' Chappell married A.T. Leake, brother of Wm. Wesley Leake.

Mary Jane and ''Wes'' moved to the Allison Community in Wise Co., Texas around 1916. ''Janie'' died on July 27, 1941 and ''Wes'' died Jan. 11, 1949, and both are buried in the Sweetwater Cemetery in Wise Co. They had three children: Ola, Manley, and Houston Leake.

Ola Leake, born Nov. 24, 1893 near Parker, married Clarence Coffey. Their children were: Marcella Coffey and Alma Christine Coffey. Marcella, born Dec. 19, 1915 at Branch, married Ray B. ''Chick'' Goforth. They were parents of Vernon Ray Goforth, born Feb. 23, 1942 at Lucas, and Jerry Clarence Goforth, born May 9, 1948 at Lucas.

Alma Christine Coffey, born Aug. 15, 1919 at Branch, married Willard Pharr. To them were born Bobbie Joyce Pharr, Carey Milton Pharr, and Linda Kay Pharr.

Bobbie Joyce Pharr married Perry Gene Fisher, and their children are: Laurie Ann Fisher, born Aug. 26, 1957; Michael Ray Fisher, born July 4, 1960; Cathey Lisa Fisher, born April 14, 1962; Sherrie Lynn Fisher, born Oct. 1, 1965; and Amy Louise Fisher, born Oct. 2, 1966.

Carey Milton Pharr, born Feb. 20, 1943, married Karen Frances Neale. The children are: Thomas Cary ''Tommy'' Pharr, born July 17, 1965; Steven Edward Pharr, born Feb. 20, 1968; and William Gregory Pharr, born Dec. 21, 1970.

Linda Kay Pharr, born Jan. 15, 1952 (3), married Scott Lee Cleveland. They have a boy, Christopher Lynn ''Chris'' Cleveland, born Feb. 14, 1971.

Manley Leake married Mae Funderburg in Collin Co., Texas. They had one daughter, Virginia Leake, who married Vance Addington. Vance and Virginia Addington have a daughter, Nancy Addington.

Houston Leake was born Oct. 7, 1903 at Winningkoff, Collin Co., Texas. He married Blanche A. Walker in Wise Co., Texas. Houston Leake died March 13, 1968 and is buried at Sweetwater Cemetery in Wise Co., Texas. They had two boys: Jack Leake and Gene Leake.

HOUSTON—DALE

Fannie Houston, daughter of James M. and Teressa H. Houston, was born Dec. 28, 1873. She married (1) W.R. Rutledge and (2) John Dale. Fannie Houston Dale died Nov. 24, 1944. Both Fannie and John Dale are buried at Farmersville, Texas.

HOUSTON—DENISON

Nancy Ruth Houston, daughter of James M. and Teressa H. Houston, was born Aug. 13, 1875 and died June 10, 1952. Nancy Ruth married (1) M.T. Rutledge and (2) W.R. ''Bob'' Denison, born Nov. 16, 1870 and died June 5, 1946. They are buried at Forest Grove.

One daughter, Tressie, married Gordon E. Kerby. They had three children: Robert, Shannon, and Billie Ruth. Tressie and Gordon Kerby are buried at Ridgeview Cemetery, McKinney.,

HOUSTON—KERBY

Minnie Houston, daughter of James M. and Teressa H. Houston, was born Aug. 7, 1878 and died Oct. 7, 1946. Minnie Houston married G. Frank Kerby in Collin Co. in 1902. G. Frank Kerby was born June 23, 1874 and died July 4, 1944. They are buried in Forest Grove Cemetery.

Their children are: Clarence Kerby, Jack Kerby, and Rowena "Bill" Kerby who married Earl Barry.

HOUSTON—KNIGHT

Annie Houston, daughter of James M. and Teressa H. Houston, was born in 1883 and died June 14, 1967. Annie Houston married Ed Knight born 1878 and died 1951. Annie and Ed Knight and an infant born in 1933 are buried in Forest Grove Cemetery. One son, Jack Knight, lives in McKinney. He and his wife have two daughters, Joan and Bess Ann Knight.

JOANNA KATHERINE HOUSTON

Joanna Katherine Houston, daughter of Jonathon and Joanna Houston, born Jan. 9, 1845 in Tenn. died Aug. 7, 1911 and is buried in the Princeton Cemetery, Collin Co., Texas. She married (1) William Jasper Chappell on Sept. 6, 1863 by S.L. Jenkins, minister, in Collin Co. They had the following children in Collin County before moving to Wise Co., Texas about 1874: J.L. born Aug. 16, 1865, died in infancy; James William "Jim" Chappell; and Mary Elizabeth (Mollie) Chappell. One daughter, Susan Burtina "Tina" Chappell was born on Sept. 28, 1875 near Audibon, Wise Co., Texas, after her father died in June of 1875. William Jasper Chappell, born Jan. 10, 1837 in Tenn., enlisted in the Civil War on Sept. 13, 1861 in Hickman, Co., Tenn. and was discharged on Aug. 7, 1863. He died in Wise Co. near Audibon of pneumonia.

Joanna Katherine Houston Chappell married (2) J. Henry Colvin, born Oct. 6, 1836. They married before 1880 in Wise Co. and to this union was born a daughter, E. Minnie M. Colvin, born Feb. 12, 1880 near Audubon, Wise Co., Texas. Joanna K. and J. Henry Colvin separated about 1885, and she moved her family back to Collin Co. settling between Lucas and Dump, where they lived until her son, James William "Jim" Chappell, bought land in 1898 south of Princeton (the old Bates place). Joanna's nephew, John Andrew Hall, and her son, James William Chappell, drove two wagons from Audubon, Wise Co., to the Wylie area where she grew up and where her sister, Elizabeth Jane Hall, lived.

James William "Jim" Chappell, born Aug. 11,

JOANNA KATHERINE HOUSTON, 1845-1911.

1869, died at Princeton Dec. 20, 1953. He married (1) Villa Calhoun and (2) Clara Dalton. They had no children and are both buried at Princeton. He lived in Wylie until 1898 when he bought a place south of Princeton (the old Bates place). His mother and sister, Minnie M. Colvin, lived with him.

Mary Elizabeth "Mollie" Chappell, born March 5, 1873, died March 13, 1951. She was married to Anthony Thomas Leake on Oct. 30, 1889 by Elder John M. McKinney. He died May 4, 1956 and both are buried at Princeton. They bought an adjoining farm to her brother, James William "Jim" Chappell, south of Princeton. They had two children: James Luther and Minnie Ellen Leake. Luther was born July 27, 1893 near Parker and died July 22, 1973. He and his cousin, Homer Myrick, went to school at Higgins. Luther Leake married Sarah M. "Sadie" Greer, May 13, 1915 at Lowry Crossing. Sarah M. "Sadie" Leake was born on Sept. 20, 1895 in Union, S.C. and died Feb. 21, 1973. Both are buried at Princeton. They had one daughter, Mary Louise Leake, who graduated from Princeton High School and Texas State College for Women. She married Charles Younger and they have four boys: James, Bruce, Blake and Michael.

Minnie Ellen Leake, born Oct. 18, 1905, married Paul Gibson Henderson on May 24, 1930. Paul Henderson taught school at Allen and was Superintendent of Princeton High School at the time of his death. He died on Sept. 9, 1957 and is buried at Restland Memorial Park, Dallas. They had two girls: Betty and Barbara. Betty Henderson, who married Jimmie Klepper, has two boys and one girl, John Paul, James Richard, and Luvenia Sue. John Paul Klepper married Karen Dianne Fugate and they have one daughter, Amy Daien Klepper, born in 1973. James Richard "Rickie" Klepper is still single. Luvenia Sue Klepper married Arvin Glen Yandell, May 26, 1973. Barbara Henderson married Bob Moreland and they have two children: Keith Moreland, who attends the University of Texas, and Paula Ann Moreland.

CHAPPELL—MYRICK

Susan Bertina "Tina" Chappell, born Sept. 28, 1875 near Audubon, Wise Co., Texas died Feb. 4, 1964. She married Thomas Theadore Myrick on Nov. 19, 1893 at Lucas by Elder J.D. Jobe in a double ceremony with his sister, Clara Bell Myrick, marrying Marion Hackler. "Tina" went to school at St. Paul (see picture of the class in 1888). Thomas Theadore "Dode" Myrick was born Nov. 29, 1871 and died Aug. 22, 1958. They were members of Wilson Chapel Church until it disbanded and they moved their membership to Wesley Memorial Methodist in McKinney. Both are buried at Wilson Chapel Cemetery. They spent most of their lives around McKinney.

"Tina" and "Dode" Myrick had one child, Leslie Homer Myrick, born Nov. 2, 1894, near Dump. He married Johnnie Belle Short on Jan. 4, 1914 at the parsonage of the First Methodist Church in McKinney by Rev. C.C. Young. Homer, Johnnie Belle, and a cousin, Luther Leake, went to school at Higgins. Johnnie Belle Short was born June 21, 1893 near Conway, Ark. Homer and Johnnie Myrick are both members of the Wesley Methodist Church, McKinney. They have six children: Wanda Roberta, Gerald Weldon, Euva Ozelle, Leslie Homer, Jr., Joanna, and Emma Sue.

Wanda Roberta Myrick, born Oct. 2, 1914, married (1) Winston F. Bomar and (2) Henry Lee O'Roark on Nov. 23, 1946. Henry Lee O'Roark died Feb. 11, 1970 and is buried at Wilson Chapel Cemetery. They had two girls: Billie June Bomar, born Dec. 30, 1935, who married Choyce David Watkins on March 3, 1961. They have two girls: Leslie Renee, born Nov. 6, 1963, and Cynthia Carol, born Dec. 12, 1964. Brenda Kay O'Roark, born May 30, 1956, is still at home.

Gerald Weldon Myrick, born Sept. 12, 1916, died May 12, 1942 and is buried at Wilson Chapel Cemetery.

Euva Ozelle Myrick, born Feb. 12, 1919, married (1) James C. Wright, who died Dec. 4, 1955 and is buried at Wilson Chapel. Children born to

this union were: Johnny Timothy Wright, born Sept. 10, 1936, married Barbara in 1957. They have four living children: Arthur, Timothy, Felicia, and Timmy. Two children died at birth and are buried at Wilson Chapel Cemetery. Lynda Gail Wright, born March 31, 1940, married (1) James Drake in 1957 and (2) Odis Clark, Sept. 7, 1962. She is mother of four children: Jim Drake, born Sept. 24, 1958; Ray Ann Clark, born Feb. 21, 1964; Beverly Clark, born Jan. 31, 1967, and Lori Lynn Clark, born Nov. 28, 1968. Gerald James Wright, born Aug. 7, 1944, married Jimmy Summers in Dec. of 1966 and had three children: Gerald James, Jr. "Sonny" born January, 1968; Amy Michelle, born July 1969; and Michael Bryan, born Dec. 31, 1971.

After the death of James C. Wright, Euva married Gary Tidwell, but had no children, and Johnny McFerrin on Dec. 31, 1970 and had no children. Euva works at Wilson Abstract Co.

Leslie Homer Myrick, Jr. born in 1921 died in 1922 and is buried at Wilson Chape Cemetery.

Joanna Myrick, born June 3, 1925 married (1) Vas Reed Grider in Nov. 1949. Born to them were three children: Leslie Michael Grider, born Oct. 19, 1950; Gary Lynn Grider, born Oct. 29, 1951 married Debbie Hale, Dec. 4, 1970; and Joanna Sue Grider, born April 9, 1954 married Ken Hampton. In 1956, Joanna married Grady Long and they had one child, Grady Long, Jr., born Aug. 19, 1957 who is still at home.

Emma Sue Myrick, born July 21, 1930, married (1) Cletus Duckworth then (2) Billy Hurst in 1953. She has one child, Pamela Dianne Hurst, born July 28, 1954, who is still at home. They both work at Collin Memorial Hospital in the bookkeeping department.

COLVIN—ELLISON—PITTS

Minnie M. Colvin, daughter of Joanna and J. Henry Colvin, was born near Audubon, Wise Co., Texas on Feb. 12, 1880. She died May 21, 1938 and is buried at Princeton. Her mother and father separated about 1885, and Joanna Colvin moved her young family back to Collin Co. where she was raised, settling between Lucas and Dump. Around 1898, the Anthony Thomas Leakes, the Thomas Theadore "Dode" Myricks, and Joanna Colvin with her son, James William Chappell, and daughter, Minnie M., moved to farms south of Princeton. Minnie went to school at St. Paul near Wylie while living there and her teacher's name was Mr. Dunn.

1890s PICTURE of old Saint Paul's School near Wylie.

Minnie M. Colvin married Zona Ellison on Feb. 22, 1905 by Rev. Abe Enloe in the home of her brother, James William Chappell, where she and her mother were making their home. (Joe Bates lived on this place later until the 1940's.) Zona Ellison was born at Gilpin, Casey Co., Ky. on July 15, 1875 and died Oct. 5, 1951 in Wise Co. in the Allison Community at the old home place on Denton Creek and is buried in the Princeton Cemetery. The Ellisons moved from Princeton and bought land in Wise Co. in 1916. Their children were a baby who died at birth, Alice and Leon.

Alice Ellison, born Nov. 15, 1907, started to school at Princeton and finished high school at Allison Community School in Wise Co. On Sept. 29, 1923, she married Willie LeRoy Pitts in Wise Co., and in 1934 they moved to Princeton. Willie LeRoy Pitts was born July 16, 1904 near Emory, Rains Co., Texas and died Sept. 4, 1955. He was a dairyman and farmer and is buried at Princeton. They were members of the First Baptist Church at Princeton.

After her husband's death, Alice Pitts studied secretarial training and worked for churches in McKinney, Fort Worth and Dallas as church secretary. St. Paul Methodist Church in Fort Worth awarded her life membership in Women's Society of Christian Service (W.S.C.S.) in 1961. Her interest in genealogy research took her to Ireland and England in 1973 where she visited the home in which her paternal great grandfather was born in 1803 and where her great, great grandparents brought up their family in Dublin, Ireland. She is active in genealogy research and member of the Dallas Local History and Genealogical Society and Plano Genealogy Society.

Alice and Willie LeRoy Pitts had one daughter, Minnie Louise, who was born Oct. 22, 1931 at the Ellison home place in Wise Co. She graduated from Princeton High school as Salutatorian (1949). Minnie Louise Pitts married Willie Elmer Spruill in 1949 who was killed in a car accident on Dec. 23, 1952. A baby girl died at birth and is buried at Farmersville. She attended Southern Methodist University (1951-1953) and graduated from Howard Payne College with a degree in music education. In 1955, she was named to Who's Who in American Colleges and Universities. Graduate study in music and education was done at Howard Payne and Texas Christian University.

On March 25, 1955, Minnie Pitts Spruill was married to Richard Glen Champ in Junction, Texas by Rev. B.W. Mantooth. Richard "Dick" Champ was born May 10, 1934 at Chattanooga, Ok. He graduated from Howard Payne and received his Master's Degree from Southwestern Baptist Theological Seminary in 1959. He is now working for Hilton Hotels Corp. as Manager of Southwestern Division Sales Office. Minnie Champ taught school several years then moved into the secretarial field. An active member and officer of The National Secretaries Assoc. Intnl., she passed the rigid exams for certification as C.P.S. (Certified Professional

JIMMIE LEE ELLISON **RAY ROLAND ELLISON**

Secretary) in 1969. At that time, she was Executive Secretary to the Chairman of the Board of Michigan General Corporation. Richard and Minnie Champ have one son, Russell Brent Champ, born Aug. 5, 1970. They attend Wilshire Baptist Church.

Leon Ellison, born June 15, 1911 on the farm south of Princeton which his parents had bought about 1908. (Mrs. Pete Mounger is living there now —1974). Leon Ellison married Annie Katherine Wardlaw on June 20, 1932 in Wise Co., and they still live on the farm that his parents bought about 1916, operating a dairy. Leon and Annie both went to school at Allison Community School. Annie Katherine Wardlaw was born Aug. 20, 1912. They have two sons: Jimmie Lee and Ray Roland.

Jimmie Lee Ellison, born July 20, 1933, married (1) Ruth Merle Caldwell and they have two boys: Jimmie Lee "Corky" Ellison, Jr., born Aug. 21, 1957; and Rory Scott Ellison, born July 21, 1959. (2) Jerri (no children). (3) Glenda (no children). Jimmie Lee is retired from the Air Force and has settled near his parents.

Ray Roland Ellison, born Dec. 10, 1937, married Gwendolyn Fortenberry on July 21, 1956, and they have two children: Sheryl Ann born March 15, 1958 and Lawrance Roland, born May 29, 1960. Ray Ellison operates a dairy near Slidell where the children go to school.
Submitted by: Alice Pitts

THE RICHARD HOWARD FAMILY

Richard Howard, born May 12, 1801, and wife, Eliza B. Pettet, born in 1808, were born in Albemarle County, Virginia. They were married November 2, 1824, in the same county of Virginia. They had two children while living in Virginia— James Sidney Howard, born October 16, 1826; and Virginia, born in 1829. Between 1829 and 1933, Richard and Eliza and their two children moved to Saline County, Missouri. In this county they settled and started farming. This is where the rest of their children, listed as follows, were born: William, b. 1833; Mary Ellen, b. 1835; Lucretia, b. March 11, 1837; Demarius Margaret, b. 1839; Elizabeth, b. 1841; Sarah Mildred, b. June 16, 1843; Ira Pettit, b. April 19, 1845; John Barnett, b. December 3, 1847; Lavinia, b. 1850; and Louisa, b. 1851.

While living in Missouri, James Sidney Howard married Martha Frey in 1854. They came to Texas about the same time as Richard and his family.

Richard and Eliza Howard settled in the Bloomdale Community, northwest of McKinney, Collin Co., Texas, about 1858. Their farm was located across from what is now Scott Cemetery. James Sidney Howard and wife settled in the Lebanon District, south of Frisco, Texas. James and his wife lived out their lives in this area. They are both buried in Bethel Cemetery, north of Frisco.

Most of Richard's children are thought to have moved to this area with him. Those known are: Virginia F. Howard, who married Sam W. McCorkle; William Howard (he did come to Texas, but it is not known just where); Mary Ellen Howard, who married a Crews and then a Thomas; Lucretia Howard first married a Mr. Hard and then a Mr. Archie McCorkle; Demarius Margaret Howard married Allen Bell, February 21, 1858, and they lived in Denton County, Texas. Elizabeth Howard married Leonard Smith; Sarah Mildred Howard married Jasper Newton Armstrong and moved to Hunicutt, Butte County, California (this is where they are buried, also); Ira Pettit Howard went back to Sedalia, Pettus County, Missouri, and married Alice Reynolds West, then moved back to the home place at Bloomdale in 1867; John Barnett Howard married Martha Jane Hunter in 1872; Lavinia Howard married three times—(1) a Mr. Faries, (2) a Mr. Brown, and (3) a Mr. Wallace; Louisa Howard married twice—(1) Jack Crane, and (2) a Mr. Runnels.

Richard's father was William Howard, born about 1760; his mother was Elizabeth Marshall. William and Elizabeth were married in Albemarle County, Virginia, December 14, 1789. All their children were born there and they lived out their lives in Fredericksburg Parish, Albemarle County, Virginia, where Richard was born.

Richard's brothers and sisters were: Mary, b. 1790, married William Wells December 15, 1808; Mildred Howard, b. 1802, married Richard Dorsey, Jan. 15, 1824; John Howard, b. 1794, married Virginia Pettet (sister to Richard's wife) December 9, 1818; William, unknown; Frances, unknown; Eli Howard, b. about 1808, married Ann Marshall, May 12, 1834; and David Howard, b. after 1810. All were born, and probably married, in Albemarle County, Virginia. It is not known if any of Richard's brothers or sisters settled in Texas, but it is thought that the David Howard descendents around Farmersville, Collin County, Texas, are possibly descendents of Richard's brother, David.

Richard's son, Ira Pettit Howard, b. April 19, 1845, married Alice Caroline Reynolds West, May 7, 1867, in Pettus County, Missouri, settled on the home place of Richard Howard, and started his life as a farmer. Ira and Alice's children were: William Richard Howard, b. February 17, 1868, married Frances Theressa Rodden, July 5, 1891, Collin County; Margaret Ellen, July 30, 1870, to November 18, 1870; Adolphus Andrew Howard, b. February 13, 1871, married Ollie Carter, October 19, 1897; Mary Elizabeth Howard, born August 15, 1873, married Robert A. Foster, June 12, 1890; Franklin Lee Howard, b. November 13, 1874, never married. He died December 19, 1931; George W. Howard, b. November 23, 1876, married Sallie Phillips, September 15, 1901; James W. Howard, b. June 18, 1880 and died July 25, 1881.

All of Ira Pettit Howard's children were born, raised, and died in Collin County, McKinney, Texas. Most are buried in Scott cemetery northwest of McKinney, Texas.

The family of William Richard Howard, first child of Ira Pettit Howard, b. February 17, 1868, married Frances Theressa Rodden, July 5, 1891, in McKinney, Collin County, Texas. Their children are listed as follows: Robert Gano Howard, b. August 10, 1892, married Thelma Young, September 19, 1927; Ophelia May Howard, b. April 20, 1894, married W.J. Bolding, January 18, 1914; George W. Howard, died in infancy, February 17, 1896; Florence Myrtle Howard, b. October 16, 1897, married Willie J. Taylor, April 27, 1921; Willie Roy Howard, b. June 1, 1900, married Vinnie Self, December 23, ——; Emmitt Pettit Howard, b. November 17, 1903, married Alta Bomar Tarvin, August 14, 19--; Otha Francis Howard, b. March 12, 1905, married (1) Celia Roselee Knox, June 23, 1935, and (2) Ethel Morton, June 4, 1955; James Harold Howard, b. April 18, 1907, never married; Jack J. Howard, b.

June 10, 1910, married Virginia Knox, August 10, 1935; Infant Howard, June 8, 1914; Vernie Wilson Howard, b. July 28, 1915, married Ruby Crawford McNatt.

All live in or around McKinney, Texas with the exception of Emmitt Howard, who lives in Junction, Jack J. Howard, who lives in Sherman, and Roy Howard, who died in a truck accident in 1965.

DANIEL HOWELL

Daniel Howell, born in Ohio in 1821, played an important part in the settlement of Collin, Denton, and Wise Counties. Prior to 1845 he settled on a 640 acre grant from Peter's Colony, just east of present day Celina. The marriage records of Old Fannin County shows that he was married in March of 1845 to Mary Ann (Polly) Bradley Ellis, the widowed daughter of Edward Bradley, another Peter's Colonist. Mary Ann, as a widow, recieved the 640 acre tract adjoining that of Daniel Howell. In 1850 Daniel, Mary Ann and their children were living in McKinney.

Record of Daniel Howell's activities in Texas are abundant. Soon after 1850 he and his family were living in Old Alton, the old county seat of Denton County, where he established himself as a merchant. As he watched the stream of immigrants moving west he reasoned that this would necessitate the formation of a new county (Wise) to the west and the establishment of a county seat. Realizing that a new county seat would need a merchandising establishment, he surveyed a likely spot where the new county seat would doubtless be located, he located his trading post at the edge of the timber near a flowing spring and this later proved to be the center of the newly formed Denton Co. Virtually all business was transacted in his trading post; it served as a post office where mail was brought in once a week from old Alton. Along with the settlers, a tribe of Delaware Indians lived nearby and came to the post to trade hides and furs for calico, tobacco, brown sugar, and whiskey. In 1857 Taylorsville, later Decatur, was formed and he moved his store to the new town.

The Civil War brought hard times and great problems to the Howells as well as other families. With no federal troops to protect them, Indian atrocities were commonplace. The Commanches were especially fierce, even wiping out the friendly Delawares. The Howells sent the women back to McKinney for safety. When Daniel Howell brought his family back to McKinney, he built a house on a 27 acre tract awarded her from the estate of her

DANIEL HOWELL, pioneer merchant.

father, Edward Bradley. Daniel Howell's grand-daughter, Bennie Parker West, lives in the home now. This house is on Howell St., named for Daniel and is one of the oldest homes in McKinney. Howell Street was the old McKinney-Denton Road then and the house set back from the road.

In 1865 Daniel Howell, as a Confederate, was suspended from his position as Chief Justice of Wise County to make room for the Reconstruction group. He sold his store and came back to McKinney, where he began again by establishing a store in one of the three brick buildings on the north side of the square. Daniel Howell died August 27, 1878 and his wife preceded him in death. She died April 18, 1878. Both are buried at Pecan Grove Cemetery in McKinney.

The children of Daniel and Mary Ann Howell were; John (1843), Nancy (1845), James Benjamin (1853), George R. (1854), Margaret (1856), and Mary (1860).
Story written by the grandchildren.

THOMAS FINLEY HUGHSTON
1842-1935

Thomas Finley Hughston was born in Shelby County, Alabama, January 2, 1842. He was the son of Archibald Hughston (1795-1872) and his

THOMAS FINLEY HUGHSTON

second wife, Nancy Finley, and was one of twelve children. He was the grandson of John Hughston (ca. 1750-1812) of Spartanburg Dist., S.C., and Mrs. Elizabeth Adair Davis, daughter of Joseph Adair, Jr., and Sarah Dillard of Laurens Co., S.C.

After spending his childhood in Alabama, Thomas served from that state in the 18th Regiment Alabama Infantry of the Confederate Army during the entire Civil War. He was in the thick of the fighting, in five major battles, survived Shiloh with a bullet embedded in the Bible he carried in his shirt pocket, was finally gravely wounded by a Minie ball which struck him in the forehead during the Battle of New Hope Church, Ga., in May, 1864. Military records list Pvt. T.F. Hughston as one of four men on the Battle of Chicamauga Honor Roll for valor from 18th Regiment, Company K, Alabama Voluntary Infantry. Then after almost a year in the field hospital and disabled camp he was given his discharge with "rations and transportation in kind" to his home. On the way home he was taken prisoner of war by the Yankees.

This was near the close of the war. Thomas was paroled at Talladega, Alabama on May 19, 1865. The following year he came to Texas, to Collin County where he settled near the present town of Plano.

204

THE HUGHSTON HOME

About the beginning of World War I, Thomas Finley made a list of the officers and privates of his "Company K, 18th Alabama Infantry," including their initials or first names. There were 12 officers and 101 privates. Ann, his wife, said, "How can you recall all those names?" He replied, "If you had been with them under the conditions we were, you too could have remembered."

In 1865, at Talladega he became a Mason, and affiliated with that organization in 1869 at Plano. In 1895, he served as Worshipful Master of that lodge, and later accepted the duties of tiler for 29 years. On his 71st birthday, the Plano lodge presented him a gold disc charm for his watch chain, with the Masonic Blue Lodge emblem on one side and his monogram and the occasion and date on the opposite side.

At the Grand Lodge session in Waco, December 6, 1933, when his son Wallace presided, Thomas Finley Hughston was interviewed by a reporter from The Waco Times Tribune. "You say you are from the Waco newspaper? Well, spell my name right and call me Thomas Finley . . . Yes, I will be 92 years old January 2nd., and I have been attending these Grand Lodge sessions over 40 years. I have been a Mason 67 years. . . . I went to Houston

when the boys voted to move the Grand Lodge to Waco. . . . The Civil War?" Then Thomas Finley pushed back his hat, fingered a lock of white hair and said by way of answer, "A Yankee Minie Ball did that. . . . I served 4 years. First battle of Shiloh, when Albert Sydney Johnston was killed. Then served under Beauregard and Bragg. That was the Army of Tennessee. . . ." The interview was cut short when a friend came by and interrupted the conversation. One reason why he requested the news reporter to call him "Thomas Finley" was because at that time there were 10 Thomas Hughstons in North Texas, and one Hughston Thomas!

Thomas Finley came to Plano in 1866 and settled near the John Beverly family, early settlers who had a land grant in Peter's Colony. Thomas married Ann Beverly, daughter of Reverend John Beverly and his wife Isabel Russell Beverly, July 29, 1871, in Plano. They were the parents of Wallace Hughston, b. 1874. He studied law in the office of his uncle, Tully Beverly, later District Judge of the 59th District Court of Sherman and McKinney. He was county attorney in 1898, for two terms, Grand Master of Texas Grand Lodge 1932, State Senator 1934; Nettie Hughston (Morgan) b. 1876; Eva Lee b. 1878 and Carrie, b. 1882 were school teachers; and Tom Allen, b. 1884, was head of the Cotton Seed and Oil Industry of Texas for several years. Each of their children graduated from Plano Institute. The Hughstons also reared a niece, Hester Henry, whose mother died when she was a baby. On June 29, 1921, Thomas Finley and Ann Beverly Hughston celebrated their 50th wedding anniversary, and ten years later their 60th anniversary. For both occasions relatives and friends came to wish them many more years of joy and happiness.

Thomas Finley had united with the Presbyterian Church when in Talledaga, but became a member of the Methodist Church when he married. He and his wife were active and devoted members of the Plano Church. Although his eye sight and hearing were impaired, he never missed a church service.

In December, 1973, the Plano School Board met to decide on names for seven future schools. It is a tradition that schools be named after local pioneers. The following paragraph is copied from the Plano Daily Star-Courier: "Another Civil War veteran . .

Thomas Finley Hughston, . . . will be the namesake of an elementary school in northwest Plano. Mr. Hughston was a farmer of several different crops near Plano, including corn, oats, wheat and cotton. The Hughston children attended the first public school in the Plano area . . . the Plano Institute. They attended school only a few months out of the year, traveling on foot, pony, horse or mule. Thomas F. Hughston was a member of the Plano Masonic Lodge for 70 years, was a charter city council member, a county commissioner (1888), Deputy Tax Assessor of Collin County and a member of the Board of Stewards for the Methodist Church for several years.''

It should be noted that in the records of the past the name ''Hughston'' is spelled variously ''Huston,'' ''Houston,'' etc. Thomas Finley Hughston's grandfather spelled his name John ''Huston.'' This is the way John's sons spelled the name until for some reason they all changed the spelling to ''Hughston'' and it became consistant that way.

It should also be noted that there is a possibility that Thomas Finley Hughston's father, Archibald, had come to Texas for a short while in 1844. Because in the Peter's Colony of Texas an ''Archibald Houston,'' single had entered on July 1, 1844. He settled in old Fannin Co. at the head of Elm For and Mineral Creek in the Cross Timbers. This Archibald apparently left before receiving a land certificate, or fulfilling the obligations required to receive one. If this were Thomas' father, perhaps his early venture to Texas influenced Thomas to come after the war.

REFERENCES:

National Archives, Confederate Records—Civil War, File No. 35876, Thomas F. Hughston

Personal Papers and Letters of Thomas Finley Hughston, in possession of Mrs. E.W. Hughston, Dallas, Texas.

1850 Federal Census of Taladega District, Alabama, September 25, 1850; Families of Arch Houston, John F. Houston.

1880 Federal Census of Collin County, Texas, Dist. No. 24, July 16, 1880, Dwelling No. 187, Family No. 198. Thomas F. Hughston.

Will of Joseph Adair, Jr. (1732-1812), Box 3, Pkg. 6, Office of the Judge of Probate for Laurens County, S.C.

Probate Records, John Huston Estate, June 8, 1812, on file Spartanburg County Court House, S.C.

Marriage Records of Old 96 Dist. S.C., Sara Erwin, Ware Shoals, S.C. 1951.

The Peters Colony of Texas, Seymour V. Conner, Texas State Historical Association, 1959.

A History of Collin County, Texas, J. Lee Stambaugh and Lillian J. Stambaugh, Texas State Historical Association, 1958.

1850 Federal Census of Collin Co., Texas, Family No. 278, John Beverly

1880 Federal Census of Collin Co. Texas, Precinct 5, Dist. 24, Dwelling No. 186, Family No. 190, John Beverly.

Beverly Family Bible Records, Birth Records, Death Records, in possession of Mrs. E.W. Hughston, Dallas.

Beverly Family Tombstone Records, copied in Old City Cemetery, Plano, Texas.

Biographical Souvenir of the State of Texas, F.H. Battery & Co., Chicago, 1889, page 79.

History of Central and Western Texas, Paddock, Vol. I., page 420, 421.

Alabama-Mississippi Confederate Military History, Evans, p. 115.

The Confederate Soldier in the Civil War, Ben LaBree, Courier-Journal Job Printing Co., Louisville, Ky. 1894.

THE JOHN WILSON HUNTER FAMILY

Mary Frances Compton, daughter of Eber and Angie Frye Compton, was attending boarding school in Bonham when she married John Wilson Hunter, a young man who then had just recently come to Texas from Tennessee. This couple continued to live in Bonham for about three years when they and their two baby sons came to make their home on a farm about eight miles south of McKinney. There they continued to live while rearing a family of fifteen children. There were eleven boys and four girls, all of whom except the two oldest were born in the same house. Here is but a brief statement about each of the family.

Eber, the eldest son, who was born in Bonham, came with his parents to Collin Co. at age three. Eber, who was later known as Dr. J.E. Hunter, was graduated from Galveston Medical school in the class of 1896. When a very young doctor, he lived and practiced medicine in Malissa and adjoining communities. He was married to Mattie Ogilvie of Malissa. She lived only a few years after their marriage, and she was buried in Highland Cemetery, near Malissa. Dr. Hunter moved to McKinney where he was associated with Dr. Wysong in the practice of medicine. In McKinney, he was married to Anne Gough, daughter of Senator J.R. Gough. Mrs. Hunter and their son William now reside in Dallas, where William is a lawyer. Dr. Hunter died in 1936 and was buried in Highland Cemetery. Robert Marshal, the second son, grew up on the family farm. He was married to Olive Cantrell of the Lucas community. This couple lived most of their married life on a wheat farm near Claude, Texas. Both are buried at Claude.

Grace May Hunter was the third child and was the first to be born to the Hunters after they came to live in Collin County. Grace was married to John Coffey of the Lucas community. She died at age nineteen when giving birth to a baby girl. She was buried at Fitzhugh Cemetery, Forest Grove.

Claud B. Hunter, the fourth of the large family, was born Sept. 24, 1876, and now in his 98th year he can tell tall tales of his long experiences as a frontier man of West Texas. Claude was graduated from McKinney Collegiate Institute in June, 1898. Two years later, he was married to Cora B. Sneed, who also was graduated in the same class. Together they taught school at Forest Grove and Princeton in Collin County before going to make their home on a farm near Amarillo, Texas. Those were the days in which they purchased unfenced and untilled land at ten dollars per acre and when the West was full of adventure and daring. Claud and Cora liked living in the West, but when time for retirement made life in the West too difficult, they moved to Austin to be near their two daughters, Nora Leta Hargis and Frances Goggan. This couple had this year, the most unusual experience of observing their seventy-third wedding anniversary.

Luther T. Hunter specialized in farm demonstration work and was, for a number of years Farm Demonstration Agent in several West Texas towns and communities. He was married to Jane Coffey of the Forest Grove Community. This couple was living in Bowie, Texas, when they were deceased. Both are buried in Fitzhugh Cemetery, Forest Grove. Maud Hunter was born in 1878. She attended school in Denton, and later taught several rural schools in Collin County and in Allen. She was married to Charlie McKinney, who was reared in the Lucas community but who at the time of their marriage was living in Fort Worth. Each died while making their home in Bowie. They, too, are buried at Fitzhugh Cemetery.

John Clarence Hunter, the seventh child to be born to the Hunters, had the tragic misfortune of being burned fatally at age five. This accident cost him his life after a few days of suffering.

Virginia B. Hunter was born January 14, 1883. She was married in 1902 to William H. McMillen of the Murphy community. Virginia now resides at Juliett Fowler Home in Dallas, where she will observe her ninety-first birthday on January 14, 1974.

Edward Lee Hunter early chose to make teaching his life work. After attending school in Denton, he completed his M.A. Degree at Colorado College. He taught first in Allen and in rural schools in Collin County. He was, for twenty-five years, principal of Horace Mann School in Amarillo. Lee died Dec. 30, 1973.

Dr. Joseph Boone Hunter was number ten on the list of Hunters born in this family. He was one of the three Hunter Brothers who had military service in Europe during World War One. He attended colleges and universities outside of Texas and taught in missionary colleges in Japan and in Syria. He was married to an American missionary in Nagasaki. She was Mary Clery of Ohio. In addition to his work as a minister of the Christian Church, Joe has made study trips to the Far East in connection with his college teaching in America.

Eula Frances Hunter is another of the family who chose to be a teacher in the public schools. She taught for four years in McKinney High School while making her home with her mother in Allen. The daily trips to McKinney were made by Interurban. Later, she taught in a Fort Worth High School until retirement time. She now lives in Fort Worth.

Oran E. Hunter was born down on the farm and was the last of the boys to leave the farm for other work. He engaged in buying cotton in Allen and with larger firms. He was married to Elizabeth Mallow, daughter of Dr. Mallow of McKinney. Oran died while living in Emory, Texas, where his wife now lives.

Hal H. Hunter was perhaps the best athlete of the family. In Plano High School competition he won first place medals, and later was all southern fullback in football, and helped by coaching football. He was living in Fort Worth, Texas, at the time of his death. He was married to Gladys Reed of Ranger.

Roy R. Hunter left the farm at about fifteen years of age to make his home in West Texas. He was a soldier in France in World War One. Returning to Amarillo, he engaged in cattle commission business. In Amarillo he was married to Ruth Coffey, daughter of Dr. John Coffey, who was formerly of Collin County. Roy and wife now live in Canyon, Texas.

Walter D. Hunter, youngest of the Hunters born down on the farm, graduated from McKinney High School, to which he made daily trips by Interurban from his home in Allen. He early engaged in buying cotton as an employee of Will Bush of Allen. Later he bought cotton for a large firm in Fort Worth before going to Waco to go into business for himself. He was married to Jennie B. Duren of Waco. They now reside in Waco, where he is with the W.D. Hunter Cotton Company.

THE GEORGE A. WILSON home place where the Jay family lived for many years. The house was later remodeled and made into a full two story house.

THE JESSE JAY FAMILY OF THE WILSON COMMUNITY

Jesse Jay was born March 8, 1867 in Murray County, Georgia. He was a descendant of a pioneer family of Murray and Walker County, Georgia. His grandparents were Mr. and Mrs. David Jay of Walker County, Georgia. He was the son of James Richard and Ellen Elizabeth Gilwreath Jay. He had three brothers, Dave, Henry and George. Two sisters, Mrs. Mary (Mollie) Thomas and Mrs. Martha (Mattie) Walls.

About 1878 his parents left Georgia via covered wagon in search of a more healthy climate for his father. They went into the Ozarks of Arkansas where his father passed away and was buried. His mother remarried a Mr. Bowman. Eventually this marriage ended in a separation. She passed away in

BAPTISMAL SERVICE at a farm tank on the Ike Dillow place. Services were for the Bomar Chapel Methodist Church. Taken in the 1920's.

SHOCKING GRAIN on the Jay Farm about 1916.

WAGONS BEING loaded with grain to be hauled to the thrasher. About 1916, Jay Farm.

SORGHUM MAKING TIME on the Jay Farm about 1917.

McKinney, Texas in 1924 and is buried in the Van Alstyne cemetery.

Jesse Jay worked as a farm hand for several years at Center Hill, Arkansas. Living with the Matthews and Neal families. This information comes from letters written to him from members of these families and dated May 23 and September 30, 1887. He first came to Grayson County, Texas where he married Minnie Jay Niell in Sherman, July 24, 1887. She too was a native of Murray County, Georgia. Their families were acquaintances in Georgia. To this union twelve children were born: James Arthur, Myrtle May (Mrs. R.C. Rankins), Nora McCoy, Allie (Mrs. Willie R. Wallis), Jessie Pauline (Mrs. Oran Wallace), Chester Pearl (Mrs. W.C. Nitcholas), Willie (deceased February 7, 1905) and Homer Henry. All of these were born in Grason County.

In 1905 the Jesse Jay family moved to Collin County, seven miles Northeast of McKinney, where they lived for eighteen years in the old George A. Wilson home place then owned by Mrs. John E. Burrage nee Mamie Wilson of McKinney. Here in this house the four younger children were born: Tomie Paris, Marguerite (Mrs. Jerry Lewis), George and Flora Ellen (Mrs. John A. Carson).

Jesse Jay was a thrifty farmer. To provide for the large family he managed the 320 acre farm. With sub-tenants and the children he cultivated the land in cotton, corn, wheat, oats, sugar cane, peanuts and vegetables. The family made and sold sorghum molasses. Chickens were raised in large flocks not only to provide meat for the table but for the sale of eggs. Two or three kerosene incubators were set each spring. There were many livestock, horses, mules, registered Duroc hogs, and sheep. Large flocks of geese, ducks, turkeys and guineas. Another side line project was a telephone exchange which started as a party line and expanded into an exchange that covered areas around the communities of Wilson, Altoga, Valdasta, Princeton, New Hope, and Woodlawn, with connections into McKinney and Melissa. This telephone exchange was known as the "Jay Exchange" until in the late 1920's when it was known as the "Altoga Exchange." It was in operation until about 1935.

Allie married Willie R. Wallis and continued to

THRASHER TIME. The little girl shown in the foreground with back to camera is spellbound with the thrasher operations.

209

COOKING SORGHUM on the Jay Farm about 1917.

TYPICAL SCENE of cotton pickers weighing cotton. Made in East Texas. Some of the Walls family, cousins of the Jay's. Date unknown.

live in the adjoining community of Wallis Chapel. And also on the adjoining farm, the Henry Wallis home place. Nora married and went to Wyoming thence to California, in the early 1920's. Later, Homer, Pauline, Chester, Tomie, George and Flora Ellen and their families moved to California and established homes. Myrtle and Allie continued to live on a portion of the farm bought from Mrs. Burrage until in the 1960's. Marguerite lived in McKinney where her husband was a well-known masonry contractor.

Mr. and Mrs. Jay sold their farm and moved to Tracy, California in 1943. Jesse Jay died there April 21, 1945 and Minnie Jay passed away there June 9, 1965. Both are buried in Tracy. Arthur Jay passed away in McKinney October, 1968, Allie Jay Wallis in January of 1969. Homer died in Tracy, California in May of 1973.

Descendants still living in Collin County are Mrs. Myrtle Rankins and son Robert C. Rankins, Jr. and his children Suzie and Cliff. Also Mrs. Marguerite Lewis of McKinney. Two grandchildren live in Dallas, Mrs. Paulien Wallis Blakely and Mrs. Jessie Rankins Vaughan and children, Donna and Jerry Vaughan. All other descendants of this family now live in California.

Story sent by Mrs. Jerry Lewis, McKinney.

JOHN H. JOHNSON
Collin County
(Legendary)

John H. Johnson, his mother and sisters trekked and carried their belongings on some of their earlier moves. Barbara Johnson, mother of John Johnson, died and was buried in Missouri. Rachael Johnson and Polly Johnson, sisters of John Johnson, came to Texas. Rachael Johnson Willis was buried in the old Denton Cemetery, Denton, Texas. Polly Johnson Younger left many descendants living in this area among them being Ada Younger Boone, Pete Younger, and Rachael Straughan.

When Polly Kimsey of Missouri fell in love with the young John Johnson, her father heartily disapproved of the marriage, feeling that the young man had no financial future, and forbade his daughter's marrying, whereupon the young Johnson and his bride-to-be stole away on horseback with a quilt or robe around the young lady to protect her from the weather.

Polly Kimsey Johnson is said to have furthered her husband's education, since he had had little formal schooling as he grew to manhood.

Mr. Johnson became a slave holder and when the Missouri Legislature voted against secession, Johnson found his sympathies lying with the South.

The War Between the States was in progress and John Johnson had leave from the Confederate Army when he returned to Missouri to bring his family to Texas. Since neighbors and brothers were fighting on opposite sides, Johnson found it expedient to ride on his horse while accompanying his family to their new home in Texas for he could disappear into the hedges or trees along the way and yet be near the wagon train until it could be ascertained as to whether strangers along the way were friend or foe.

If the Negro slaves chose to remain in Missouri, they were given their freedom and land to cultivate as they wished.

John H. Johnson organized a company of men to fight in the Confederate Army, and, as the conflagration of war burned more brightly, it literally burned more brightly near St. Joseph, Missouri, for the new home that the Johnson Family had left there was razed by fire by those who had chosen to

THE JOHN H. JOHNSON home on Anthony Street in McKinney.

THE LARGEST MONUMENT in Collin County stands above the graves of John H. and Polly Kimsey Johnson in the old Johnson Cemetery of McKinney. The site of the cemetery was chosen because it was his old "deer stand" under a big elm tree and a favorite spot.

remain with the Union.

At a more propitious time Mr. Johnson dispatched his eldest daughter, Dade Johnson Mallow, and her husband, A.C. Mallow, to return to De Kalb County, Missouri, for the sole purpose of selling what remained of the property there. The young people travelled by wagon and carried the money from the sale of the property in an old coffee pot.

John Johnson became known as "Rutabaga" Johnson, a fiery political figure, whose writings were often published in the newspapers of the state.

Although Mr. Johnson had to take his education where he could find it, he was a firm believer in education, and sent some of his sons to Virginia for training in law. One son, Louis F. Johnson, was killed in a friendly croquet game at Washington and Lee University just prior to his graduation. It has been said that the friend who was responsible for the accident became so disturbed over the accident that he was later committed to a mental institution. Another son, Merrill W. Johnson, practiced law and it was the father's dream that one or more of his sons should enter politics as he had done, but it has

been said that even though Merrill Johnson practiced law it was his ambition to be a preacher, and he did often find himself being called upon to occupy various pulpits over the county. At any rate, none of the children became interested in politics.

Education for young ladies had not become so prevalent at the time, and even though Mr. Johnson was a firm advocate for higher learning for boys and young men, he hardly appreciated the necessity for educating the girls of the family. After all, the girls were only going to get married and rear families, and Johnson evidently had not become convinced that

"Educate a young man and you've educated an individual;

Educate a young lady and you've educated a family."

John H. Johnson and his wife Polly Kimsey Johnson, as are many of their descendants, are buried in the Old Johnson Cemetery, four miles east of McKinney. The cemetery platte was carved out of some of the original land purchased from the government for one dollar per acre.

During the Civil War one son, Benjamin W. Johnson, was not well and one day he said to his father, "Pappy, when I die I want to be buried under the old elm tree by my deer-stand." The "deer-stand" where the young son had hunted deer was on the higher north east corner of the farm, and to this day various members of the family chose to be buried in the Old Johnson Cemetery in spite of its sometimes lacking in care, or of vandalism which has destroyed parts of some of the older monuments. But the impressive monument marking the resting places of John H. and Polly Kimsey Johnson remains much as it has looked for some sixty or seventy years—a landmark worthy of sturdy pioneers.

—Nadine Holder Honaker

THE KERR FAMILY

Three Kerr brothers came to Texas from Tennessee: Major Green William, James Orr, and John Whitfield. Major Green W. Kerr came alone in 1858 and bought 590 acres of land in the Vineland Community, northwest of McKinney. He then went back to Tennessee and returned with his family and slaves. He and his wife, Mariah Henderson Kerr, were the parents of nine children, Jerome B., Elizabeth, Lawson, Malinda Jane, Ruth, John Steele, A.W., A.D., and Will M. Jerome died in the Battle of Shiloh, Elizabeth married T.H.B. Hockaday in Tennessee and came to Texas with her parents. Their daughter, Ella Hockaday, established the famed Hockaday School at Dallas in 1913 and donated the school to the City of Dallas in 1942, and became President Emeritus until her death March 26, 1956. She had one sister, Emma Hockaday Johnson, and four brothers, Fred, Jim, Brown, and Albert.

Lawson Kerr engaged in farming and religious work. Malinda Jane Kerr Sneed was a teacher, while Ruth Kerr Dowell did social work and taught music. John Steel Kerr served in the Civil War and after the war was in the nursery business in Sherman with his brother, A.D. Kerr. John S. married Amelia Rutherford Murray and they were the parents of five children. He died in Sherman October 4, 1925.

James Orr Kerr was born in Tennessee November 10, 1813 and was married June 1, 1837 to Elizabeth Naomi Blackwell. They came to Texas in 1860 and were the parents of ten children: Mary F. (Molly), married Billy White; Lavenia; John Blackwell, married Rebecca Ferguson, daughter of Samuel Ferguson of Boling Green, Kentucky; James G., never married; Samuel J. drowned in Little Elm Creek on his way back from Denton where he had bought a marriage license; Thomas Jefferson (Tump) married Willie Jones and had one son, Sydney; William Whitfield married Isola Looney and had one son, William Cloyd, who ran a drug store in Prosper and after his wife's death, married Betty Bell Sneathen; Elizabeth, married Will A. Gossett and had the following children: Hattie, Ray Gossett of Celina, and Dr. John Gossett, a well known veterinarian of McKinney. Jerome Botford Kerr married Emma Orr and their children were Sydney, Marie, Whitfield, and Fred. Eugenia Alice Kerr and her husband, Robert Kerr, had the following children, Bernard, Finis, Sadie, Roger, and Florence.

John Whitfield Kerr, brother of Greene W. Kerr and James Orr Kerr, was born in Tennessee September 2, 1834. He married Sallie Scott in 1858. After her death, he married Mary E. Scott, a cousin of his first wife. They were the parents of four sons and a daughter who died young. The sons were Julian B., Dave W., Frank S., and Albert S. After the death of his second wife, John W. married a sister of George McWhorter, a pioneer of west Collin County. John W. served as a lieutenant in the Civil War, was wounded twice and captured once. He settled at Celina in 1871 and died there February 28, 1925.

John Blackwell Kerr was a farmer and lived in the Foote Community, one mile west of the old Foote Store and half a mile north. He lived on this farm all his life except the time he was away serving in the Civil War. He and his wife, Rebecca Ferguson Kerr, were the parents of six children: Thomas Leslie who lived in Missouri; Granville who lived in Oklahoma; Ethel married Andrew Martin Griffin; Lillian Cloyd married Thomas H. Cunningham; Sallie Naomi who married Bill Lively; and Edwin who married Gertrude Leigh Cline.

Ethel Kerr, third child of J.B. and Rebecca Kerr, spent part of her married life in Collin County, then in Hale County. Their eldest son, William Marion Griffin was a Presbyterian minister and held pastorates in Texas, Missouri, and Arkansas. The Rev. Griffin married Marie Wilson and they were the parents of two sons, Martin, a computer technician, and Warren of Austin, Texas.

The second child of Ethel and A.M. Griffin, Rosalie, married James Floyd Baxter. The couple spent most of their lives in Collin County, and most of their children still live there. Luther Martin, third child of Ethel and A.M. Griffin, was a businessman and veterinarian in Amarillo prior to his death. Their other children were Sarah Ethel who married Hiram Attaway, Raymond who died in infancy, Rebecca married Dawson Allman.

Lillian Cloyd Kerr, fourth child of J.B. and Rebecca Kerr, married Thomas H. Cunningham, a farmer and stockman of the Walnut Grove Community and after his death his wife moved to McKinney. They lost their only daughter in infancy, but their sons were Vincent, Paul, T.H., and T.C. The elder Cunninghams are buried in the Walnut Grove Cemetery.

J. Edwin Kerr, youngest child of J.B. and Rebecca Kerr, is now retired from the ministry and lives in Meeker, Oklahoma.

Story written by Mr. and Mrs. James Baxter.

THE ISAAC KIMSEY FAMILY

The Isaac Kimsey family came to Collin County in the year of 1864 from Missouri. They settled southwest of Farmersville where he purchased a large acreage. He married Margaret Adams who was born in Wilkes County, North Carolina on January 7, 1827. Their children were Mary Abigail, James M., William Hugh, Mattie, Thomas J., and Robert Lee. All of the children were born in Missouri except the youngest son, Robert Lee, who was born in Leonard, Bonham County (1866). Isaac William Kimsey was a Captain in the Quartermaster Corp of Shelby's Brigade of Price's Division during the Civil War.

A grandson, Clifford Carpenter, lives in Farmersville. Mrs. Herman Goldblotte also lives in Farmersville. A grandson, Kim Carpenter, lives on the home place. Other relatives living in the area are Mrs. M.L. Rickerson of Mesquite, Mrs. Gladys Bickley Watson of McKinney, and Mrs. Maxine Kimsey Watson of Farmersville. C.T. Kimsey, Mrs. Hubert Kimsey and a grandson, Alton H. Kimsey still live on the Robert Kimsey homeplace, although the government has bought much of the land for Lavon Lake.

Robert Kimsey had seven grandchildren, Alton H. Kimsey of Farmersville; Robert B. Kimsey of Garland; Eunice Kimsey McDonald of Blue Ridge; Margaret Kimsey Harrington of Farmersville; Linda Watson Yeats of Shreveport, Louisiana; Jeanette Bickley Bland of Richardson, and Rita Bickley Roose of Farmersville. Robert Kimsey has 21 great-grandchildren.

Story sent by: Mrs. Hubert Kimsey, Farmersville, Texas.

ELBERT WILEY KIRKPATRICK

General E.W. Kirkpatrick was born near Whitesburg, Tennessee on October 12, 1844. His father and mother were Jacob M. and Sarah Jane (Campbell) Kirkpatrick. He had one younger brother and seven sisters.

The family arrived in Collin County in 1854. A year or so later the father died and young Elbert, then 13 years old, took complete charge of running his mother's farm. For the most part, he was self-educated, however he did attend a private school a few miles south of McKinney for a few months.

When the Civil War broke out, the recruiting officer, knowing that his mother needed him to operate the farm, refused to let him enlist until he was 18, the latter part of 1862. At that time he enlisted as a private in Company I, Martin's Texas Partisan Rangers, DeMosse's Brigade, Cooper's Division, Marmadukes' Corps, Trans-Mississippi Department. After the war ended he was honorably discharged in South Texas in May 1865, and returned to his home in McKinney to take charge of his farm.

In 1872 he taught the first public school in Collin County. He was always a strong advocate of Free Schools although at the time there was strong opposition to the idea of free schools for every child.

On November 5, 1874 he married Emily Terrell Clive of McKinney and to this union were born six children. Mr. Kirkpatrick began growing, experimenting, and improving trees and plants of all kinds and in 1874 he established his first nursery at White's Grove. When the Texas Nursery Company of Sherman was organized, he was elected president and served in that capacity until his death. He also served as President of Whitesboro Fruit Company, the Nueces Land and Immigration Company, and was a director in the Durant Nursery Company, the Collin County Mill and Elevator, New Century Milling Company, and the Burrus Milling Company of Dallas. He served as president of the Texas Industrial Congress in 1908 and 1909. He helped organize both the state and national Nurserymen's Association, and served as president for several years in them. He was a charter member of the National Nut Grower's Association and served as president for several years. He was active in forming a State Nut Growers' Association and on May 29, 1906 it was formed and he served as its first president.

Gen. Kirkpatrick helped to organize the Throckmorton Camp, United Confederate Veterans, No. 109, at McKinney in 1888. He was Commander of the camp at the time of his death. Each year he entertained the veterans at his home.

During World War I he served as a member of the Texas State Council of the Y.M.C.A., War Fund Committee, and as a member of the food conservation organization of the State of Texas. He was a Mason, an Oddfellow, an Elk, and a Rotarian. He was an active member of the McKinney Chamber of Commerce, being Chairman of the Agricultural Committee.

He died of pneumonia March 24, 1924 at Rincon, New Mexico, where he had gone on a business trip.

The story written by Martha Schubert who still lives in the palacial old home on Parker Street, McKinney

THE KIRKPATRICK HOUSE.

The Kirkpatrick House, one of the historic homes still standing in McKinney, was built by Gen. Kirkpatrick in 1900, and has sheltered Kirkpatricks ever since. Alice Kirkpatrick, Mrs. Charlie Waide raised her two children here, Martha Waide Schubert and son Elbert. Martha's two sons, Jay Crum now with CBS Radio in New York and Tom Waide Crum, a Waxahachie attorney, grew up in the ancestoral home.

THE LAWSON FAMILY

The Lawson Family came to Texas from Cleveland, Tennessee around 1873. Jerry Lawson and Jim Moreland who married Mantooth sisters came first, then worked on the railroad enough to bring their families. The families rode a train to Anna, then went southeast to the present Altoga. This was before the first store at Altoga which was established about 1880.

Mr. and Mrs. Jerry Lawson had seven children— John, Evaline, Billy, Jim, Lizzie, Rowe, and Elmer. All of these children are now deceased. Several grandchildren, great-grandchildren, etc., still live in Collin County. Grandchildren who are still living include Mrs. Hattie Baxter, daughter of John; Mrs. C.N. Gerron, daughter of Evaline; Wilfred Lawson and Troy Lawson, sons of Billy; Royce Lawson, son of Rowe; and Walter Lawson and Reno Lawson, sons of Elmer. Great-grandchildren living in Collin County include Glen D. Lawson, Billy Lawson and Herman Lawson sons of Troy; Mrs. Jean Roebuck, Mrs. Radean Herron, and Weldon Lee (Bud) Lawson, children of Walter; and George Lawson, Joe Lawson, Sammy Lawson, and Billy Lawson, sons of Reno.
Story sent by: Herman Lawson, Principal of Finch Elementary School, McKinney, Texas.

THE LOVEJOY FAMILY

The family of the Rev. John L. Lovejoy was one of the earliest of Collin County's pioneers. John L. was born in 1800 in Georgia and brought his family to Texas in 1835, crossing Red River at Mill Creek, and lived both in Lamar County, and Grayson. In 1845 he settled near Wilson's Mill on Sister Grove Creek and stayed there about one year. In 1846 he settled at Buckner and opened a general merchandise store. Old notes record that on the day they moved into Buckner he sent his son, James H., to the log cabin of William Davis to borrow fire.

His children were George, John L., James H., and Una. His store was a gathering place for the sparsely settled community and he did a good business selling to the settlers and trading with the peaceful Indians who lived here at the time. In 1848 when an election was held to relocate the county seat of Collin County, there was a lot of controversy about the proper site. Some favored the spot where McKinney now is, and some the land south of McKinney near the old underpass on Highway 5. The night before the election, a flooding rain fell and no one could cross the swollen waters of the creeks so only those in the vacinity of Buckner could vote. Lovejoy decided to follow the county seat and on May 1, 1848 his little store was hauled across three miles of prairie by 16 oxen driven by Manse Wilmeth. It was placed on the northwest corner of the present square on May 3, 1848, the first store in McKinney. The family lived in the back room of the store and it later became the Foote House. He later sold the location to the Alexander brothers and moved to Denton where he also put in the first business.

James H. Lovejoy, son of John L., came to Collin County with his parents at age three (born February 3, 1832 in Hot Springs, Arkansas).

James served in the Civil War, at first serving under Vol Young, and helped take Ft. Washita. He helped raise Co. D, Stone's Regiment at Old Mantua with Captain Bowen and served in Arkansas and Missouri. After the Battle of Pea Ridge he returned to Collin and helped organize Martin's Regiment, Burford's Regiment, and Stone's 2nd Reg., then rejoined his company at Holly Springs until the end of the war. He served two terms as sheriff of the county.

John Lemuel Lovejoy, son of George Lovejoy, was born in Paris, Lamar County, Texas, August 22, 1848 and came with his parents to Collin County in 1848, settling at White's Grove. He was a successful business man in McKinney for many years, serving as president of the First National Bank, director of the Texas Electric Railway, director of the Texas Cotton Oil Company, vice president of the McKinney Cotton Oil Mill, vice president of the McKinney Dry Goods Company and a number of other interests. He married Carrie Louise Emerson, daughter of Francis Emerson. The late Mrs. C.G. Comegys was his daughter, and her sons, George Wilkins Comegys and J.L. Comegys, continued to serve the town in many areas. The third generation is still active in business and civic life of Collin County.

Sources: Microfilmed newspapers at Lib.
Biog. John L., April 28, 1931
Biog. May 25, 1920
Feb. 6, 1908
Capt. Hall's notes made from interviews.

FROM HISTORY OF LUCAS FAMILIES
By Mrs. John Shipp

Peter F. Lucas was one of the early settlers of this community. His log cabin was three-fourths of a mile northeast of the present Lucas stores. He and his family lived there in mid-1850. His son, Gabriel H. Lucas and his wife, Nancy Wetsel Lucas, daughter of Mr. and Mrs. James Wetsel, were the parents of eleven children, three of whom now live in McKinney: Mrs. J.B. Hammock, Mrs. Walker Thurman and Tull B. Lucas. Prior to Peter Lucas' death in October of 1868 (according to his granddaughter, Mrs. Thurman), the area was to be granted a post office. Peter Lucas sent in the name "Lucas" to honor his son, Gabriel or Gabe, as he was called.

Another early settler, Joe McKinney, sent in the name "St. Jo," but the Post Office Dept. of Washington selected the name "Lucas." According to General Services Administration, Washington, D.C., a post office was established May 11, 1888 and discontinued Sept. 30, 1903.

Following are the names of the postmasters of Lucas, who were also merchants:

Postmasters	Date of Appointments
Gabriel H. Lucas	May 11, 1888
George W. Bradley	July 17, 1890
James M. Gallagher	May 15, 1891
John G.J. Moss	Oct. 8, 1891
Robert H. Coffey	June 29, 1892
Samuel L. Renfrow	Oct. 26, 1897
Stockley T. Armstrong	Nov. 2, 1898
John A. Armstrong	Jan. 29, 1903
Rufus E. Morrow	June 5, 1903

At one time in Lucas' early history, there were three or four stores, two barber shops, blacksmith shop, cotton gin, grist mill, school and two churches. And, in the early days it seems there was always a resident doctor. Dr. John Armstrong, a bachelor, was the first doctor to locate in Lucas. After his death, Dr. J.C. Coffey arrived. Dr. R.E. Morrow followed Dr. Coffey. Later Dr. Morrow moved to the Winningkoff community, but continued to look after the ills of most of the Lucas people.

Lucas was incorporated in 1959. The following served as mayor from that date to 1973: Gene Biggs, Dale Spurgin, Ray Parr, O.E. Spurgin and Jim Outlaw.

A water system was organized and in 1970 Lake Lavon water was available to the area.

BAPTIST CHURCH

According to courthouse records the first church in Lucas was organized and given the name Willow Springs Baptist Church in 1881. The first building erected on the land donated by Mr. and Mrs. John Spurgin burned many years later and was replaced on the same site. Later Mrs. Bob Coffey donated one-half acre of the Coffey estate that joined the church yard. The congregation continued to worship there until 1966 when the old building and land was sold to the Nathan Strains and a new brick building was erected one-half mile west on FM 1378.

LUCAS CHRISTIAN CHURCH

The Lucas Christian (Disciples) Church was established around the turn of the century. Prior to its establishment those of that faith attended the Forest Grove Christian Church.

UNITED METHODIST CHURCH

Blyth Chapel, a Methodist Church established on land donated by a Mr. Blyth before the turn of the century (we were told) in Winningkoff community.

Since so few members of the church lived in that area and most of them lived at Lucas, the church was moved here in February of 1967 and given the name First United Methodist Church of Lucas. We were told that in the early days the whole Winningkoff community attended church at Blyth Chapel. In 1971 a parsonage was added on the three-acre plot belonging to the church. The Lucas Christian also has a home for their ministers on the church grounds.

Written by Mrs. John Shipp
As Reported by Tressye Click

THE MAYES FAMILY

Adolphus Barbee Mayes came to Texas with his parents, Dr. Robert B. Mayes, one of Collin County's earliest physicians, and his wife Nancy. His family had come from Green County, Kentucky and settled on Panther Creek, later known as Mayes Creek, four miles northeast of present Frisco. They bought land and settled here. The following children came with their parents to Collin County, A.B. Mayes, William, Berenice, Mrs. Margaret McWhorter, Mrs. William Allen Abbie, Mrs. John Rhea (Veronica).

Adolphus and Nancy Mayes were already married when they came with the elder Mayes to Collin County, and were the parents of two sons, John and Joe Rhea. Rhea was killed in the Civil War and his widow later married T.J. Ferguson.

A.B. Mayes, who was eight years old when he came with his parents to Collin, also served in the Civil War from 1861 to 1865, joining at old Mantua in September of 1861. He was in Company D. 6th Texas Cavalry with T.H. Bowen as Captain. This company went in with 76 members and came out with 26. Bowen was succeeded by William A. Rhea. William Mayes died in the war, as did Dr. Robert B. Mayes, their father.

Adolphus Barbee Mayes was married in Kentucky in 1869 to Pernie Allen, a sister of the Texas State Senator, William Allen. The couple returned to Collin County to farm.

The children of Adolphus and Nancy were Edgar E. Mayes, Lillie Mayes who married Dr. J.C. Greer in 1897, James Cole Mayes, Robert and Ida both died in infancy, Addie Mayes who married Dr. I.E. Webb, Dr. Joe A. Mayes, and Alva Mayes who married T.A. Hartsfield.

There were 22 grandchildren, one of whom, Rosabel Greer, now Mrs. McCarty Dowell Sr. lives in McKinney.

Mr. and Mrs. Mayes moved from the farm to Bradley Street in McKinney in 1886 and he was one of the early merchants in the town, owning "Mayes and Porter Stock Feed Store." Mr. Mayes was a large land owner and cattleman.

THE GEORGE McGARRAH FAMILY

George McGarrah was born March 8, 1804 at Caney Fork, Tennessee, the son of Col. George McGarrah. Soon after young George's birth the family moved to Missouri. Col. George McGarrah had three sons, John (Jack), George, and William. All three came to Fayetteville, Ark. in 1823 and were among the first settlers of that city. They helped build the public buildings there.

Young George McGarrah came to Collin County in 1843 and headrighted one square mile of land in the present Bowlby Community west of McKinney. The land is now the George McGarrah Survey. While still living in Arkansas, George's wife died at the birth of a daughter, Harriett, March 25, 1838, and is buried in Sun Valley Chapel Cemetery. The children of this marriage were Martha, Merinda, Louisese, James and Harriett.

On November 22, 1841, George McGarrah married Mrs. Sarah Ford. Mrs. Ford had one son, G.W. who joined a caravan of 150 others for the gold rush in 1849 in California. They went by way of El Paso, Texas and lost all their animals in raids by plains Indians. Only half the men reached California. Men from around present McKinney making the trip were Jack McGarrah, G.W. Ford, Thomas McDonald, and Tola Dunn. Jack McGarrah and Tola Dunn both died from yellow fever. McDonald and Ford returned to Collin in 1850.

George McGarrah died July 3, 1879 and his wife, Sarah, died December 26, 1896. They both lie in the McGarrah Cemetery on the land he headrighted. All of their children, except one, married and went to live in California. Harriet married Henry Ottenhausen in 1867 and she and her husband continued to live on the old headright of her father. Harriett came with her parents to Collin County when she was five years of age.

JOHN F. (JACK) McGARRAH, FOUNDER OF BUCKNER

It is impossible to separate the story of Jack McGarrah from the beginning of Collin County. In 1843 he began a trading post at the site of Old Buckner, primarily to gather hides and furs from the Indians from the western parts of the county.

He was born in 1805 (a twin of George), on Caney Fork, Tennessee. In 1820 he married Polly Graham, one quarter Indian, in Missouri. Polly's full name was Mary Pauline and she lies in the McLarry Cemetery three miles north of McKinney.

Before coming to Collin County, the McGarrah family migrated to Arkansas and helped found the town of Fayetteville. Jack and his twin brother, George, helped to build most of the public buildings there. At this time Jack served two terms in the Arkansas State Legislature. His eldest child, Elizabeth, was born in Missouri in September 15, 1821 and married James Herndon. She became the mother of 12 children. Those living to grow up were Mary E., John M., George H., Joshua, Virginia, James W., Ella N., and Harrison. She and her family joined her parents at Buckner in 1847 to make their home in Collin. Their children grew up in Collin County, married sons and daughters of other pioneers, and so began many old families of Collin.

Also joining Jack McGarrah was the second daughter, Cynthia Ann, who was married to George Herndon. Their children were Henry C., Thomas, and James who was the first white child born in the newly formed County of Collin.

Sarah McGarrah came to Collin with her parents in 1843 and married Tola Dunn, also a settler at Buckner, who headrighted land north of McKinney and has scores of descendents still in Collin County. Tola went with his father-in-law, Jack McGarrah to the gold rush of 1849 and never lived to get home.

Eliza Jane, another McGarrah daughter, came with her parents in 1843 and later married Dr. G.A. Foote, a pioneer physician. He had served as a surgeon in the Rangers and took his pay out in land here, thus becoming one of the largest land owners in the county. The children were Edward, Ludd, Henry, and Mrs. Rhea.

Randolph, another of McGarrah's sons, married Nancy King of Denton County. Many of their descendents still live in the county.

Conway McGarrah, another son, served in the Civil War with a Company organized in McKinney, married Mary Ann Wilson in 1868 and leaves many descendents in Collin County.

Mary Margaret McGarrah came to Collin with her parents, married Edward R. Stiff January 15, 1856, and had fifteen children.

Seburn G.S. McGarrah (born in 1835). No records except that he shared in his father's will read in 1855.

McGarrah and the other pioneers encountered many trials in their efforts to build this first settlement. In February of 1843 he and his friends, J.H. Wilcox, David Helms, Joe Harlan, Blankenship and Rice were putting up logs for the trading post. A Dr. Calder from the new settlement where Dallas now is, but then called Cedar Springs, rode by and asked if there were any hostile Indians near. They assured him they had seen none. He had scarcely ridden 200 yards when he was set upon by two Indians, dragged into a clump of trees and scalped. Soon 60 or more Indians rode out of the woods and began firing arrows at the men. After daylight 11

men left Buckner and went to get Dr. Calder's body. The Indians set fire to the prairie in an effort to stop them, but they got it back to camp. Whistler and Clements buried the body. During the summer of 1843 no other settlements were attempted, but McGarrah stayed on at his place. September 21, 1846 lots were sold in Buckner at auction from land given by McGarrah in an effort to attract new settlers. Lots were sold an average of $22 per lot which were 80 by 80 feet. In 1846 John L. Lovejoy opened up a dry goods store in Buckner, and in November 25, 1846 Buckner was made a post office with McGarrah the first postmaster.

In 1846 the state government appointed a committee to find the exact center of the county and select two places near there, one to be made the county seat. The committee was composed of John McGarrah, J.C.M. Hodge, Thomas Rattan, Ashley McKinney, and Pleasant Wilson. When the County Seat was moved to McKinney, it spelled the end of this historic old settlement. The McGarrah family and others continued to live in Buckner, but with the passing of time nothing remained but the old Cemetery with its crumbling stones, dotted with the Trees of Heaven that Ben Milam had brought as a gift to Collin McKinney's daughter. At present a new community is growing around the spot where Buckner stood. The Riley Boren home stands on the spot where the store and blacksmith shop once served the pioneers.

By Capt. Roy F. Hall

COLLIN McKINNEY
Written by Clara McKinney Reddell

Collin McKinney, leader in establishing Christian Churches in Texas, land surveyor, legislator, signer of the Texas Declaration of Independence, and member of a committee of five who drafted the declaration, was honored by having both Collin County and the town of McKinney named for him.

Of Scotch descent, Collin McKinney was born in New Jersey, April 17, 1766, one of the ten children of Daniel (1740-1809) and Mercy Blatchley McKinney. When Collin was a small boy the family moved to Lincoln County, Kentucky and settled at McKinney's Station, near Crab Orchard. Since Kentucky was sparsely settled at the time, Collin had many harrowing experiences with hostile Indian raids on the white settlement. It was here that Collin married Amy Moore on February 10, 1794. Of this union four children were born, Ash-

THE COLLIN McKINNEY pioneer home now in Finch Park at McKinney, Texas. The home was given to the City of McKinney by Collin's descendents and is a project of the McKinney Garden Club, who helped restore it after a tornado in 1948 damaged the building. It is open to the public and has an interesting display of pioneer living.

ley, Jimmy, Emeline, and Polly. Jimmy and Emeline died in infancy. Collin's wife, Amy, died May 6, 1804. His second marriage was solemnized April 14, 1805 to Betsy Coleman and to this union were born William C., Amy and Margaret (twins), Anna C., Eliza S., and Younger Scott.

In 1823 Collin moved with several families to a point six miles east of present Texarkana, arriving there September 15, 1824. In 1831 they moved farther west and settled at Hickman's Prairie on Red River, which was then Miller County, Arkansas, but is now Bowie County, Texas. Prior to 1846 he moved his family to a point which is near the line of Collin and Grayson counties, where he farmed the rest of his life. Collin died September 8, 1861 at the age of 95 and is buried in a marked grave in the cemetery at Van Alstyne, Texas.

When a new county was created from Fannin County in 1846 it was named Collin in his honor, and when the county seat was moved from Buckner, to a point more geographically centered, he was honored by naming the town McKinney, thus perpetuating the memory of his full name.

While at Hickman's Prairie, Collin was the political helmsman for that section of the Red River

District, which at that time covered a large portion of North and East Texas. In 1835 he was elected a delegate from that section to the meeting at San Felipe. He was elected the next year to the convention meeting March 1, 1836 at Washington on the Brazos. He and four others were appointed by Judge Richard Ellis to draft a declaration of separation from Mexico, which later became known as the Declaration of Independence, and which document bears his signature. Collin represented Red River District in the first, second and fourth Congress of the Republic.

Although Collin was not a graduate of any school, he read and studied much. It was said that he was a man of very fine natural ability, and as the responsibilities of life fell to his lot he was fully prepared to meet every requirement. He was never known to turn anyone away who was in need, if it were possible for him to help in any way. In appearance Collin was six feet tall, full chested and well built, with an average weight of 165 pounds. He had a high forehead, a prominent nose, keen dark eyes, thin lips, cheek bones not overly prominent, and a pleasant well-rounded face, always clean shaven.

Collin McKinney was religious in nature. Early in life he was a Free Will Baptist and later became connected with the Stone Wing of the Christian Churches (Disciples of Christ). He was leader of the first group of ''Christians only'' who came into Texas, stopping near the present town of Texarkana. This group was a whole family clan, the McKinney family. From 1844 to 1846 Collin acted as guide for people coming from Kentucky and Tennessee to settle in north Texas. He made eleven of these trips horseback.

To him, probably more than to any other person, is credited the present shape of the several tiers of counties along the northern part of Texas. He contended for counties as nearly thirty miles square as circumstances would permit and he largely succeeded in his demands.

Collin McKinney was a Magistrate in Kentucky from 1805 until he came to Texas, and here too he was made a Magistrate, serving for some time. He was a citizen of eight different governments during his life. He was born a subject of King George III, later a citizen of the Colonial government of the thirteen states, a citizen of Mexico, a citizen of the Provisional government established by the Texans in 1835, a citizen of the Texas Republic until annexation, then of the United States, then of the Southern Confederacy.

Collin's home was moved from near Anna to McKinney and placed on Highway 75 during the Texas Centennial of 1836, where it was on exhibition. Over 10,000 people from 33 states, Washington D.C., Canada, and Scotland registered in a two month period during the year. It was later moved to Finch Park, McKinney, where it stands today, a shrine for Texans and a monument to that staunchest of patriot pioneers—Collin McKinney.

JOHN BRICE McKINNEY

John Brice McKinney, a grandson of Joseph B. Wilmeth, and a great-grandson of Collin McKinney, was an apiarist and a farmer. In 1900 he and Mary E. Annie Magers were married at the Wilmeth Chapel. They lived their entire married life at the old Wilmeth homestead. All seven of their children were born in the home: Drury Metz, Joe Magers, Collin Leak, Clara Belle, J.B., Armyn Odell, and Ridgell Murphy.

This old home stood almost a century holding within itself a wealth of history of the pioneer days of Collin County. The home changed ownership only three times. It was built by J.B. Wilmeth, then

JOHN BRICE McKINNEY HOME.

owned by John Brice McKinney's mother, Martha Marilea (Mrs. Daniel Leak McKinney) and following her death by John. The old home was razed in 1941 but much of the materials were used in the modern home now occupied by Mr. and Mrs. McKinney's only daughter, Clara McKinney Reddell.

John Brice McKinney, born June 18, 1877, east of Van Alstyne, Grayson County, Texas, son of Daniel Leak and Martha M. Wilmeth McKinney. He married Mary E. Annie Magers, born February 9, 1879, in Lincoln County, Tennessee, daughter of Willaim Lafette Magers and Luella Parr Magers. They were married July 22, 1900, prior to church service at Wilmeth Chapel, north of McKinney, Texas, by Reverend W.G. Reynolds of Denton County. John Brice was a farmer and apiarist. John Brice died March 2, 1968; Mary E. Annie, June 8, 1968. They are buried in Pecan Grove Cemetery, McKinney, Texas. They lived their entire married life at the old J.B. Wilmeth homestead, which they owned.

Their children were:

Drury Metz McKinney, born June 22, 1901 and married Rubie Tom Barnes, born March 9, 1896, died March 28, 1971 married April 15, 1920, and had one child, Pat G.

Joe Magers McKinney, born December 15, 1902, died November 5, 1972, married on January 14, 1927 to Chloe Grace Chesnutt, born March 2, 1907, had one child, Joe Charles.

Collin Leak McKinney, born November 9, 1905, died January 7, 1929.

Clara Belle McKinney, born January 31, 1908, married June 6, 1931 to Eugene Randall Reddell, born July 7, 1909 and died May 20, 1939, had one child, Shirley Ann.

J.B. McKinney, born July 7, 1909, married November 4, 1930, to Jackie Parris, born July 20, 1907.

WEDDING PICTURE of John Brice McKinney and Mary E. Annie Magers, July 22, 1900.

Armyn Odell McKinney, born July 25, 1911, married August 22, 1933 to Mary Elizabeth Hughes, born November 15, 1910, and had one child, Mary Carmyn.

Ridgell Murphy McKinney married first on November 9, 1939 to Preble (Peggy) Douglas, born January 31, 1917 and died January 16, 1967 and married second to Fay Blaske in 1969.

Clara Belle McKinney, daughter of John Brice and Annie Magers McKinney, was born January 31, 1908, at McKinney, Texas. She married Eugene Randall Reddell on June 6, 1931, at Durant, Oklahoma. Eugene, son of Frank W. and Maggie Wilkerson Reddell, was born July 7, 1909, at Palmer, Ellis County, Texas. An electrician for Texas Power & Light Company, he was killed in his line of duty on May 20, 1939, at the company's substation at Buckner Orphanage, east of Dallas. He is buried in Pecan Grove Cemetery. Clara McKinney Reddell, office secretary for the McKinney Chamber of Commerce for 33 years, is also a past secretary-treasurer of the Chamber of Commerce Manager and Secretaries Association of East Texas. They had one child, Shirley Ann Reddell.

Shirley Ann Reddell was born June 24, 1935, at McKinney, Texas. She married Chester Don Cooper, son of John Chester and Jewel Cooper of Perryton, Texas. Don was born August 27, 1935 at Shaddock, Oklahoma. They were married June 7, 1957 in the First Christian Church at McKinney, Texas, by Dr. T.R. Leen. Don and Shirley are both graduates of Texas Christian University, Fort Worth, Texas, receiving their degrees in May, 1957. Shirley Ann was awarded the Master of Arts Degree in English at the Thirty-ninth Annual Commencement Exercises of Texas Tech University, at Lubbock, Texas, May 2, 1965. Prior to their move to Perryton, she was an instructor in the English Department at Texas Tech. She is now teaching senior English at the Perryton High School. Their children are Timothy John Cooper, born August 21, 1958 at Lubbock, Texas, and D'Ann Cooper, born August 9, 1961 also at Lubbock.

(Compiled by Clara McKinney Reddell)

THE JOHN M. McKINNEY FAMILY

Elder John M. McKinney was born in Green County, Missouri on April 14, 1832 and died January 1, 1918 at his home on Benge Street in McKinney. He was the son of John Meyers McKinney, a pioneer settler of Green County. The family settled in the Forest Grove Community and after the death of his parents, John M. lived with "Uncle Billy Snider." He had five brothers: Giles McKinney, who was for many years a prominent businessman of McKinney; Nelson; Jim; John and William. He was first married to Eliza Jane Snider who died in 1852. They had one son, Jim McKinney. In 1857 he married Polly Ann Coffey, the daughter of a pioneer settler, Salathiel Coffey. To this union were born the following children: Joe D., George Washington, Mary Ellen (m. Cook), Giles McKinney, John S., and Wiley Benton. He was elected Tax Assessor and Collector for Collin County and served several terms.

When news of the new county seat being moved to McKinney from Old Buckner, Elder J.B. Wilmeth felt that the first thing that a new town should have was a church and on April 1, 1848 a little band of Christians who met on Sundays at the Wilmeth home for worship, went about where the present courthouse stands and organized the First Christian Church under a big tree. (It was not until May 3, 1848 that the Lovejoy store was hauled across the prairie and placed on the northwest corner of the present square.) At the close of the worship service John M. McKinney expressed a wish to be baptised. The group went to Wilson Creek south of McKinney and he and Pete Wetsel were baptised by Elder Frank Wilmeth. After that he preached the gospel for 52 years and as he said never took a penny for his services, not that he was against the practice, but he was a successful farmer and stockman and owned extensive property.

His wife, Polly Ann Coffey, was born June 22, 1840 and died just one week after her husband's death. She came to Collin County with her parents in 1854. She had 16 brothers and sisters; all grew up in Collin County. There are many descendants of this fine couple.

The children of John McKinney's son, Jim were George, Pearl Watson, Bess Willis, Aline Pennington, Arliegh, Johnny Marley, and Eugene.

Joe D. McKinney and his wife had four children; Agnes McDonald, Mattie Lou Quesenberry, Garrett, and Henry.

Mary Ellen (m. S.F. Cook) had six children, C.M. Cook, Lee Cook, Vone Bowman, Myrtle Faulkner, Florence Berry, and Lawrence Cook.

Giles McKinney and his wife had five children, Eddie Norton, Cecile Thomas, Eustace, Anna Lee Mallow, and Hershal.

John S. McKinney and his wife had four children, Dr. Walter McKinney, Edgar, Ruth, Harold, and Florence Sparlin.

Wiley M. McKinney and his wife had four children, Juanita Floyd, Mary Wiley Czarawitz, Collin, and Bryan.

George Washington McKinney died in childhood.

This story from biography in microfilmed newspaper at McKinney Public Library under the date January 2, 1918. Further notes furnished by Eva Ellen Alexander and Berniece Straughan, great granddaughters of Johnny McKinney.

SAMUEL JEFFERSON McKINNEY FAMILY

Samuel Jefferson McKinney was born in Montgomery County, Arkansas, in 1837, the son of William McKinney and Alia Wilkerson. He came to Blue Ridge in 1861 and was married to Virginia Griffith, the daughter of John Fletcher Griffith and Edith Elvira Morrill who was born in Tennessee in 1846. Samuel died in 1904 and she in 1930. Both are buried in Blue Ridge Cemetery.

Their children were: Albert Clarence who died in infancy, James Jefferson who married Missouri Jane Cantrell, Elvira who married A.K. Johnson, Leannah Helen who married James Pinckney Dotson, Albert who died in infancy, Emma who married Lon Cox, and married a second time to Oliver Loher, Charles Alvin who married Beaula Ford, Birdie married Arthur Baird, Edgar Angus married Georgia Cook, and Virginia married William Burns.

THE COMFORT ALLEN McMILLEN FAMILY

Comfort McMillen, one of the early pioneers to settle at Murphy, was born in Arkansas, January 29, 1818. He was the son of Lewis and Charlotte Joy (daughter of Comfort Joy of New York). When he was very young, the family went to Illinois to live and there the father died. Comfort McMillen married in 1841 and became converted to the Christian faith the same year. In 1845 he brought his family to old Buckner and camped on Wilson Creek one mile south of Alf Chandler. With him came his wife and six children; Jim Maxwell and wife and two children; Henry Maxwell, wife and six children; Lewis Marshall, wife and one child; Jim Williford, wife; and Bill Williford.

All came overland by ox teams pulling the wagons and driving herds of sheep as they came. The night they camped on Wilson Creek, raiding Indians killed an entire family nearby and they were uneasy about staying. He headrighted 640 acres of land. Game was abundant, including bear and dear but bread was hard to get since he had to travel many miles to buy a bushel of corn that had to be brought home and ground into meal in a small hand mill.

Mr. McMillen married Liddie Maxwell, daughter of James Maxwell of Tennessee. Six children were born to the couple—William A., James R., Martha J., and Mary E. lived to be grown.

JOHN McMINN

The John McMinn family trace their coming to Texas to 1849 at which time he received a grant from Gov. Wood for 1600 acres, now known as the McMinn Survey near Copeville. John McMinn, born Feb. 27, 1809, in Bedford County, Tennessee, came to Lamar County in Texas in 1843 and was married to Evaline Ladd Majors. In 1849 they settled on the land granted them. The land was hog-wallow land, none suitable for cultivation and was the home of bands of wild horses, wild turkey, and all kinds of game which came to water at the creek running through the land. It was a lonely life. The nearest neighbor was in Millwood; Terrell was the nearest town where the family journeyed once a year to buy groceries and other supplies. As the community grew John McMinn gave land to build a Presbyterian Church, a cemetery and a school. They were named for him and served the community until moved to Nevada. He died Dec. 27, 1898, leaving seven children: Milton Polk Mc-Minn, Mary Jane, Oliver, John, Dave, Mattie, and Lula. He gave each of his children 200 acres of land. Lula married George McSpadden of Tennessee and lives on the original homeplace.

Submitted by Mrs. Ray McSpadden, Nevada, Texas (1969).

MERRITT FAMILY

Robert Clarence Merritt was born in McKinney April 2, 1872, the son of Captain William Washington and Virginia Compton Merritt. Captain Merritt served under General Shelby's command during the Civil War. In 1874 he was elected sheriff of Collin County and later served four years in the Texas Legislature. Mrs. Merritt was the daughter of Eber Compton from Giles County, Tennessee and was a very early settler of the Forest Grove Community.

The Merritts moved to a farm near Melissa and their children attended school at Melissa, Stony Point, and Chambliss. Clarence graduated from Texas A&M College in 1893 and was given an appointment to West Point but illness prevented his going. He first worked in the county Clerk's office and read law at night. In 1895 he was admitted to the bar to practice law in the state and federal courts.

On November 15, 1899 he was married to Leslie Pearson, the daughter of Judge and Mrs. J.M. Pearson. In 1902 Clarence Merritt was elected County Attorney, serving two terms. For six years he was Chairman of the Democratic Executive Committee of Collin County. He was one of the "immortal forty" delegates to the Convention in Baltimore in 1912 where the 40 delegates voted in Woodrow Wilson as a presidential candidate. He was also a delegate at the 1920 Convention in San Francisco.

June 8, 1914 he was appointed by Woodrow Wilson as District Attorney for the Eastern District

ROBERT CLARENCE MERRITT

LESLIE MERRITT

of Texas. He served for six years then went into private practice in McKinney and Dallas. He is listed in the 1922 edition of Who's Who in America.

He was a member of the Christian Church, a member of St. John's Masonic Lodge, the Modern Woodmen of the World, and was always active in the civic and political life of McKinney and Dallas. Clarence Merritt died April 28, 1927, survived by his wife, two brothers, Jim and Eber Merritt of Mc-Kinney. He was buried in Pecan Grove Cemetery of McKinney.

Leslie Pearson Merritt, his wife, died October 14, 1973 in McKinney and was buried in Pecan Grove also. She is survived by two adopted daughters, Elizabeth Pearson Finch of Little Rock and Sally Pearson Elliott of Irving, Texas, two grandsons, Curtis Finch Jr., Leslie Merritt Finch, and one granddaughter Mary Belle Findley, and six geat grandchildren.

William Washington Merritt married Virginia Compton. Their children, John Thomas Merritt, William Brandy Merritt, Robert Clarence Merritt, Eber Washington Merritt (married Lotaine King), Minnie Merritt (married Harry Q. Smith), James Hansel Merritt (married Rosabel Hynds).

Story sent by: Mrs. Houston Elliott, 4230 Belclaire, Dallas, Texas.

THE MATHIAS MILLER FAMILY

Mathias Miller, a native of Kentucky, was born in Casey County of that state on December 17, 1826. His father was Thomas Miller also a native of Kentucky and married Cynthia Rubards, a daughter of Samuel Rubards an early settler of Kentucky. Thomas and Cynthia Miller had six

WEDDING PICTURE of George Washington Taylor and Nancy Ellen Miller (1896). Both were children of pioneer families.

GEORGE WASHINGTON TAYLOR, pioneer nurseryman, horticulturist, and newspaperman of Collin County.

children; the second of these was Mathias Miller. He grew to manhood in Kentucky and in 1851 married Anna Prindle, a daughter of William Prindle, a native of Virginia but who settled in Kentucky. To this union were born eight children: William F., Mary J., Thomas, Samuel, James M., Eliza, Nancy E., and Jonah. In 1856 the Mathias Miller family came to Collin County where he bought 255 acres of raw land and settled down to improve it. He added to his land holdings until he had several farms, his homeplace having 585 acres.

During the Civil War he served the Confederacy, but having been crippled in one of his feet as a boy, he could not fight in the field. He served throughout the war in the commissary department.

Nancy Ellen Miller married George Washington Taylor in 1896 and to this union were born the following children: Mathias Armstead Miller (Tice), Bettie Jenette, George Samuel, James Thomas, May Tabitha, and Nancy Ellen. George Washington Taylor's father came to Collin County in 1853 and was a cabinet maker and also made coffins, who was married to Tabitha Jane Scott, daughter of Preston Scott, an early pioneer of Collin County, who served in the legislature from this dis-

trict. George was a horticulturist and spent his life developing new plants and experimenting with new varieties of fruits, vegetables and flowers. He ran a nursery on North Tennessee Street a number of years. Besides his activities in this area he was a typesetter and worked on the old newspaper "The Messenger" as well as on *The Examiner* and *The Democrat.*

POSSIBLY THE oldest house in McKinney. This was known as the "Two Bit" Taylor Inn, since travelers could find a room and food here for "two bits."

223

The Inn, built and operated for years by George's father, A.J. Taylor, still stands on South Chestnut Street in McKinney. This was a popular stopping off place for travelers before the Civil War since one could get a good bed and breakfast for two-bits, as the quarter was then called by the people. It became to be called "The Two-Bit Inn."

George Samuel Taylor married Lilly Pearl Jay, the daughter of pioneer settlers of north Collin County, and to this union were born 10 children.

MILLIGAN FAMILY

William and Liza Milligan, pioneer settlers of Collin County, came to Texas in 1856 from Missouri and settled east of McKinney in what has since been known as the Milligan Community.

William was crippled, but during the Civil War, he hauled supplies for the Confederacy to a Prisoner of War camp close to where Bonham now is located. As Quantrell's Raiders had swept through the community, taking away all good horses, William had to use a mule to carry his supplies.

Descendents of William and Liza Milligan were: Jack Milligan, Christopher Milligan, Jim Milligan, Charles Milligan, George Milligan, Missouri Milligan, Molly Molligan, Ellen Milligan, Rosa Milligan, and William P. Milligan.

After William and Liza settled, many other families came to make their home in this good farming community. Milligan School house was built and a Milligan church held regular services. Many of the leaders of the county were educated in this school. Story sent by Mrs. Clifton Dowell, a granddaughter of McKinney.

EARLY B. MILSTEAD
AND HEDRICH FAMILY

Early B. Milstead was born August 22, 1929, in McKinney, Collin County, Texas, the son of Early Brite and Lanie Cummings Sisco Milstead.

His maternal grandparents, Robert Theodore and Lou Ella Jordan Sisco, moved from Hohenwald, Murray County, Tennessee to Nevada, Texas in 1910. They purchased a farm northwest of Nevada which they operated until the death of Mr. Sisco on April 24, 1945. The paternal grandparents, Nancy Rains and John Beecher Milstead moved from Tennessee to McKinney, Texas about 1885. They also purchased a farm which they operated until the death of Mr. Milstead in March 1939.

EARLY B. MILSTEAD   LENA V. MILSTEAD

Early B. Milstead married Lena V. Hedrich of Blue Ridge, Texas, July 25, 1964. They have one daughter, Holly Beth, born December 28, 1965.

Mr. Milstead received his formal education from Texas Christian University, Fort Worth, Texas, and Southern Methodist University, Dallas. He entered the real estate business in 1960. His work consists of real estate brokerage, appraisals, and counseling. He attends the Westside Church of Christ in McKinney, Texas, where he is a deacon, Bible school teacher, and served as chairman of the building committee. He is a member of the McKinney Rotary Club, a Knight Templar, a 32 degree Mason and Shriner. He serves on the board of governors of Collin Memorial Hospital, director of Town and Country Savings and Loan Association, chairman of the Collin County Democratic Executive Committee, and past president of the Collin County Board of Realtors.

MORROW FAMILY

Mr. and Mrs. John Morrow were early settlers of Lucas community. Their sons: W.D. (Dave), Dr. R.E. Morrow and John Dick. These three had a half-brother, Everett Morrow. Dave Morrow, born in 1879, died in 1960 in Lucas. He married Miss Bessie Johnson, born in 1883 and died in 1957. They had one son, Winston (deceased). Dr. R.E. Morrow married Miss Ida Campbell, daughter of Mr. and Mrs. Arch Campbell. They were the parents of three children, one of whom died young. Their son, Dallas C. Morrow and daughter, Venita, grew up in this area. Dallas married Miss Ruth Lewis. They live in south Texas. Venita Morrow married Linch McMillen (deceased). She lives in Jasper, Texas.

John Dick Morrow married Miss Missouri Pettis Snider of this area (both deceased). To this union was born a son, Forest Morrow, and three daughters: Ettie, who married N.P. Lynge of Allen (both deceased); Naomi, married Curt Lane (deceased); and Serilda (Pril) married Richard Miller of Dallas (deceased). Both Mrs. Lane and Mrs. Miller live in Plano.

Everett Morrow married Miss Ellie Sanders. They lived in the Winningkoff area. (See Sander's family history.)

MOSES GENEOLOGY
Motto: Dumspiro Speri—
"While I breathe I hope."

John Moses was a Virginian and a Revolutionary War soldier. Later he married and moved to Georgia (1783) where they became the parents of four sons: Neal, Hiram, Philip, and David.

Neal Moses was born in Edgecomb County, North Carolina but grew up in Georgia where he farmed. He served in the War of 1812 and was stationed in Georgia. When the Creek Indians ceded their land to Georgia, 1828, Neal moved there and helped survey the land, settling in Senoia. He married Mrs. Nancy Manning Graham on October 17, 1822 and they became the parents of six children: Norton, Elizabeth, Egbert, Ansley, Lynton, and Nancy.

Norton Moses, son of Neal and Nancy, was born in Georgia in 1823 and was the oldest of the six children. He was 13 when his father died. He was educated in private schools of Fayette and Coweta Counties and later taught school and helped his mother educate the other children. In 1845 he and two companions started for Texas and landed at Galveston on January 1, 1846. He located in Washington County in what was called Jones Prairie. He taught school and visited the First Legislature that was in session which ratified the Articles of Annexation of Texas to the Union. Norton went back to Georgia and married Ann Ealy Johnson, then came back to live. To this union Ealy Johnson Moses was born. Norton's wife, Ann Ealy died in 1849.

Norton Moses married a second time to Miss Nancy Ann Moore of Washington County in April 4, 1850 and to this union three children were born: Amzy, Lauretta, and Egbert. Nancy died April 5, 1855.

Norton Moses married a third time to Mary Emily Hill of Tennessee and they were the parents of two children: Samuel Neal and Mary Edna. Mary Emily and infant Mary Edna died in 1859.

Norton Moses married a fourth time to Mrs. Lucy Ann Binkley in 1860 and to this union six children were born: William, Norton Jr., Inez, Dayton, Martin, and Andrew. About 1862 Norton Moses moved to Georgetown where he operated a general store until about 1864 when he sold his business and moved to Burnet County. He served as County Commissionary of Burnet County in 1864-65, during the time the South was engaged in the Civil War. Norton Moses, a consistant Democrat, was elected to the 15th Legislature in 1876, where he helped to fight against the Texas and Pacific Railroad Company to save 7 million of choice acres of Texas land forfeited by that company. He was a member of the Baptist Church for 60 years and for 17 years was Moderator of the Baptist Association. He was a Master Mason, Knight Templer and served as Grand High Priest of the Grand Royal Arch Chapter of Texas in 1872 and 1873. For 48 years he was a regular attendant upon the Grand Bodies, missing but three meetings. Lucy Ann Moses died September 22, 1899 and her husband, Norton Moses, on May 21, 1908.

Martin White Moses, son of Norton and Lucy Ann Moses, was born at the Moses Ranch near Strickling, Burnett County, on October 11, 1871. After his schooling was finished he worked in the Lampasas Post Office, later returning to Burnet County and worked in a general merchandise store. Eight years later he bought an interest in Stokes Brothers and Co. and remained until 1914 when he sold his interest and formed a new partnership with J.H.H. Berry, Nell Berry, and Nancy J. McGuyer. They operated a general merchandise store at Rogers, Bell County, Texas. In May of 1917 they moved the firm to McKinney and the store was in operation until 1927 when they sold out.

Martin Moses entered the life insurance field, where he was so successful that he became Manager of the Austin District of the Prudential Insurance Company. He retired in 1958 at the age of 87 years. He celebrated his 102nd birthday on October 11, 1973 at the home of his daughter, Christine Moses Stidham and her husband, R.M. Stidham.

Mrs. Lenora Lewis Moses was born at Oatmeal, Burnet County, on July 14, 1872. She was from a historic family, one of her greatgreatgreat grandfathers, Col. Fielding Lewis, having married Betty Washington, sister of George Washington, "Father of Our Country." She died in Austin on October 7, 1959 and is buried in Pecan Grove in McKinney.

Martin White Moses and Lenora Lewis Moses were the parents of nine children, Andrew (named for Gen. Andrew Moses), Robert Lewis, Martine, Madeline, Josephine, Leon Oliver, Allie Florine, Mary Christine, and Norine.

Andrew Moses was born on the Norton Moses Ranch January 30, 1894. After A&M graduation, he entered the First Officer Training Camp at Leon Springs when World War I began, and was commissioned a Lieutenant and when World War II began he volunteered in 1941 and was made a Captain. After the war he was made manager of the Texas Liquor Control Board, San Antonio District. He was first married to Clarissa Woodring and after they were divorced, married Ida May Maple. They live in San Antonio and have no children.

Robert Lewis Moses was born July 7, 1895 and after A&M, volunteered and after officer training at Camp Leon Springs, he was commissioned a Lieutenant in a Machine Gun Battalion. He went overseas with the famed 36th Division, serving in France from 1917 to May 1919. He was severely gassed and never recovered from the effects. He spent 15 years in Veteran's Hospitals. After his release from the hospital he was employed by the government. He was first married to Mary Little of Pearsall on March 17, 1918 and to this union two sons were born, David Martin and Robert Lewis. After a divorce, he again married, to Oneta Harrell of Tucson, Arizona. They became the parents of two sons, Robert Lewis Jr., and Andrew Douglas. Robert Lewis Moses Sr. died in the Veteran's Hospital at Legion, Texas on November 1, 1971.

Martine Moses was born April 3, 1897 and married Love P. Moore of Rogers, Texas on December 16, 1917. They were the parents of two children: Mary Love Moore and Love P. Moore Jr. Love P. Moore Jr. was killed in an airplane crash on October 31, 1949. Martine Moses Moore and Mary Love Moore still live in Rogers, Texas.

Madeline Moses was born in Lampasas, Texas on January 12, 1899 and graduated from high school at Rogers, Texas with the highest honors. After moving to McKinney she entered the McKee Business College at McKinney, and a month after graduation became associated with the Collin County National Bank, starting as a secretary. She remained at the bank for 47 years, resigning in 1968 as Vice-president and Cashier. She has always been active in the civic life of McKinney and Collin county, and in January of 1974 received her Life Membership in the McKinney Chamber of Commerce. Since 1956 she has secured 723 new members for the Chamber of Commerce. She lives in the homeplace at 205 North Church Street in McKinney, the home is a pictoral example of an old his-

HOME OF Miss Madeline Moses, McKinney.

toric Victorian home. It was built in 1887 of lumber hauled by mule train from Jefferson, Texas and is put together with square-headed nails. It is trimmed with intricate gingerbread work and is an example of the gracious homes of the Gay Nineties.

Leon Oliver Moses was born at Lampasas on October 9, 1900 and received his degree in law from Baylor University. He practiced law for a while at Idalou and Post, Texas, coming back to McKinney where he served four years as Assistant District Attorney under Dist. Judge, W.C. Dowdy. He then served four years as an Assistant Attorney General under William McCraw. At the end of that term he was employed by the Texas Wholesale Liquor Dealer's Association as general attorney, which post he held until he was made States Attorney for O.P.A. with headquarters in Ft. Worth. He later came back to McKinney and entered a partnership with Luther Truett under the name of Moses and Truett, Attorneys-at-Law, occupying the same office as Governor Throckmorton once used. He was married to Lucile Kerby of McKinney on July 19, 1924 and to this union two children were born: Billy June and Sandra, the latter dying in infancy. He died in March of 1969 and is buried in Pecan Grove, Lucile Kerby Moses still lives in McKinney.

Allie Florine Gateley was born in Lampasas February 4, 1904 and married John R. Gateley. They were the parents of two children: Sharon Lynn and John R. Gateley, Jr. They were later divorced and she became associated with Neiman Marcus Company in Dallas where she remained until retirement, and is now managing an apartment complex in Dallas.

Mary Christine Moses was born in Lampasas on October 24, 1906 and was after school days a secretary for the late Hon. W.R. Abernathy, an attorney of McKinney. She was also employed by the Ashburn Hospital but is now with the Social Security Office in Austin. She married R.M. Stidham and they, with her father, live in Austin.

Norine Moses (Bill) was born in Lampasas in June 10, 1909 and after graduating from the Baylor School of Nursing became supervisor of Cooke Memorial Hospital at Ft. Worth, Texas. She was married to Gentry Warren Stuart on September 29, 1933. They are the parents of four children: Thomas Edward, Joel Gentry, Christine Elizabeth, and Amy.

Story sent by Madeline Moses, McKinney

AUDIE MURPHY

Audie Murphy was the most highly decorated soldier of the Second World War. Born the son of a Hunt County share cropper, he was a victim of the depression of the 30's and learned early to work hard at whatever he was called upon to do. He had a hard time getting into the armed forces because of his size—he was five feet three inches tall and weighed 112 pounds.

He was a battlefield genius. Officially he is credited with killing or capturing 240 Germans in the 39 months he served in the European Theater of Operations, World War II.

He won the Congressional Medal of Honor, the Distinguished Service Cross, the Silver Star, the Purple Heart three times, the Bronze Star, the Legion of Merit, the French Croix de Guerre, the Belgian Croix de Guerre, and dozens of other medals.

The day he won the coveted Congressional Medal of Honor he was faced with a desperate situation—the Germans were advancing on his cut-up company from three sides. Sizing up the situation, he climbed on top of a burning army tank and turned its lone machine gun on the enemy. When the smoke had cleared, more than 100 Germans lay dead in the snow. His refusal to give an inch saved his company from encirclement and destruction, and gave his division time needed to regroup.

After the war he took his younger brothers and sisters from the Boles Home near Quinlan where they were staying and rented a home in Farmersville so they could live with an older sister. He went to Hollywood under a long term contract with Universal Pictures, Inc. and starred in many motion pictures. Perhaps his best known film was *The Red Badge of Courage* (1950) based on his own life. He

AUDIE MURPHY . . . in scene from movie
(Photo Courtesy Greenville Herald-Banner)

also played in many western movies. His motion pictures were well received by the public and are frequently re-shown on television. In these parts he played roles that were almost opposite to his own personality, brash characters with ready answers and a certainty that they were always right. In real life he was actually of a retiring nature and very sensitive. He was twice married and had two children. His book ''To Hell and Back'' told of his life.

He died tragically on Memorial Day of 1971 when his chartered plane struck a mountain in Virginia and killed him and the other people aboard.

Many honors have been given him by Farmersville, Greenville, and by Government markers.

(Materials furnished by Audie's brother, Buck Murphy.)

WILLIAM H. MURRAY

William H. Murray, one time Governor of Oklahoma, and affectionately called ''Alfalfa'' Bill Murray, was born near Collinsville, Texas on November 21, 1869. His mother died when he was only two years old and at age twelve he left home and struck out on his own. In those early years he did many kinds of work, he worked as a cowboy in Wise County, taught school in Parker County, also taught in Limestone County and Freestone, and Navarro Co. At one time he was a reporter for the old Ft. Worth Gazette. He read law on his own and passed the state bar, practicing law in Corsicana and Ft. Worth. Later he moved to Tishamingo, Indian Territory where he practiced law, farmed and engaged in ranching. He served in many areas of the newly budding state, President of the Chickasaw-Choctaw Commission, and was a member of the Sequoyah Convention seeking statehood for the Indian Territory. He was elected a delegate to the Constitutional Convention in 1906 and served as President of the convention and after statehood served as the first Speaker of the House and later was a member of the 63rd Congress serving Oklahoma as the Representative at large. He became Governor of Oklahoma, the climax to a long and dedicated career of public service.

Many people knew him in Collin County at the beginning of his career. At one time he covered the area around Copeville and Farmersville selling books for Rand-McNally and Company, calling at every house in the area.

The McKinney papers February 27, 1918 said of him, ''It is no surprise to us to learn of his success, for all Collin County knew this young man for his pluck and energy, and no matter what his employment at the moment, he held his head high and gave the job his best, never used the word 'failure.' '' A complete biography may be read at the McKinney Library on microfilmed newspapers. February 27, 1918.

THE NAYLOR FAMILY

By Donald Covey Naylor
Decatur, Georgia

My great grandfather was my grandfather's brother! That's right. James Decatur Naylor, my great grandfather and one of the founders of the Collin County village of Millwood was the older brother of my grandfather, William Commodore Perry Naylor, which will be explained later in this narrative.

James and Commodore and six or seven other brothers and sisters were born in Tennessee; the children of John Naylor, who was born in Maryland in 1787, but lived most of his life in Shelbyville, Tennessee, where he died in 1855.

James Decatur Naylor was born in Shelbyville in 1822 and died in Austin, Texas in 1912, where he is buried in the Confederate Veterans Cemetery.

His younger brother, my grandfather, William Commodore Perry Naylor, left Tennessee on horseback in 1849, bound for the California gold rush. He went by way of Missouri where he met and fell in love with a girl named Sarah Emaline Bryan, to whom he said farewell forever, he thought, as he pushed on toward California and hoped for gold. But he got only as far as Arizona where thirst, hunger and Indian attacks caused him to give up and turn back in the direction of Texas. Five or six years later, by purest accident, he again met Sarah and her family on a lonely Texas trail, seeking a homestead. He went to work for her father, and a year or so later, he and Sarah were married.

Meantime, James D. Naylor had stayed in Tennessee, because he was married and had two children. But he moved his family to Texas in 1850 and bought land in the Millwood area of Collin County.

We are not sure what caused James to leave Tennessee, but research indicates that his first cousin, John McMinn, a pioneer citizen of Nevada, Texas, was living in Collin County as far back as 1835, having moved there from McMinnville, Tennessee. (J.D. Naylor's mother was a McMinn.) So, it is logical to assume that John McMinn may have influenced James to migrate to Texas where land grants were plentiful and cheap.

As a leading citizen of Millwood, James Decatur Naylor was a prosperous farmer and owner of the old grist mill, saw mill and flour mill from which Millwood got its name. (One of the grinding stones he used is still in the back yard of Ike Emerson, Route 1, Royse City, close to the site of the original mill.)

He also operated a general store and was the postmaster of Millwood in 1857 and 1859. And he was a Collin County Commissioner in 1860 and 1862. (The Millwood Post Office was discontinued in 1907.)

During the Civil War, J.D. Naylor was the Captain of Company F, Fitzhugh's 16th Cavalry, formed in Millwood. He donated the property for the old Millwood cemetery where his 2nd wife, Jennie Covey Naylor, as well as my father and mother, two oldest brothers, countless Coveys and other of my relatives are buried. This cemetery is just a few hundred yards below where Captain Naylor's two story home stood.

He also donated the land for the second Millwood school, founded about 1889.

MILLWOOD SCHOOL CLASS OF 1911. Left to right, top row: Mary Ratcliff, Thomas Williams, Anatell Knight, Oscar Emerson, Ina Ratcliff, Lloyd Naylor and Stella Naylor, Ivan Foote, Mamie Morris, Dolly Watkins. Second row: Jim Spearman, Ola Morris, Allie Watkins, Clayton Russell, Lena Williams, Jimmy Ratcliff, Jennie Kitty Knight, Lucy Ratcliff, Maudie Spearman, Unidentified, Pearl Huffman and the teacher, Thomas E. Nelson. Third row: Aubrey Huffman, Frank Naylor, Eula Spearman, Houston Watkins, Maudie Knight, Oran Suiter, Edith Ratcliff, Rosa Lee Borckey. The others are unidentified.

DR. H.T. EMERSON, on the right, with a friend or patient in front of his office in Millwood, in 1909.

JAMES LAFAYETTE NAYLOR children in 1914. Back row, left to right: Frank Aubrey Naylor, Stella Maud Naylor Baber, James Lloyd Naylor. Front row, left to right: Raymond Leroy Naylor, Donald Covey Naylor.

JAMES LAFAYETTE NAYLOR AND Clara Clyde Covey Naylor at the time of their wedding in Millwood in 1890. She was the granddaughter of James Decatur Naylor on her mother's side and he was the nephew of James Decatur Naylor on his father's side. Both of them died in Millwood in 1914.

JAMES DECATUR NAYLOR and his first wife, Martha Davis Naylor, in Millwood, about 1870. He was born in Shelbyville, Tenn., in 1822 and died in Austin, Texas in 1912. She was born in Mississippi and died in Tennessee in 1874, while on a visit. She is buried in Tennessee.

James Decatur Naylor's seven children by his first wife, Martha Davis Naylor, were William E., Susan Frances, John A., Robert, Lula, Mary Alice (my maternal grandmother) and Rebecca Jane, who married W.B. Newsome, a prominent pioneer citizen of McKinney. His great grandson, W.B. Newsome, lives in Dallas and his great granddaughter, Dorothy Newsome McGeorge, lives in New York City. (The first two children were born in Tennessee, but the other five were born in Millwood.)

Captain Naylor's oldest daughter, Susan Frances, married Dr. R.A. Taylor in Millwood in 1866. He was a grandson of former Governor of Texas, James W. Throckmorton. Dr. Taylor and his wife are both buried in the Millwood cemetery. His house was still standing in 1973, but unoccupied, close by where Captain Naylor's home was and adjacent to the site of the home where I was born in 1910, across the road from where Ike and Willie Emerson still live (December, 1973) Ike's father, Dr. H.T. Emerson, delivered me and my brother, Raymond, and hundreds of other Collin County babies in those long ago years.

While on a visit to Tennessee in 1874, James Decatur Naylor's first wife died; following which, he returned to Millwood, where in 1876 at the age of 54, he married 19-year-old Mary Virginia (Jennie) Covey. Contrary to some reports, he had only two wives, not three. By Jennie, he had seven more children, all born in Millwood. They were Isaac A., Sarah H., Lesley Earl, Anna, Kate, Carl and Joe Foster Naylor.

Jennie died in 1893, and in the years following, he and his children lived in many places. Records are not complete, but we know that he first lived with his daughter, Rebecca Newsome in McKinney, then with the Coveys in Josephine. Later he operated a grocery store in Vernon, Texas. He then moved to Marlow, Oklahoma and operated a freight line in Indian territory and next, he returned to McKinney. In 1910 he was living with his son, Joe Foster Naylor in Decatur, Texas, and for a while in Denton, Texas with another son. In 1911, he was admitted to the Confederate Soldiers Home in Austin, where a year later he died at the age of 90.

Meanwhile, on October 12, 1868, Captain Naylor's daughter, Mary Alice, married William Henry Covey in Millwood. They had one child, Clara, my mother, born November 4, 1869. Mary Alice suffocated in a grass fire in 1873 and is buried in the Millwood Cemetery. In 1875, William Covey married Laura Perry Bourland in Millwood.

Children by this marriage were Oliver, Venie, Charles, William, Ruby, Elmer, Evan and Houston. (As of December '73, all but the last three were dead.)

But back to James Decatur Naylor's younger brother, Commodore Perry Naylor. In 1856, he married Sarah Bryan, by whom he had 13 children. Among them my father, James Lafayette Naylor, born in 1861. In his late teens and early 20's, my father was a cowboy, working on many cattle drives from Texas up through the Indian territory of Oklahoma, to Kansas, the Dakotas and Montana. On one such cattle drive, to New Mexico, he met the notorious outlaw and cattle thief, Billy the Kid, who was killed in 1881 at the age of 22.

In 1890, my father settled down and married Clara Clyde Covey, granddaughter of James Decatur Naylor, who was my father's Uncle. And that is the complicated explanation of how my great grandfather was my grandfather's brother.

James L. and Clara Naylor had seven children: Claude; Lester; Lloyd and Frank (all deceased); Stella Naylor Baber; Raymond Naylor, living in California as of December '73; and Don Naylor in Georgia.

In 1914, when both my father and mother passed away, we were living on a small farm, abstract No. 437, Collin County, three miles from Royse City. I still own this property.

In July of 1914, we moved to Fort Worth, and the decendents of James Decatur Naylor have since scattered to the four winds. Most of them are living today in various parts of Texas, California, New York and Georgia.

My wife is Flora Hill Naylor of Atlanta. And we have a son, Larry Naylor, of Atlanta and a daughter, Penelope Naylor Bailer, of Berkeley, California. Both of whom have two children, as of December, 1973.

Submitted by: Donald Covey Naylor

THE NICHOLS FAMILY

J.M. Nichols came to Texas from Tennessee before the Civil War and was one of the pioneer settlers of Collin County. His father was George Washington Nichols and was born about 1815 in Rhea County, Tennessee, 30 miles east of Knoxville. The family first settled in Uvalde County in 1859, then moved to Missouri where George Washington Nichols was killed by the Quantrill gang.

J.M. Nichols was only 17 years old when they came to Texas. He was a Texas Ranger for four years under Captain Bush in Alexander's Regiment. Later he served in the Civil War with the Confederates. After the war he returned to his farm near Melissa where he lived for fifty years.

J.M. Nichols had several sons who lived in Collin County. A.M. Nichols was a Collin County merchant, Joe Nichols farmed near Melissa, Charlie Nichols was a farmer near Blue Ridge (he also served as a County Commissioner for several years), Burl Nichols of Celina, and Miss Dora Nichols a school teacher. Many of these families still live in the area.

Sent by Mrs. W.T. Dungan.

THE HENRY OTTENHAUSEN FAMILY

Henry Ottenhausen was born in Germany in Hannover, September 15, 1839. In 1844 he came with his family to America. He was the son of William Ottenhausen and Christina Ousenkoff Ottenhausen. The family became American citizens September 21, 1855 by an oath of Julius Eggeling and John Sohnauty attesting to the fact that they had resided within the United States for five years.

Henry's father first settled in San Antonio, Texas then moved to Seguin and later to San Marcos. The father died there and is buried on the farm he owned, now known as the Knypsil Place. Henry's mother died March 7, 1904 in McKinney and is buried in the McGarrah Cemetery. As a child Henry played on the old stone walls of the Alamo while the family lived nearby. In 1858 he joined the Texas Rangers, first with Burleson then with Rip Ford. During the Civil War he served in Texas, Louisiana, and Arkansas under Capt. John S. Ford's Co. of Volunteers. He came to Collin County to live in 1866 and married Harriett McGarrah. To this union seven children were born: Christina, George W., Henry Elmer, Mattie, Ida Mae, Inez, and James R. George and Mattie died in their youth, Henry and James lived in Batesville, Texas and Christina lived with her parents until their death. Ida Mae married Doctor Wootson Hill, son of Frances (Tuck) Hill and Mary Quintillia Graves Hill, on March 15, 1898. Inez married Claude Paysinger in 1910.

The children of Inez and Claude Paysinger born in McKinney were William Henry, Annie Harriett, Louise Ludie, and Jimmie Inez. The children of Ida Mae and Doctor W. Hill were Marian Ardelle (Truett), Maybelle (Hilliard), and Ralph Henry Hill.

Story by Maybelle Hilliard of McKinney (a granddaughter).

JOHN RANDOLPH PARKER

JOHN RANDOLPH PARKER

(1838-1909)

John Randolph Parker was born September 10, 1838, near Waverly, Tennessee, the son of William S. and Josephine Rudolph Parker. His grandparents were also from Humpherys County, Tennessee, Joshua and Mary Patterson Parker and Elijah and Susan Stewart Rudolph.

Shortly after the death of his mother, John Randolph Parker came to Texas with his mother's sister, Jane Bernice Rudolph Cloyd and her husband, J.B. Cloyd. They made the trip overland in a wagon, stopping for a while at Honcy Grove, Mr. Cloyd became McKinney's first gunsmith and goldsmith.

Information from the National Archives reveals that John Randolph Parker enlisted in the Confederate Army in McKinney. He was mustered into company E, Steven's Regiment of the 22nd Cavalry in the Indian Territory at old Ft. Washita. In 1864 he was serving in the same company as a First Lieutenant.

On March 11, 1879, he was married to Margaret Howell, daughter of Daniel Howell, a pioneer McKinney merchant. The marriage ceremony was held in the old Christian Church, with the bride's attendants her sister, Mary, Howell, and Flora Benge. The groom was attended by S.D. Heard and Joe W. Waddill. Following the wedding a reception was held at the home of Ben and Nannie Howell Estes, older sister of the bride. As was the custom of the times, the couple was given a charivari by the young men of McKinney.

John Randolph operated a gun and locksmith shop just west of the square, on Virginia Street. He served as Alderman from southwest McKinney for twenty-five years and as a member of the school board for about the same number of years. Miss Cecil Abernathy (1880-1971) told of his visits to the school and the children's enjoyment of his talks to them. He was a member of the Cumberland Presbyterian Church. Parker Street was named for him.

The children of John Randolph and Margaret Howell Parker were; Bennie Parker West (Mrs. Edward G. West), who was born in 1880 and is now living at the Howell-Parker homeplace. The couple's son was John Howell Parker (1884-1946).

Following a long illness, John Randolph died on June 25, 1909 and is buried in Pecan Grove Cemetery in McKinney.

PARR-HALL FAMILIES
Compiled by Mrs. John Shipp
As reported by Ruth and Ray Parr

William Madison Parr and his wife, the former Sally Ann Pike, came to this area from Kentucky around 1890. The following children were born here: William M. married Mattie Corbitt of Wylie; Preston married Stella Marchant of Wylie; Hurbert married Monica Corbitt; Henry (no wife); John R. married Lucy Dunlap of Wylie; Robert S. married Mary Cassie Hall of Lucas; Clarence married Leona Moss of Lucas; also Roy, Jennie and George Parr. George married Elsie Corbitt of Wylie. For a time Henry, Clarence and Hurbert Parr continued to live in this area, but only Robert (Bob), has remained on his farm in Lucas and George (Pete) on his place in Forest Grove. Mr. and Mrs. Bob Parr are the parents of six children: Ray, married Ruth Russell of Clear Lake; Naomi, married Si McCreary of Parker area; Beola, married G.T. Woodard of Paris, Texas; Gladys, married Leslie McCreary of Parker; Paul R. married Ila Rae Leapard of Athens, Tex.; Fay, married Randall Humphries of Garland. Of the group only Ray, Gladys and Fay and their families still live in this area.

THE PATTERSON FAMILY

William and Elizabeth Ann Patterson were Peter's Colonists, coming to settle in Collin County between 1845 and 1848. Willaim was born in North Carolina in 1805 but was living in Morgan County, Illinois when they decided to come to Texas. To this marriage the following children were born, Elizabeth Ann (1836) married William C. Hall, H.G., a son was born in 1838, M.J., a daughter, was born in 1842, William C. (Cull) was born in 1844, and Mary Ann (1846) married John A. Gibson.

Andrew Jackson was born June 22, 1849 in Collin County to William and Elizabeth Ann Patterson. His mother died soon after his birth and is buried in Collin County. Andrew was a wheelwright and farmer, and was born in McKinney.

The Patterson land grant was from Fannin County and was issued by word on April 3, 1850, the grant being 640 acres. It had been surveyed by the Colony contractors but could not be designated because there was no map or field notes in the possession of the commissioners at the time.

William Patterson remarried on April 17, 1855 to Sarah K. Tenney, by whom he had five children. They were Elinor (January 1, 1856), John (1860), Jordon (1862), Jane (1864), and William (1866).

In 1856 William Patterson sold his land to Henry Maxwell and he and his family moved to Parker County, where they took up another land grant about 10 miles from Weatherford. By 1870 Sarah had died and William and his son, Andrew J. and daughter, Mary Ann, and his five younger children, moved home to Collin County. In the fall of 1870 they moved to Bell County where William died.

Both William C. Hall and his father-in-law, William Patterson, served with the Confederate forces. William Hall was with Martin's Regiment under Capt. Leonidas M. Martin's 6th Regiment, Partisan Rangers. This later became Company K. Martin's Reg. of Texas Cavalry, 10th Btn. of the Texas Cavalry. He was mustered in at McKinney on July 5, 1862 for three years. (He was listed as having a horse valued at $175.00 and equipment valued at $25.)

William C. Patterson, age 19 years, mustered in at McKinney July 5, 1862, also with Captain Leonidas Martin and served until February 17, 1865.

Written by: Mrs. Margaret Hawkins, Corpus Christi, Texas 78403.

PEARSON FAMILY

James Madison Pearson II was born September 4, 1843 in Dadwile, Alabama, the son of James Madison Pearson and Elizabeth Ann (Brown) Pearson. On his paternal side they were English and some were members of William Penn's Colony. On his mother's side the family was Scotch-Irish.

His early education was in schools of Alabama, later went to Emory College in Georgia and later the University of Alabama. At the outbreak of the Civil War he ran away from school and enlisted in Company E. Thirtieth Infantry of Alabama. He soon became a 2nd Lt. and served in eastern Tennessee under Kirby Smith. He was in the Kentucky Campaign and fought several battles in Mississippi. He was taken a prisoner during the battle at Vicksburg, May 22, 1863 and taken to Johnson's Island in Lake Erie, where he was held for 22 months. He later said that during this long confinement he memorized Paradise Lost and Paradise Regained. In March of 1865 he was returned to the South where he began to study law. He was admitted to the bar in Mississippi. In 1871 he entered the law department of Washington University and in 1873 won his L.L.D.

In 1875 he came to McKinney to practice law. In 1878 he married Mary Belle Powell and made his home at 318 South Tenn. In 1893 he became McKinney's first mayor and served five terms, unopposed. During his tenure he established the first water-works system, established the first sewage system, built the first public school, improved the streets and sidewalks, extended the city limits, revised the City ordinances, and received $1.00 as mayor.

In 1901 he was appointed by the Governor to entertain Eastern Capitalists, the New York Chamber of Commerce, and eastern merchants who wanted to tour Texas. In his speech he referred to McKinney as "the diamond pin on the bosom of Texas," a term that was widely used by the press. In March 31, 1903 he was appointed judge of the 59th district of Texas by Governor Latham. He served for three terms until ill health forced him to retire. He died May 1, 1915.

Judge Pearson was a Confederate soldier, a member of the Masonic Lodge, the Odd Fellows, and the Benevolent Order of the Elks. He is written up in the Encyclopedia of Famous Texans, p. 92, published by Southern Publishing Company in 1880.

James Madison Pearson, son of Judge Pearson, was born in McKinney February 8, 1887. After finishing school, he entered the real estate business

JUDGE J.M. PEARSON, McKinney's first mayor, elected in 1893, a noted attorney and District Judge.

with his cousin, Dan Jones, and helped promote the suburb of Urbanton, built on the Interurban route. Pearson Street was named for him.

In April of 1914 Matt Pearson passed the state bar examination and was licensed to practice law. December 1, 1914 he was killed turning on a light in his parents' home. He is buried in Pecan Grove in McKinney.

Elizabeth Ann Pearson was born in Alabama near Bell's Landing on a plantation. She was the daughter of John B. and Isabella Johnson Powell. She came with her family to Texas in 1870 and located in Van Alstyne and later settled in McKinney. After her marriage to James Madison Pearson they made their home at 318 South Tennessee Street. They were the parents of Leslie, Annie Belle, J. Matt. She was a sister of Yancy Powell. Story sent by: Mrs. Houston Elliott, 4230 Belclaire, Dallas, Texas.

LEANDER MARION HAMPTON (H.M.) PENLAND

Leander Marion Hampton (H.M.) Penland was born in 1875 near Newport, Tennessee. The son of Lorenza Dow Penland and Emmaline (Bell) Penland. Descendants of Charles and Wesley Penland, two brothers who were from Scotland.

Maggie Nola Metcalfe Penland (1878 to 1956) was born in the Cherokee Nation near Ashville, North Carolina. She was the daughter of William Irving Metcalfe (Cherokee Descendant) and Nancy Cook Metcalfe (Irish descendant).

H.M. and Maggie Penland arrived in McKinney, Texas from Dorchester, Virginia on April 23, 1908, with five children: Bertha (Garner), Bailey, Charles Dewey, Hagy, and Henry. They had six more children born after they arrived in McKinney, Levi, Vergil, Nancy, Walter, John, and Morris.

Charles Dewey Penland married Geneva Guy on July 3, 1926 in Bay City, Texas. The children born to this union were Charles Guy Penland and Peggy Jean Penland. They also has a foster child, Claudia Penland, who married Billy Womack Jones from Andrews, Texas.

Charles Guy Penland married Betty Jane Hooten (descendant of W.T. Hooten by marriage) on December 25, 1950. There were two children from this marriage, Geneva Elaine Penland and Elizabeth Jean Penland.

Peggy Jean Penland married Leo Boils on July 3, 1952. There were three children born to this marriage, Charles Leo Boils, July 24, 1953, Mary Ann Boils, Nov. 20, 1955, and Kimberly Jean Boils, April 25, 1962.

MARION A. GUY

Marion A. Guy (1879 to 1934) was born in Coosa, County, Alabama December 6, 1879, the son of J.E. Guy.

Mary Cordelia (Cordy) Colley (1881 to 1955) was born in Marion County, Texas January 13, 1881, the daughter of Wm. G. Colley and Melissia Colley.

Marion A. and Cordy Guy married in the Excelsor Hotel lobby in Jefferson, Texas in August, 1902 and came to Collin County following the marriage ceremony. They resided in Collin County until December of 1924.

Born to this union were three children: William Coleman Guy, July 17, 1903, Thomas Henry Guy, May 12, 1908 and Geneva Gertrude Guy, Jan. 23, 1910.

Geneva Guy married Charles Dewey Penland on July 3, 1926 in Bay City, Texas. The children born to this union were Charles Guy Penland and Peggy Jean Penland. Claudia Penland married Billy Womack Jones.

Charles Guy Penland married Betty Jane Hooten (descendant of W.T. Hooten by marriage) December 25, 1950. There were two children from this marriage, Geneva Elaine Penland and Elizabeth Jean Penland.

Peggy Jean Penland married Leo Boils on July 3, 1952. There were three children born to this marriage, Charles Leo Boils, July 24, 1953, Mary Ann Boils, Nov. 20, 1955, and Kimberly Jean Boils, April 25, 1962.

D.N. PHARR FAMILY

D.N. Pharr and his wife, Margaret Gallgher Pharr, and five children came to the Lucas area from Mississippi in 1879. They were the parents of four sons and two daughters: Carey, Dallas, Ellis, Lennie, Cora and Lester. The latter was born in Lucas.

Casey married Dean Cook, daughter of Mr. and Mrs. J.W. Cook of Lucas. Dallas married Susan Malinda Sneed, daughter of Mr. and Mrs. Robert S. Sneed. Ellis married Mattie Anderson, daughter of Mr and Mrs. Bet Anderson of Lucas. Lester married Clara Spears, daughter of Mr. and Mrs. Will Spears of Lucas. Lennie married Joe Lee Cook and Cora married Charley Cook, both sons of Mr. and Mrs. Bet Cook of the Lucas area.

Carey, Dallas and Ellis Pharr lived in Lucas the remainder of their lives. Mr. and Mrs. Carey Pharr were the parents of two sons and a daughter: Norman Pharr married Alice Russell of Clear Lake. Willard Pharr married Cristine Coffey, daughter of Mr. and Mrs. Clarence Coffey of Lucas and Willa V. Pharr married Osborn Blackmon of Houston. Norman Pharr and his mother are the only members of the family still in Lucas. He is farming the land that belonged to his great grandfather, Johnathon H. Cook. Mr. and Mrs. Norman Pharr are the parents of two daughters and a son: Norma Ann married Kenneth Lewis of Lucas, son of Mr. and Mrs. J.T. Lewis. Carey Beth Pharr married Johnny McQueary of McKinney and Willie Pharr married Darla Looper and he and his family live in Cleburne, Texas.

Mr. and Mrs. Ellis Pharr were the parents of two daughters: Jessie and Clodia Mae. Jessie married Edward Gunter of this area and they have a son, James Ellis Gunter. Clodia Mae married Randy Pace of Dallas.

THE POWELL FAMILY

John B. Powell and Isabella Johnson were married December 20, 1842 in Alabama. They made their home on a plantation on the Mobile River. They were the parents of William Ripley, Laura S.,

LESLIE JOHNSON POWELL, cotton buyer in McKinney in the early 1900s.

WILLIAM RIPLEY POWELL, pioneer cotton broker of McKinney.

Pichney Putman, John Leslie, Mary Belle, Blake Rose, Frank I., and Yancy Powell.

After the Civil War they lost their plantation and came to Texas by way of Jefferson. They came on a ship bringing only their clothes and one bale of cotton, raised on the plantation. Inside the base of cotton was a brass and cut glass candle stick and a pair of brass andirons. They bought an ox team and set out for Van Alstyne, the journey taking six weeks. While living in Van Alstyne Mr. Powell died and the family moved to McKinney. Mrs. Powell died in 1903, leaving two sons, Leslie, and Yancy and a daughter, Mrs. J.M. Pearson and her grandchildren, J. Matt Pearson, and Mrs. Clarence Merritt. Both John B. and his wife are buried in Pecan Grove Cemetery in McKinney.

Leslie Powell was born September 15, 1850, the

YANCY POWELL, cotton broker and Tax Collector of Collin County for years.

son of John C. and Isabella Powell of Monroe County, Alabama. Leslie was a cotton buyer in McKinney for many years and had a large warehouse for his cotton. He died in 1903 and is buried in Pecan Grove.

William Ripley Powell, also the son of John C. and Isabella Powell, married Maude Benge, daughter of early Collin County pioneers. They had one son, Jack, who died at age 18. Rip Powell was a cotton broker and at one time was Tax Collector for Collin County. He too is buried in Pecan Grove Cemetery.

Yancy Powell, son of John C. and Isabella Powell was born March 25, 1861, the youngest child. Yancy was a cotton broker and was for many years Collin County Tax Collector. He died November 17, 1947 and was buried in Pecan Grove Cemetery.

PRUETT FAMILY HISTORY

The Pruett name was formerly spelled Pruit. W.C. Pruett married Jane Cantrell, a widow with three children, James Richard, George, and Mary. They are both buried in the Grounds Cemetery north of Blue Ridge. To the union were born these children: Newt Pruett moved out of Collin County and settled at Archer City. Thomas Albert Pruett was born October 7, 1855 and died January 30, 1931. His wife, Ardena Bell Mulder, was born February 8, 1861 and died December 27, 1933. They lived on a farm one mile north of Blue Ridge and are buried in Pecan Grove Cemetery. John Pruett went to Archer City. Laura Pruett married Julius Conner and lived in Dallas. Martha Pruett married Jerry Worden and made her home in Farmersville and their children were Eugene, Lester, Will, Arlie, and a son. Darthaulia Pruett married George Akin and lived in Blue Ridge where they reared their children, Cleo and Ermine. Hettie Pruett married Dr. Robinson and settled in West Texas.

These are the children of Thomas Albert and Bell Pruett, William Walter (January 8, 1880—July 21, 1940), Mary Paralee (February 27, 1882—July 17, 1930) and married Labe Anderson, Bertye Annie (March 13, 1885—November 18, 1970) and married L. Howard Evridge. They have a daughter, Mrs. R.N. Jenkins of Marshall. Harvey Melvin (August 18, 1887—January 28, 1960) married Ethel Lawrence and lives in Princeton. Their children were Bertie, Viola, Ellen Lynn, Welson, and Kenneth. John Elmer, the fifth child (February 4, 1890—1943) married Kate Wardlow,

Albert Ben (January 18, 1893—May 21, 1961) served in World War I, Linnie Mae (September 27, 1895—January 14, 1971) married Clarence Barrett, Henry Lewis Pruett (September 13, 1898—March 20, 1933) married Esther Farmer of Melissa.

Nannie Pruett was born on September 7, 1904, married J.G. Williamson and lives in Ft. Worth. They had one daughter, LaVerne.

These are the children born to W.W. and Ida Pruett. W.W. married Ida Mae Houk on July 8, 1900, a native of Broadhead, Kentucky. W.W. owned the McKinney Monument Works. Their first child, Mary Leona, was born November 25, 1901 in Blue Ridge, and was a graduate of Mary Hardin-Baylor in 1923. She married Oran Albery Ballou on May 23, 1926 and to this union were born Carlene Beatrice, who now is a teacher in Colorado Springs, Colorado and William who is pastor of the Rosenberg, Texas Calvary Baptist Church. The second child of W.W. and Ida Pruett was Gladys Modena (August 28, 1903) born in Blue Ridge, also a Baylor graduate, she married John G. Moore, December 22, 1926, and to this union were born Margaret Jo, John Robert, and Gladys Ann. Gladys Ann and her family are missionaries in Indonesia. The third child was Burnice Houk (December 8, 1905—March 19, 1907). The fourth child was Willie Carlos (March 7, 1908—January 21, 1960) married Reba McLaughlin April 20, 1930 and had two sons, Donald Paul and Ronald, both living in Kansas City. Kermit Edwin, the fifth child (April 20, 1911—May 30, 1968) married Connie Agnello, November 7, 1943 at Mostagnum, North Africa. Connie was a nurse and he was in the Army. They had a son, John Nichols born April 20, 1955, who at present is at West Point. The sixth child was Margaret Eloise (January 8, 1922) married Frederick Henry Ogilvie on May 13, 1943. To this union were born Ida Margaret and James William. Fred retired from the army as a Lt. Colonel in 1970.

Written by Mary Leona Pruett Ballou, McKinney, Texas.

THE RANDLES FAMILY

Three Randles brothers, Jim, John and Joe migrated from England about 1847. Jim settled in Tennessee, Joe in New York State, and John came

JOHN AND HARRIETT RANDLES, pioneers of Valdasta and Sister Grove Area.

to Texas.

John Randles married Martha Harriett Hodges, who was half Indian. Her mother was a Cherokee from the tribe living east of Sister Grove Creek near Valdasta in northeast Collin. Harriett was born and died on the same farm. To this union were born eleven children, of which only five lived to be grown, three girls and two boys, Vira, Sam, Myrtle, Horace and Ettie.

Sam Randles married Lillie Hemphill in 1901 and to this union were born 12 children, five boys and seven girls. The children were Lovie, Lessie, Lena, Elbert A., Inez, Owen, Asalee, John, Doris, Troy, Mary, and Billy Joe. Seven of the 12 attended college and five became school teachers.

E.A. Randles has taught school 43 years in Collin County. He is married to Juanita May from Blue Ridge. They had one daughter, Barbara, who is married to Tom P. Jester Jr., a Denton attorney. The daughter and her husband have two small daughters, Angie and Jill.

Both E.A. and Juanita Randles are involved in all phases of community life and service. He was named "Man of the Year" in Plano in 1952, was Worshipful Master of Lodge 768 in Plano, was for five years president of the Collin County Fair, was Director of the Chamber of Commerce for six years

THE SAMUEL Elbert Randles family.

E.A. AND JUANITA RANDLES of McKinney. Both taught school for many years.

and a member of the McKinney Park Board of McKinney for 15 years. He is a Deacon in the First Baptist Church, Past District Deputy of the Lions, member of the Chamber of Commerce for 22 years, member of the Masonic Lodge, a Shriner (thirty-second degree), Secretary to the Collin County Livestock Association. He was a District President of the Ag Teachers Association, and holds the honorary degree ''Lone Star Farmer.''

Juanita Randles holds both a Bachelors and Masters Degree and taught thirty-four years in the Plano and McKinney school system. She is past President of the Business and Professional Women's Club and of the Art Club. At present she is President of the City Federation of Women's Clubs and also serves on the Library Board.

RATTANS

The year 1840 found all eyes in America and western Europe turned on Texas. She had declared her independence of Mexico March 3, 1836 and, seven weeks later, had won it, April 21, 1836, at the Battle of San Jacinto. The leader of Texas was Sam Houston, a romantic figure, who had been Governor of Tennessee, and Indian Chieftain and a United States Congressman. Andrew Jackson was President of the United States and Houston had served on his staff. Through such associations and personal friends, exactly one year from the day that Texas declared her independence of Mexico, she was recognized as an independent nation by the Senate of the United States.

With her political independence assured, Texas was still beset by the perils of prairie, stream and Indians. The agents of the Mexican Government turned the Indians against the American settlers in every part of Texas. Thus, she faced hostility from both Mexicans and Indians—for the next four years, and from 1836 to 1840 all of Texas was ablaze with Indian warfare. Besides this, she found herself faced by the still more desperate perils of ignorance, poverty and social unrest. One can readily see that by the keep to God, and the courage of men who were men and women who were women, all would eventually be well in Texas!

The land was to be cleared, the soil was to be stirred for crops, domestic animals were to be raised, thus furnishing the three necessities of food, shelter, clothing.

The stirring events of the Texas Revolution, with the gripping tales of the Alamo, Goliad, and San Jacinto, had riveted all eyes on Texas and had thrilled the hearts of thousands of Americans citizens in their old home states.

The Congress of the Republic of Texas was most anxious that settlers should come as rapidly as possible—Texas was beckoning. There were two main reasons for this desire: first, that settlers might give protection to one another against the Indians; second, that the Republic might develop its resources and wealth.

Accordingly, Congress made liberal laws, even offering actual settlers free land and liberal business inducements. The territory, open to settlers, ran from the Red River, near Denison, through Grayson, Collin, Dallas, and Ellis Counties to near Waxahachie. Hence, more than 30,000 of the most adventurous spirits of America, had come to Texas to seek homes, fame and fortune! This was a vast and princely domain, larger than some states in the United States and larger than some nations in Europe.

Each family was to receive from 320 to 640 acres, and, in order to secure it, they had to live on it at least three years; had to build a log cabin on it and had to cultivate at least 15 acres of land.

THE THOMAS RATTANS

Thus, Thomas Rattan (the first Thomas, they still follow) got the yen to come to the new land. So, he came in 1840 and staked his headright about three miles southwest of the present town of Anna. Despite the hazards of travel and the mode of travel—just remember there were no roads and the means of transportation was "one-horse-power-hay burner"—despite all this, Thomas Rattan made nine trips back to Carrollton, Green County, Illinois from whence he came. He had made acquaintances along his route, and could stay overnight anywhere or borrow anything that he needed for his purpose.

Thomas Rattan was a descendent of John Rattan, a Revolutionary soldier, also of Illinois, so Thomas Rattan was well ensconced in Illinois when he pulled stakes.

He was short, energetic, stockily built and a thorough man of business. He was born in Illinois, October 4, 1789 and died on the Rattan headright November 11, 1854. He is buried in Throckmorton Cemetery east of the land he staked out.

He married Gilliam ("Gillie") Hill March 5, 1807, the daughter of Isaac Hill, the earliest settler of Bond County, Illinois, and the builder of Hill Fort. She was born September 25, 1792 and died in 1870. She, also, was buried in Throckmorton cemetery beside her husband.

Within the last few years, a Mr. Arrington, from New Jersey, whose mother was a Rattan, removed their bois d'arc markers and replaced them with granite.

Thomas Rattan sold out preparatory to coming to Texas. He was a slave owner and the History of Greene County states that he sold eleven of his slaves in the sum of $1,100.00. Therefore, "Gillie," his wife, was accustomed to servants, and liked to be waited upon, as well as keep everyone around her busy.

He had held high offices, besides his business ventures. In Illinois, the Governor had appointed him Justice of the Peace. In Carrollton, he had contracted and built the first Court House in Greene County. He was one of the most active and energetic men in the county and was said to have contributed more to its development than any of his contemporaries. He had built the Rattan Building in which he was elected to several offices. He was elected commissioner, then was elected to the State Legislature, having served in both Houses before coming to Texas.

He had met with hardship and reverses in his native state but had also mastered success. So, this man of toil was ready to face clearing land of its forests and tilling the soil for life's necessities. He and Gillie built their cabin, dug their well for water, and settled down to the fine task of having and rearing a family of fourteen, five of them being born in Texas. Life for them was no bed of roses as they had crude homes, crude furnishings, no conveniences, no good roads and no fast transportation. It took real men and women and that's just what these pioneers were!

Following are their children and marriages. These are given because their marriages were made with well-known names who were instrumental in the development of Collin County.

Names and marriages of the children of Thomas and Gillie Rattan will be given because several are names familiar to Collin County and more, especially, to McKinney: William S. Rattan, never married, died on his way to the California Gold Rush, and was buried at sea. Merrell E. Rattan married Melvina Negos, then Ann Morfoot. Wade Hampton Rattan married a Miss Pyle and was killed by Indians near Carrollton, Texas. Martha Patricia Rattan married Isaac Brown, then Henry Blanford. John Rattan married America Broyles. Clarinda Rattan married William Pyle, then Mr. Moore. Temperance Rattan married John Mace Kencaid. Lucy A. Rattan married Hugh Jackson. Harriett Rattan married Andrew Jackson Witt. Sarah Rattan married Carroll McKinney. Louisa Rattan married Hogan Witt. Mary Rattan married William Fitzhugh. Ann Rattan married Dr. James W. Throckmorton. He later became governor of Texas. Thomas Hempstead Rattan married Rebecca Jane Coffman.

Most of these fourteen children of the original Thomas Rattan who came to Collin County from Greene County, Illinois, lived normal lives and moved about to different states. But there were two of these children who accomplished enough that they are written up in several histories of Texas. The first, Ann Rattan, who married Dr. James Throckmorton, and Wade Hampton, who was the first white man to be killed by the Indians in the vicinity of Dallas.

An account of Ann Rattan will be given first. She was born March 5, 1828 in Carrollton, Illinois; and died October 30, 1895 at McKinney, Texas. Governor Throckmorton was born February 1, 1825 at Sparta, Tennessee, and died April 20, 1848 at McKinney, Texas.

They were married in Illinois, January 20, 1848. They were distantly related as his mother was Susan Jane Rotan, which is a variant of Rattan.

A portion of the history of Collin County, in its first settlement, is very closely allied to that of Dallas. In the month that John Neely Bryant camped at Dallas (November, 1841) Dr. William E. Throckmorton, from Fannin County, settled and headrighted land on Throckmorton Creek, near the

THE THOMAS H. RATTAN home on the original Rattan headright. In this home Ann Rattan and Dr. J.W. Throckmorton were married. James D. Rattan was born in the home. This is a frame house.

Rattan settlement and just south of Throckmorton Cemetery. He was father of Dr. J.W. Throckmorton, who had studied medicine in the Mexican War.

As one can see, in the thesis of Pyramus and Thisbe, of Greek Mythology fame, ''propinquity threw the young people together and acquaintance ripened into love.'' So Ann Rattan settled down to the fine avocation of wife and mother. He had studied under the supervision of an uncle, Dr. James E. Throckmorton, had an extensive practice and was reputed to be a skilled physician. This is mentioned here to show his wife's great responsibility. She was well-educated and read extensively to keep abreast of the times. These newspapers and magazines, while few in number, were carefully read and kept as are our deluxe editions today.

As can be seen, Rattans have large families and Ann Rattan was no exception. Ten children were born to this union and she reared them in a log cabin, sans conveniences, took his patients into her home and cared for the critically ill. The doctor had good relations with the Indians, but when a chief with feathers on his fantastic headdress bent over her baby or took it up and played with it, her blood ran cold. She dared not offend him. She said, ''I thought I should die of fear and loathing, yet for the sake of peace, it must be endured.''

Her reading, also, consisted of reading Dr. Throckmorton's medical books. He was away from home a lot on missions of mercy so this pioneer mother ''took care of emergencies.'' A little boy, almost in convulsions, was brought to her. He had a piece of a broom handle broken off in his foot and the wound had closed. She got down her husband's old instruments, cut open the foot, removed the stick and bound up the wound. A doctor was summoned and he told her that her quick action had saved the child's life.

She had kept a very ill, almost blind little girl in her home for a year. When the child became better, she did not want to go home.

She clung to Ann Rattan Throckmorton, almost screaming. The parents were amazed and hurt. They took her, but had to return her to the Throckmorton home for almost a year's stay and care.

There are countless cases of this mother's courage and skill—and willingness to keep humanity in her primitive way.

Both she and Governor Throckmorton are buried in Pecan Grove Cemetery in McKinney. After serving as Governor and getting a taste of politics, he became a lawyer and never practiced medicine further.

All the Governors' wives' inaugural gowns are in

the art building of Texas Women's University at Denton. The mannikins are very similar to these ladies and their elaborate gowns are very beautiful. Mrs. Throckmorton is represented as petite, with red hair and a plum-colored dress, adorned by a black lace scarf about her shoulders.

WADE HAMPTON RATTAN

The other Thomas Rattan off-spring in history is Wade Hampton Rattan, who had met John Neely Bryan, Captain Mable Gilberts, John and James Beeman. Mr. Bryan built his 10 x 16 log cabin in Dallas and the latter families, accompanied by others, moved on to Bird's Fort. They had sent men back to Red River for supplies, and when, after six weeks, they did not return, Hamp Rattan and three others were designated to go search for them. On Christmas Day in 1841, they found a bee tree. While they were busy cutting down this tree for the honey, they were discovered by Indians, who killed Hamp Rattan. Five days after the Indians had killed him, the body of Hamp Rattan was found by the returning wagon. His faithful bull dog was still guarding his body when found, else it would have been ravaged by vultures and wild animals. The remains were conveyed to Bird's Fort, and there, in a rude coffin made of an old wagon body, committed to the earth. Mrs. Rattan, wishing to enclose the grave, was assisted in her labor of love by the Beemans and John Cox, who, with the widow, went in an ox wagon to the camp of John Neely Bryan.

The Thomas Rattan headright was north of the Throckmorton survey, camp site, and creek. This was one of the centers of social and religious life of these pioneers. As they stirred up the soil for a subsistence, they also stirred up a social life, which consisted of camp meetings, and picnics at Throckmorton camp grounds, and square dancing in the homes.

John Coffman headrighted adjoining Thomas Rattan on the north. Then 1½ miles southwest of Anna and east of the Thomas Rattan place, was the Isaac Shelby survey, a descendent of General Joseph Shelby, undefeated rebel of Kentucky. He was also the first Governor of Kentucky. The Shelby survey is mentioned because Mrs. James D. Rattan's mother was a Shelby. And these surveys are mentioned to show that propinquity really does propinque as these families all intermarried.

These original Rattans married neighbors. Thomas Hempstead married Rebecca Jane Coffman. The Coffmans and Slaughters married Sherleys, the Rattans married the Milligans, of the Shelby line, and the Throckmortens married the Rattans. A Slaughter and Coffman even "swapped" sisters. It was all very well kept in the family.

Thomas Hempstead had one of the first homes built of lumber. It was built on the first Thomas Rattan land, and in it Governor Throckmorten married Ann Rattan, his sister, and also delivered his son, James Dow Rattan. The home was 1½ stories and has long since been razed, much to the regret of the present Rattans. Dow Rattan, son of John Hampton Rattan, brother of James Dow, bought it and owned it up to his death a few years ago. His, Dow's daughter, Sue Evelyn Rattan, now owns the land and occupies the large brick home her parents built on the original home site.

The only two Rattan brothers remained in Collin County. Also, one sister lived at Melissa. The children of Thomas Hempstead Rattan were: Mary (Sis), married Isaac Jones; Ann, married Will Moore; Dorothy (Dollie), married John Mallow; James D. Rattan, married Minerva Jane Milligan; and John Hampton Rattan, married Dirie Strother.

The Joneses moved to Tucumcari, New Mexico. None survive.

The Moores moved to Ft. Worth and one daughter, Agnes, now lives in Arlington.

The Mallows (Dollie Rattan) both died at Melissa. They had no children and are both buried at Melissa.

John Hampton Rattan was accidentally killed by a horse as a young man on August 26, 1904. He was born November 11, 1859. He and his wife had three children, two daughter and one son. His wife, Dirie Bell Strother Rattan, was born April 13, 1864 and died at Anna on November 14, 1950. Their children are as follows:

Dow Rattan, married Edna Lindsey, of Van Alstyne. They are parents of a son and daughter. John Hampton (Hamp), born July 12, 1905, died in 1971. He was educated at Anna and Rice Institute at Houston. He married Eunice Vermillian and they have one son, John Hampton Rattan, age 23 years. He is a graduate of West Texas State and is married.

Sue Evelyn Rattan, their daughter, owns and still lives in the lovely country home. She is a graduate of McKinney High School, attended S.M.U. where she was a member of Pi Phi Sorority. She received her B.A. degree at Huntsville, Texas and taught in Anna Schools until her parents' health required her to retire.

Miss Lee Rattan, was born April 15, 1887 and married Sam Houston McAnally and had two daughters, Louise and Fay Bell.

Lillian Rattan, youngest of the three, born at Anna, graduated from Anna High School and attended Kid Key Woman's College at Sherman. She married Arthur W. Powell March 19, 1914, who graduated from Anna High School, attended Decatur Baptist College and Baylor University. They have two sons: Raymond is engaged in farming and livestock. He married Alma Thornton September 16, 1936. They have no children. Arthur Weldon attended Texas A&M and served in World War II as T-Sgt., in the European Theatre for 21 months. He married Betty Lou Gorner June 5, 1947. They have two daughters, Rebecca Elaine and Debra Jane. They reside in Amarillo where he is a Manufacturer's Representative of a Drug Company.

JAMES DOW RATTAN

James Dow Rattan, son of Thomas Hempstead Rattan and Rebecca Jane Coffman, was born April 11, 1857 and died January 18, 1924. He was married by the Reverend A.M. Douglas, First Christian Minister of Van Alstyne, on November 29, 1882 at the Edward Milligan home southwest of Anna. The bride was the daughter of Edward Milligan and Ruth Ann Shelby.

Minerva Jane Milligan Rattan was born at Kachtown, Pennsylvania on April 23, 1862 and died in a Dallas hospital on April 18, 1961.

These pioneer couples married to settle down to the fine fulfillment of establishing a home and rearing a family. Mr. and Mrs. Rattan bought 300 acres of land south of the Coffman cemetery, where they lived until they bought a farm west of Coffman School. Then they bought the Milligan home, the Shelby Headright, where they had been married and, where several of their children were born. This farm was held in the Rattan family until it was sold to settle the estate, in 1972. In 1914, the Rattans built a large home in Anna, where they finished rearing their children. The home is now owned by a daughter, Mrs. Jewel Rattan-Bralley, who still resides there.

To Mr. and Mrs. Rattan were born eleven children, four sons and seven daughters: Zora (Zoe), Beatrice (Bea), Ursa (Jackie), Nola (Tony), James Laud, Jewel, Thomas Edison, Jim Minerva, Ruby Ruth, Paul Milligan, and Benjamin Rupert.

There were several, five to be exact, of the James Dow Rattan children who lived or are still living in the vicinity of Anna. They are: Zora (Zoe), Laud, Jewel, Thomas, and Ben.

Zora (Zoe) Rattan, born October 22, 1883, died May 17, 1966. She attended Hardin College, Missouri St. Ursala's Convent, Dallas and graduated from Texas Christian University. She married Otis C. Cartwright on October 22, 1907, at Anna Christian Church. He was born at Van Alstyne November 10, 1872 and died May 28, 1936 at San Angelo. They had no children. They are both buried at San Angelo, where he was with Central National Bank his last forty years. At his death, Mrs. Cartwright moved to Anna to live with her widowed mother, the last 30 years of her life.

James Laud, born September 11, 1890, died October 6, 1972. He was educated at T.C.U. and the University of Texas in Pre Med. Then he decided on farming. He married Arlyn Graves of McKinney and a teacher at Anna and a graduate of North Texas. To them were born a son and daughter: James D. Rattan II, a graduate of Annapolis and now a Lt. Commander in the Submarine Service in Monterrey, California. He married Miss Elaine Valchuis of Boston, Massachusetts. They have three children, James Dow III, Janelle, and Dow Todd.

The daughter, Dana, graduated from Anna High School, and attended North Texas State University. She married Roy Adams of Van Alstyne, April 18, 1957 at the Rattan home in Anna. He is a CPA with a Dallas firm. They live in Plano and have four children, Dawn, Darja, Adam and Alicia.

Jewel Rattan, born March 3, 1893, is now living in the old Rattan home in Anna. She earned her diploma at C.I.A. in Denton in 1916, her B.A. degree in 1932 and M.A. at the present Texas Woman's University at Denton.

She married, in 1917, Ernest Bralley, son of Dr. and Mrs. F.M. Bralley, President of the University from which she graduated.

Ernest Bralley graduated from North Texas and attended the University of Texas. He was flying instructor at Kelly Field No. II at San Antonio, Texas in World War I. He was born in 1893 and died in 1970. To them were born a son and a daughter: Ernest Meade, Jr. was born March 14, 1920, and was educated in Dallas Public Schools. He took Premedical at S.M.U. and Washington and Lee University in Virginia. He was in the first graduating class of Texas University Medical School, in Dallas, 1944. His fraternity was Phi Chi Medical. The sons and sons-in-law of Mr. and Mrs. James D. Rattan, as well as their grandsons and grandsons-in-law all served their country in various wars since World War I, inclusive, as did their forebears. But Colonel Bralley has a longer service, of thirty years, as he decided to make a career of the Army. Therefore he was made a First Lieutenant upon graduation from medical school, and was immediately sent to Germany duringWorld War II. He served in various towns in Germany, Vienna, Lebanon, and finally Nuremberg, where he helped organize Masonic Lodge No. 828 and served as Worshipful Master.

He was later sent to Korea, to serve in the "Little Police Action" for eight months. He was with the 24th Regiment of the 25th Division and served as Chief Medical Officer from Pusan to the Middle of North Korea. He was awarded his Majority, the Combat Medical Badge and the Bronze Star for valor in action.

He served for one year as Deputy Commander of the hospitals in South Vietnam in 1971-72. He retired in March 1974 as a Colonel in the Army after 30 years' service. He practices medicine in Huntsville, Alabama. He married Marilyn Spencer, a nurse at Parkland Hospital, where he was House Physician.

She now does "Home Nursing" for their seven children. One son, and six daughters as follows: Marilyn Minerva, born in Germany, Sept. 12, 1947; Carolyn Jane, born in San Antonio, April 1, 1949; Kathryn Ann, born in San Antonio, Nov. 22, 1950; Ernest Rattan, born in Denver, Jan. 8, 1953; Suzanne Jewel, born in San Antonio, May 26, 1955; Victoria Lynne, born in Germany, Aug. 22, 1957; Roslyn Elizabeth, born in Fort Belvoir, Va., Oct. 30, 1959;

Betty Jane Bralley, born in Dallas, January 21, 1923, lives in Washington, D.C. She married January 16, 1944. Her husband was Ensign Paschal O. Drake Jr. of San Angelo. She graduated from Woodrow Wilson High School in Dallas in 1939 and from Hockaday Junior College, Dallas, in 1941, after attending Christian College in Columbia, Missouri. Ensign Drake was graduated from San Angelo High School in 1939. He was in the Navy in World War II, was a Lt. and Hellcat Pilot, based on the Saratoga "Flat Top" off the coast of Japan. After the war he attended A&M University, where he procured his B.A. and M.A. degrees. He is now with the Department of Agriculture in Washington, D.C. They have one daughter, Cydine, who is married to Wade Burleson. They have three children, Tracy Drake, Taylor and Betty Jane. They also live in Washington, D.C.

Thomas Edison Rattan was born October 28, 1895 at Anna. He maintains homes in College Station, west of Anna. He is a graduate of Anna High School, and served in France in World War I. He married Frances Oates on April 8, 1927 at her

home in McKinney. She graduated from McKinney High School and attended T.W.U. at Denton. She taught in several schools in Collin County. He was administrative assistant of the U.S. Division of Agriculture. They are now both retired. They have two children, Thomas Oates and Frankie Jane Rattan.

Thomas Oates graduated from high school in College Station then took his masters degree at Texas A&M University. He married Sherley Brown of Anna on January 20, 1951. She graduated from Allen High and attended T.C.U. He was not privileged to serve his country as he lost his right hand in a tractor accident. It was then that the "kids" in the family dubbed him "Captain Hook" due to his artif al hand. They are the parents of four children: Victoria Scott, married; Rebecca, married; Thomas Andrew (the youngest Thomas Rattan), and Mona Minerva, she and Thomas Andrew are twins. They are attending T.C.U. and West Texas State, respectively.

Frankie Jane Rattan, born at McKinney on June 21, 1929, married William W. Howell Jr. of Waycross, Georgia, a jet pilot in World War II who was stationed at College Station. He has a masters degree from "The Citadel." She is a graduate of College Station High School and Texas Woman's University. They now live in Atlanta, Georgia where he is with an oil company. They have three children still in public schools, Laura, Melissa and William Whitehead III.

Benjamin Rupert (Fuzz), born January 26, 1906, west of Anna, was the youngest of the eleven children. He married Velma Thornton. By natural inclination, they were "drop outs" before it was fashionable, which lead to a teenager marriage. He went back to the vocation of his forbears and was a natural for livestock raising and farming. They have no children and are retired (1974) in their very liveable brick home half a mile west of Anna. And he brings to an end the living generations of the descendants of Thomas Rattan, who first headrighted in the vicintiy of Anna to Throckmorton Creek.

Following are the six of the eleven James D. Rattan sons and daughters who lived in neighboring counties:

Beatrice (Bea) Rattan was born at Anna on January 20, 1885 and died at San Angelo August 17, 1959. She married John Augustus Miller of Montgomery, Alabama on October 25, 1911, at San Angelo. He was a graduate of the University of Alabama. She attended Hardin College, At. Ursula's Academy, Dallas, and T.C.U., where she continued the study of violin. She taught violin in San

Angelo for over 40 years. The following is a tribute paid her in The San Angelo Standard:

"Mrs. J.A. Miller qualified as one of the great lovers of the violin as an instrument of enjoyment and technical beauty. Her violin choirs, made up of members of her classes, not only promoted the cultural front of San Angelo, but they performed in recitals and at church and civic functions throughout her forty-nine years of service here as a teacher.

The talent of many was strengthened and beautified under her direction. Musical appreciation was brought to full flower, also, as a part of her contribution to the cultural life of San Angelo. Her death removes from the ranks of our musicians one of the most talented."

One son was born to Mr. and Mrs. Miller. He, Jon, was born August 26, 1923 at Dallas. He lives in Houston with his father, J.A. Miller, and his teacher of English in Houston Junior College. He is an accomplished violinist and pianist. He was educated in San Angelo High School, S.M.U., Rice Institute and the University of Arkansas, where he recieved his masters degree. He served in the Seavees in World War II, on Guadal Canal. There he was organist to the Chaplain, as they put it "between Japanese Air Raids." He married Dollie Woodall of Dallas on November 15, 1951. She earned her masters degree at the University of Texas and teaches English at Corpus Christi, in Junior College. They have one daughter and two sons: Beace, John Stuart and Robin Reynolds.

Ursa Rattan, born December 6, 1886, died at Nocona, March 15, 1962. She married Hugh Carson, a graduate of Texas Christian University and Air Ensign in World War I. He accompanied war supplies to Europe. He died in Nocona, where he had been with the F&M Bank for many years. She was a graduate of North Texas and taught for several years in Anna and Nocona.

To them was born one daughter, Patricia. She attended Oklahoma City University, Trinity University, received a degree from Stanford, and her Law Degree from Golden Gate College, San Francisco. She is now, in 1974, practicing law in San Francisco. She received the President's Award at Stanford for being the most outstanding student. She and her partner had also won first place for Stanford in the National Debate Meet in Denver.

She married Dr. Robert A. Major in Nocona, Texas, January 13, 1956. He is a graduate of Baylor Medical College and is a physician and surgeon in San Francisco. They have four children, two

sons, and two daughters: Leslie, Robert Jr., Hugh Geoffrey and Maritza.

Nola Rattan was born in West Texas and now resides in San Angelo, Texas. She was educated in Anna High School and graduated from North Texas State College at Denton. She was accomplished in voice and piano, and taught in Anna, Sherman and Dallas Schools. She married L.L. Farr, Jr., June 4, 1920 in a beautiful home wedding in Anna. He was a graduate of San Angelo High School and a graduate of Rice Institute. He was prominent in athletics there. He was a rancher, but left to serve as a captain in a machine gun corps in the famous 36th Division. He died, at San Angelo, April 8, 1960.

To them were born two sons and two daughters: Louis Lee III, Jim Rattan Farr, Ellen Elizabeth and Minerva Jane.

Louis Lee Far III was born in San Angelo on June 4, 1921. He was educated by a governess on the Bar S. Ranch and graduated from Culver Military Academy in 1940. He served in the Tank Corps, in Germany, in World War II. He was a First Lieutenant and was awarded the Bronze Star and other citations.

He married Lou Dickey Baucus September 13, 1940 in Kansas City where she was reared. She was an honor graduate and received a scholarship to Linwood College where she graduated.

To them were born four children, one daughter and three sons: Penelope Ann, born August 13, 1942, is now in Japan, where her husband is serving in the Army. Louis Lee IV, born March 4, 1944, is a doctor of veterinary medicine in Hereford. William Baucus, born August 25, 1946, was educated in San Angelo and at A&M University. He is now in Dallas where he is Marketing Manager of Livestock Producers of America. Philip Sawyer, born August 3, 1949, was educated in San Angelo and at Texas A&M, and is in business in Lubbock.

Jim Rattan Farr, born February 28, 1923, was taught by a governess and attended Culver, T.C.U. and Rice. He was in World War II in the Pacific Theatre, where he served with the Marines. He was at Manila when General MacArthur issued the statement, "we shall return."

He married Margaret Toombs in November of 1947 in her home in San Angelo. She was born in Houston and educated at S.M.U., Dallas. To them were born two daughters and one son: Phyllis, born May 2, 1949, married, was in the service with her husband, in Germany. Kathleen, born September 5, 1951, is in Texas Tech. Tom Lee, born May 31, 1956, is in Uvalde High School, where his parents live on irrigated farm and also ranch.

Ellen Elizabeth, born on the Bar S. Ranch on September 18, 1924, was educated at San Angelo High School, St. Mary's at San Antonio, Hockaday Junior College, Dallas. She married Lt. Russell Lee Heitkamp during World War II. He served in the Tank Corps in Germany with Louis Lee Farr III. He was awarded a Bronze Star for valor in action and made a captain. They live in Alexandria, Louisiana, where he is in the automobile business.

Minerva Jane, born December 5, 1927, is now living in Cuba, New Mexico. She was educated by a governess and at Hockaday, Dallas, and in New York City. She is married to Harold McDonald. They have three sons and one daughter.

Jim Minirva Rattan, daughter of James Dow and Minirva Milligan Rattan, was educated at Anna, T.C.U. and Texas Woman's University where she earned a degree in 1922. She was accomplished in voice and piano. She studied at Bush Conservatory in Chicago. She studied voice with Arthur Meddleton, Stella Owsley, Miss Ethel Rader and Dr. William Hemphill.

She married Fred Cunnigham, son of Judge Cunnigham of Sherman. He was educated in Sherman and attended Stanford. He studied voice with William Hemphill, and evangelized with Dr. George Truett, Baptist Minister, for a Corporal, was given a Medical Discharge. He was with the Bureau of Internal Revenue, Dallas. He died May 26, 1966. Mrs. Cunnigham lives in Dallas. They had no children.

Ruby Ruth Rattan was born Dec. 11, 1901 at Anna. She resides in Dallas with her daughter and son-in-law, Dr. and Mrs. Reginald McDaniel.

She was educated at Anna and received her B.A. from Texas Woman's College in 1923. She earned her Master's Degree from North Texas University in 1950. She is an accomplished pianist and also studied voice. She taught in Van Alstyne for several years, then in Garden City, Texas.

She married Rupert P. Richer, graduate of the University of Texas and an attorney in the University oil field. To them were born a son and a daughter:

Prince Rupert Richer, born at McKinney, August 30, 1933, attended school at Anna and Garden City. He attended Virginia Military Institute and received his B.A. Degree from the University of Texas. He served with the Armed Forces in France in World War II as a First Lieutenant.

He married and has three sons and two daughters. He was in the oil business with his father at Midland until his father's death. He, Prince, is now retired and lives in El Paso.

Cindrette Richer, born at San Antonio, October 39, 1935, was an honor graduate of Garden City High School. She attended Southwestern University, Georgetown; and, also, Texas Woman's University, Denton. She married John W. Benson, August 22, 1957 at the Rattan home in Anna. He was a graduate of Virginia Military Institute, and served as a First Lieutenant in the armed forces in France. They had a son and daughter, John and Paige. He died May 4, 1966 of a heart attack. Several years later, she married Dr. Reginald McDaniel, and they reside in Dallas where he is a pathologist.

Paul Milligan Rattan, M.D., was born March 27, 1904 in Anna. He now lives west of Howe, Texas on his cattle ranch, and practices in Dallas. He is a heart specialist and diagnostician. He was educated at McKinney High School, S.M.U., and Baylor Medical College when it was in Dallas.

He married Miss Mary Rae Abbott, a Registered Nurse from Canada. She was head nurse in a hospital in St. Louis and in San Angelo, Texas, where Dr. Rattan was practicing medicine. They later moved to Dallas. They have one daughter, Paula Rae Rattan, born February 3, 1942. She graduated from Hockaday Girls' School in Dallas in 1960, attended finishing school in Columbia, Missouri, and earned her B.A. from the University of Texas.

She married William Fenton Scott of Houston whom she met in the University. He served in the Marines in World War II, until he met with a serious accident, which led to medical discharge. He is in business in Dallas, where they now reside. They have three little daughters: Stacey, born February 13, 1967; Ashley, born July 9, 1969; and Robin, born June 29, 1972.

Thus, ends the whereabouts and businesses of the posterity of the Rattans—of Thomas and Gillie Rattan who blazed the trail from Illinois to Texas in 1840. Those two who cleared forests, tilled soil, stood in awe of Indian attacks, and bore hardships with fortitude, to help build a Texas—A Texas such as we, we their posterity enjoy!

THE RHEA FAMILY

Capt. William Alexander Rhea was born in Sullivan County, Tennessee on Feb. 24, 1833, the second of his parents' five children. He was the son of Joseph R. Rhea and a nephew of John Rhea who for years represented his district in Congress. His mother was Emaline Alexander, the daughter of William and Mary Alexander. The family came to

Collin County in 1855 and settled near Walnut Grove. W.A. grew up on his parents' farm in Collin and at 19 years of age attended the Blount Academy in Tennessee. He engaged in business with Larkin Adamson at Weston, and for a time taught school at Mantua. In 1857 he and his brother James entered into a partnership and operated a mill for building machinery. The location they selected grew into Rhea Mills, ten miles northwest of McKinney. By the time the Civil War came the operation had flourished and they were operating an extensive carding machinery, corn and flouring mills.

In 1861 W.A. Rhea joined the Confederate Army, enlisting as a private in Company D., Sixth Texas Cavalry, and at the reorganization of the company in the following spring he was elected Captain. At the Battle of Corinth he had his left foot torn away by grape shot. He returned to Texas in 1863 and was elected to the legislature, then appointed Adjutant General by Gov. Murrah and aided Gen. Griffith in organizing the state troops. After the war the mills were extended and business expanded. A mercantile store was added to serve the community.

Capt. Rhea was married the 16th of July, 1868 to Ella Foote, daughter of Dr. G.A. Foote. Six children were born to them: James F., Emogene, William A., Lawrence J., Mary E., John Edwin.

James C. Rhea was born in Roane County, Tennessee in April 11, 1837. In 1855 he immigrated with his parents to Collin County and settled 10 miles northwest of present McKinney. He and his brother, W.A., built and operated the wool-carding machines that started the famous Rheas Mills. The flour mill was added in 1860. He too served in the Confederate Army and he was twice wounded at the Battle of Corinth. After the war he and his brother continued as partners in the growing business. At the organization of the militia of Texas in 1871 he was elected Captain of Company G. 85th Regiment. In 1876 he was appointed postmaster at Rhea's Mills when the mail route was opened. He was appointed notary public by Gov. Ireland and again by Gov. Ross in 1889. His home, "Sunnyside" contained over 1000 acres and he had business interests in the North Texas Mill and Elevator Co.

He was married to Mary A. Gossett of Kentucky, Sept. 14, 1875. She was the daughter of Rueben and Harriett Gossett. Three children were born of this union—William J., Robert L., and James L.

Story from newspaper biography and Capt. Hall's notes.

THE RICE FAMILY

William Rice came to Collin County, Texas in 1843 from Benton County, Arkansas, around Fayetteville. Rice came with the Throckmortons and built a cabin at Buckner, the first county seat of Collin County. It seems that the Rice family moved from Virginia to Tennessee where he married Abigail, a half Cherokee Indian. Abbey, as she was called, was born December 6, 1807 in South Carolina (Indian Territory as some family records called it). She died November 18, 1889 and is buried in the Clear Lake Cemetery.

William came to Collin County as a Peter's Colony settler and received 640 acres of land. He settled northwest of McKinney and patented his land on January 19, 1855. He was a farmer and served as a private in the Mexican War, enlisting in Captain Andrew Stapp's Company, Mounted Volunteers (1846). His son, Charles P. Rice, and his nephew, Paschal H. Rice, also enlisted from Collin County.

William Rice bought four lots in the town of McKinney on June 27, 1850 and sold them in 1852. He later moved to the Hardin T. Chenoweth survey about three miles northeast of McKinney. The Rice family had 10 children, Charles P. Rice (1827), and died 1847, his father received payment for his service in the Mexican War. The second child was Joseph P. Rice (1830-1844). He was scalped by the Indians at about the same time the Muncey-Jameson massacre on Rowlette Creek. He was buried in a small cemetery on Wilson Creek, west of McKinney, which no longer exists. The third child was John L. who was born in Tennessee in 1832 and died around 1860, the fourth child was Margaret (1834-1850 to 1860).

Alexander Rice (1837) was born in Arkansas and married Mary Ann Crabtree who was born in Missouri (1839). To them were born eight children.

Other children were E. Rice, a female born in 1839; Julia Ann, born in Arkansas in 1841; William, born in 1843 in Arkansas, and died at the hand of robbers in New Mexico; Martha Ellen Rice, born May 12, 1846 near McKinney. On December 14, 1865 she was married to Peyton Russell Jordon (born July 8, 1839 in Georgia) and became the parents of five children.

The tenth child was Caroline Wilmine Josephine Perusa Rice (February 22, 1848—September 22, 1922). She first married Thomas Jefferson Davis in 1870 (divorced), then married Phillip James Soden (July 6, 1841). She and her second husband are buried at Clear Lake Cemetery.

Martha E. Rice and Peyton R. Jordon were the parents of the following children: Julia Ann who married Tinah Haywood Poland, May Rella who married John Calvin Jones and settled at Nevada, William Ludwell married Monte Swope and settled at Josephine, Dudley Everett married Cornelia Godrey.

Caroline Rice and Jefferson Davis had two daughters: Julia Ann who married William Greenbury Robbirds and Alta Boyd who married Roy Gann.

Sallie Ellen Davis (1875-1945) married Walter Price Addington, the son of John Wesley Addington and Martha Jane Price. To this union were born nine children: Faye Hodges and Grace Poor, both of McKinney; Ollie of Wylie; Opal A. Long of McKinney; Elsie Smith of Richardson; Delia Bull of San Clemente, California (mother of George Bull, the author of this story); Elmo of Brooklyn, New York; Vince of Dallas; and Oleta Arnsen of Thermal, California.

Caroline Rice Davis and Phillip Soden had four children: Owen P., who died young; Thomas Phillip, who married Ida Mae Preston (they had one daughter, Hester Phennel, of Clear Lake); and Katie Elvira Soden who married Luther Hays Harris and had nine children: Lillie Springer of Pomona, California; Tennie Seinfield of Claremont, California; Eva Harries of Rockwall; Soden Harries of Garland; Daisy Prince of Royce City; Robert Pershing Soden married Ruth Woods of Grand Prairie; Arsie Harris of Garland; and Maxwell of New Boston, Texas.

Martha Soden married Henry Lee Smith and they had six children, Faye Simmons, Pearl Mounger of McKinney, Luther Smith of Clear Lake, Thomas L. Smith of Wylie, Anna Mae Smith of Tracey, California, and Cora Bess McCoy of Mesquite.

Pascal and Martha M. Rice had these children: George (1851); Johnny (1853); Mary Esther (1855); who was married to John William McGraw, who was born in 1848 in Ireland; Dorothy A. (1857) married Joseph Harding, the son of America Harding.

Polly Rice (1859-1930) married Lo Newby.

Ellen Rice (1861-1904) married Phillip Corbitt, both buried at St. Paul. Jackson Rice (1863), and Mattie Rice (1874).

Mary E. Rice and John W. McGraw had a number of children: John (1874-1952) married Minnie Lee Sperry, Margaret D. (1878-1956) married Ab Boyer and settled at Culleoka, Mary (1880), William Thomas (1876-1940) married Agnes Nesbitt, Joseph P. (1885-1951) married Etta Strickland, James Patrick (1888-1963) was twice married, first

to Pearl Paris then to Rosa Peters, George Lawrence (1890-1952) married Katie Ann Akin, Hamilton David (Jack) married Nannie Bell Highsaw, Ernest Everett (Pete) born 1894 and died 1972, married Vera McDaniel. Most of these children settled in Collin County.

Dorothy Rice and Joe Harding had the following children: J. Willie, Rose Marie who married Pitt Kellog Babcock, Claude J., Peter J. who was killed in the Battle at Argonne Forest, France in World War I, Susie Bell married Willie Townsend.

Ellen Rice married Phil Corbett, son of William and Elizabeth Corbitt, early settlers of the St. Paul community near Wylie, and they were the parents of Mattie who married William F. Parr, Mary Ellen married John P. McEntee, William, Margaret who married first Francis Brennan, and second John McGarth.

Monnica (1885-1970) married Joseph H. Parr, Annie R. (1887-1944) married Edward Miller, Joseph P. (1888-1940) married Lillie Boyer. Robert Emmett (1890-1968) married Minnie Dodd.

Dorothy Elizabeth (1892-1943) married Charlie Cotter, Elsie married George M. Parr and settled at Wylie, Dennis Phillip, Katherine Delia married Virgil Heard, and Frederick Corbitt (1901-1906).

William Rice came to Collin County in 1843 and helped to make a county out of a wilderness and hundreds of his descendents now live here and enjoy the fruits of this pioneer and his labors.

Data sent by George Bull, San Clemente, Calif.

THE RIKE (REICH) FAMILY

R.A. Rike (Reich) came to Collin County in 1850 from North Carolina, settling on Pilot Creek, three miles west of Farmersville. He was born in Salem, North Carolina, October 22, 1821 and christened in the Moravian Church. He married Maria Seitz (Sides) and there were three children who lived to grow up: Henry, John, and Lewis. The family left Salem in April of 1850; the caravan of settlers included his two brothers, Owen and Agustus. Owen settled at Bonham and Agustus went back to North Carolina. Also in the party was Lewis Sides, brother of Maria. After the death of Maria, her husband was married to Martha Griffin and to this union were born Emma, Mattie, and Sallie and a son, Charles, who died young.

R.A. Rike was a member of the Regular Texas Cavalry of the Confererate Army, as shown by the muster rolls of the 5th Martin Cavalry of 1862 with

J.K. Bumpass the Captain. Henry Rike, his son, was also in the army at the time.

John Rike, son of R.A., was Justice of the Peace and was the first mayor of Farmersville, 1973. R.A. Rike had the first hotel in Farmersville in the 1860s on Main Street. George Rike was a partner with E.H. Pendleton and W.B. Yeary in Farmersville's first drug store in 1885. Charles J., son of George Rike, was associated with this drug store for 45 years. The business sold in 1965 to Billy Harrison after 81 years of Rike ownership. Rike Street in both McKinney and Farmersville are named for R.A. Rike.

Story sent by Charles J. Rike, Box 287, Farmersville.

U.S. REP. RAY ROBERTS

Congressman Ray Roberts, Democrat of McKinney, was born March 28, 1913 in Collin County. He was educated in the local public school and later attended A&M, North Texas State, and the University of Texas. He began his public service in 1935, as director of the National Youth Administration of Texas under Lyndon Johnson, and in 1940, he joined the staff of House Speaker, Sam Rayburn.

Roberts is a combat veteran of World War II and also served in the Korean War, retiring from the Naval Reserve as a Captain. He is married to the former Elizabeth Bush of McKinney, and they have a daughter, Mrs. Tom R. Murray II, and two grandchildren.

Roberts is the 10th ranking member of the Public Works Committee and 4th ranking member of the Veterans' Affairs Committee. As a member of the latter, he serves on its Hospitals, Compensation and Pensions, and Housing subcommittees. He is chairman of the new Public Works subcommittee on Water Resources, created by combining three subcommittees, Rivers and Harbors, Flood Control and Internal Development, and Conservation and Watershed Development. He is also a member of the subcommittees on Transportation, Public Buildings, and Grounds, and Energy.

Congressman Roberts has been a leader in the development and conservation of the nation's resources. He was a principal author of the important Water Resources Development Act of 1973 and has sponsored legislation promoting water pollution abatement, flood control, river and harbor development, economic development of the under-developed areas, and the improvement and expansion of the nation's highway system. He guided passage of legislation authorizing the Sabine River development, Trinity River project improvements, navigation of the Red River, and the enlargement of Lavon Reservoir. As a ranking member of the Veteran's Affairs Committee, Congressman Roberts has sponsored legislation to improve housing, education, pensions, compensation, health, and other benefits for veterans.

Story and photograph sent author by Congressman Roberts.

JOHN WESLEY ROBINSON SR.

John Wesley Robinson was born to an old Tennessee family on January 21, 1876 at Bushgrove, Tennessee. As a young man he came to Plano to join family friends who had settled in Plano, the Carlisles. His knowledge of farming and ranching soon made a place for him in his new home. He married Mary Isebell Pirtle of Tennessee, who had come with her family and settled south of Dallas. To them were born four sons, James Gipson Robinson, John Wesley Robinson, Eugene Quentin Robinson and Leland Howell Robinson while living at Hebron on the farm he had purchased. Mrs. Robinson died in April of 1925. Being left with four small sons to rear was not easy, and in July of 1926 he married his son, James', school teacher, Mary Elizabeth Price, the daughter of A.G. Price of Denton. The new family settled west of Plano in the Haggard Community. Four children were born to this union, Mary Ellen, Lewis Jacob, L. Vernon, and Tom Ellis Robinson. He spent his life farming and ranching, and the family was always a part of the community activities of school and church. Mr. Robinson died in a traffic accident September 10, 1963 at age 87. Six of the sons still live in Plano, as did Mrs. Robinson until her death, October 22, 1973.

Story sent by the grandchildren.

DR. SAMUEL LEGGETT ROBINSON

A beloved doctor well known to pioneer residents at Nevada was Dr. Samuel Leggett Robinson. He was born February 9, 1823, at Charleston, South Carolina. Harriett Benjamin Jordan became his wife on July 22, 1853. She was born in Bertie County, North Carolina on Dec. 2, 1840. He studied at Charleston, South Carolina for his M.D. Degree. After their marriage, they first came to Athens,

Texas, in 1858 and two years later he moved to Nevada, Texas, and set up practice. Mr. and Mrs. Robinson were members of the Church of Christ.

Their twelve children were as follows:

Anna Robinson was born Aug. 2, 1856. She married Newton J. Stinebaugh on Aug. 13, 1877. He was born in 1856 in Missouri. He was a son of Granville Stinebaugh whose family settled early at Nevada. They were of the Baptist faith. Their children were Charles, who married Ora Jones, and Lela, who died in infancy. Anna died in 1937.

Maston W. was born Jan. 2, 1858 and died July 24, 1866.

Samuel I. was born March 30, 1859, and died Jan. 22, 1878.

John T. was born Dec. 6, 1860. He married Mary Sue Buchanan on May 26, 1884. Their children were David Guy, Mary Crow, Willie J., Lottie Mae, Alvie, and Ida Inez.

James J. was born April 22, 1862. He married Dora Lee Stinebaugh on March 31, 1885. She was a daughter of Sam Stinebaugh. They were blessed with twelve children.

Henrietta E. was born Nov. 19, 1863. She married W.H. Buchanan on Jan. 19, 1883. They were members of the Church of Christ. He taught at the Old Karo School. Their children were: Novae, Russell, Vista, and Clarence. Henrietta died Jan. 9, 1941.

Martha E. was born July 15, 1865 and died March 14, 1866.

Miriam E. was born Jan. 20, 1867 and died June 23, 1887.

Pompey was born Nov. 13, 1869 and died in 1931. He married May Taylor and second to Lovace Rodgers. His children were Faye Nell, Gladys, and Oma May by his first wife. By his second wife, Obed.

Horace Oscar was born Dec. 10, 1871 and died Feb. 1, 1888.

Jerome was born April 14, 1874 and died Jan. 25, 1890.

Ila was born Aug. 11, 1876. She married W.A. Hambrick on Jan. 11, 1890. She died July 10, 1890.

Dr. Robinson died March 2, 1887 and was laid to rest in the Bear Creek Cemetery. No citizen contributed more to the progress, health and happiness of the pioneer communities around Nevada than Dr. Robinson. His wife passed away Jan. 28, 1925.

Submitted by Paul Russell, Box 1524, Grand Prairie. Texas 75050, December 28, 1973.

THE RUDOLPH FAMILY

The members of the Rudolph family who came to McKinney from Waverly, Tennessee during the middle of the 19th century made important contributions in skilled mechanical workmanship, musical talent, and newspaper knowledge the life of the community. After four of their children had settled in McKinney, Elijah Rudolph (1794-1870) and his wife Susan Stewart Rudolph (1793-1877) moved to McKinney and made their home with their daughter, Jane Bernice Rudolph Cloyd, and her husband, John B. Cloyd. A letter written to his son, Dave of Waverly, Tennessee, gives a clear picture of what life was like in frontier McKinney. (1869).

The first of the family to arrive in McKinney were Abe and Harriet Rudolph Hall, in 1852. Abe operated a blacksmith shop near the square on Louisiana Street for twenty years before moving northwest of McKinney to a farm, for which he paid $1600. in gold. During the Civil War when Collin County was isolated by blockades, he operated a train of carrying cotton from the area to markets in Mexico.

Another daughter, Elizabeth Rudolph Batson (1833-1912) and her husband, Thomas Batson, came to live in McKinney in 1860.

A son, Thad L. Rudolph (1835-1874) was a talented musician. With John P. Lillard, he furnished music for the ball held at the Cannon Hotel in McKinney on August 14, 1868, in celebration of the nomination of Seymore and Blair as the candidates of the Democrats for President and Vice-president of the United States. In the Civil War he served as 3rd Lt. in Company K, which was organized in McKinney in 1862.

Robert M. Rudolph, another son (1818-1880), whose wife was Elizabeth Kirkpatrick Rudolph, was a minister of the Cumberland Presbyterian Church. He operated a wagon and machine shop during the week and also served as one of the first District Clerks of Collin County.

The sons of Robert and Elizabeth Kirkpatrick Rudolph were prominent in the life of the community of the last half of the nineteenth century. The four brothers, Sam K. Rudolph, Lige K. Rudolph, Jim K. Rudolph, and Hugh K. Rudolph were fine musicians and had their own band, which they called The Silver Cornet Band. They became quite famous over the state and were called upon to play at political rallies and at the Governor's mansion in Austin. Sam Rudolph headed a locally famous Barbershop Quartet which entertained

LIGE KIRKPATRICK RUDOLPH

customers at the Northside Barbershop. Their favorite songs were "Sweet Adaline" and "I'll take you home again Kathleen".

The Rudolph brothers (Lige, Sam and Jim) were connected with newspapers. Lige began working for Thomas H. Bingham when he was only 12 years old, and at 15 was foreman of the shop in publishing the "Advocate." The three brothers published "The Collin County Mercury" in 1887. The Mercury entered the statewide fight for prohibition and Lige wrote stirring editorials on the subject.

A daughter of Robert and Elizabeth Rudolph, Betty Rudolph, and her husband, Paul Gallis, owned and operated the "Opera House" at Greenville.

MAYOR AL RUSHHAUPT OF McKINNEY

Al Rushhaupt was reared in Victoria. He and his wife Gerry came to McKinney to make their home from Ft. Worth in 1947. His is a long and consistant record of public service to his community and church. In 1964 he received a standing ovation at the Chamber of Commerce banquet when he was named "Outstanding Citizen of the Year" for his work on the McKinney Development Committee and other projects. He was the organizer of this committee. He has operated the McKinney Office Supply business in McKinney for over 25 years and has expanded it to other towns. The East Texas Chamber of Commerce named him "East Texan of the Month."

There is no area of community life that has not been benefitted by his work. Some of the offices he has held are, committeeman for both the Boy

AL RUSHHAUPT, Mayor of the City of McKinney

Scouts and McKinney Council of Camp Fire Girls, Director of Collin County National Bank, Board of Directors of the Heard Museum and Wildlife Sanctuary, Library Board, past president of the Rotary Club, as well as of the United Fund, president of the high school PTA organization, and chairman for the McKinney Advisory Committee.

In April of 1973 he was elected Mayor of McKinney and in May was elected to the Executive Board of the North Central Texas Council of Governments. He also serves on the Regional Health Planning Council of this organization.

He and his wife are the parents of three children, Judy, Janet and Richard. Mr. Rushhaupt is a teacher and leader in the United Methodist Church.

JAMES V. RUSSELL FAMILY

James V. Russell and his family settled at Wylie, Texas, in 1860, having immigrated from the State of Missouri.

Hiram Russell, the father of James V. Russell and his wife who was a Graham, were both natives of North Carolina. After their marriage in 1820 they settled in Logan County Kentucky. This family later moved westward in 1837 to western Missouri in Polk County.

To this union was born seven children:

Abner, the first, died in early manhood in New Orleans, La.

Mary Polly, born in 1823, married Granville Stinebaugh and came to Texas in 1860, settling at

J.V. RUSSELL of Wylie, 1827-1920.

Nevada, Texas. Mr. Stinebaugh owned the farm on which Nevada was built when the cotton belt came through in 1888. Their children were Nancy Mildred, who married Buster Boyd; Mary Ann, married Blunt Harris and Jack Odom; Newton married Anna Robinson; and Sarah married Hiram Cook and Tom Letson.

Lavena Russell, another daughter, married Fountain Mayfield who settled at Wylie at an early date. Their children were Jim, Will, Lee, Marion, Molly Randall, and Eureka Parish.

Rebecca married Riley Harper. Their children were James Riley who married Matilda Bateman of Wylie; William, John, and Jane the wife of Theo Brooks.

Sarah married Jacob Wilkinson who came to Texas in 1860. Three unmarried boys were John, Jacob, and Lewis. Ruth married James Flowers.

John Russell married a niece of Jacob Wilkinson.

After the death of his first wife, Hiram Russell married Matilda Harper, in the 1840's. To this union were born two daughters; Martha who married Landrum King of Wylie and Harriet who married John Lewis and Ike McDowell of Wylie. Both of these daughters were born in Missouri. Hiram Russell died in Missouri before the Russell family came to Texas. His wife was the mother of Nancy Jane Russell and many of the Harpers who settled in the Wylie area. She died in 1888 and was buried in the old Decatur Cemetery near Murphy.

James V. Russell, son of Hiram, was born in Russellville, Kentucky, Sept. 15, 1827. He was a volunteer in the Mexican War of 1846 and served with the 3rd Regiment, Co. K, Missouri Mounted Volunteers Infantry. He was also a veteran of the Civil War serving in the 16th Regiment as 2nd Corporal of McKinney's Company, Fitzhigh's Regiment, Johnson Brigade, T.M.V. Collin County. He served under Captain John McKinney.

In 1850, J.V. Russell joined the vast immigrant train of fortune hunters in the famous gold rush to California.

In 1849, he married Nancy Jane Harper. She was born in Kentucky in 1832 and had immigrated with her family to Missouri in the late 1830's. Their first two children died in infancy.

Mary Ellen, the third, was born in Missouri in 1855 and died in 1861 at Wylie.

Dorcas, the fourth, was born in 1857 in Missouri and married Jim Brown of Wylie. He donated the land on which the First Christian Church was built. The first school in Wylie was conducted in this building. Dorcas died in 1891 and left one son, Seth.

Fountain Russell was born in Missouri in 1859 and married Elizabeth Dowdy of McKinney. They reared two boys, Edgar and Raymond. He farmed at Wylie and died in 1926.

In 1860, James V. and Nancy, along with her mother, Matilda Harper, and the Jacob Wilkinson family all immigrated to Wylie where J.V. bought a farm and put up a home. This farm covered the north section of Wylie. His first land purchase at Wylie was out of the S.B. Shelby Survey. One section of 200 acres was purchased at the price of eighty cents per acre. He also purchased land in Denton County near Argyle and engaged in the ranching business. He and his wife were charter members of the Wylie Christian Church and also served the Cotton Wood Church of Christ in the 1870's.

The first child born in Texas was John who married Josephone Sullivan. He was born in 1861. He operated a sorghum mill at Wylie and later moved to West Texas.

James W. was born in 1864 and died in 1866.

Jim Wilson was born in 1867 and in 1892 married Lelia Edens of Wylie. She was a daughter of E.H. Edens from Judsonia, Ark.

Landrum was the last born to J.V. Russell family in 1870. He married Eva Smith. He died young at Argyle, Texas.

James V. Russell died in 1920 at the age of 93, his wife preceeding him in death in 1905.

Submitted by Paul Russell

JIM W. RUSSELL, 1967, pioneer of Wylie, Texas.

JIM W. RUSSELL FAMILY

Jim W. Russell and Leila O. Edens were married at Judsonia, Ark. Nov. 20, 1892, in the Baptist Church. They left immediately for Texas.

Mrs. Russell was born Dec. 26, 1873 at Judsonia, Ark. Her mother died at an early age and she was reared by her oldest sister, Betty, who married Moses Andrews. At the age of 12, she moved to Texas with her father, E.H. Edens, and with the Andrews family. With this move also came three brothers, George, Bill, and Bob and another sister, Susie. Mrs. Russell made confession to the Christian faith and united with the Wylie Christian Church in 1894.

Jim W. Russell was born in 1867 to James V. Russell and Nancy Jane Russell in a log house which was situated on the northern edge of present Wylie. They came to Texas in 1860 from Missouri.

He and his brothers all attended the old Nickleville College near Wylie.

Mr. Russell built his home on North Ballard in Wylie in 1893 and later moved the home onto old 78 on the South side. He taught school for many years around Wylie and in 1898 was selected the principal of the Wylie Common School District. He served as Mayor of Wylie in the early 1900's. For many years afterwards, he owned and operated a dry goods business in Wylie and also owned and operated stores at Denison, Fort Worth, Corsicana, and Gordon, Texas, during the coal boom of 1918. He edited the Wylie Herald in the 1930's until his retirement.

Mr. and Mrs. Russell had two daughters and four sons.

The first son was Vaughn (1893-1943) who married Maude Adams at Austin, Texas.

Dorcas, the second child, a daughter, was born in 1895 and died in 1900.

Lloyd (1897-1973) married Agnes Watson of Wylie. They lost a son, Ralph, in World War II.

Kathleen, the fourth, was born in 1899. She was married to John Green of Wylie.

Clyde (1901-1972) married another native of Wylie, Gladys Paul.

Paul, the last son (1904-1971) married Ruth Pruitt of Dallas.

Mrs. Russell passed away on April 1, 1939, on the same day her sister, Mrs. Betty Andrews, died, after an extended illness. A double funeral was conducted at the Methodist Church.

James W. Russell died in November 1941. Both he and Mrs. Russell were members of the Wylie Christian Church.

JOSEPH RUSSELL 1799-1882

Joseph Russell was born in North Carolina on December 31, 1799, according to his tombstone in the Bowman Cemetery northwest of Plano, Collin County, Texas. The 1850 federal census of Collin County would have him been born in 1801. The 1880 census gives the information that his mother, whose name we do not know, was also born in North Carolina, and his father in Pennsylvania. We believe his father was the Thomas Russell whose name appears on the Romny payrolls of Captain William Hatcher's company of Virginia on November 2, 1775. Two things support this conjecture; first, the tradition of several families agree that they enjoyed close fellowship with this Russell family in Virginia long before the families of John D. Brown and William Beverly began their migration to Texas; and second, there is listed on the above payroll of John Beverly, thought to be the father of William Beverly. In January 1880, William Beverly wrote, ''father John Beverly, was born in Virginia in 1743, and died August 23, 1829. He was a captain in the Revolutionary War—my son, John Beverly, was born in Roane County, Tennessee, on July 6, 1829, and came to Texas with me.''

During his childhood, Joseph Russell lived in North Carolina, Virginia and Tennessee. As a young man, he moved to Missouri, about 1823, possibly in Kentucky, Joseph married Elizabeth Grey, born April 16, 1803, in Madison County,

252

Missouri. She was the daughter of Levin (Leavin) Grey, whose name appears on the 1800 tax list on Madison County, and his name did not appear on the 1790 list. Joseph and Elizabeth had five children, all born before the family came to Texas. Family tradition says the family was at Independence, Jackson County, Missouri.

The promise of new land in Peter's Colony, south of Red River, caused Joseph to move into Texas in 1845. The John D. Brown family were traveling companions. With Joseph Russell were; his wife Elizabeth, his widowed daughter, Mary Russell Stone and her three year old daughter, Nan Stone; Joseph's two unmarried daughters, Elizabeth and Isabel; his married daughter, Nancy, and her husband Samuel P. Brown, son of John D. Brown. Also, traveling with the group was a single man, James Stone, who was probably a brother of Mary Russell Stone's deceased husband. James Stone received three hundred and twenty acres in Peter's Colony which he sold unlocated after 1850. Members of the John D. Family were William A., Robert H., Eliza, Elizabeth, Sara, and Charles M.

The group crossed the Red River into Texas at Old Warren, north of Bonham, on December 18, 1845. When they came to the river, Isabel Russell, 13 years old, wanted so much to be the "First girl in Texas" that she jumped down from the wagon and mounted her horse and rode across at a gallop through the shallow water of the ford. Although the water was shallow here the river was dangerous because of quicksand. She had to ride right back because the men decided to wait until morning to cross with the wagons. All wagons were lightened as much as possible so they could cross quickly to avoid bogging down in the quicksand.

After the successful crossing the Russell and Brown families soon parted company for a while, the Browns going west to Old Buckner, the first county seat of Collin, but soon on the Cottage Hill community area where they settled.

The Russells with their son-in-law Sam Brown and with James Stone, moved on southward to a point three miles north of present Plano. Joseph Russell's 640 acres in Peter's Colony grant was patented in two tracts, about a mile apart with Rowlett Creek running through both tracts. First, the family settled on the lower easterly tract near Old Indian Hole, a deep water hole at a sharp bend of the creek on Muncy 640 acre tract which adjoined them on the north. If the Russells did not know, they surely heard that less than a year before the Muncy family had been savagely murdered and mutilated by Indians at that spot. Although that tragic

event is said to have been the last great Indian depredation in Collin County, the Russells lived in constant fear and dread of the Indians who frequently came to the cabin demanding food. Elizabeth tried to keep hot bread baked to appease them because they seemed to favor that. When they demanded meat, she gave them a cow.

The Russell family suffered a grievous loss when their young married daughter, Nancy, died. This was two weeks after the crossing into Texas. The death is believed to have resulted from a combination of premature childbirth complications, the rugged trip and the severe winter weather. There was no wood with which to build her coffin. Her saddened family had to tear apart the bed of a wagon for her father to fashion a coffin. They lined it with one of her mother's handmade quilts, and buried Nancy on the new land just after Christmas, 1845. Her young widower, Sam P. Brown, returned to his family at Cottage Hill, but kept in close touch with the Russells. In 1846, he married their widowed daughter, Mary Russell Stone. He took her and her daughter Nan to settle in Dallas County where they were living at the time the 1850 census was taken. By that time they had two little boys of their own.

On November 15, 1847, the first Methodist church in Collin County was organized in the Joseph Russell home. On the 100th anniversary of the Methodist Church of Plano, the church published a history which says in part: There were thirteen charter members, Joseph Russell, his wife Elizabeth, his son and three daughters. Also, John D. Brown, his wife Rebecca, their two sons and two daughters, and James Stone.

The first 100 years of history and growth was commemorated in a sermon by Bishop Charles C. Selecman at the morning service. In the afternoon, Mr. Wallace Hughston, a great grandson of Joseph Russell, gave the response the welcome address.

On November 15, 1973, a group of about 100 members of the Plano church met at the site of the Joseph Russell home at six in the evening. A short worship service of prayer and hymns was held by the pastor of the church. A message of praise was given by Bishop McFerrin Stowe at this place and later a sermon in the Plano church. For this occasion there were six descendents of Joseph Russell present.

Sometime before 1850 the Russells moved to their other tract of land about a mile and a half west. This second tract was in a fork formed by West Rowlett Creek which passed through the northeast corner, and by what is now called Russell Branch which passed through the southwest corner of the

JOSEPH RUSSELL

tract. The house they built there, which no longer stands, was their home the remainder of their lives.

Death claimed the life of Mary Russell Stone Brown in the early part of 1856.

In March 1856, Nan chose Sam P. Brown as her guardian, and her estate was valued at $500.00. She was fourteen years old, and later that same year she married Frank F. Morrill of the Cottage Hill community, living there the remainder of their lives and rearing a family of six children.

Isabel "Ibby" Wilburn Russell (Jan. 5, 1832-April 20, 1911) married Reverend John Beverly, Methodist minister, son of Captain William Beverly and Nancy Delozier, April 11, 1849, and lived about two miles and a half south of their parents' home. Their first of twelve children, Joseph William was born May 2, 1850 and died in 1934.

Joseph and Elizabeth gained another of the Brown boys as a son-in-law on Jan. 2, 1850, when their daughter Elizabeth (b. March 22, 1834-d. Nov. 23, 1910) married Robert Harvey Brown, a brother of Sam. The young newly married couple were living in the Joseph Russell household when the 1850 census was taken.

Joseph Warren Russell married Julia Ann Bowman in March 1867. She was born February 1, 1840. On September 4, 1868, their only child John Joseph "Little Johnny" Russell was born and his mother, Julia, died the following day. Less than four years later the child was orphaned when his father Joseph Warren Russell died February 16, 1872. On March 22, J.W. Bowman was made guardian of "Little Johnny." Johnny often stayed with his grandparents Russell before their deaths a few years later.

Joseph was a farmer and a carpenter. He and Elizabeth lived long happy lives together, dying within a few years of each other. Elizabeth died December 2, 1876, and Joseph on November 10, 1882. His last few years were spent in blindness; the 1880 census states that he was blind then. His death resulted from an accident due to the handicap. He was visiting at the home of a relative in Pilot Point, Denton County, and was sitting in a rocking chair on the porch. Failing to realize he was near the edge of the porch, he rocked over the side and died of the resulting injuries or shock. He and Elizabeth are buried in the Bowman Cemetery.

REFERENCES

Collin County, Texas court records—Deeds; Probate; Marriages.

Collin County, Texas Federal Census, 1850, 1880

Collin County, Texas Early Land Survey Maps

Correspondence with Mrs. Edna Russell Parr, Alice, Texas, Miss Eva Hughston, Dallas, Texas, Mrs. Foy Thomas, McKinney, Texas.

Dallas County, Texas Federal Census 1850

"First One Hundred Years of the Methodist Church of Plano, Texas, 1847-1947"

Madison County, Kentucky, Tax Lists 1790 and 1800

"The Peters Colony of Texas," Conner

The Quarterly, March 1967, "Beverly Family Records"

Revolutionary War Records, Virginia State Library, Richmond

Tombstone Records, Bowman Cemetery, near Plano, Texas

Tombstone Records, Old City Cemetery, Masonic

Tombstone Records, Routh Cemetery (see The Cemetery Quarterly, June, 1972)

SANDERS FAMILY

L.H. Sanders married Jimmie Walls, a native of Arkansas. They came to this area around 1890 and settled between Lucas and Branch.

Mr. and Mrs. Sanders were the parents of five children, three sons and two daughters: Ellie May married Everett Morrow of Winningkoff. (Both are deceased.) Dured married Emma Welburn of Branch. They reside in Garland. Duel married

Lizzie Riley of McKinney. Allie married Jim Heifner of Lucas. Clifford (deceased) married Alah Talbert of Winningkoff.

Mr. and Mrs. Evertt Morrow were the parents of a son, Chester, and daughter, Lorene. Both attended local and McKinney schools.

Chester Morrow married Gertrude Harvell of Winningkoff. They live on the Everett Morrow farm and are the parents of two sons: Glen and Jerry. Glen and his family live in Garland and Jerry lives in the Everett Morrow home-place.

Lorene Morrow married Jack Kerby of the Winningkoff area. They are the parents of a son, Frank, who is a student in NTSU, Denton.

Cliff Sanders (deceased) and Alah Talbert Sanders lived in Lucas many years. They had five children, four daughters and a son: Joann married Kenneth Housewright of Wylie; Peggy married James Goodwin of Rowlett; L.T. married Evelyn Chastinne ot near McKinney; Nancy married Bo Dickerson of Wylie; Dian married Norman Morris of Caddo Mills. Mrs. Sanders now lives in Wylie.

JOHN HARVEY SANDIDGE

John Harvey Sandidge was born December 12, 1869 in Tennessee. He was the oldest of three boys. Will Sandidge lived in McKinney for many years. Charlie left Collin County and purchased a large acreage at Hail Center and later oil was discovered in the area and his land had producing wells. He married Mary Russell, a relative of Charlie and George Russell of McKinney. The three brothers were reared by their grandmother, Mary Sandidge Dobbs. Her son, Dr. Jess Dobbs, was a well known Altoga Community physician.

John Harvey Sandidge bought land three miles north of Altoga when he was 20 years old. Four years later he married Josephine Emylee Munger, who was born June 20, 1873 in Mississippi, the daughter of Mr. and Mrs. Hiram Munger. She had three brothers, Berry, Pomroy, and Jim. Berry was a barber for many years at Van Alstyne. His daughter, Mary Munger Knott, was the mother of Clifford Knott. Hiram Munger was three-fourths Cherokee Cherokee Indian and was eligible for free land in Oklahoma but would never claim the land. He served in the Confederate Army and lost the fingers of his left hand, was captured and held prisoner for two years. In later years he would never listen to a brass band because during a battle the band would play to drown out the screams of dying men and horses.

At the time of J.P. and Josephine's marriage she was living with her sister and her husband, the Henry Johnsons of Stony Point Community. They were the parents of three children, George, Mrs. Otis Johnson, and Mrs. Ross Fagala of Princeton.

J.P. and Josephine lived for 60 years on the land he bought as a youth, and both lie in Stony Point Cemetery, a beautiful place on a hill overlooking the land both loved and tended so long. Both were a leader in the religious life of the community, serving where there is need.

Story sent by Martha Fagala, Box 401, Princeton, Texas.

JAMES PRESTON SCOTT
1809-1858

James Preston Scott was born in Wilson County, Tennessee, October 23, 1809 and died in McKinney on March 13, 1858. He is buried in the Scott Cemetery six miles northwest of McKinney. He and his wife and children came to Collin County along with the Robert Foster family and the A.J. Taylors, about 1852. He bought several hundred acres of land in the Bloomdale Community and gave several acres of his land to the community for the Scott Cemetery. His granddaughter, Mary Taylor, was the first person buried in the beautiful cemetery.

James Preston Scott was elected to the 6th district of the Texas Legislature in 1857 and served until his death. The senator serving from the district at the same time was J.W. Throckmorton, later to become Governor of Texas.

He married Jennie Craighead Caruth in Tennessee and they were the parents of seven children, Malinda Caroline Scott. Robert Henry Foster in Tennessee on November 10, 1852. To them were born six sons and two daughters, Willie P., Sam H., Thomas H., Robert A., Lucy J., Joe H., Sarah Idella, and John who died young.

Tabitha J. Scott married Armstrong J. Taylor and several children were born to them. Elizabeth M. Scott married J. Dud Doak on August 9, 1855 and he served Collin County as its sheriff from 1858 to 1860. Andrew Jackson Scott married Margaret Ann Smith and to them were born two sons and four daughters, John, Laura, (who married Frank Neely and had three sons, Claude, Erwin, Earl). Lizzie Scott married James Preston Hayes and they were the parents of Ida, Roy, Verbie, and Ona.

Mattie Scott married John L. Applebee and they were the parents of Jean and Leonard. Lula M. Scott married L. Dow Franklin and they had two children, Alma and Lora. He had a son, Joe Scott, by his second wife. Thomas B. Scott married Margaret N. Magner and they were parents of Estella E. Scott who married Jim J. Smith and Rhea P. Scott who married Nola Howard. Rhea's children are Helen, Dorothy, Audrey, Edith, Faye Delle and Earl Wayne.

James W. Scott moved to Oklahoma and no history is available. Mary F. Scott married D.C. Flippen and they reared a large family on the farm in Bloomdale Community. The children were Fred, Bill, Ruth, Mae, and Pearl.

James Preston Scott was a large land owner, a good farmer, a leading citizen of his community. He left many descendents still living in McKinney and Collin County, all good citizens, good businessmen, and leaders in their church and community.

JOHN SCOTT FAMILY

John Scott was born in 1820 in Lebanon, Wilson County, Tennessee. On October 23, 1845 he married Martha Ann Barclay of Lebanon. Two daughters and one son were born there. In 1852 he and his family came to Texas, spending the first year in Red River County. In 1853 they they came to Collin County and settled in the Bloomdale Community, where four other children were born.

During the Civil War he followed his trade as a miller for the government, making flour at an old crudely constructed mill that was located near the city limits of McKinney. This mill later became

THE CHILDREN of John and Martha Scott: Tobiatha Scott Andrews, Dr. John T. Scott, Retta Scott Horn, Frank Scott, and Jim Scott.

JOHN SCOTT, pioneer of the Bloomdale Community.

the Burrus Gin and Mill location. The family worked to establish the Church of Christ in the area. John served also as County Commissioner in 1866.

"Uncle Johnny" as he was called in the community, died March 4, 1883. His wife, Martha, died December 24, 1899. Both are buried not far from the site of the pioneer home.

Their descendents are now into the sixth generation and number into the hundreds, a large number of these still live in this area and are some of McKinney's well known citizens.

The children of John and Martha Scott were:

Tobiathia Elizabeth Scott (September 15, 1856) was born in the Bloomdate Community. She married W.C. Andrews a widower with five children. Her husband was a Confederate soldier and her son died in battle in World War I.

Dr. John Thomas Scott, a pioneer in the field of Psychology, he wrote two textbooks, "Simplified Psychology" and "Scott's Psychology." He was a well known teacher and speaker.

Retta Scott (born Bloomdale, September 29, 1866) wed J.R. Horn, a member of another pioneer family. They had five children.

B.F. (Frank Scott) was born February 7, 1859 at Bloomdale. He married Mattie Andrews on December 28, 1882. They had twelve children. They ran the "Delightful Inn" on Tennessee Street for many years.

J.W. (Jim) was born April 19, 1851 in Tennessee. He married Emma Hunsaker, member of a pioneer family. He attended Hackberry School as a boy. A firm believer in education, he saw eight of his children through college.

Lucy Scott married L.M. Darnell, a jeweler at Pilot Point. They had three children.

Fanny Scott married Dr. J.L. Harmon of Virginia. He also ran a Photography Shop in early day McKinney. They had three children.

Submitted by Kay Steenerson, 3000 NW 11, Oklahoma City, Oklahoma (a descendant).

LOUIS ALFRED SCOTT FAMILY

The history of the Scott family extends back to the time when they were prominent in the affairs of the British Government, from the time of Cromwell up until the colonization of America. Several members of the family were among the first settlers of the thirteen colonies.

Captain Thomas Morton Scott, grandfather of Louis Scott, was born June 24, 1824 in Cadiz, Ohio, and was the son of James and Harriett Arnold Scott. The family moved to Louisville, Kentucky in 1851. Capt. Scott married Elizabeth Matilda Shirley, daughter of Lewis Shirley, a soldier of the War of 1812. An ancestor was a soldier and officer in Cromwell's Army and while a member of the Parliament, signed the death warrant of King Charles Stuart of England. Capt. T.M. Scott served in the Mexican War and later served in California commanding troops against the Indians. Capt. Scott also served during the Civil War.

Louis Alfred Scott was born in Louisville, Kentucky on April 16, 1852, the son of T.M. and Elizabeth Shirley Scott. His mother died May 19, 1922. Her father settled in Melissa in 1852. Capt. Scott purchased a farm he called "Belmont Farm" four and one-half miles east of Melissa and here the family lived while Louis was growing up. Because of a lack of public schools in Texas he attended a log house school erected on his father's farm and taught by his mother. He later attended Carlton College in Bonham after which he himself taught in rural schools of Collin County for several years before beginning his career in business. He established a mercantile store in Melissa, where for 25 years he was the agent for the H&TC Railroad.

He moved his family to McKinney in 1900 and engaged in many local businesses. He served as president of the McKinney Ice and Coal Company, who also provided the city with light and power. He was an executive of the Collin County Mill and Elevator Company, a Director of the Collin County

JOHN HARVEY and Emylee Josephine Munger Sandidge, settled at Old Stony Point Community.

National Bank, and served on both the Melissa and McKinney school boards. Because of his taking an active part in building a junior high school building for McKinney, the school was named for him.

January 19, 1881 he married Louise Allen, the granddaughter of Jonathan Allen who settled in Collin County in the late 1840's, and served as the first County Judge of Collin County. Her father was M.W. Allen, who was appointed to survey the Fannin District out of which Collin County was formed. He was a Colonel in the Confederate Army and was stationed at Denton to guard against Indian raids from the north. Later he served in the Texas Legislature, author of the Land Bill, and instrumental in getting eastern capitalists interested in building the first railroad in Texas between Houston and Harrisburg.

Mrs. L.A. Scott's mother was Virginia Royal, daughter of R.R. Royal who was one of the original founders of the Republic of Texas. He was one of the twelve men who wrote the Declaration of War against Mexico.

The L.A. Scotts were the parents of Velma Hunter, Alfred Malley Scott, and Louis Allen Scott. Mr. Scott died February 19, 1934.

(Story taken largely from *Who's Who In Texas* (1945) and newspapers. Microfilmed at McKinney Library.)

ROBERT MARION SCOTT

Robert Marion Scott was born in Tennessee and wed Nancy Jane Chilton on June 17, 1857. She was the 15 year old daughter of a Nashville, Tennessee policeman. The family moved to Texas in 1872,

ROBERT M. and Nancy Scott, pioneers of Bloomdale.

bringing their six children. They were met at the train in Denison by brothers John and Enos who had settled much earlier in the Bloomdale Community. Robert was a brickmaker and brick mason by trade, and several of the early brick buildings in McKinney were built by him. He operated his brickyard where the Pecan Grove Dairy later located. One of his sons also became a brick man in McKinney and served as a County Commissioner in 1882.

Their children were W.W. (Bud) Scott, Charlie, Dee, Tom, J.L. (John), Fannie (m. Oliver Hart), Nannie (m. Dr. James Rutledge). Maggie Quisenberry Hockett, and three who died young, Henry, Enos, and Nennie. The father died at his home in Blue Ridge November 19, 1906 and is buried in Highland Cemetery.

Story sent me by: Kay Steenerson, 3000 NW 11, Oklahoma City 73107.

DR. AND MRS. MARSHALL MAYES SEARCY

Marshall Mayes Searcy, M.D. was born in Dallas, Texas August 15, 1917, the son of Henry Clay and Rebecca Senter Searcy. He was educated in the Dallas School system, and spent two years in the Edinberg Junior College (no longer in existence). He graduated from the University of Texas School

of Pharmacy, graduating first in his class. He then attended the University of Texas School of Medicine in Galveston, Texas, graduating in the upper 10 per cent of the class 1943.

Dr. Searcy was commissioned into the U.S. Navy as Lt. J.G. and received his internship at the Navy base in Norman, Okla. He went aboard the USS Dolphin and served as chief medical officer in the Pacific theater of war. The USS Dolphin was one of the ships that survived the battle of Okinawa. Sen. Talmadge of Georgia was commander of the ship.

After his completion of duty with the navy and post graduate work in the VA hospital in McKinney, Texas, he began the practice of medicine in McKinney.

Dr. Searcy is a member of the First United Methodist Church, and has served as past chairman of the board. He is a member of The AMA-TMA and Collin County Medical Assn., serving as past president of the county society and past chief of staff for Collin Memorial Hospital. He is a member of the McKinney Rotary Club.

Dr. Searcy married Evelyn Williamson of Houston in 1943. To them were born four children: Marsha; Marshall, Jr.; Evelyn Susette and Marcus G.

Mrs. Marshall M. Searcy (Nee Evelyn Williamson) was born in Houston, Texas Sept. 15, 1919, the daughter of E. Franklin and Mae Brown Williamson. She was educated in the Houston public schools and received her degree in Nursing Education from the University of Texas 1943.

Mrs. Searcy is a member of the First United Methodist Church, and has been active in church duties during her lifetime. She is a member of the Owl Club of McKinney and has served as president in 1958-59 and 1968-69. She was selected to serve as editor of the Owl Club's proposed publication, "Heritage Homes of McKinney". Mrs. Searcy is on the board of trustees for the Heard-Craig Woman's Club of McKinney, Texas.

Mrs. Searcy deems her greatest accomplishment to be rearing and educating her four wonderful children.

Marsha (Mrs. Don Harris) was born in Newport, R..I. on November 7, 1944, educated in McKinney schools, graduated from the University of Texas on the honor roll, and married Don Harris, an engineer with NASA. They have two children, Jeffrey and Shannon.

Marshall M. Searcy Jr. graduated from University of Texas (Phi Beta Kappa), graduated from University of Texas School of Law in the upper 10 percent of his class, served on the Law Review while in law school and received an award for the most outstanding paper on constitutional law. He married the former Miss Ann Urguehart of Houston, also an honor graduate of University of Texas. They have two children: Marshall M. III and Amy Meridith. Mr. Searcy practices law in Dallas.

Evelyn Susuette Searcy, born in Dallas June 18, 1948, attended University of Texas in Austin. She married William G. Hall, a graduate of the University of Texas whose disciplines are in accounting. They have no children. Mr. and Mrs. Hall live in Ft. Worth, Texas.

Marcus G. Searcy was born in McKinney, Texas July 17, 1951. He attended the University of Texas at Arlington then transferred to the University of Texas School of Pharmacy with intentions of following in his fathers footstep and becoming a physician. Marcus was on the Deans List with the designation of highest honors. On Dec. 17, 1972 Marcus died in an accidental death. At the time of his death, he had a scholastic average of 98 with hopes of a 100 per cent. Marcus was intered at Hillcrest Mausoleum in Dallas, December 20, 1972. Although it was a December day, four days away from Christmas, the day was as warm as if God had made this day especially, just for Marcus.

Submitted by Mrs. Marshall M. Searcy

THE SETTLE FAMILY

William Thomas Settle came to Collin County, together with several brothers, from Kentucky and settled around Prosper and Rhea Mills. Leslie Simon Settle, son of William and Georgia Ann Drain Settle, was born January 17, 1894 and died December 27, 1965. He was the 10th of 11 children born to his parents. After school days, Leslie Settle was a salesman, covering Collin County and surrounding counties. He was a veteran of World War I. He married Clefa Belle Johnson, the daughter of Oscar Childs Johnson and Sarah Leona Conwell Johnson. Oscar Childs Johnson and Boone Johnson (who established the Johnson Furniture Company in McKinney) were two of the thirteen children of Mr. and Mrs. Robert H. Johnson of Princeton.

William Thomas and Clefa Belle Settle were the parents of the following children: Billy Childs (1925-1925), Joyce Marie Settle Kee (1929), Leslie Clifton Settle, Nennie Lee, Clyde Monroe,

MRS. JOYCE KEE, Postmaster, Melissa.

Georgia Ann Settle Smith, Ida Belle Settle Bennett, Barbara Settle Bennett, and Gloria Suzanne Settle Metheny.

Joyce Marie Settle Kee has been the postmaster at Melissa for almost twenty years. She was married April 7, 1951 to John Monroe Kee, son of Mr. and Mrs. Joseph E. Kee. They are the parents of four children: Jaqueta Marie, the eldest is married to Ronnie Dale Hardin a teacher at Lake Highlands High School in Richardson, and music director at Dunn Memorial Baptist Church, near New Hope. Other children of the Kee family are, Joseph Simon, a nineth grader at Melissa Schools, Julie Melissa is a third grader, and Jonna Merri Eve is a Kindergarten student at Melissa. Joyce Kee has been the Correspondent for the *Examiner, Dairy Courier-Gazette,* and *Sherman Democrat* for ten years. The Kee family has been active in all areas of civic endeavor as well as in the work of their church.

JESSE SHAIN

Jesse Shain, prominent businessman of McKinney, in the latter part of the last century, was born October 8, 1849, the son of Tom Shain. Jesse came to Collin County with his parents when two years old. His father was a farmer, but did blacksmithing too and a few years later was appointed Deputy Sheriff of Collin County. In 1860, tragedy befell the family. The father was shot and killed while trying to capture a horse thief. Jesse learned early to be the man for the family. At 18 years of age, with no capital at all, he began to deal in real estate and stock. Later he operated a livery stable and many young swain rented his rigs to take a girl to social affairs for his were always fine animals and good rigs. Since the mother of the family died the same year as the father, young Jesse and the other three children lived with Burl Stiff, an uncle.

For 30 years he operated a mercantile business, still dealing in real estate. He never sold a piece of property he bought for he had great faith in the future of the village that McKinney was when he first came. He served the City of McKinney as an Alderman for 20 years and was an official in such companies as the Cotton Oil Mill, Compress, President of the Texas, New Mexico and Pacific Railroad, and served as a member of the World Fair Committee.

He was married to Fanny Eubank of Sherman. One son was born to them but died at the age of three years. The couple adopted Maggie Shain who married Fletcher B. (Bud) Pope. Jesse was a member of the First Christian Church. He died at age fifty-six, a self-made man of wealth and prominence in the county.

Source: Biography printed at the time of his death in McKinney papers. Microfilmed at the Public Library, April 26, 1906.

E.G. (PAT) SIMPSON'S FAMILY

The Washington Simpson family settled in Grayson County in the early 1850s near the Collin-Grayson line near Elmont. Part of his land was in Collin County but the home stood on the Grayson side. The family came here from Simpson County, Kentucky. As soon as the family was settled, Washington Simpson built and ran a stage coach inn one mile south of Elmont and operated it all through the Civil War. The inn was called The Buckhorn Tavern, and from this came his nickname, Buckhorn Simpson. He served at one time as Sheriff of Grayson County.

John Simpson came with his father, Washington Simpson, from Kentucky. He lived most of his life on the farm they settled. He served in the Confederate Army for the duration. After the war he operated a freight service with wagons and oxen from Sherman to Jefferson until the early 1870s.

Walter Simpson, son of John Simpson, was born in 1873 between the communities of Elmont and Warden. He married Miss Corda McLain in 1902, the daughter of James F. McLain, who had come to Collin County from Jasper, Alabama soon after the Civil War. James McLain had served in the Confederate Army, joining at age 17, and upon returning from the war found his family all lost, so he came to Collin County to make a home. He was a farmer and a land owner and lived in the Kelly Community and in Anna until his death in 1929. He was married to Miss Phoebe Miller in Collin County by the Elder R.C. Horn.

E.G. (Pat) Simpson, son of Walter and Corda McLain Simpson, lives in McKinney, married to Georgia Douglas, daughter of pioneers of Grayson, County. They have one son, Bill and two grandsons.

SIMPSON FAMILY OF PRINCETON

Ollie Simpson was born at Brownwood, Texas on November 1, 1889 and moved to Denton at an early age. He was the son of Mr. and Mrs. John Simpson. On June 11, 1911 he married Mary Lindy Davidson in a double ceremony with Sam and Ola Clements. She was the daughter of Thomas Jefferson Davidson of the Higgins Community. To this union were born 10 children: Odie Mae, Rosie Lee, Lilly Catherine, Margaret Moyelle, Effie Faye, Merril Cole, and twins who died, Geneva Ruth.

Ollie Simpson worked in many areas, threshing, farming, dairying, railroading, truck farming, and carpentry, besides farming his own farm. Due to bad health, he retired in 1957 and died November 7, 1964 at the age of 75 years and is buried at Wilson Chapel in Lowery Crossing.

Merril Cole Simpson was born in Collin County on November 30, 1926 and attended grade school at Enloe. He married Peggy Ann Young who was

OLLIE AND MARY SIMPSON.

THE OLLIE SIMPSON FAMILY OF LOWERY CROSSING.

born near Renner. Her parents were the E.B. Youngs. Their children are Kathy, Nancy, Carol, Ollie Merril, David, and Susan. They attend school in McKinney. Merril is City Councilman for the city of Lowery Crossing and Trustee of the Grace Baptist Church (once called Milligan Church). Peggy is the news correspondent from the community to the McKinney newspapers.

ROBERT BROWN SIMS
Biography
By Bessie Sims Sheppard

Robert Brown Sims, born Nov. 18, 1825, in Jackson, Hinds Co., Miss. Parents unknown.

He married Margaret Leek Brinlee, daughter of Hiram and Betsy Ann Brinlee, Sept. 15, 1856, by G.Y. McKinney, J.P. of Collin Co., Tex. Recorded in Vol. I, p. 369.

Robert Brown Sims was a farmer, who raised cotton, corn hegari, and canes.

His father-in-law, Hiram Brinlee, deeded 49 acres to him and Margaret Leek when they got married.

Margaret and the children would pick the cotton, harvest the corn, and strip the cane for making sorghum syrup.

Children:

Houston Sims, born Feb. 25, 1858, died Oct. 7, 1859, between two and three o'clock, at the age of one year, 7 mos. and 12 days.

John Sims, born in Texas in 1859, married Sarah Rebecca Hendricks at McKinney, Texas

Robert B. (Bud) Sims, Jr. born April 6, 1862,

ROBERT BROWN SIMS, father of Ben Sims.

married Lenora E. Howser.

Mary Ann Sims, born August 10, 1863, married James Ed. Brinlee, a cousin.

Laura Jane Sims, born July 28, 1865, married Tommy Homer Stevens.

George Sims, born January 27, 1867, disappeared. Foul play suspected. Fate unknown.

Benjamin Sims, born July 1, 1874, married Mary Jane Thetford.

All these children were born in Stony Point Community, Collin Co. Texas a community North-

ROBERT BROWN SIMS, JR., son of R.B. Sims and Margaret Leek Brinlee. He married the former Lenora Ella Howser.

JOHN SIMS FAMILY—Left front, Rebecca Hendricks Sims, Raymond Sims, Jessie Rose, John Sims. Back row, left to right, unknown, John Lewis Sims, unknown, and Effie Sims.

LENORA ELLA HOWSER SIMS, wife of Robert B. Sims.

east of McKinney about 15 miles.

George Sims rode off horseback in the company of two men. Later they returned, bringing George's horse and saddle, and saying they bought them from George and they did not know where he went.

Robert B. Sims served as Pvt. Co. H. Anderson's Regiment, Texas Cavalry, C.S.A. Jan, 1865.

In private life R.B. Sims struggled heroically against tremendous handicaps to produce food and fiber for his family. His farm was located on Sister Grove Creek Bottoms. He raised hogs, cattle, mules, chickens and horses.

On Feb. 18, 1861, ordered by court that R.B. Sims be and is hereby appointed overseer of the Lower Bonahm Road Precinct No. 2, beginning at Reuben Moores' and extending to Sister Grove Creek, and the followings hands were assigned to him: G.P. Carroll and Negro, H. Brinlee's hands, J. Hendrix, L. Hendrix, and hands, G.R. Brinlee, G. Arrington, and all that are assigned to him for the performance of road work.

During the County Court Term of Nov. 29, 1865, R.B. Sims is again ordered to be overseer of the road in Precinct 2, of Lower Bonham Roads. Hands: Matt Coffee, G. Coffee, R.M. Brinlee, and others.

He was also a carpenter by trade. His children and grandchildren are all well educated. Robert

MARY ANN SIMS and James Edward Brinlee, her husband.

LAURA JANE SIMS

Brown Sims had attended college in Jackson, Miss.

The illustrious men and women were also leaders who performed great services for Texas, both before and after the War Between the States.

Borrowing a coal of fire from was an occasional happening, although each household tried to see that the coals were well covered with ashes to preserve the valuable necessity.

Some bills were paid with cord wood, or by washing all day for 50 cents, or sewing, quilting, hauling hay, etc.

Robert Brown Sims was separated from his family, and was living with a family when an argument arose, and he was hit in the head and killed. He was killed July 5, 1889, near Stony Point.

He is buried in the Brinlee Cemetery. He rests beneath silent sentinels of cedar and juniper, and bluebonnets in the spring.

His descendants are scattered throughout the world.

DR. B.M.E. SMITH

Dr. Smith settled in McKinney in 1853 coming here from Tennessee. He was educated in Louisville, Kentucky before coming to Collin County to practice medicine. Doctors were so scarce at that time that he had to work all over Collin County and surrounding counties, going by horseback with his supplies in saddlebags, always ready to stop at pioneer homes along the way. Soon he was joined by two other physicians, Dr. Fitzgerald and Dr. Westfall and the three of them founded Smith Drug, still doing business on the east side of McKinney's square and is the oldest continuing business in Mc-

BENJAMIN SIMS

MARY JANE Thelford Sims

Kinney.

Dr. Smith served two terms as President of the Medical Examiners for the district. When the Civil War came he joined Col. J.B. Wilmeth's company and served on the Texas coast.

Dr. Smith was twice married, first to Amelia Tinsley and then to Mrs. Wheat of Clarksville. He died November 15, 1886.

Source: Biography in McKinney Democrat on the date of his death.

C. TRUETT SMITH OF WYLIE

C. Truett Smith, prominent business man and civic leader of Wylie, comes from two lines of pioneer families who settled in Collin County at its beginning. His maternal great-grandfather, James Anderson, came to Peter's Colony as an emigrant and headrighted 640 acres of land in 1850. A son of James, Sylvester Anderson lived on this land until his death in 1935. C. Truett Smith's paternal grandfather was John Wesley Smith, a former County Commissioner of Collin County.

C. Truett Smith is married to Rita Gallagher Smith, who is also a descendent of early settlers of the St. Paul and Wylie area. The Gallaghers were active in establishing the Catholic Church here in the early 1850's, the first Catholic Church in North Texas. In the early 1850's several Irish families sailed from Liverpool, England and after a

ST. ANTHONY'S CATHOLIC CHURCH in Wylie, established in the 1850s. This picture was taken in 1966.
ST. ANTHONY'S CATHOLIC CHURCH in Wylier, established in the 1850s. This picture was taken in 1966.

six week voyage landed at New Orleans and made their way to the Wylie area. Included were the Gallaghers, Millers, Neilons, and in 1855 they were joined by the Boylan and Corbitt families. Father John Martinere rode horseback from Galveston and organized the old St. Paul Church in the home of James Gallagher.

C. Truett Smith is president of the Texas Banker's Association and has been a banker since 1945. He is Chairman of the Board of Governors of Collin Memorial Hospital in McKinney and has served in that capacity for 16 years. He is a past president of the East Texas Chamber of Commerce and was one of the original organizers of the North Texas Municipal Water District and has served on its board of directors since its organization.

Data sent by Mr. Smith.

GEORGE WASHINGTON SMITH

From Red River County, Texas the entire family of George Washington Smith and his wife, Elizabeth Briggs Smith, moved to Collin County about 1852. He lived out his years on land he bought north of Blue Ridge. He is buried in the old Grounds Cemetery just a short distance from his home. Two of his four daughters are buried beside him.

Looking back to the land grant, Number 456, George Washington Smith came to Texas in 1834 and was a citizen of old Fannin County. When the War for Texas Independence came along he joined with his neighbors and went away to help the cause. He was a seasoned soldier, having fought in the Indian Wars with Andrew Jackson and was in the Battle of New Orleans before he was 20 years old. When not in actual combat, he returned to his home to plant a crop. He was an expert in scouting and knew the way of the woodsman well. He went into the Battle of San Antonio with Ben Milam and family tradition says that he was the first man to step to Milam's side when he called for volunteers to go with him into battle. Smith was near Milam when he received a fatal wound and held his head in his arms as Milam died. He then fought under Johnson and was in the Battle of San Jacinto. Later he went to help drive the Mexican soldiers back across the border. Along with others he was captured after the Battle of Mier and was doomed to prison and the Black Bean episode, but managed to escape.

After much hardship he managed to make his way back home to Collin County. Volume II of the

GEORGE WASHINGTON SMITH

History of Texas by John Henry Brown, lists Smith's name in Pierson's Company of the 42 men of the Guard who escaped at the river.

After the fighting was over, Smith settled down on his farm on Bois d'Arc Creek and took his place in the affairs of his community. When the War with Mexico began, he again joined his neighbors and went into the wars once more. He was discharged because of illness while in Mexico and made his way back home. He served as a Constable in Fannin County and after moving to Collin County he became a leader. His home was the voting place before and after the Civil War.

Smith was born in Tennessee in 1795 and his wife, Elizabeth, was a native of North Carolina, born in 1800. She was the daughter of a Cherokee Indian mother and an Irish father. They had four daughters, Mary Smith, born in Kentucky in 1818 (Mary married First William J. Hart and had the following children; Nancy who married Wylie Langham, George R., John T., William J. Hart Jr. Mary married a second time; this time to Jack J. Smith. They had one son, Ruben.

The second daughter of George and Elizabeth Smith was Jerusha who was born in 1825 in Alabama. Her first husband lived only a few months and she remarried, this time to James Hanson.

Their children were: Mary Jane who was born in Alabama in 1840 and James N. Hanson Jr. who was born in 1845 in Missouri. Jerusha's third husband was Hezekiah Worden. Their children were: Parilee who married Newt Vernon and lived in Rockwall, Fox Worden, and Hezekiah Worden Jr. Mary Jane Hanson married Isaac Dotson. James N. Hanson married Elizabeth Dotson, a sister of Isaac.

The third daughter was Jane Martha Smith. She married Richard Cantrell but was left a widow soon after coming to Texas. Their children were: James R. Cantrell who was born in Missouri in 1845, George W. Cantrell who was born in Texas in 1846, Mary E. Cantrell was born in 1850 in Texas.

James R. Cantrell married Malissa Smith and their children were: Arris who married Ed Tillet, Rosa M. who married Jenkins, Alice married Mac Alexander, Cora married Press, Missouri Jane married James J. McKinney, Jerry Cantrell, Mary E. married James Barnet, George Cantrell married Samantha ——, Jane Martha Smith Cantrell married a second time to William Pruet. Their children were: Newton born in 1853, Thomas born 1855, Martha born 1858, Laura born 1861, John born 1863, Alice born 1866 and Darthula born in 1869. All were born in Texas.

The youngest daughter of George and Elizabeth Smith was Hester Ann who married Williams Worden Jr. in 1849. Their children were Alonzo born in 1853, Charles Todd born 1855, and Missouri born 1856 and married J.W. Christian. Williams Worden was always connected with the sheriff's office while he lived in Collin County. He died at the home of his son, Todd Worden, in Oklahoma City.

George Washington Smith died after 1870 and his wife survived a few years. Both are buried in the old Grounds Cemetery, north of Blue Ridge.

(Just before his death, Capt. Hall was trying to obtain a state historical marker for Smith's grave.)

THOMAS Z. SMITH FAMILY

Thomas Z. Smith was born Jan. 31, 1830, at Adairsville, Georgia. He came from rugged farmer stock and was of English blood. He was married to Elizabeth Ann Shaw (Bettie) and to this union were born eight children, the last surviving member being Henry W. Smith who died in 1955 at Farmersville. Mrs. Smith was born in 1829 and died Nov. 3, 1895.

Thomas Z. Smith was a confederate veteran. One related incident told by a member of the family was that during the Civil War he was shot in the left leg and in later years the bullet came out under his right leg.

The Smith family first moved to Jefferson, Texas, and later on in a covered wagon in 1878, they moved to a place near Nevada and lived on Mr. Dick Harris' farm for a year in a log house. In 1879, they purchased a farm at the Cowskin community which is about three miles north of Nevada.

Mrs. Smith only lived 17 years after moving to Nevada. She was a citizen who knew what a frontier life meant as a wife and mother, having indulged to the fullness in its hardships and joys. Both she and Mr. Smith felt that they had been humble instruments in the hands of an all wise providence for the up-building and development of this part of Collin County where they lived. Both were devoted Baptists and served their church faithfully. Mrs. Smith, in a sorghum mill accident, had lost her arm up to the elbow and used the stub of her arm to knead her bread.

They reared a large family of children who were intermingled by marriage with many southeast Collin County families. A brief account of each of their children follows:

William Charley Smith was born Oct. 24, 1852, at Nannie, Ga., and died May 2, 1925. He married Dialphia A. Carmichael Dec. 3, 1876, at Toonigh, Ga., by Dr. W.H. Dean. She was born April 26, 1857, and died April 18, 1946 with her burial at Nevada. They reared seven children, were Baptist people and lived south of Nevada.

Mollie Smith was born July 24, 1854, and was married to Steve B. Morris. He was born Sept. 2, 1847 and died July 22, 1915. He was buried at the South Church Cemetery south of Nevada.

John Lewis Smith was born July 3, 1856, and died Mar. 25, 1925. He married Martha Ann Cox on Nov. 28, 1878. She was born Feb. 2, 1858 and died in childbirth on Oct. 17, 1902, being buried in the Thompson Cemetery north of Lavon. They were Baptists and lived south of Nevada. He married the second time to Mrs. Jane Cannon Popham in 1903. She was from Cleveland, Tenn., born in 1865 and died in 1942 at Nevada. He reared ten children by his first wife and four by his second wife.

Dora Smith was married to Bob Westbrook. She died July 31, 1894.

Mattie Smith married John Atchison and their home was at Nevada.

W.T. Smith and his wife Lula lived at Vernon, Texas.

James M. Smith was born at Dalton, Georgia, on June 26, 1861, and died Sept. 28, 1931. He married Bertie Lee Harris on Oct. 10, 1889. She was from Alabama, born in 1873 and died at Nevada in 1904. They built a home near the Cowskin Community and later moved to Nevada in 1895. They were Baptists and farmed. He married second to Miss Jane Parlier in 1905. She died May 6, 1929. They lived near Harlingen, Texas, and later moved to Riverside, Calif. He reared seven children by his first wife and two by the second marriage.

Henry Washington Smith was born Dec. 23, 1866, in Georgia and died at Farmersville on Jan. 30, 1955. He married Laura Ida Penn on Dec. 17, 1891. She was born at Rockwall, Texas, on Jan. 18, 1871, and died Jan. 31, 1944. They are both buried at Farmersville. He owned the land owned by his father which was located at Cowskin North of Nevada. Their children were:

Alma Lehalla born Dec. 12, 1892. She married James L. Vaughn on Sept. 5, 1915. They had two children, Mary Elizabeth and Clyde Smith.

Frank Leslie Smith was born Feb. 27, 1896, and married Oma Bell Buck at Nevada. She was from Royse City and they had two children: Walter Henry who married Josephine Kirby and Frankie Lougenia who married Jimmie Richie.

Ruby Nelcine was born Aug. 10, 1897. She married Macon James of Nevada and had two children; Billie Max and Peggy.

Shelley Lenota Smith was born Aug. 1, 1894. She married John Walter Akin on June 29, 1913 in a home wedding. He was born Jan. 1, 1880 in Tennessee. He was a widower with two children when they married. For many years he taught school at many points in the southeastern part of Collin County. Their children were: Wayman and Raymond twins who died young. Henry Max, Laura Louise born at Clear Lake who married Carroll Leary Webb of Nevada. Dorothy Nell was born at Clear Lake and married Clifford Rosengren. John Weldon was born at Princeton and married Pauline Green of Wylie. Wilma Sue was the last born to this family.

Submitted by John W. Akin

Great-Grandson of Thos . Z. Smith

SNEED FAMILY

Robert Seales Sneed was born March 20, 1835 in Davidson County, Tennessee. He was a civil engineer and surveyed the railroad from Tennessee through Mississippi, Louisiana and into Texas. He married Malinda Jane Kerr of the Vineland community northeast of McKinney in 1860.

During the Civil War Robert Sneed went ahead of the Army and built pontoon bridges across the rivers. During his absence their first child was born in May, 1862 and died in 1863.

Following the war, Robert S. Sneed and Malinda Jane Sneed established their home on a 140 acres blackland farm in the Lucas community and remained there for the remainder of their lives. He and his wife were charter members of the Corinth Presbyterian Church, Parker community. He died Jan. 1, 1894. They reared 10 children to be grown, all active members of the Parker Church.

The children of Robert S. Sneed and Malinda Kerr Sneed who lived in the Lucas community to be grown were: Jerome Hardeman Sneed, born Feb. 25, 1864, died March 26, 1950 and was buried at Pecan Grove Cemetery, McKinney. He married Susan Elizabeth Batson of Fitzhugh Mills community in 1889. He taught school in Cottage Hill, Forest Grove and Princeton. He and Mr. Alma Wilson established the first store in Princeton (according to the family history). Later he operated Sneed's Book Store in McKinney. He also served as District Clerk of Collin County for four years and during World War I he was appointed to the Texas Legislature to fill an unexpired term and was re-elected twice to that office. Mr. and Mrs. Jerome H. Sneed were the parents of six children. five of whom lived to be grown, but none lived in Lucas.

Laura Henderson Sneed was born in June, 1866 at the Sneed home in Lucas community. She married James Adam Snider of Lucas in 1888. They were the parents of eight children. Their first child, Clarence Snider, was born in the Lucas area in 1890, the others were born near Brady, Texas. She died in Brady in 1952. Her husband died in April, 1911.

Mary Eliza Sneed was born in August, 1868. She continued to live at her home in the Lucas community until her marriage to Joseph Gideon Hedrick in November of 1888. She died in August, 1915, and was buried in the family lot in Fitzhugh Cemetery, Forest Grove. William Bush Sneed was born in February of 1870. He attended Collin County schools and at age 18 went to Nashville where he died in 1944.

Thomas Jackson Sneed was born in January of 1872 at the Sneed family home at Lucas and grew to manhood here. He married Oda Bowman, daughter of Mr. and Mrs. John Cox Bowman of Lucas. Their four children were born and reared in the Sneed home (his mother's home in Lucas). When his

mother died in 1919 he bought the interests of the other heirs and continued to live on the 140 acres farm in Lucas (now the Ranch Estate area). In 1921 Thomas Sneed moved his family to Waxahachie, Texas to continue his children's education at Trinity University. He died Dec. 26, 1945.

Sara Ruth Sneed was born in April, 1874, at the Lucas Sneed home. She married Felix Agustus Klutts. They established their home in Princeton where they lived until 1926 when they moved to McKinney. They were both teachers in the public schools of Collin County. They were the parents of four children, none of whom live in Collin County.

Glenn Lawson Sneed, born in Lucas, attended local school, Trinity University, A&M, Columbia University and Union Theological Seminary. He was a minister, United Presbyterian U.S.A., and was pastor of Trinity Presbyterian Church, Dallas from 1907-1930. He married Miss Leta Higginbotham of Prosper. She died 41 years later.

Cora Bethenia Sneed was born in March, 1878, in Lucas where she grew to womanhood. She married Claud Basil Hunter. They both taught for several years in the public schools in Collin and Denton counties after which they moved to the Texas Panhandle.

Susan Malinda Sneed, born in February of 1880 at Sneed home in Lucas, married Dallas Pharr, son of Mr. and Mrs. D.N. Pharr of Lucas. They established their home in this area and their three children were born here. One died in infancy. Mrs. Pharr died in August, 1924 and was buried in Fitzhugh Cemetery, Forest Grove. Their children were: Leonard Sneed Pharr who died July 1, 1933 and Margaret Malinda Pharr who married James Paul Boone and now lives in Austin.

Bessie Viola Sneed, born in April, 1883, died Nov. 29, 1865. She attended Lucas School, C.I.A. (now TWU) Denton. She served in the mission fields many years.

Mr. and Mrs. Thomas Jackson Sneed were the parents of four children. Thomas Jackson Sneed was the fifth child of Mr. and Mrs. Robert S. Sneed who established their home on a 140 acre farm in Lucas community following the Civil War. The Thomas J. Sneed children are as follows:

Vera Edith Sneed born at the family home in Lucas attended local school, Trinity University, and T.W.U. in Denton. She was home economics teacher in high schools of Texas and served in the Extension Service as County Home Demonstration Agent.

Fred Bernard Sneed, born in Jan., 1905, at the family home in Lucas, died in January, 1951. He married Faye Passmore of Beeville. They had no children.

Hugh Bowman Sneed was born in July, 1907 in Lucas. He attended the local school, Waxahachie school and Trinity University. He married Virginia McCaskill of Childress, Texas. They have two sons who live in Mississippi.

Eunice Elizabeth Sneed was born at the Sneed home in Lucas and lived here during her early childhood. She and her sister, Vera Sneed, returned to the homeplace in Lucas in the 1930's and lived for a time. She is a graduate of Trinity University and NTSU, Denton. She started her teaching career in the rural school in Parker community and later taught in Wylie. She is at present teaching in Dallas.

AARON SNIDER FAMILY

Aaron Snider was born January 1, 1836 in Greene County, Illinois to William and Mary Sandusky Snider. William was descended from John Snider, a Revolutionary soldier served with the Virginia 8th Army, German Regiment.

Aaron was born in Illinois and came with his parents to near Allen when he was nine years old. At age 21 he was married to Rheuhammy Elizabeth Scott and to this union the following children were born; Albion (1858), Nancy Ruth (1859), James Adam (1862), William Adam Allen (1867), Joseph Benjamin (1868), Missouri Pettis (1970), Charles Marion (1871), Cordie Elbert (1875), Mary Catherine (1877), and Albert Henry (1882).

James Adam Snider married Laura Sneed and they were the parents of: Clarence, Raymond, Robert Alvin, Mary Pettis, Malinda Rheuhamma, Cora Ruth, and James Aaron.

Robert Alvin Snider married Fannye Eudoxie Lyle and they were the parents of Doris Jeanette and Robert Newton. Robert Newton and Viola B. Snider were the parents of Robert Newton Jr. and James Bowman, and Susan Lynn Snider.

Joseph Benjamin married Lilliam Browne and they became the parents of two children, Herman L., and Hester A. Snider. Herman and May Snider were the parents of H.L. Jr. Hester A. and Lucile Blair Snider were the parents of William Allen and Joe Ben Snider.

William A. and Helen D. Snider had the following children; Brenda Dianne, Patricia Beth, Susan Elaine. The children of Joe Ben and Elaine T.

Snider was Sandra Kay.

Charles Marion married Della Kerby and became the parents of: Mary Delmina, America Almenda, Paralee Blythe, Truett Hastings, and Marion Benjamin.

Albert H. Snider married Lena Nesbitt June 20, 1912 and to them was born these children; Connaly Ruth, Albert Wiley, Lavauda Faye, and Frances Wynell. Albert Wiley and Ida M. Snider are the parents of Marianne (married to Robert A. King) and James Albert Snider. Lavauda Faye Snider married Verr Garland Branch and they have one son, Kenneth Garland Branch.

Story submitted by Lavauda Snider Branch, McKinney.

THE WILLIAM SNIDER FAMILY

Between 1844 and 1848 William Snider, his wife, and their nine children came to settle in Collin County. William Snider was born March 22, 1806 and died in Collin County on June 12, 1882.

On July 20, 1825 he was married to Mary Sandusky Maxwell and to this union were born these children; John Durham (1827), Polly Ann (1828), James Madison (1830), Sarah Louise Elizabeth (1832) who married Thomas Bradley, Jane Snider (1834), who married John M. McKinney, Aaron (1836), who married Rehuhammy Elizabeth Scott, William Thomas (1838), Catherine (1839) who married Dan Bradley and later Joe Scott, Emily (1843) who married George Fitzhugh, Amandy (1844), Martha Melviny (1849) who married Hiram Wilmeth, Missouri Ann (1851) who married Dallas Sparlin, Alvin Lorenza (1853) who married Uatus Bellew.

William Snider brought with him from Kentucky his skills as a carpenter and is listed on census records as a wagon maker. When they came to Collin County the family settled on a 640 acre land grant southeast of McKinney. On the land at the time was a lake which came to be known as Snider Lake. William helped to build the first corn mill in that part of the county. He also operated a Bois d'Arc mill. This thorny tree was very popular among the early settlers for fences. Snider ground the apples and put them into barrels of water. After a few days the pulp floated and the heavier seeds dropped to the bottom of the barrel. After drying, the seeds were sold and was a valuable crop. He also raised horses as well as bees. He even had a bee hive under glass in his log home.

William Snider died June 12, 1882 and Mary on January 14, 1889. Both are buried in the Fitzhugh Cemetery at Forest Grove.

James Madison Snider, third child of William and Mary Snider, was born June 2, 1830, coming to live in Collin County as a child. He married Sarah Jane Fitzhugh and the following children were born to them; John P. who married E.J. Cornelous, Mary E. who married Taylor Coffey, Lutishia Ann who married J.B. Spurgin, Sarah Alice who married Dan Faulkner, Martha Ellen who married W.W. Wetsell, James Harrison who married Sibbie Mayes, Gaberiel Solomon who married Mary Serepta Armstrong, Emily Catherine, Missouri Jane who married Stokley Armstrong, and Susan Frances.

Gabe Snider, son of James Madison and Sarah Jane Snider, married Mary Serepta Armstrong and to them were born four children; Theron Gerald, Naomi A., Vemon C., and Dorothy who died at age 7.

Theron Gerald Snider married Lena Nelson and to them four children were born; Frances Elizabeth Milroy, Theron Gerald Jr., Bennie Gabe, and Paul Edward.

Frances' children are Barbara who is married to James Woodruff and the mother of Brenda and Glenda, and a son Bill Woodruff. Theron Gerald Jr. married Margaret Selby. They are the parents of these children, Theron Gerald III, who is married to Kathy Davis, and has a daughter, Melissa, Enid, Sherill who is married to Louis Bullard and has a son, Tony, Timothy who is married to Jody Branch and has a son, Jason, and Randy who is married to Charlyn Evans.

Bennie Gabe Snider is married to Joyce Stiles, and they are the parents of Craig, Leia Ann, and Kimberly.

Paul Edward Snider is married to Gwen Smith and they are the parents of David and Rhonda.

Naomi, daughter of Gabe and Sarah Jane Fitzhugh Snider, married George Raines Morris and lives in the historic Waddill home on Lamar street in McKinney, where she operated her own business.
Story furnished by Naomi Snider Morris

SPEARS FAMILY
Written by Mrs. John Shipp
As reported by Ruth Spears Brooks of Wylie

Mr. and Mrs. Will Spears, she was the former Mary Ann Wright, came to Lucas from Caddo Mills, Texas. They were the parents of five children: Ruth, Tina (deceased), Edgar, Sadie and Clara. Ruth married Willie Brooks of near Wylie. They were the parents of four children, all of whom were very much a part of Lucas as they grew up. Mr. and Mrs. Brooks now live in Wylie. Edgar Spears married Florence Spurgin, daughter of Mr. and Mrs. Cordis Spurgin of Lucas. To this union were born seven children, all of whom lived in this and the Chambersville communities and attended schools at both places. None are living in Collin Co. at present. Sadie Spears married Johnny Akers. No children. Clara Spears married Lester Pharr of Lucas. They had one son, Gene. The Lester Pharrs live in McKinney. Mrs. Johnny Akers is the only members of the Spears family still living in Lucas.

THE JOHN JORDON SPORTSMAN FAMILY

John Jordon Sportsman came to Texas from Dodge City in 1890. He was the father of John Robert (Jack), George Arthur, Laura, Betsy, Emma, Elizabeth, James and Harvey. John J. and his family settled near Valdasta and later moved to McKinney. Here he engaged in the livery stable business with his sons, Jack and George. Jack later became a farmer, livestockman and auctioneer. He was elected as County Commissioner and served two terms. At the end of his tenure he was urged by friends to make the race for Sheriff, but declined. In appreciation of his many friends and the support they had given him in his political venture, he staged a huge barbecue and invited everyone to attend. A huge crowd turned out and partook of barbecue beef, pork, and mutton along with pickles, onions, corn on the cob and cold drinks. The Municipal band furnished music for the gala affair. Jack became an auctioneer and was a familiar figure all over the county where an auctioneer was needed. For a time he auctioneered horses for the British government following World War I.

The children born to Jack and Harriett (Osborne) Sportsman were, Beverly, Charles, George, and Edna and all attended the McKinney schools. Beverly graduated from West Texas State University and taught school at Parker and Blackwell in West Texas. He was employed by the City of Tulsa then for several years operated a Food Market at Refugio where he formed a partnership with his brother, George. He later sold out to George and opened Sportsman's Man Shop at Six Points in Corpus Christi. Beverly and Ann were the parents of a son and a daughter, Charles H. and Beverly Ann. Beverly is now deceased.

Charles (Choc) was graduated from North Texas University and after a year as Deputy District Clerk of Collin County, became a member of the Physical Education staff at North Texas University. He served as Head Track Coach and Assistant Football Coach for 13 years. When World War II broke out he enlisted in the United States Navy and served 45 months as Military Training and Physical Fitness officer. He was retired from duty with the rank of Commander. He attended graduate School at the University of Southern California and completed work on his Master's Degree, afterwards he joined the staff of the San Diago State University where he was head track coach for 20 years.

He retired in 1968 and served as coach of the Olympic Team of Greece for track and Field for the Summer Games at Mexico City. He and his wife Jennie Tunnell Sportsman are now retired and living in Ben Wheeler, Texas. Their two children are married. Beverly Ann has two sons and two daughters Charles W. has a son and two daughters.

George Sportsman after High School joined Beverly in Tulsa and worked for the City of Tulsa. Together the brothers operated a business in Refugio. He is now deceased. He and his wife were the parents of two sons, Jack and Jerry, who live in Refugio.

Edna married Gilbert Garland and lives in McKinney. Edna attended North Texas University after High School. Edna and Gilbert are the parents of two sons, John Gilbert and Kenneth. John Gilbert is an attorney in Houston and is President of American Steel Building Co. Kenneth is a High School Coach in Denton, Texas. Edna is an employee of the Collin Memorial Hospital where she has worked for years.

George A. Sportsman and his wife, Etta Hitchcock Sportsman moved to their farm after leaving the livery stable business. George Sportsman was a successful farmer making their home on the Hillranch north of Celina. Their children were Norma, Verda, John W., Jennie Lou, Glenn, and G.A.

Laura married Jesse Carroll and they were the parents of Margaret, Bertha, Earl, and Bob. Jesse Carroll was a successful farmer living east of Melissa in the Stony Point Community.

Betsy married Elmer Hodges and they settled at Valdasta, later moved to Calera, Oklahoma. Their children were Opal, Charles, Jesse, John, Leonard, Fred, Ernest, Kalli Marie and Ethel.

James and Jennie Thompson Sportsman were the parents of Mary Catherine Dan, and LeRoy. Jim was a salesman for Paris Grocery in McKinney for many years, but later moved to Refugio.

Harvey Sportsman worked in the oil fields for many years in South Texas and around Tulsa, Oklahoma. He and his wife, Holly Mae, were the parents of Jack, Tommie, Gene, Richard, and Emma Lois.

Emma married M.J. Wiggins and they had no children. Elizabeth married Ott Madison and they had two daughters, Rose Mary, and Shirley Jane. Shirley Jane died at an early age. Ott was a rural mail carrier.

SPURGIN AND FUNDERBURG FAMILY

As reported by
Mr. and Mrs. Ollie A. Spurgin
Contributed by Mrs. John Shipp

David F. Spurgin came to Collin County in 1854 from Tennessee. He lived north of Wylie 25 or 30 years, married Ellen Gallagher, a native of Collin County and moved to the Winningkoff community in 1901.

Mr. and Mrs. David F. Spurgin were the parents of six children, four daughters and two sons: Sally, who married R.J. Russell of Clear Lake (Collin Co.); Agnis, married Elmo Funderburg; Emma married Mason Funderburg of Greenville; Ethel married Mack Gooch of this area (Lucas); Joe married Annie Merritt of near Wylie; and Ollie married Elizabeth Funderburg of Winningkoff in November, 1911. They moved to Lucas in 1941. Of the children, only Ollie A. Spurgin and Emma Funderburg (of Greenville) are living (1973).

Ollie A. Spurgin and Elizabeth Funderburg Spurgin are the parents of eight sons and two daughters: Noble, married Cora Campbell of Winningkoff; Zelda married J.C. Copus of Rockwall; Olen (Buck) married Mary Tom Acuff of McKinney; Orval (Cotton) married Estelle Heifner of Lucas; Edward (Sandy) married Jean Wise of McKinney; Jack married Dorothy Estep of Anna; Truman married Jimmie Lowery whose parents, Mr. and Mrs. J.M. Lawrey, live in Lucas; Marie, married Edward Phelps of Dallas; Vernon (Billy) married Virginia Hawkins of Washington state; and Dale K. married Barbara Cavender of Garland.,

The children of Mr. and Mrs. Ollie A. Spurgin attended school at Winningkoff, Lucas, Plano and McKinney. Of the above children the following continue to live in Lucas: O.E. (Cotton), Edward (Sandy), Truman, Billy and Dale. O.E. Spurgin and

Estelle Heifner Spurgin are the parents of two daughters: Janet and Mary Helen, both students at North Texas State University (1973).

Edward Spurgin and Jean Wise Spurgin are the parents of a daughter, Cathy, and a son, Jeffrey. Jeff is a senior in McKinney High School. Cathy married Terry Cupit of Van Alstyne. They now live near her parents in north Lucas.

Truman Spurgin and Jimmie Lowrey Spurgin are the parents of two children: Alan Ray and Annette. Alan Ray married Patricia Humphrey of Plano. They and son Michael live near his parents in Lucas. Annette is a student in McKinney High School.

Billy Spurgin and two daughters, Lori and Lisa live in Lucas. The girls are both students in Allen High School (1973).

Dale K. Spurgin and Barbara Cavender Spurgin have three children: Sandra, Keith and Kevin. The boys attend Lovejoy School and Sandra goes to school in Sherman.

Buck Spurgin and Mary Tom Spurgin lived in this area several years and owned a farm in Lucas. They sold their place in 1968 to Mr. and Mrs. Kenneth Jones and bought a farm near Leonard. They have two daughters: Louana and Deborah, and a son, Wyatt. While living in Lucas Louana married Bill Guthrie of Tom Bean. They have a little daughter, Katie, and now live in Oklahoma where Mr. Guthrie is in the Air Force.

Deborah, a graduate of Texas Women's University School of Nursing, is now in the Air Force and is stationed at Air Force Hospital, Altus, Oklahoma.

FUNDERBURG FAMILY

James Funderburg and Leon Reed Funderburg, both natives of Arkansas, were early settlers of the Winningkoff community. They were the parents of seven children: Johnny, who married Lucille Persohn of McKinney; Elmore, married Agnes Spurgin; Maggie, married Milton Scott of Winningkoff; Louis, married Hallie Crouch of Parker; Elizabeth, married Ollie A. Spurgin of Winningkoff; Cecil, married Gladys Spurgin; and Ed, married Brina Rosseter of Parker. Of the seven children only Cecil, Ed and Elizabeth are living, and only Elizabeth (Mrs. O.A. Spurgin) lives in Lucas. (1973)

JOHN SPURGIN FAMILY

John Spurgin was born in Missouri in February, 1819. He came to this area as a young man and it is said that he operated the first cotton gin in the Lucas area. He also had a grist mill here. John Spurgin married Miss Martha Ann Vick of this area. To this union were born five children: Oscar, born in March, 1869, died in May, 1892. Robert P. (Bud), born in February, 1872, died in Nov., 1835 in Lucas; Ida, born in Jan., 1874. She is still living at age 99 in Oklahoma (1973). Estelle, born Feb, 1876, died July, 1896 in Lucas. Benjamin, born Aug., 1878, died in infancy. Both Ida and Bud attended Westminster (Collin County) Baptist College. Ida Spurgin married G.W. Armstrong and the family moved to Oklahoma around 1912.

Bud married Miss Willie Cook, daughter of Mr. and Mrs. J.W. Cook of Lucas. To this union were born twin daughters: Tressye and Ressye. The latter died at six months of age. Tressye married John H. Click (deceased) of Farmersville. They had no children. Tressye Spurgin Click still owns and lives on part of the land owned by her grandparents. It was her grandparents who gave the land on which was established the first church in Lucas.

STINSON FAMILY
Sent by Mrs. John Shipp
Our thanks to Mrs. Jack McCreary
and Velma S. Spurgin.

James Francis Stinson was born in Akron, Ohio in October of 1846. He was orphaned when young, migrated to Missouri then to Collin County, Texas when a young man. He came by wagon train with a family by the name of Roundtree and settled south of McKinney where he went to work for Benjamin F. Biggs. In 1876 he married Margaret Catherine Biggs (born Jan., 1859, died in 1947). She was the oldest daughter of his employer.

They started housekeeping on a small acreage he bought on what is now Parker Road. Mr. and Mrs. Stinson added to their small farm from time to time until they owned around a thousand acres of land in various places. The nearest schools in the area in that early day was a one-room school located southwest of Parker, and also a one room school at St. Paul, which is east of Parker. When the need arose for another school Mr. and Mrs. James Francis Stinson donated the land, and another one-room school was built on the west side of the Stinson farm, and it was called "Stinson School." It was also called "Who'd A Thought It." That was the exclamation from a man who passed while the school was being built and the name stuck. It was the school that all the Stinson children and other nearby neighbor children attended in that early day. In later years the schools were consolidated, and a larger school house was built, more centrally located in the Parker area, and this land was donated by Mr. and Mrs. F.L. Myrick (the late Mrs. H.R. Stinson's parents).

Mr. and Mrs. James F. Stinson were the parents of 10 children, eight of whom lived to adulthood. In 1920 Mr. and Mrs. Stinson deeded each child 50 acres of land.

Four of the children were closely connected with the Lucas community through the school, churches and other activities. They were: Lucy Jane, born in 1877, died Dec. 1961; Lula Maude, born in 1890; Henry Robert, born Aug. 1895, died June 1946; and Clara Edith, born in Jan. 1902.

STINSON—TOMBERLIN

Lucy Jane Stinson married W.R. Tomberlin. Mr. Tomberlin, born in November, 1865, and died in February, 1959. They were the parents of seven children, of which six lived to be grown, and all attended neighborhood schools and churches. The oldest son, Arlee Tomberlin, married Katherine Parrish and they live in California. Noel Tomberlin married Della Atchley and are now living in Van Alstyne. Nona Tomberlin married Martin Heifner (deceased). They were the parents of two children, Maurell Heifner, who married Iola Rolf and lives in Winningkoff community, and a daughter, Fay, who married Gene Dobbs and lives in McKinney.

Alleen Tomberlin (deceased) married Marion Welborn of Farmersville, who is also deceased. Julia Tomberlin married Delbert Meuir of Princeton and they now live in McKinney.

J.C. Tomberlin married Ollie Gandy of Clarksville. The J.C. Tomberlins still live on part of the original W.R. Tomberlin (or Mrs.) farm. They have two daughters, Venita, now Mrs. J.R. Ellis of Lucas, and Irene, who lives in Yuma, Ariz. Both girls attended Lucas School and graduated from Plano High School.

Mr. and Mrs. J.R. Ellis have two sons, James Ray and Don, and one daughter, Judy Kay. The children attend the local school and are the fourth generation to live on the W.R. Tomberlin farm.

STINSON—L. McCREARY

Lula Maud Stinson married Loy McCreary. (Mr. McCreary died in March, 1967.) They were the parents of three sons and two daughters. The daughters died in infancy. All the children were born in this area, but only Leslie, the oldest, attended school in Lucas. The family moved to Parker Road-Plano School district and all the children finished school there. They were: Si (deceased), who married Naomi Parr, daughter of Mr. and Mrs. R.S. Parr of Lucas. Mrs. Si McCreary now lives in Garland.

Robert McCreary married Merry Lee Merriman of Plano. They now live at Blue Ridge (Collin Co.) Leslie McCreary married Gladys Parr, daughter of Mr. and Mrs. R.S. Parr of Lucas. They have two daughters, Zada and Martha Joyce. Martha had a twin sister who died in infancy. Zada married Randall Nicholson of Plano.

STINSON—McCREARY

Zada and Randall Nicholson are the parents of three daughters, Connie, Lisa and Beverly and a son Ken. The Nicholsons built a home on the Leslie McCreary farm, the children attend school in Plano and the family is active in the Lucas Christian Church.

Martha McCreary is a student in Texas Women's University, Denton. The Leslie McCrearys and Martha are also active members of Lucas Christian Church. Mrs. Loy McCreary (Lula Maud Stinson) now lives in Plano.

STINSON—W. McCREARY

Clara Edith Stinson married Watson (Jack) McCreary. (Mr. McCreary died in May, 1965.) They were the parents of one child, a son, Watson McCreary Jr. He married Janelle Cole of Jacksonville, Texas. They and their two sons, Charles and Mike, live in Shreveport, La.

Mr. and Mrs. James F. Stinson had a granddaughter, Sadie Margaret McGuire, who was a missionary in Africa. She married Roy Echols who was also a missionary there. At one time Mr. and Mrs. Stinson had five grandsons and a grandson-in-law in the service of their country during World War II at the same time. They were: Nathan Strain (six years), Harold Stinson, Watson McCreary Jr., Stinson Phillips (20 years), Paul Stinson and George Hennig.

THE MYRICK FAMILY

Fountain Lee Myrick and Della Hall were married at the old Hall home place in south Lucas by the Rev. Johnny McKinney, Christian Church minister. After their marriage they moved into a house on what is now "Seis Lagos Ranch" in South Lucas, which was near the Hall home place. It was here that their first child, and only daughter, Allie Ethel Myrick, was born in September, 1893. They had three sons, one of whom, Leonard Myrick, lives at Parker, one is deceased and the other, Fred, lives in Fort Worth.

STINSON—MYRICK

Henry Robert Stinson married Allie Ethel Myrick, daughter of Mr. and Mrs. Fountain Lee Myrick of Parker. They were married Dec. 25th, 1916, in Wylie, Texas by Rev. Hanson, who was pastor of St. Paul Methodist Church. They moved into a house on the James F. Stinson place in Lucas, which was part of the 50 acres of land deeded to him by his parents, Mr. and Mrs. James F. Stinson, in 1920. Other acreage was added and in 1922 Mr. and Mrs. Stinson built a new, modern (for the time) home where they spent the rest of their lives. Mrs. Stinson died in August, 1970.

They were the parents of four children. One died in infancy. The three are: Jana B., Velma and James. All attended Lucas School—the girls graduated from McKinney High School and James finished at Wylie High School.

Jana B. married George Hennig of Rowlett. They have two sons, George Henry and Don, and one daughter, Sara. Jana B. and George live in Dallas. George Henry and his wife, the former Joyce Moore of Irving, bought a home in Forest Grove Estates in North Lucas. Don married Betty Crumbley of Cooper, Texas and they reside in Gainesville, Tex. Sara married Larry Leggett of Ft. Worth. They now live in Boston, Mass., where she attends Boston College.

Velma married Milford Spurgin of McKinney. They have no children. Both are active members of the First United Methodist Church of Lucas.

James Stinson married Emma Spears of Lucas. They are the parents of two daughters, Velinda, who was born on the homeplace here and Jana, born after the family moved to Irving, where they now live.

Mr. and Mrs. H.R. Stinson left each of their children a farm and James drew the home place here at Lucas, though all the farms are in the city limits of Lucas. Mrs. H.R. Stinson's mother, Mrs. F.L. Myrick, who was an invalid, lived with Mr. and Mrs. Stinson 32 years with the exception of a year or two spent elsewhere. Mrs. Myrick died in June, 1962.

Dorothy Stinson, daughter of Mr. and Mrs. Bill Stinson of Parker (now of Arlington) married Ridley Trail of Tennessee and she and Ridley bought and lived for several years on the Anderson farm just east of the Lucas store. They sold the farm to Earl Pillard and moved near Trenton, Texas.

JAMES M. AND PULLEY SLEDGE of Prosper.

JAMES MARION TERRELL AND FAMILY

James Marion Terrell and Pulley Parthene Sledge were married August 16, 1887 in Toccopola, Mississippi. In the fall of 1900 they left their home for Texas and with them came their four children, Lillie, Minnie, Dock, and Wesley. It took the family over a month to travel the 900 miles in a covered wagon before they reached Altoga. Two young men made the trip with them, walking behind the wagon, Jim Henderson and Tutor. The family settled at Prosper area about 1928.

James Terrell was a self-made veterinarian and blacksmith, serving his community in both capacities. They were members in the Baptist Church at Prosper. Both Mr. and Mrs. Terrell are buried in the Mount Olive Cemetery. Two of their children still live in Collin County, Dock lives in Prosper and Wes lives in Celina.

Dock and Alma's children are Billie, J.W., Marlin, and Elton, and Juanice. Juanice was born near Prosper in 1929 and was officially called "Little Miss Collin County of 1929" since she was the first child born in the county that year. After finishing the Prosper schools she married Doyce Lee Stanton, who is a veteran of World War II and received the Purple Heart for injuries sustained while in combat in the Phillipines Islands.

He is the son of W.M. and Jimmie Bell-Stanton. They are the parents of two children, Edward Duane and Leesa Kay. They are active in all civic and religious affairs of the community. He has long been a member of the school board and is a volunteer fireman, as well as an elder in the church. She contributes news to the newspapers each week and is interested in recording local history.

JOHN W. THOMAS

John W. Thomas, pioneer newspaperman of Collin County, was born Jan. 19, 1826, the son of John P. Thomas of Jefferson, Missouri, who served with the Colonists in the Revolutionary War. His mother was Sarah Christopher Thomas, a native of Kentucky. The Thomas family migrated to Texas in 1845 where he worked as a surveyor, a school teacher and in 1859 they settled in McKinney and opened up the first newspaper in the county, *The McKinney Messenger*. This was the only paper in the county during the Civil War and was an influential news media.

Thomas was a great admirer and personal friend of Sam Houston and his *McKinney Messenger* was the first newspaper to suggest his running for Governor of Texas. Other papers then got behind the movement. Thomas served as Postmaster under President Pierce, Buchanan, Johnston, Grant, Hayes, Garfield, Arthur, and Cleveland as well as serving as County Treasurer for several terms. He was married to Mary William Smith of Clarksville, Texas. One son, James P. Thomas. Mr. Thomas died in McKinney Nov. 9, 1906.

Microfilmed Newspapers

HISTORY OF
THE THOMPSON FAMILY

Dr. Francis Marion Thompson and his wife, the former Sarah Roberta Mack, came to McKinney in January, 1877, with their eleven-year-old son, William Clinton. Dr. Thompson was engaged in the real estate business, contributing much to the early development and growth of McKinney. He died in 1909.

William Clinton Thompson (1865-1954), better known as Clint Thompson, received his education in the McKinney Public Schools and the old Hawthorne Academy, also at McKinney. At an early age he began his newspaper career as a printer's

CLINT THOMPSON owned "McKinney Examiner" for many years. He was the first of three generations to own the paper.

"devil" on the McKinney Advocate, later joining the staff of the McKinney Enquirer, where he learned the rudiments of printing and journalism. In 1886 he established the McKinney Gazette. In 1897, on account of ill health, he sold the Gazette, and a year later bought the McKinney Examiner. Thereafter, until the close of his active career, only a short time before his death, he was its editor and publisher.

Editor Thompson was an Elder in Trinity Presbyterian Church of McKinney, a member of the lodge of Knights of Pythias, and other civic organizations. He was one of the oldest members of the McKinney Chamber of Commerce and a member of the Texas Presss Association for 65 years.

On June 5, 1895, William Clinton Thompson married Anna Belle Wofford, daughter of a Presbyterian minister, the Reverend J.H. Wofford. They became the parents of the following children: Mrs. Marion Thompson Purnell; Miss Katherine Thompson, a retired McKinney school teacher; Mrs. Nina Thompson Kressly, for a number of years a feature writer in the Women's Department of the Dallas Morning News; and Wofford Clinton Thompson, associated with his father in the publication of the Examiner.

The death of this veteran editor and publisher occurred at McKinney on November 2, 1954, and concluded a career which, for length of useful service and professional integrity, has had few equals in the annals of the region.

Wofford Clinton Thompson (1902-1971) received his education in the McKinney Public Schools, Trinity University, and Southern Methodist University. He joined his father in the publication of the Examiner in 1940, becoming managing editor and publisher on the retirement of his father, a position which he held until his own death in 1971. He continued to uphold his father's high standards and ideals in publishing the paper.

He was a long and faithful member of Trinity Presbyterian Church, where he served as an Elder, a Sunday School teacher and superintendent. He was a member of the Masonic Lodge, the McKinney Chamber of Commerce, the Texas Press Association, and the McKinney Rotary Club.

In 1929 he married the former Elizabeth Carr. They have one son, Wofford Clinton Thompson, Jr., who became co-editor and publisher with his father in 1958.

Wofford Clinton Thompson Jr. (1930-) was also educated in the McKinney Public Schools and Trinity University. He is continuing to publish the Examiner, promoting the same high standards of Journalism upheld by his father and grandfather.

He is also an Elder in Trinity Presbyterian Church, a past-president of McKinney Rotary Club, a member of the Chamber of Commerce and Texas Press Association.

In 1955 he and the former Nelma Jean Bernard were married. They have a teenage son, Wofford Douglas, who, it is hoped, will follow in the footsteps of his father, grandfather, and great grandfather. They also have three adopted children: Pam, Mary, and Rick.

(GRANDFATHER of JIM T. WILSON)

JAMES J. THOMPSON

James J. Thompson was born December 18, 1835 in Hopkinsville, Kentucky, the son of George Overton and Margaret Thompson. When he was quite a young man, he went west as Horace Greenley advised. He came to Collin County and McKinney in the early 1860s. The Civil War was just beginning and he enlisted in a company being organized in McKinney, the company made up of Collin County men. There were 95 men who enlisted for a period of 12 months, but when that time was up they all re-enlisted for the duration of the war. The company took part in many areas and were in the Battle of Shiloh where his commander

JAMES J. THOMPSON and his grandson, George Thompson Provine.

and many of the men lost their lives.

Following his war years he returned to his boyhood home in Kentucky, but the pull of pioneering prompted him to return to Texas, this time to make his home. He settled in the Rock Hill Community, west of McKinney. Here he farmed his 320 acres and built his home fronting on the old Preston Road, the most traveled road leading north from Dallas. He married Dollie Field, daughter of a very early pioneer family from Missouri, Jesse Field. Two children were born to them, George Field Thompson and Margaret who became Mrs. G.H. Provine.

Besides farming, Thompson operated his own gin and general store and served as postmaster for a while. His wife died while the children were small.

In 1888, while still maintaining his farming operations, Thompson and his family moved to McKinney and bought a home built by R.H. Parker in 1877. The home was surrounded by 125 acres and was situated on Rock Hill Road near the city limits of McKinney on the west. The home was built along colonial lines with lumber hauled by ox-wagons from Jefferson in east Texas. It was surrounded by huge oak and pecan trees estimated then to be 100 years old, a picture of beauty, ready for gracious living. Thompson married Mrs. Anna

THE JAMES J. THOMPSON HOME, owned by the family over three quarters of a century. Located on Rock Hill Road, McKinney.

Allen Gatewood, a widow who had come with her son, Allen from Moscow, Tennessee in 1883.

Four children were born of this marriage, James Jason, Rebecca (Mrs. J.B. Crockett), Ruth (Mrs. Paul K. Wilson), and Rachel (Mrs. Aubrey B. Griffin). Jim, Ruth and Rachel still live in McKinney.

George Thompson joined his father, James J. Thompson, in the gin and became its manager in 1909. Jim Jr. owed a surburban grocery store called Thompson's Suburban Grocery. When World War I came, Jim Jr. enlisted, but after the war was over, he returned to his business which he carried on for 43 years.

Many of James J. Thompson's descendents still live in Collin County.

His descendents recall an incident that happened back in the end of the last century, an incident that bears out the quote from an old paper that called him "the gentleman with the Chesterfield manners." While living on Rock Hill Road the notorious outlaw, Sam Bass, and his gang appeared in his store one day and declared their intention of robbing the store. Thompson stepped aside and told the robbers to help themselves, even helped them carry out heavy objects. After a bit Sam Bass came back into the store and told Thompson that they had intended taking everything he had but they had been treated so politely that they weren't taking a thing. Thompson's small son, who had been hiding under a counter, rushed to the house to report the incident.

The homeplace is still owned by the James J. Thompson heirs.

Story written by Ruth Wilson

THE J. WILBUR THOMPSON ANCESTRY

Both J.W. Thompson and his wife, Helen Johnson Thompson, come from pioneer lines in Collin County.

Alexander D. Buckley, grandfather of J.W. Thompson, was born in Lewis County, Missouri, January 14, 1833, and was reared a farmer. His father, Joseph B. Buckley, was born in Virginia on February 9, 1801 and married Nancy H. Bass, daughter of Captain Bass. He was the father of five children, Alexander D being the third. He was a Christian leader in the pioneer community. Nancy H. Buckley was born on Christmas Day, 1811 in Campbell County, Virginia and died December 26, 1881.

Alexander D. Buckley lost his father at age four and had little opportunity for education since it fell to him to help support the family as soon as he was old enough to work. December 15, 1853 he married Martha J. Morris, daughter of L.T. Morris, a native of Butler County, Kentucky, a farmer of substantial means and a Justice of the Peace. In 1858 the Buckley family came to Texas, arriving with a few hundred dollars with which he purchased land at $7 per acre. Before they were settled, he was called upon to serve in the Confederate Army, and in 1861 he enlisted in Company K, 16th Texas Cavalry and took part in the engagements in Louisiana and Arkansas. At the Battle of Pleasant Hill, in Louisiana, he was struck by a minie ball in the right foot. He was taken prisoner and after six months in the hospital, he was sent home, crippled for life. It was several years before he was able to resume his farming activities but the farm of 420 acres was one of the productive farms of the time, and here he and his wife and six children enjoyed a comfortable life. The children were Susan A., who died as a child; Joseph L.; Mary L.H.; William E.; Sarah F.; and Rosa J. Rosa married W.D. Thompson and was the mother of J.W. Thompson, prominent business man of McKinney. He is married to Helen Johnson Thompson, and they are the parents of three children.

John M. Kincaid, great-great grandfather of Mrs. J.W. Thompson, was born in Bath County, Kentucky, August 31, 1814, the son of William T. Kincaid. William T. was the son of Andrew and Martha Kincaid. William was a native of Pennsylvania but in early childhood moved with his parents to Kentucky; then in 1818 to Illinois. During the War of 1812 he served as a private, winning several commendations for his bravery; he received two wounds and was taken prisoner at the Battle of Raisin, January 22, 1813. He was married to Elizabeth Mace Kincaid who died in 1835. In November, 1841, the Kincaid family moved to Texas from Illinois, locating in Fannin County which included Collin County at that time. In 1846 he served with the Texas State troops in the war with Mexico. When Collin County was formed in 1848 he was elected Justice of the Peace. In 1863 he entered the Confederate Army, Company C, Second Texas Infantry. In 1837 he was married to Temperance Rattan, a daughter of Thomas Rattan of Illinois. To this union were born three children, Harriett, Elizabeth, and Virginia. Harriett was the mother of Alma Wilson, who was the father of Nancy Harriett Wilson Johnson. Nancy Harriet Johnson was the mother of Helen (Johnson) Thompson.

George A. Wilson was born in Sumber County, Tennessee, January 1, 1828, son of Addison Wilson, who was a native of Sumner County. A farmer, he came to Texas in 1849 and died in Collin County in 1868. His wife, Annie Moore Wilson, died in 1882. George A. Wilson was reared at his homeplace in Tennessee and came to Texas in 1845, settling in Collin County. He served in the Mexican War of 1846, returning home at the close of the war, engaging in the carpenter trade, also farming and raising stock.

In 1855 he married Harriet Kincaid, daughter of John M. Kincaid. The couple had eleven children: Almarine, John J., Bettie, Jenny, Lucy, Benjamin, Tollie, George, Wallace, Addie, and Mary.

In 1866 Mr. Wilson was elected Sheriff of Collin County, which office he held for four years during the perilous Reconstruction times when the entire country was in a time of change. Later he entered the real estate business.

George A. Wilson was the father of Almarine, who was the father of Nancy Harriet (Wilson) Johnson. Nancy Harriet Johnson was the mother of Helen (Johnson) Thompson of McKinney.

Story given by Helen Thompson. Facts from "Biographical Souvenir of the State of Texas, F.A. Battey and Co., 1889.
Sent by Wilbur and Helen Thompson

THE THROCKMORTON FAMILY

No Collin County family's roots go as far back in Collin County history as the Throckmortons. Up until 1842 Collin County land lay untouched by the hand of the white man. It lay as the forces of nature had made it, virgin and primitive, inhabited only by a few Indians and abundant wild game. The first exploring party departed from present Bonham to see if the rumors were true about the land lying at the headquarters of the Trinity River. The party consisted of Dr. Daniel Rowlett, Jabez Fitzhugh, Edmund Todd, Pleasant Wilson, Littleton Battan, William R. Garrett, and Dr. William E. Throckmorton. They were so impressed with the land that they returned to bring all their families and supplies. In January, 1842 the wagon train arrived in Collin and the first settlement was established seven miles north of McKinney around a huge spring that is called Throckmorton Spring.

The Republic of Texas was just getting on its feet and were powerless to protect early settlers against the raiding Indians from the west. James W. Throckmorton said, in later years, that in the early days every cabin was a castle and every man a soldier, but the settlers banded together and set up their own code of laws with Throckmorton the leader. Dr. Throckmorton married Mrs. Wilson in 1842. He died the next year, leaving the leadership of the little settlement to his son James W., who was later to become the Governor of Texas. During these pioneer days, young James was farming and studying law at night. The death of the elder Throckmorton left the settlement without a doctor, and before young James reached manhood he was treating the sick with the help of the few medical books his father left him. When the second war with Mexico broke out he left with Capt. Robert Taylor's Company for the border, where he served in a medical capacity for the duration of the conflict.

Governor James W. Throckmorton served the public of Texas for 30 years. He was born in Sparta, Tennessee on February 1, 1825 and grew to manhood in that state. He studied medicine with great success and was surgeon in Major Mike Chevallie's Texas Rangers in the Mexican War. After the Mexican War he settled in Collin County and began the practice of medicine until 1859. He was elected to the Legislature in 1851, 1853, and 1855. In 1857 he was elected to the State Senate. It was said by his constituents that no man did more to protect the frontier, help the Peter's Colony people when their land titles were endangered, and encouraged the building of railroads and establishment of a system of public schools. He was reared a Whig politically and when that party ceased to exist, he threw in with the Jeffersonian Democrats.

When the subject of secession came he opposed

that method of settling the south's grievances. He was elected to the Secession Convention by both the South and the Union and sat by turns in the two opposing seats. When the vote on secession was taken he voted against it. A single man sitting in a gallery above him hissed. With dignity as always, Throckmorton rose to his feet and made his famous remark—"Mr. President, the rabble may hiss while the patriots tremble." Only seven voted against it, but Throckmorton had already confided in the convention his strong feeling against war to settle the differences and told them plainly that if war came he would have to shoulder his musket and stand with the South. The convention respected his feeling and held him in great respect for it. True to his word he commanded a company that took Ft. Washita and Ft. Arbuckle. He served with the 6th Texas Cavalry as Captain until ill health sent him home. When recovered he served with the Stones 2nd Regiment as a Major and later the governor appointed him a Brigadier General in the State troops. In 1865 he was appointed by Gen. E. Kirby Smith.

At the end of the Civil War he was elected to the reconstruction convention by President Johnson. When an election was held under the new constitution, he was elected Governor of the State of Texas by a vote of 4 to 1. While in office he made every effort to renew friendship with the north and to restore peace in the country. On August 9, 1867 after little more than one year of service he was deposed by three lines of pen marks from an officer of the United States Army who was in command of all military affairs in Louisiana and Texas. Like thousands of other Texans he was disfranchised until 1874 without even the right to vote. But in 1876 he was again elected to the state senate by a vast majority, where he served several terms, retiring when his health broke.

Governor and Mrs. Throckmorton (Ann, daughter of Thomas Rattan) had the following children: Hugh J. (m. Miss Turner) and died a few years later; Jennie (m. Dr. Moore of McKinney); Tollie (m. Robert Dowell) and lived in McKinney; Edward (m. Miss Stiff); Hattie (m. E.F. Reeves) of Dallas; Ben E. was a physician practicing in Collin, Lucy, James, Annie, and Florence. He died April 21, 1894.

The Historical Society placed a Medallion on his Law Office still in use on Virginia Street just off the square in McKinney and his statue stands on the northeast corner of the courthouse plaza.

Written by Roy F. Hall

LUTHER TRUETT

My father was Luther Jeremiah Truett and he was born in Clay County, North Carolina, August 22, 1869. My mother was Addie Lee Grimmette who was born in Franklin County, Texas, October 7, 1878. My mother and father were married June 12, 1900 on the day after her graduation from the then female college at Belton, Texas. He was a graduate of Grayson College, Whitewright. They resided at McKinney, Texas thereafter, at which place my father had lived for two years.

My father was the son of Charles Levi Truett and Rebecca Kimzey and my father was a seventh generation descendant of George Truett who was the original member of their family to come to the United States from England.

My mother was the daughter of John Lee Grimmett who had earlier lived in the community of Rome, Georgia, and of Nancy Ann Weems. John Lee Grimmett's father was James Grimmette and of French extraction; his mother was Charlotte Sturdivant and of Dutch extraction. Nancy Ann Weems' parents were from Tennessee and moved to Texas while Texas was a Republic.

My mother and father, Mr. and Mrs. Luther Jeremiah Truett, had four children born to them and which four children are all residents of Collin County, Texas, living at McKinney and are as follows:

Annie Lee Worthy, wife of W.W. Worthy.

Dr. H.K. Truett, whose wife is Ruth Marcom Truett.

Luther L. Truett, whose wife is Hilda Thomas Truett.

Addie Grimmette Warden, wife of William Warden.

(Compiled by Luther Truett)

THE WADDILL FAMILY

Judge R.L. Waddill was born February 11, 1811 in Shelby County Kentucky. He was educated at the Princeton College of Kentucky as a student of law. He practiced law in Kentucky and was for two terms a legislator from his district. In 1853 he and his step-son, George S. Morris, then a boy, rode horseback to Collin County from Kentucky. They located in McKinney and his wife soon joined them. He practiced law in McKinney and from 1860 to 1865 he was the District Judge, his district taking in 11 counties. As there was no railroad, he rode the circuit on horseback.

His wife was a daughter of a pioneer family of

Culpepper County, Virginia. Her father, Benjamin Shackelford, was an attorney and served as District Judge for 40 years. Her mother was Francis Paca Dallam, a native of Maryland, and also served a term as Governor Of Maryland.

R.L. Waddill was born August 1, 1850 in Hopkinsville, Kentucky, the son of Judge R.L. Waddill Sr. and Elizabeth Waddill. Her mother was Betty Martin, Belle of Baltimore, niece of William Paca, signer of the Declaration of Independence. At 23 she married George Morris, a lawyer and politician of Henderson County, Kentucky. He was nominated as the Whig candidate for Governor of Kentucky but died before the election. Ten years later, 1846, she married Judge R.L. Waddill. Of this marriage 4 sons and 1 daughter were born.

George Shackelford Morris, brother of R.L. Waddill, was born in Hopkinsville, Christian County, Kentucky on August 16, 1835. He was the son of George S. and Sarah Elizabeth Morris (Sarah Shackelford). The husband died in 1836 and in 1845 Elizabeth married Robert Lawrence Waddill, and came to McKinney to make their home in 1853. George Shackelford Morris and Alice Rains were married in 1885. They were the parents of one son, George Rains Morris. George served during the Civil War in Martin's Regiment and later General Gano's Brigade. He was wounded in the Battle of Cabin Creek, Indian Territory. After the war he studied law at Louisville and there was admitted to the bar. In 1874 he returned to McKinney, serving as Deputy County Clerk under Joe Waddill. He died in McKinney, May 27, 1910.

Fannie P. Waddill, daughter of Judge R.L. and Sarah Elizabeth, was born in McKinney November 17, 1856. She was one of six children. She was born in the Waddill home built on a high ridge overlooking McKinney, now Waddill Street. She attended a private school taught by Elder James S. Muse in the school he built near them on Waddill Street. (recently restored and owned by the Walter P. Bomar family). Her father, Judge Waddill, was always a friend of education, and he built a school on the lot just north of the present Methodist Church. Fannie was one of the teachers in this school and was one of the best of the early educators in McKinney. She died at age 82.

Joe W. Waddill was born in Kentucky, the son of Judge R.L. and Sarah Waddill and came with his parents to McKinney in 1853. He was educated under the tutorship of Payton A. Hamilton. He served as Deputy Sheriff under W.W. Merritt and under William Warden. In 1882 he was elected County Clerk and served three terms. In 1892 he was again elected County Clerk and served one term. He died at age 53.

Gaston Meers Waddill, son of Judge and Sarah Waddill, was born in Hopkinsville on November 1, 1852 and was an infant when they moved to Collin County.

Mrs. Elizabeth Waddill Muse was the wife of Professor Roger B. Muse, an early Collin County educator. They were married in 1912 and she died August 18, 1916.

The old Waddill homeplace was laid off in town lots by Lawrence Waddill and Waddill Street was opened. The Muse heirs joined the movement and continued the street north through the Elder J.M. Muse farm. The two families had been neighbors since pioneer days and worked together to promote this new part of McKinney. The big old Waddill home was destroyed by fire.

George Rains Morris, son of George Schackelford and Mary Alice Rains Morris was born in Abilene, Texas. He married Lillian Rook and of this marriage two children were born, George Rook Morris and Mary Alice Morris. (Love).

Mary Morris Love married James Alley and lives in Michigan. They have one daughter, Karen Alley.

Lu Love married Bruce Kingsley, the son of Dr. Kingsley of Dallas. They are the parents of a daughter, Kristan Kingsley.

George Rook Morris married Marguerite Hall and one child was born of this marriage, Gail Morris now married to James Hitchcock.

In 1940 George Rains Morris was married to Naomi Snider. George Morris is deceased but Naomi Snider Morris still lives in the Waddill homeplace and is a successful businesswoman, operating her own downtown business.

Story furnished by: Naomi Snider Morris McKinney

PETER RANDOLPH WALLIS

The Matthew Wallis and the Meadows families came to America together and settled in the county of Iredell, North Carolina near the town of Statesville. Matthew's son, Allen, was born in Iredell Co. in 1791. Sarah Meadows, daughter of the Meadows family, was also born in 1791. Allen Wallis and Sarah Meadows married in 1841 and to them were born the following children: Alfred, Peter Randolph, Malinda, Myra, Joel A., Sarah, Allen Jr., Charles G., Robert F., and Jeptha, the youngest child, who was born in Bedford County, Tennessee in the village of Bell Buckle. Allen and Sarah had migrated to Tennessee with the Wilsons, Wallaces, and Moores, all of whom had been close neighbors in North Carolina.

Peter Randolph Wallis was married to Martha Catherine Wilson in the village of Gallatin, Tennessee on September 23, 1847. Martha was a daughter of Add and Ann Moore Wilson. Peter and Martha were the parents of the following children: William N., Laura N., Henry O., Sarah A., Ora A., Elmer L., and Lou E. Laura was born in the pioneer town of McKinney, Texas where the family had just settled, awaiting the section of land they were to purchase. He operated a blacksmith shop on the southeast corner of the square. Their home was on the site where McKinney's mayor, Mr. Rushhaupt operated an Office Supply business. Peter bought 640 acres of land, paying $1.25 per acre for it. The land was located seven miles northeast of McKinney on the Bonham Road. He built a large two room house, the back room for the family to live in and the front room for his wainwright machinery until a shop could be built. April 1, 1853 their son, Henry Orman, was born.

There was much blacksmith work and woodwork for the next two decades and Bois d'Arc wagons to be built, besides building a larger home. When the Civil War came he began making flour and groats for the Army with the help of his teenage nephew, A.M. (Gus) Wilson. The mill operated until 1864 when it was feared Grant would send men by boat into the Gulf Coast area, he and Gus decided they were needed more in the Army. P.R. Wallis joined Speight's Battalion and A.M. Wilson was now old enough to get into the service. He rode horseback to join Speight but met others from that troop riding back home with the sad news that Gen. Lee had surrendered.

In the early 1870s the home burned so the family moved into the blacksmith shop while another home was built with Evans Wallace and J.P.A. Wallace the chief carpenters and architects.

The P.R. Wallis family were charter members of the first Presbyterian Church organized in Collin County, the Cumberland Presbyterian Church of Melissa with a Rev. Brockett serving as the first pastor. He was a Mason for many years. He died in October of 1877 and is among the first buried in the Woodlawn Cemetery, now known as the Noyes Cemetery. His wife died in October of 1915.

Almost 200 descendents are proud of the grandparents who stood tall in the new west.

Contributed by a granddaughter, Effie Wallis Roberts (Mrs. (Mrs. Ralph Roberts).

THE WARDEN AND WORDEN FAMILIES

The Warden family has been prominent in the affairs of Collin County for well over a century. The founder, Williams Warden, Sr., was born in Kentucky on February 2, 1808. He later moved to Missouri and on April 15, 1844, he and his family crossed the Red River into Texas north of Bonham. The trip, which required six weeks, was made in ox wagons. The Wardens brought with them thirty to forty head of Durham cattle. They camped for ten days at Lick Skillet (also known as Pilot Grove) in Grayson County. Later they camped again, this time for six weeks at a spring a mile south of Melissa, while the father looked the country over for a suitable location for a permanent home. For a short time they lived at White Rock Creek in northern Dallas County but hostile Indians forced them to return to Bonham. In 1851 they moved to Climax, twelve miles east of McKinney. Soon thereafter Warden secured a patent on 640 acres of land north of Weston.

He and his wife, Hulda, were married in Cooper County, Missouri, in 1825. To this union eleven children were born: Williams, Jr., W.A. (Chief), Hezekiah, F. Marion, John, Att, James, Robert, Mrs. J.P. Hunter, Mrs. Robert Fitzhugh, and Mrs. John Rike. Williams Warden Sr. died on his farm north of Weston in 1858.

Williams Warden, Jr., was born in Jackson County, Missouri, on April 15, 1833, and came to Texas with his parents in 1844. On March 15, 1849, he married Hester Ann Smith and they had three children: A.P., C.T. (Todd), and Mrs. J.W. Christian. After the death of his first wife he married Nancy McCarley on February 22, 1860. To this union were born six children: Hezekiah, Floyd, Mrs. Ben E. Throckmorton, Mrs. W.A. Bristol, Mrs. Ed. Mayes, and Florence, who died young. On November, 5, 1876, he was married to Mrs. M.A. Wilson. They had no children. She died on September 25, 1906.

Williams Warden, Jr., was a versatile man. He was at times a farmer, a cattleman, an Indian fighter, a Confederate veteran, constable, county commissioner, postmaster, deputy sheriff, and sheriff. In 1862 he enlisted in Alf Johnson's Spy Company at McKinney and saw service in Texas, Arkansas, Missouri, and Louisiana. After the close of the Civil War he lived on a farm near Blue Ridge and was constable in that precinct. There he also served as postmaster for four years. In 1868 he moved to Fitzhugh Mills where he farmed. There he was elected constable in 1870. Six years later he was elected county commissioner from precinct 3 and in 1878 he was elected sheriff, serving three terms. For fifteen years he served in some capacity in the sheriff's office. He died at the home of his son, Todd, in Oklahoma City on December 12, 1911.

W.A. (Chief) Warden was born near Bonham on August 3, 1849. He was a deputy sheriff for over fifty years.

Hezekiah Warden was captain of a company in Colonel William Fitzhugh's Sixteenth Regiment of Texas Cavalry during the Civil War. There were a William Warden and a John Warden in his company but the relationship is uncertain.

F. Marion Warden was born in Missouri in 1835 and came to Texas with his parents in 1844. He was married twice. Children by his first marriage were Hez, Mrs. Nannie James, and Mrs. Charles Martin; and those by his second wife were T. Ben, Henry W., General John Warden, and Mrs. Gibson Caldwell.

Hez Warden was the father of fifteen children, thirteen of whom are living in 1957. These are: Henry J., Clarence, O.B., Jack, Lester, Chief, Willie, J.B., Mrs. Mattie Routsong, Mrs. Dessa Dickerson, Mrs. J.M. Drake, Mrs. Bonnie Barrow, and Mrs. Lonnie York.

T. Ben Warden graduated from Texas A&M College in 1903. He was a member of the Texas State Board of Control from 1947 to 1953 and is now an engineer in Austin.

Henry W. Warden was born in Collin County on August 9, 1876, and was a prominent businessman of McKinney. For many years he served the Collin County National Bank, both as vice-president and as president.

John A. Warden was born in Collin County on July 31, 1886. In 1908 he was graduated from Texas A&M College as a civil engineer. During the same year he was commissioned a second lieutenant of cavalry at Ft. Leavenworth, Kansas. He was a veteran of both World Wars. In 1941 he was promoted to the grade of brigadier general. In 1947 he retired from the army and has since lived at 609 West Lamar Street in McKinney. In 1950 he was elected representative from Collin County and served two terms—in the Fifty-second and the Fifty-third legislatures. General and Mrs. Warden had three children, John A., Jr., Henry E., and Mrs. Jim Love.

John A. Warden, Jr., graduated from Texas A&M College in 1936 and was commissioned a second lieutenant in the army at Ft. Logan, Colorado, the same year. He is now in business in Pennsylvania.

Henry E. Warden is a colonel in the United States Air Force.

William Warden, one of Collin County's earliest pioneers, was born in Missouri in January of 1833. In 1844 his family started for Texas and after six weeks of travel they crossed Red River at Beale's Ferry, 20 miles north of Bonham which at that time had only one log cabin and one log store that had little merchandise except a barrel of whisky and an assortment of coon hounds. They came to a spring south of present Melissa and camped for six weeks. Warden made daily horseback rides over the countryside looking for a good place to settle. He rode to Buckner then to White Rock Creek 12 miles north of Dallas. Indian scares drove them back to Bonham where they settled 640 acres and built a log cabin. When the title to the land proved to be bad, the family came back to Collin County and settled at present Climax in 1857. He was the first settler there. William's father, William Sr., was born in 1808 in Kentucky and after arriving in Collin County headrighted 640 acres of land near present Weston. He was a veteran of both the American Revolutionary War and the War of 1812. He died at Weston in 1850.

The younger William Warden married Hester Ann Smith in 1849 and had three children, one of them was Todd Warden, who figured largely in the early life of the County. After his wife's death he married Nancy McCurley in 1869. After her death he married Mrs. M.A. Wilson in 1876. William served in the confederate Army in Alf Chandler's Spy Co. of McKinney as a First Lt. in 1862. He was with the troops who surrendered at Appomattox. After the war he lived at Blue Ridge, serving as Constable and farming. He was also postmaster. In 1868 he moved to Fitzhugh Mills and served as Commissioner of his district. Later he was sheriff for three terms.

THE WEEKS FAMILY

George and Amiel Weeks came to this country from Devonshire, England about 1635, landing at Dorchester, Massachusetts. According to deeds and records found in Floyd County, Virginia, Elijah Weeks, a descendant of this Weeks family left eleven heirs at his death to share his estate.

Elijah's sixth child, Louis Weeks, born July 15, 1811, married Betsy Ann Thomson, born July 28, 1815, in Floyd County, Virginia—near Hylton,

Virginia. To this union were born one girl, Louise, and three boys: one died young, one was killed in the Civil War, the third son, Abaslom Clark Weeks, born July 30, 1836, came to Texas prior to the Civil War. After war broke out, he enlisted as a private in the Army of Virginia. When the war ended, Absalom returned to Texas and lived for a time around Weston. He was by trade a master carpenter and helped to build some of the older pioneer homes and buildings of Collin County. Absalom also lived at Rhea Mills for a time and it was while living there that he helped build the old J.O. Kerr home, then about the best in all this section. He next helped build a house for W.H. Horn, Sr. It was while doing so that Absalom met, wooed and won for his wife Mildred Jane Horn, the daughter of W.M. Horn Sr. and wife Martha Caruth Horn who were prominent pioneer settlers and land owners in the Vineland Community. The young couple were married in the bride's home on December 28, 1870.

After his marriage, A.C. Weeks bought a farm in the Vineland Community and soon became a model farmer, building barns, sheds, lots etc. that were models for both convenience and stability. He purchased the best machinery and tools and took excelent care of them thus saving much money. In 1888, Absalom's parents, Louis and Betsy Weeks came to Texas to live out their lives and are buried in the Horn Cemetery northeast of Bloomdale. Absalom Weeks was an obliging neighbor, always upright in his dealings, a faithful church member, always on time at the regular services and ready to bear what he considered his part.

Absalom and Mildred Jane Weeks were the parents of ten children—seven of whom lived to adulthood: Nova Louise, who married Ollie Hall; Betty Ann, who married Sam Sproles; Floyd Clark, who married Annie Henry; Carl Lee, who married Ethel Lewis; Jasper Leroy (Jack) who married Ailene Claycomb and after her death, Ruth Campbell Horn; Ella Mildred who married Lem Vernon; and Leta Gertrude, who married Forrest Currell.

Of the seven children of A.C. and Mildred Weeks, the girls were gifted seamstresses and the boys were all good carpenters and farmers. Carl and Ethel Weeks continued to live on the old Weeks place until Carl's death.

Carl and Ethel had five daughters: Cleva, who married Ernest Martin; Aline, who married Dee W. Snodgrass; Ida Jean, who married T.A. Johnson; Floyd Jane, who married Bill Harper; and Louise who married Even Babin. Mrs. Martin and Mrs. Snodgrass presently live in Dallas; Mrs. Johnson lives in San Angelo, Texas; Mrs. Harper lives in Longview, Texas; and Mrs. Babin lives in Chicago, Illinois.

The other son of A.C. and Mildred Weeks, J.L. (Jack) Weeks, survives. Jack has lived in Collin County all of his life, and owns land in the old Vineland community yet, but has lived in the city now for over fifty years. Jack is a fine businessman, good neighbor, with a friendly smile for everyone he meets. For forty-eight years, he had a sausage making plant in the south part of McKinney where he slaughtered and sold his own sausage for sale county wide. When he first started this business, one could also buy a good bucket of lard, but as the years passed, lard was replaced in the home by vegetable shortening. Jack and Ailine Weeks were the parents of two children: Allen Clark Weeks who married Mattie Ruth Winston of Waco, Texas, and their children are Betty Joyce Kaiser, Charles Leroy Weeks, and Margaret Ellen Clark. The second child of Jack and Ailene Weeks was Elizabeth Ailene who passed away in 1943 having never married.

Allen Clark Weeks and wife and oldest daughter, Mrs. Charles Kaiser and family live in Jasper, Texas; Charles Leroy Weeks and family live in Dallas; and Mrs. Wm. D. Clark and family live in Maryland.

Numerous descendants of this fine family yet live in Collin County.

CAPTAIN FRANCIS HENRY WELCH

Captain Francis Henry Welch was born in Monroe County, Alabama, July 26, 1831 and died in Collin County February 22, 1904 and is buried in Pecan Grove Cemetery in McKinney. He acquired the title of Captain by being the commander of a Mississippi River steamboat in his early years. Captain Welch, his wife, Rebecca Ann Brown, and his two sons, Munson F. and John Seawright Johnson Welch, migrated to Texas in a covered wagon in 1859, settling at Mantua.

Capt. Welch enlisted in Company D, 6th Texas Cavalry at Camp Barto, Dallas, Texas on September 7, 1861. Company D fought in some of the fiercest battles of the war. In the Battle of Corinth they went in with 76 men and came out with 36, wading through the Mississippi Swamp they placed the tallest man at the front so that when the water came up to his neck, they knew it was time for the rest to swim. After they finally made their way through the swamps they learned of the surrender.

After the war, he returned to his family at

FRANCIS HENRY WELCH, Captain of a Mississippi river boat, who settled at Mantua, now a ghost town in north Collin County.

Mantua. Besides the two sons, they had a daughter, Rebecca Ellen Welch who was born at Mantua. Another son, Samuel Andrew Welch was born in Alabama in 1856 on a trip the family made to the old home. The family settled on a farm a half mile west of Anna, which was not a town then. The children attended school at Mantua.

In 1872 the family moved to McKinney and Capt. Welch was associated with the firm of Board, Nenney, and Welch Dry Goods and later he and his son Samuel were agents for New York Fire Insurance Company. He built a home west of Anna on his farm in 1901.

Story sent by granddaughter, Rebecca Ann Welch Brune.

THE WHISENANT FAMILY

The first of the Whisenant family to settle in Collin County was Robert Caldwell Whisenant and John Whisenant, settling near present Allen. Robert was born in Georgia in 1811 as was his first wife. Their first child was born on the journey to Texas (Mary E.) and the family stayed in Barry County, Missouri until 1834. Here two other children were

MR. AND MRS. A.B. WHISENANT

born, William Hugh and Martha. They settled in Allen in 1844 and the wife died soon afterward, leaving three small children. He married Matilda Rosenburg and to this union were born seven children, Nancy Sue, Robert Benton, John Wesley, Amanda Jane, Matilda Ann, Margaret Isabelle, and Mathew Mark.

After several years, Robert decided to build his family a new home and went back to Missouri for logs. On the way back to Texas, a storm came up and he and his floating cargo were lost (1856 or

R.B. WHISENANT, age 93 and Edwin Lynge.

283

J.M. (JOHNNY) WHISENANT, president of the Collin County National Bank of McKinney.

1857). His son, John William Hugh, only 16 years old, took charge of the young family left behind. At the outbreak of the Civil War, William joined the Confederate Army and served under Captain William M. Weaver's Company, Martin's Battalion, Mounted Partisans Rangers. He married Mary Elizabeth Blackmore and to this union were born nine children, Helena Elinor, Robert William, Tolbert Riland, Benjamin Christian, Thomas Bedford, Martha Della, Marvin Benton, Edna, and Ida Myrtle. In 1886 this family moved and settled where the town of Hollis, Oklahoma now stands.

Robert Benton Whisenant, another son of Robert Caldwell, enlisted February 20, 1860 and served in Captain G.S. Fitzhugh's Company of Texas Mounted Rangers, with Col. M.T. Johnson in command. He engaged in campaigns against the Kiawas, Kickapoos, and the Commanches in the Indian Territory. In 1861 he enlisted in Joe Dixon's Company under Saur Bell Maxey and in 1862 he was with Captain R.M. Board's Company No. 1 of the 9th Regiment of Texas Infantry under Col. William B. Young.

Milton Whisenant, son of R.B. and Harriet Whisenant, was born near Allen and was married to Ola Stancell of Allen in 1908. One son, John M. Whisenant, was born to this union, June 21, 1919. After service in the United States Navy, he returned to Allen and married Miss Ruth Lindley, a descendent of early settlers of Collin County, Abe Hall. John M. Whisenant has been in banking since 1955 and now serves the Collin County National Bank as its president. He has been a moving force in all civic activities of the community, having served as president of the McKinney Lions Club, Chamber of Commerce, McKinney Jaycees, and the first president of the Industrial Foundation as well as the United Fund. He is a deacon and a teacher in the First Baptist Church of McKinney.

Three children were born to them, John B. (Ben), Bill, and David Whisenant.

GEORGE WILCOX

George Wilcox was born in Collin County October 1, 1862, the son of James M. and Nancy (Throckmorton) Wilcox. His father was among the "Forty-niners" seeking gold in California but returned to Missouri in the early 50's.

After graduating from the University of Missouri he returned to Collin County and became the first merchant of Weston. Later he bought a tract of land in the Rowlett Creek community but in 1872 he moved to Plano where he established the first lumberyard in that town. In 1881 he founded the Wilcox Lumber Co. at McKinney.

During the Civil War James M. Wilcox enlisted in R.W. Carpenter's Company from Collin County and served in Martin's Regiment. He died March 12, 1912 at the age of 84.

George's mother was the daughter of Dr. W.E. Throckmorton, who brought the first settlers into Collin County, and the sister of James W. Throckmorton who was Texas' eleventh governor.

George's grandparents were Lazarus Wilcox of Virginia and Lucy (Helm) Wilcox of Kentucky who moved, after marriage, to Missouri where they organized the first Baptist Church ever organized in that State.

The subject attended the common school of Plano and entered his father's lumber business at the age of 17. Upon his father's death he became president and general manager of the Wilcox Lumber Company in McKinney which he developed and extended becoming supervisor of yards in Melissa, Anna, Princeton, and Allen.

He was organizer and for many years president of the McKinney Building and Loan Association, organizer and director of the McKinney Cotton Mill, on the board of directors of the Collin County National Bank, served more than twenty years on the McKinney School Board and was a member of the Baptist Church.

Mr. Wilcox was married to Maude Wilson, daughter of Lake C. Wilson, a native of Arkansas, on January 10, 1894 and are the parents of the following: Dorothy, wife of Kent D. Allen, an attorney in Dallas; Mary Wilcox, who attended Hollins College in Roanoke, Virginia; Bertha Garnett, wife of John D. Reece, an attorney in McKinney; Maud

Lake Wilcox who attended Christian College in Columbia, Missouri and studied art in Paris, France; and Billy Jean Wilcox who graduated from Hockaday School for Girls in Dallas and attended Baylor University in Waco.

The subject died on August 25, 1928.
Story by Roy F. Hall

THE J.B. WILMETH FAMILY

Joseph Bryson Wilmeth was born in North Carolina, September 11, 1807, the son of William and Mary (Crawford) Wilmeth. When he was still a child the family moved to McNairy County, Tennessee and on December 26, 1826 he was married to Nancy Ferguson, daughter of James and Martha (Hogge) Ferguson, who was a granddaughter of Major Patrick Ferguson who died commanding the British troops at the Battle of King's Mountain during the Revolutionary War. It is interesting to note that Major Ferguson's son, Nancy's father, also fought at the Battle of King's Mountain, but on the side of the Colonists.

In the fall of 1831 Nancy's father headed a wagon train made up of ten families related by blood or by marriage and after a long journey landed in Lawrence County, Arkansas. Here they engaged in farming, raising livestock, and J.B. preached the gospel. During these years he also served as a soldier and helped escort the Choctaw and Cherokee Indians from their homes in that section to the newly formed Indian Territory (later Oklahoma). This march is called by historians "The Trail of Tears."

In 1845 an agent for the Peter's Colony visited their community and J.B. became interested in going to live in this new land just opening up for settlers. In October of 1845 his wagon train moved out, headed for Peter's Colony. The train consisted of the Wilmeth family, Frank Wilmeth, Jordon O. Straughan, and three young men hired to help with the teams. It was a long and hazardous journey, sometimes they had to stop and camp for several days while trees were cut and a bridge built so they could cross uncharted rivers and even small streams. On December 26, 1845 they reached the present site of Dallas and made camp near John Neely Bryan's cabin while the men looked for a suitable location to homestead.

In later years, Martha Wilmeth McKinney wrote, "I remember the Bryan cabin well. It stood on the bank of the river. It was built of unhewn logs and none of the cracks were filled except a few on the north side. It had a cowhide for a door that was

JOSEPH BRICE WILMETH, who established the McKinney Christian Church in 1848.

hung at night on the two pegs above the door. They had a fire built in one corner of the cabin and the smoke went where it could. He had a swinging shelf that held his goods he sold." On New Year's Day of 1846 J.B. Wilmeth and Jordon O. Straughan selected adjacent sections fronting on the river near present Grande Prairie. Life was pleasant for them, game was abundant, a snug cabin was soon built but Indian raids in other settlements kept them on edge.

J.B. told in later years how he was working in his blacksmith shop when a shadow fell across the door. It was an Indian girl and she had come to warn the settlement that plans were to raid this settlement on the next full moon. After much discussion, the wagons were loaded and the site abandoned and they headed back the way they had come, going back to Tennessee. There is a story told about why they did not actually go back home. When they camped one night on the bank of a stream, thinking it was Red River. When the time came for loading the wagons for another day of riding, Nancy took a seat and said that she personally intended to stay forever in this new land. After discussion the wagons were unloaded for the last time and sites were selected for homesteads, not on Red River but on the East Fork of the Trinity two miles north of present McKinney.

An old family receipt dated June 15, 1846 says

285

THE OLD WILMETH CHURCH, 1890.

THE OLD WILMETH home two miles north of McKinney (no longer there). The upper floor was used for one of Collin County's first schools, and for church services with J.B. Wilmeth preaching.

"Received of J.B. Wilmeth two hundred and eight dollars in full consideration for the improvements (cabin) whereon I now live, it being publick land." Signed by M.G. Wilson. With a cabin ready to live in, the family turned at once into making it a home. Wilmeth's first concern was to fence and turn the rich land were unloaded he set up his blacksmith shop and Nancy her loom.

Besides farming he was active in forming the new county. In 1849 when the new courthouse was built he was the District Clerk and later County Judge.

Two years after coming to Collin, he opened a school in a small log cabin just north of the old power house. He and his sons and daughters taught the school until 1855 then moved it to the unfinished upstairs of his two-story home being built. Others taught in the school from time to time— E.W. Kirkpatrick and Anson Mills.

In Collin County, as in Arkansas, Wilmeth made his home a place of worship and in the years that followed he organized many new churches over north Texas. In 1846 he helped organize a church at Liberty and in 1847 organized a church in his home with F.C. Wilmeth, Henry Webb, John Larimore, and James Masters as officers. When the new county was formed, the group decided that the first thing in a new town should be a church, so on Sunday, April 1, 1848, the people, meeting at his home for worship, went to the newly selected site of McKinney and under a big tree, about where the present courthouse is, organized the First Christian Church.

The Civil War brought many changes in the family. J.B. Wilmeth, his eight sons and three sons-in-law all served in the Confederate Army, with J.B. holding the rank of Colonel. Two sons were killed in the war, J.B. Jr. at the Battle of Corinth and W.C. lost in 1864. Only the women and slaves remained at home to keep the farm going. Nancy furnished her soldiers the clothes they wore through the war by spinning and weaving her own wool.

The Wilmeth children were Mary Jane, Mansell W., Martha Marille, Keturah Miranda, James Ransom, Joseph Bryson, William Crawforn, Hiram Ferguson, Nancy Ann, John Ficklin, Andrew Jackson, Collin McKinney, and Sarah Elizabeth. J.B. and Nancy Wilmeth died one day apart in January of 1892 and lie in the McLarry Cemetery.

They have hundreds of descendents, some still living in the area, the Crump family are descendents of Mansell Wilmeth, Clara McKinney Reddell and her brother Ridgell are descended from Martha. The author of this book, Captain Roy Hall, was born in the Wilmeth home and is also a descendent, as is his sister, Mrs. Ora Craft of Sherman.

ADDISON WILSON

Addison Wilson and family came to Collin County from Tennessee in 1849 with a number of other settlers, comprising a caravan of fifteen wagons and carryalls. He settled in the Ash Grove community, six miles north of McKinney. During the same year his son-in-law, Peter R. Wallace, built a log house and a board blacksmith shop on the southeast corner of the square in McKinney. Tom B., Addison, Jr., and Gus hauled supplies and lumber from Jefferson, Pine Mills, and Houston to McKinney, using ox teams.

George A. Wilson preceeded the other members of his family to Texas, arriving in Collin County in 1842, from Tennessee. After serving in the Mexican War he returned to Tennessee and accompanied his parents and family and other settlers to Collin

THE PIONEER HOME of the Add Wilson family built in 1850.

County in 1849. He married Harriett Kincaid. In November, 1867, General J.J. Reynolds appointed him sheriff of Collin County, which office he held until December, 1869. The following children of George A. and Harriett Wilson attended the annual Wilson reunion at Finch Park in McKinney on June 10, 1934: T. Ben, Mrs. W.A. Straughan, George M., Wallace C., Mrs. J. Frank Smith, Mrs. W.A. Massie, and Mrs. George E. Burrage.

Thomas Benton Wilson was born on November 22, 1840, in Tennessee and came to Collin County with his parents in 1849. He had only the meager education obtained in the rural schools but he had great natural ability, so with application he became proficient in mathematics and surveying. In 1861 he joined the Confederate Army but was later given a medical discharge. He and two of his brothers then engaged in farming, stock raising, and freighting. In 1869 he was a deputy sheriff under his brother George. In 1870 Governor E.J. Davis appointed him county surveyor of Collin County, to which position he was later elected five times, serving until 1882.

Always a good businessman, he was one of the organizers of a private bank which is now the Collin County National Bank. He served as a director from the time of its organization until his death on September 3, 1913. In 1908 he owned 5,000 acres of land and offered the state of Texas 460 acres as a site for an A&M College, but this state school was located at Lubbock.

On December 3, 1883, he was married to Henrietta Estes. A son, Add G. Wilson, is a former city commissioner of McKinney, a former president of the Central State Bank, and now resides in McKinney.

Augustus M. (Gus) Wilson was born in Tennessee on February 8, 1845, and came to Collin County with his parents in 1849. He never married and lived his entire life in the log house which his father built in 1850. Shunning every touch of modern life except the automobile, he was as typical in pioneer habits and dress as was his father who brought him to Texas. His funeral expenses were all paid nine years before his death, which occurred on October 1, 1935. He was buried in the family burial grounds adjacent to the house, where his parents and some other members of the family are buried. A life-sized reproduction of his faithful dog rests on top of his tombstone with the name ''Joe'' carved on it. The epitaph is simple: "Wilson. Joe and I are going home. A.M. (Gus) Wilson. 1845-1935." As unassuming in death as in life, he was one of Collin County's greatest philanthropists. During the last few years of his life, Mr. and Mrs. Cliff A. Robinson lived in the house with him; so he gave the farm and home to them.

On October 23, 1935, the Texas State Senate passed the following resolution as a memorial to him: . . . .

Senate Resolution No. 7

Whereas, There has come to the attention of this body the death of A.M. Wilson, distinguished philanthropist of Collin County;

Whereas, This illustrious citizen has during his lifetime distributed among his fellow citizens his entire fortune of $800,000.00 among worthy citizens and for worthy purposes;

Whereas, He has paid salaries of school teachers when this state failed to pay them;

Whereas, He has built churches without regard to denomination, built schoolhouses, saved farms from foreclosure and has been a helpful friend to the poor and oppressed; therefore, be it

Resolved, That a committee of three members of this body be appointed by the presiding officers of this body to procure and have prepared a portrait of said A.M.Wilson and that it be hung in this senate chamber as a guiding inspiration to aid in bringing about unselfish service in behalf of the needy and that $500.00, or so much as may be necessary, be appropriated out of the contingent fund for that purpose.

Westerfield
Isbell
Burns

Uncle Gus Wilson, Philanthropist

When A.M. (Uncle Gus) Wilson died he left behind one of the most philanthopic histories in Collin county. It was known that he gave away $750,000 during a period in which that amount of money would equal millions today.

Not only did Uncle Gus give away money, but also big farms. When automobiles were new to the county, Wilson went to a Dallas car dealer with intentions of purchasing a dozen new cars to give away. Dressed as usual in shabby overalls, Uncle Gus caused suspicion in the mind of the dealer when offering a check for his purchase. The dealer called the bank in McKinney to determine if the check was good. The reply was, "If you put a price on your dealership, Mr. Wilson can write a check to cover

it."

Wilson was described this way in a piece written by Jack Estes for the Farm News in 1916.

"Texas has a citizen who conducts a peculiar business, an undertaking which throws him into a field of little or no competition. This man, a stirring pioneer of Texas soil, is engaged in making others happy—doing good for his fellow man, providing homes for worthy farmers and educating poor children. He works quietly and cautiously and above all, modestly."

Estes continued, "Simplicity is his watchword—next to modesty. He finds worthy, hard-working families struggling with the proverbial 'wolf at the door' and many other adversities that many other problems that many tenant farmers wrestle with every day in the year, and presents them with small farms; he sees men toiling from sun to sun to pay off the mortgages on their homes, and makes them a present of their mortgage.

"Then he picks out a community without school facilities and builds school houses and endows them handsomely for their maintenance."

One of Wilson's favorite ploys was to drive on back roads on Saturday afternoon when most farmers were in town enjoying life on the shady front porch of the country store, or perhaps a saloon. If Uncle Gus happened to see a share-cropper chopping cotton at this time of day, he might very well buy the farm and deed it to the industrious worker.

As the photograph accompanying this article will attest, Uncle Gus Wilson lived modestly. He died penniless.

Elder R.C. Horn of the Christian Church paid the last tribute to the pioneer who gave away all of his worldly possessions. Wilson was buried in the now overgrown family plot, only a few paces from his faithful dog that died some years earlier.

It is so typical that the dog has a handsome tombstone.

THE JOHN K. WILSON FAMILY

This branch of the Wilson family came from twin brothers; Zackies and David Wilson's parents were from Ireland but they were born in Pennsylvania.

Zachies Wilson moved from Pennsylvania to Mecklinburg County, Carolina in 1796. Later he moved to Sumner County, Tennessee. Zackies Wilson married Keziah Alexander and the couple had two sons, Johnathan and John. Johnathan Wilson married Narcissa Wilson, a cousin. They had five children, Margie, Hiram, Addison, Thiresa, and

William.

Addison Wilson married Ann Moore and had the following children: George A. Wilson married Harriet Kincaid, Martha C. married P.R. Wallis, T.B. Wilson who married Etta Estes and A.M. (Gus) Wilson.

George A. Wilson was born January 1, 1828 and died March 6, 1895. He married Harriet Kincaid and had 13 children. Alma Wilson, the first child, married Nancy Elizabeth Straughan and their first child was John K. Wilson. He was named John Kincaid Wilson for his great grandfather.

John K. Wilson first married Jimmie Lee Graham on December 26, 1905 and Jimmie Lee died June 24, 1912, leaving two small sons, Wilbur and Malcolm. Malcolm Wilson still lives in McKinney and Wilbur in Tyler. John K.'s second wife was Miss Emma Lee Anderson (January 1, 1914). Two daughters were born to them.

Both John K. Wilson and his father and mother never lived out of Collin County, living out a lifetime here helping to build a county.

HOGAN WITT FAMILY

Hogan Witt was born in Jefferson County, Tennessee, July 21, 1824, and is the tenth child of a family of thirteen born to Eli Witt, of Virginia, and his wife, Nancy McNealy Witt, daughter of an Irish gentleman. When but five years of age, Hogan was taken by his parents to Greene County, Illinois, and there he lived with them until 1844, when he came to Texas, and in 1846 located a headright of 320 acres, on which he has ever since resided, in Collin County, Texas.

Having improved his raw land to some extent, Mr. Witt served eleven months in the Mexican War in 1847; in August, 1848, he married Miss Louisa Rattan, daughter of Thomas Rattan, of Illinois legislature, came to Texas in 1844, and here ended his earthly career. The quiet farm life of Mr. Witt was rudely interrupted by the breaking out of the Civil War, but it was not until 1863 that he enlisted; he then entered Captain Throckmorton's company, Stone's regiment, in Magruder's command, and served in Louisiana and Arkansas chiefly until the close of the war, when he returned to his home and has ever since enjoyed a peaceful life. To his marriage were born six children, named Laura A., John W., Lucy, William E., Orleana C. and Mary J.

Mrs. Witt departed this life on September 5, 1880.

The Examiner, McKinney, Texas, February 20, 1941
Came To Collin County
Nearly Century Ago

These three Collin County pioneers, long since have crossed the Great Divide, are, left, James M. Graves, a short sketch of whose life is given in the current chapter on the Anna church history; center, Hogan Witt, and right, Robert H. Brown, father of the late George P. Brown.

Hogan Witt was born in Tennessee, July 21, 1824. He was the tenth child of 13 children born to Eli Witt, a Virginian, and Nancy McNeal Witt.

His parents moved to Illinois in 1829, from where Mr. Hogan Witt came to Texas in 1844 in company with John Coffman and others. In 1846. he headrighted 320 acres of land 13 miles southwest of McKinney, and two years later became a charter member of the Rowlett's Creek Baptist church. In that same year, 1848, Mr. Witt married Miss Louisa Rattan, daughter of Thomas Rattan, who also came from Illinois in 1844.

Bro. Hogan Witt was a veteran of the Mexican War and of the Civil War, serving under Capt. (later Governor) Throckmorton's Company, in Stone's Regiment, Magruder's Command. Bro. Witt died in 1905, in his 82nd year.

Robert H. Brown was born in Virginia in 1827. His grandfather, Lon Brown, served with George Roger Clark in the American Revolution and was present when Clark captured Vincennes. Mr. Brown came to Texas, crossing Red River at Old Fort Warren, a few miles north of Bonham, December 18, 1845. Mr. Brown married Miss Elizabeth Russell in 1850, and built a log cabin home on Rowlett's Creek, later locating on Spring Creek about three miles northwest of the present city of Plano. He passed away in 1889, according to his son, the late George P. Brown of McKinney.

CHARLES H. WYSONG

Charles Hopkins Wysong, one of the pioneer settlers of the Highland Community, was born in Franklin County, Virginia, the son of Jacob and Mary Hopkins Wysong, the daughter of Charles Hopkins who was one of the Hopkins family of Pennsylvania. Four children were born to this union. Charles H., the third child, was reared on his father's farm and early learned the art of a tanner's trade. He was also a blacksmith and a wheelwright who became famous for his Bois d'Arc wagons that were much in demand among the freighters. In 1846 he moved to Missouri and in 1849 came to Texas to settle. He was first married in Missouri to Sarah M. Foster, daughter of James Foster of Virginia, and to this union were born four children, two dying in infancy. Theresa and James H. survived. Sarah died soon after coming to Texas April 29, 1850. On September 27, 1866 he married Elizabeth R. Slaughter daughter of James Slaughter, a a native of Kentucky and a descendant of Captain James Slaughter, a Revolutionary War veteran. To them were born the following children: Anna M., Charles L., Louis W., Mary L., Hampton S., Alice M., and Walter Scott.

At the beginning of the Civil War, Charles H. Wysong was a member of the State Militia and was appointed by the confederacy to be chairman of a group of prosperous farmers whose purpose was to keep the troops fed and the war widows and their children fed also. His assignment was to design and make machinery that could be used on Collin County farms to replace the manpower that the war effort had taken away. When the Conscript Act was amended to take in men 45 and over, he joined the Confederate Army and was a part of Burnett's Batallion for the duration of the war and was serving in the Houston area when the war ended.

He came home from the war and he and his brothers-in-law, I.N. and James H. Foster, reopened the blacksmith shop and continued to supply the freighters with wagons until the coming of the railroad in 1872 put an end to the freighting from Jefferson.

When Highland became the first post office north of McKinney, he was appointed postmaster. He also served Collin County as a County Commissioner, as a Justice of the Peace, and as the County Tax Assessor-Collector. In politics he was an old line Whig, and was an active supporter of such men as Horace Greeley, William Henry Harrison, and Henry Clay. He was a Baptist by faith, and was high in Masonic circles. He organized more Masonic Lodges than any other individual in the State of Texas, and held many offices.

Dr. Walter Scott Wysong, the youngest son of Charles Hopkins and Elizabeth, became one of the most prominent surgeons in the Southwest. He was born at his father's farm March 9, 1880. He decided on a medical career early in life, in fact he was a young boy and was chopping cotton beside the road leading to his home when a doctor came to attend one of the family. He was well dressed and driving a beautiful horse hitched to a fine buggy and made such an impression on the child that he decided then and there that a doctor he would be. He worked hard and won a teacher's certificate at age 17, and by saving his money he earned teaching for two years, he was able to continue his education in the medical field. He graduated from the Texas Medical Branch at Galveston in 1903 and was awarded resident physician at John Sealy Hospital, a teaching institution associated with the University of Texas.

He returned to his home in Melissa, Texas in 1904 and on March 4, 1905 he married Mary Lee Dudley, a graduate nurse from John Sealy Hospital, who worked beside him and shared the responsibilities of his work.

Walter Scott Wysong was the first to perform major surgery in Collin County. He moved to McKinney in 1913, where he gained his reputation as a surgeon. Many of the major operations from 1905 until 1920 were performed in the home of the patient, and until 1915 most were done on the kitchen or dining room table. Mrs. Vernice Jones, whom he personally trained in surgical techniques, was his assistant from 1913 to 1920. In 1915 a portable operating table became available and he purchased one. In 1916 he moved his family into a large 12 room house. Five of the rooms were used as a hospital for the care of patients. The above mentioned table was set up in the front room and when the operation was completed, the table was dismantled and stored in a closet or put in the back of the automobile for use in the next operation.

In 1920 the City of McKinney began planning and building a City Hospital and Walter S. Wysong was a moving force in its operation. His work here won him the Fellowship in the American College of Surgeons.

In 1930 Dr. Wysong built and equipped one of the finest clinics in the Southwest and in 1961 a sixty-five bed hospital was added to the medical center. He, always the chief, and his three sons, Scott, Dudley and Charles, operated the clinic and hospital alone until the patient load necessitated the addition of other physicians to the staff. In 1974, the staff consists of: W.S. Wysong, Chief Surgeon, H. Dudley Wysong, M.D., Proctology and Surgery, Charley E. Wysong, M.D., Obstetrics and Gynecology, M. Irondo, M.D., General Surgery, J.W. Frank, DSP, Podiatrist, Billy R. Boring, M.D., Medicine and Obstetrics, S.M. Fantony, M.D., Pediatrics and Medicine, B.J. Parnell, M.D., Radiology, T.E. Adams, M.D., Consultant in Pathology, L.B. McCarley, D.D.S., Dentistry.

Charles Bradford Wysong, son of Dr. Charley E. Wysong, a 1973 graduate of the University of Texas Medical Branch at San Antonio. H. Dudley

Wysong Jr., and David Charles Wysong, the sons of H. Dudley Wysong, run the business offices of the medical complex. On March 6, 1967, the Wysong Nursing Center, a 112 bed complex for the care of the elderly, was dedicated to the memory of their mother and father by the three Wysong sons.

Walter Scott Wysong was a modest and humble man who received many honors and awards for his humanitarian work. He was a 32nd degree Scottish Rite Mason and Shriner of Hella Temple. He died February 13, 1965. Here was a man who began his practice of medicine from a horse drawn buggy, and who progressed to the practice of medicine in as well equipped clinic and hospital as can be found. There must have been a great satisfaction in the realization of the dreams of the little cotton chopper.

Story submitted by his sons.

ENOCH YANTIS

Jacob Yantis, father of Enoch Yantis, was an original landed proprietor of Lancaster, Pa. He migrated from his native Germany prior to the Revolutionary War in which struggle he valiantly participated in a number of battles. Later he settled on Dick's River in Lincoln County, Kentucky, and here married Ruth Chrysman, daughter of a prominent farmer and stockman of that section of Kentucky. From that union five sons and three daughters were born, John, Mary, Amos, Rebecca, Aaron, Enoch, Jesse, and Polly.

Enoch, the fourth son, was born December 4, 1794 and on June 11, 1816 he was married to Eleanor Wolford, daughter of Major John Wolford. They became the parents of five sons and five daughters, John, George, James, William, Jesse, Ruth Jane, Mary Ann, Emily Carolyn, Amanda, and Elizabeth Margaret. By trade Enoch Yantis was a tanner who followed that trade until 1835 when his home burned, destroying all his records and possessions. He farmed until 1852 and in 1859 left Kentucky to join his son, George Reynolds Yantis, in Collin County. In that same year he served as Deputy Tax Assessor-Collector for Collin County under John M. McKinney. Enoch succeeded Mr. McKinney in the office. Politically he was a Whig until the Civil War, after which he became a staunch Democrat.

At the close of the War George R. Yantis was left destitute as so many were. He joined his father in tax assessing, he also served as deputy under Sheriff W.H. Bush. George R. Yantis was elected first Tax-Collector under the new constitution which

CAPT. R.M. BOARD

separated the office of Tax Assessor and that of Sheriff. Mrs. Enoch Yantis died on October 26, 1871 and Enoch died October 11, 1879. Both lie in Rowlette Cemetery.

Story sent by great granddaughter, Mrs. Ollyne Yantis (Sterling) Bailey, head of the DAR Chapter in McKinney.

CAPT. ROBERT MILTON BOARD

Capt. Board was born in Virginia in May of 1837 and came to McKinney to live in 1856. He served in the Confederate Army and when Dixon was killed at the Battle of Shiloh, Lt. Board was made a Captain, one of the youngest in the army. After the war when he surrendered in Alabama he returned to McKinney and became a partner of I.D. Newsome and on April 25, 1866hhe married Mrs. Newsome's sister, A.E. Willingham. Board and Newsome operated a successful general merchandising store and were the first to buy cotton locally, even taking cotton in on accounts, shipping it to Jefferson, by wagon. An old clipping tells how Board ordered a wagon load of cow bells one time to accommodate the farmers who were having trouble keeping up with their cows that ran loose everywhere. He died April 10, 1931 at the age of 94.

Microfilmed biographies at McKinney Library: October 29, 1930, April 11, 1931.

ISAAC JEFFERSON DOTSON
C.S.A. Soldier
1831-1903

Isaac Jefferson Dotson, son of Thomas Jefferson Dotson and Sally Ann Dotson, was born near Russelville, Arkansas in 1831 and came with his parents to now Blue Ridge Collin County, Texas sometime in the 1840's. In 1856 he married his distant cousin, Mary Jane Hanson, daughter of James and Jerushia Hanson, and granddaughter of George Washington Smith, who fought in the War of Texas Independence, and who had early settled in this "Ridge" settlement.

The young couple were happily making themselves a home on their land—Ike Dotson trades his horse and saddle for his land, where the present Blue Ridge High School stands—near her grandfather's when the Civil War began. Taking his own horse and gun Ike enlisted at once. Young Mary with two baby daughter and expecting a third child, courageously carried on the clearing and planting with the help of their one good slave couple, Wylie and Becky, who had a family of small children of their own.

In August, 1861, Isaac Dotson was badly wounded at the Battle of Wilson Creek near Springfield, Missouri. With other wounded, both Union and Confederate, he was carried from the field and became a prisoner-patient at an old Catholic institution being used as a Union hospital. Here he was given medical attention and his wounds dressed but the minnie ball was too near his heart to be removed and he carried it the rest of his life.

The Union doctors and staff must have liked this quiet young Texian. They treated him better than he ever expected. When Christmas came that year all the Northern patients around were receiving gifts and packages. Ike, of course received none, but a young Union patient near him spoke up: "Say, this dam Rebel here hasn't got a thing. I'm going to give him part of mine."

Isaac had been raised by hardworking Baptist parents, who frowned upon card playing, but in spite of this, he had learned to play a pretty good game of poker. As soon as he was able to sit up, he was indulging in this pastime with the other patients at the hospital. Even the doctors and staff members joined in the game sometimes, it was said.

So it was, that later on, when he was exchanged, this young Texian came riding home with quite a few "Yankee" dollars in his saddle pockets. These went to buy some black waxy acres near his own small place. It was not the Yankee money, how-

ISAAC JEFFERSON DOTSON, CSA Volunteer Mounted Cavalry.

ever, that caused the most commotion in the Ridge neighborhood—No!—that was this wounded Confederate's sincere statement: that actually "Some Yankees were good people!"

After a short time of convalescense, Isaac Dotson went back into service. On March 1, 1862 he was mustered into Capt. Hezekiah Warden's Co., 16th Reg., Texas Cavalry Volunteers. Commanded by Col. Wm. Fitzhugh of Collin County.

Later on we find Isaac Dotson stationed at Ft. Washita in the Indian Territory north of Red River, serving the Confederacy as dispatcher between Ft. Washita, Boggy Depot, and Ft. Smith and between the armies of Van Dorn and Price.

For him this was a good assignment. He was near enough home that an occasional furlough enabled him to help and advise Mary on running the farm and her other endeavors, which by this time included a project sponsored by their Collin County friend, James W. Throckmorton, who was gaining influence in the Confederate administration. He managed to get a contract for the women to weave material and make it up into suits for the men and officers of the Confederate Army. Mary, being an accomplished seamstress, was a leader in this patriotic work.

**THE OLD DOTSON PLACE, Blue Ridge, Texas.
After Battle of Wilson Creek, while a prisoner,
Isaac Dotson was impressed by the fine big farms
up north. He came back and bought one as soon
as he could afford it.**

Isaac continued at Ft. Washita until the end of the
war, enjoying a game of poker with the boys whenever he had a chance. As the Confederate notes
grew less and less in value his winnings, which he
continued to take to Mary "to put into land or
something useful," became so bulky as to nearly fill
a trunk it was said.

One "useful" thing these notes probably bought
was baby dresses. Their fourth child, a son, was
born July 5, 1865, and the little long dresses which
awaited him were of "cream colored calico with a
tiny pink rosebud," which Mary had purchased of
Ben Rhine's Store at McKinney—paying the price
of thirty-five dollars per yard in Confederate money.

After the war, with his surviving neighbors,
Isaac came home hoping to work his land and live in
peace as before.

In 1866 Throckmorton was elected governor of
Texas and began at once to bring back order to the
country. He proposed a plan whereby, if agreed to
by both parties, freed slaves could remain in their
homes and sharecrop their former master's land.
This would provide a way for both the ex-slave and
the ex-master to feed their families in this time of
terrible hunger and hardship. Wylie and Becky
chose to remain, as did many other Negroes in the
Blue Ridge area.

But the ax fell again! General Phillip Sheridan,
the popular hero of Northern Radicals because of his
bold blows on the dying Confederacy, was made
commander of the 5th Military District, which
included Texas. The hard blunt Sheridan welcomed
a chance to punish and humiliate the people of the
South. He soon removed the elected Texas Governor, James W. Throckmorton from office and the
country was at the mercy of Carpet Bagger rule!

Loyal Negroes like Wylie and Becky were persuaded or forced to leave the land and protection of
their former masters, while many of the weaker and
less intelligent, became victims of unscrupulous
whites and were led into lives of crime.

But President Johnson finally got up the courage
to remove Sheridan by giving him another assignment, and at last, people could start rebuilding their
ravaged country again. Isaac and Mary Dotson lived
out their lives at Blue Ridge. Of the twelve children
born to them, eight daughters and one son lived to
have families of their own, so their descendants in
Collin County are many.

The daughters were: Parlee, married Gabe Wor-
den; Nancy, married Sam Jones; Elzora, married
Ben Eakle; Alice J., married George McCoy;
Annie C., married Tom Wyrick; Nettie C. married
Ferd. Simmons; Edna, married Lige Parker; and
Mollie, married Green Dowland.

The son was James Pinckney Dotson who married Leanna Helen McKinney. Later they moved to
the Chickasaw nation in the Indian Territory. He
was given the appointment by Gov. Johnston of the
Chickasaw Nation to survey and settle Indians on
their allotments.

JAMES McKINNEY

James Jefferson (Pony) McKinney was born in
the Ridge settlement, now Blue Ridge, on October
25, 1862, at the home of his mother's father, John
Griffith—as his father, Sam J. McKinney, was
away in the Confederate Army.

As a small child, he recalls many incidents of the
bitter Reconstruction Days, like the times armed
military men from Pilot Grove rode up and demanded Simpson Dixon, then searched the house—
came back a number of times.

Mrs. Clarissa Griffith Dixon, who lived at Blue
Ridge, was stepmother of General Dixon, cousin of
Simp, and was a sister of Mrs. Sam McKinney.

The entire Blue Ridge area was terrorized by the
Peacock-Boren gang during the years after the war.
The Sam McKinney home place was one mile west
of "The Ridge," on a hill widely known as
"McKinney Hill." "A hard pull for a load of
cotton," they said.

Right after the war, three young men put up a log
store in the settlement. They were Myers, Burg-
houser, and Pace. One of the three gave the name

293

JAMES M. McKINNEY on his 98th birthday.

LIST OF SCHOOLS

Mr. McKinney taught first at Rock Rest School, a "free" school situated some three or four miles East of McKinney, when he was about 20 years of age and received $40.00 per month pay. Because he had typhoid fever, the school was put off until after Christmas, and was finally started early in January, 1883. He boarded at Wilson's for $9.00 per month.

In the fall of 1883, he taught at Johnson School in Sister Grove, 12 or 13 miles east of McKinney for $50.00 per month and boarded at Allen Mantooth's.

His third school started in 1884, Moreland School at Blue Ridge and boarded at Hans Johnson's, his brother-in-law.

He started the fall of 1885 at Red Oak and taught eight years there. He was married on Dec. 26, 1886. About 1892-94, he taught one year at Valdasta for $50.00 per month. He went back to Red Oak School in 1894-95 at $50.00 per month and stayed four years there.

From 1898-1901, he taught at the Flowers School, three miles north of Red Oak, for $50.00 per month and returned to Red Oak in 1901 for one year,

He moved to Jones County in October, 1902, and taught four years at Liberty Hill at a salary of $65.00 per month.

Leter he moved to Coke County in January, 1907, where he taught for seven years at the Powell School, for $50.00 per month.

He quit in 1914 to run his ranch, consisting of two sections of land in Coke County, and his store and post office at Divide, Texas.

Blue Ridge to the settlement, since the location was on a Blue Ridge—easily seen from a distance—long called "The Ridge."

He attended his first school in about 1867. His father, Sam J. McKinney, was teacher and the school house was a log cabin, split log benches and dirt floor, supposed to have been built before the war just north of the "Ridge" on the George W. Smith land.

Mr. Smith, a veteran of the Texas War of Independence and a progressive pioneer settler, had a great number of grandchildren; so was, no doubt, instrumental in getting the school built. These grandchildren and great grandchildren attended this first Blue Ridge School, the Pruetts, Harts, Cantrells, Wardens, Dotsons, Langhams, Hansons. And from then on down to the present, every term of Blue Ridge School has had its quota of George W. Smith's descendants on its rolls.

One of the great granddaughters, Missouri Jane Cantrell, married her teacher at the Red Oak School. The teacher was James J. McKinney.

In 1872 the log school house was moved to Blue Ridge town, dressed up with a new puncheon floor, and used for about nine years more. Then it was torn down and the "Old" Blue Ridge School was built on the ground.

JAMES BOYS AND QUANTRILL IN COLLIN COUNTY

The James brothers and their men were frequent visitors to Collin County during the Civil War and the years following. To better understand why the people of Collin County and McKinney were always glad to see them one must understand the conditions as they were in the county after the war. The people were almost to the point of destitution as there was little or no money to be had and most of the capital was controlled by the northern people that swarmed to the south to take advantage of the land and businesses they could take over by one means or another. Sometimes their methods were not so gentle and most of the time were not even legal. But the north had appointed the judges and

294

magistrates in the defeated south and they proceeded to work with the carpetbaggers in acquired misgotten gains and waht they called "spoils of war." So it is easy to see why the south made heroes of the James boys and other bandits that were performing depredations only against the north and northern held institutions.

In the fall of 1866 General Sherman sent mule buyers all over north Texas to purchase mules to replenish the stock lost in the recent war. The purchasing agnet assigned to McKinney and the surrounding area was Col. George Brackett. Colonel Brackett worked through buyers he sent out to gather the mules and to bring them to McKinney to keep in big enclosures of the city, called mule pens. At this time there were about 400 mules in the huge corral awaiting inspection by Col. Brackett the following morning. The Collin County Sheriff, Bill Warden, was eating supper at the Wild Cat Tavern when a local man of his acquaintance stopped at his table and asked the sheriff if he did not have some business out of town for an hour or two. The sheriff declared that he did need to check on a few things and left. In twenty minutes men began gathering behind the Wild Cat Tavern. Cole Younger, Jim Cummings, and Frank James arrived first followed shortly by Jesse James and several others. The men, fourteen in all, mounted horses and rode into the brush behind the tavern and circled around to the corral where the mules were kept.

The man guarding the stock was surprised and disarmed. Quickly now the mounted men herded the mules from the enclosure and gently started hazing them north. There was no trouble driving the herd along and five miles north of McKinney the guard was given his emptied pistol back and was told he could return home now if he so desired. The man quickly declined this by stating that the "Feds" would not believe he was innocent anyway and would prefer to stay with them if they would so allow. Just before noon the next day they reached and forded the Red River a mile above the Colbert Ferry. After letting the herd graze for a period, they drove the mules into Fort Washita as the army had a quartermaster there. The quartermaster was happy to get such fine stock and paid the men $56,000. The James boys and a few of the old Quantrill riders promptly pocketed the money and rode away. Just before dark a rider arrived from McKinney with details of the theft and was laughed at by the Colonel in charge for he believed this was just a plot to gain payment for the mules twice; for after all he had in his files a note to pay the herd drivers upon delivery of the mules.

And the note was signed by Col. Brackett, so as far as he could see the matter was closed. No other payment of any kind was ever made and ano amount of persuasion convinced the Colonel that the note was a forgery. Of course, the gang was persued from McKinney as soon as the theft was discovered by Sheriff Warden. The posse proceeded north about six miles, where they set up camp and went hunting. They saddled up the next day and returned to McKinney where they reported the thieves, who ever they were, had escaped into Indian Territory to the north and were gone as far as persuit was concerned.

After the war most of the Quantrill followers went home and took the oath of allegiance. But not so the James brothers and many of the old band. When the activity in Missouri became lax or when things began to get too hot for them, they would come to McKinney where they had many friends and could feel safe. They made their headquarters at the spacious Graves ranch on the outskirts of the city, and there was very good reason for this as this ranch was a social gathering place for a lot of the old Civil War veterans of the county. Many of the men that gathered there were old riding comrades of the James and Quantrill.

In fact, Graves set aside two rooms for the Quantrill men to use when ever they were in the vicinity. If more than the usual number of men arrived at the same time, they were allowed to take their ease in the huge barn. Needless to say, this Graves ranch was the perfect place for the Quantrill men to stay and appreciate. They were well known and liked on the streets of McKinney as the following statement will show. Once when Frank James was staying at the Graves home he decided to ride to the town of Denton to th west. At the time he decided to take this trip, there was a Federal Govt. man staying at the old Tucker Hotel in town.

Somehow the Govt. man heard that Frank James was on his way west of the city alone and proceeded to enlist the aid of some McKinney men to help him bring in this famous outlaw as most of them knew Frank on sight and he did not. As the men in the posse raced west on the road James had taken some of the men beginning shouting the old "Rebel Yell." The Govt. man was well pleased with his posse as he heard them yelling in their excitement. Ahead on the road, Frank James was in no hurry, riding slowly and enjoying the brisk fall morning as he made his way to Denton. Hearing the old "Rebel Yell," he immediately turned and rode back to meet the riders from McKinney, most of whom he knew immediately. As he drew to a stop, the Govt.

man demanded to know his name and what he was doing out on this road. Before he could answer, a man in the crowd spoke up and announced that this was John Smith, or something like that, and asked Frank if he had seen anyone riding west as they were in hot persuit of the desperate outlaw, Frank James. Frank replied that he surely had seen someone riding toward Denton in a big hurry. At this the posse rushed off westward trying to overtake Frank James. As soon as they were out of sight, James returned to McKinney to the home of Tuck Hill and was sitting on the porch with Tuck when the posse came back in a couple of hours. Tuck Hill called to the men and asked what such a large group of men was doing riding around the country. Some of the men in the posse replied that they were helping the Government by trying to chase down Frank James, and surely didn't Tuck know what a dangerous man James was. The posse disbanded at the old Rock Front Saloon, a favorite of the James boys, and had a few drinks to toast the great help they had been to the Federal Government. To understand the feelings of these men it must be remembered that Collin County had given and lost over 1000 of her finest young men to the war and feelings were still that if one could he would do anything to hurt or hinder the hated Yankees.

During and after the Civil War there were many deserters and draft dodgers from both the north and the south hiding in a great swamp just south of McKinney. This swamp was called Jernigan's swamp and was where Finch Park is now located. These renegades were called ''Bushwhackers'' and made life miserable for the surrounding area. At night they would slip out and steal food and anything else they could find. With nearly all the able bodied men of the county away at war, they had things just to their liking. At last the people of McKinney sent an appeal to Quantrill, who was camped at Sherman, Texas, to come down and give them some relief from these bushwhackers. Quantrill immediately arrived with a company of his best men and surrounded the swamp. As the day progressed, Quantrill's men captured 42 bushwhackers and marched them to the town square. Once there Quantrill's men hung all 42 men from a limb on the southeast corner of the square by the large public well. So much blood ran into the well, it was covered over and never used again. A new well had to be dug on the northwest corner of the square.

In the town of McKinney there were not many people who were not all for the South and its cause, but there were a few union sympathizers. Not too much is known of the only battle fought in the war

happening in Collin County, if a battle it could be called. It took place in 1863 on south Tennessee street.

At that time Quantrill and his partisan riders had arrived in McKinney from Sherman and had taken rooms in the Tucker Hotel on the northeast corner of the square. They had come, they said, to kill the sheirff of Collin County, one James Reed. The reason they were going to kill him was not made known. When Reed heard this news, he gathered together some of his followers about him and rode to the southwest corner of the square. But since Reed had only eighteen men and Quantrill had sixty, Reed and his men withdrew down Tennessee street and took cover in the mill that was not completed and had lots of large rocks lying about. As Reed's men took shelter behind the large rock, Quantrill and his men took up positions a short way to the north and began firing. Many shots were fired on each side from mid-morning until into the evening when it got too dark to see a target. All of the sheriff's men had their horses killed and some of his men were gravely injured. As soon as dark permitted, all Reed's men went home, leaving only Reed and one other man. This man was J.M. McReynolds from Kaufman County. He was in Collin Co. searching for the robbers that had robbed and killed his neighbor, Mr. Lackey. Lackey had been killed earlier in the week and McReynolds was here on their trail. Why he was with Reed that day and didn't leave him is not known. As darkness covered their escape, Reed and McReynolds borrowed horses and attempted to get away down the old Millwood road. As Quantrill had many sympathizers in McKinney, he was soon advised of the escape route and made haste to capture the two before they got away. The next afternoon Quantrill and his men caught up with the pair and proceeded to hang them from a large cottonwood limb overhanging the Millwood road. Reed left only one son whereas the luckless Mr. J.M. McReynolds left a very large family of children.

As has been stated, the James boys had not many enemies in Collin County. In the year 1866. there was to be a great dinner party given at the house of one of the leaders of the community of Rhea Mills. The people invited were the Union sympathizers and carpetbaggers now infesting the County. Needless to say the poor farmers of the county were not invited as were not any but those whose feelings lay in the north. This had been a poor year for crops and agriculture and many were to the point of desperation in their search for either food or money so as to feed their families. On this particular night of the party, several men gathered just outside the community of Rhea Mills. If any one saw these men no one commented to the authorities as the constable was not one of those invited to the banquet. As soon as it was dark, the men, now masked, stole to their places around the large house. The revelry was very loud inside and no one suspected anything until masked men, revolvers held ready, burst in every door with the order not to move. The great table was loaded with food the likes of which no one in the county had seen in many years. Also were gifts to each of the guests of reportedly great value. As the amassed guests stood with their mouths agape, each table covering was folded loosely around its contents and sprited away into the dark. After a brief warning to the assembled guests not to be so rash as to try to follow, the remaining raiders swept away into the night. Later that same night the citizens of McKinney were invited to come to the square in town and pick out something to take home to their families or to eat on the spot for there was four tables set up on the street with fancy tablecloths. The food for the most part was a little mashed but to these folks nothing could have been finer. No one asked where the food had come from as they knew if Frank and Jesse James and Cole Younger wanted them to know, they would have told them. It was not until the next day the story of the raid was known and then to the disgrace of most people, it was discovered that most of the dinner guests at Rhea Mills had been armed and di not have the nerve to draw and fire their weapons. This amde the humiliation complete and also to turn away any sympathy they might have gotten from the people of Collin County.

There were many instances of the James boys doing fine things for the people of Collin County but it would be very hard to find a family in the county that would speak harshly of them even after a hundred years. They may have been wrong in most of the things they did, but it is not for mortal man to say.

BOYD FAMILY

When the 1850 census was taken in Henry County, Tennessee, Joseph Boyd, age 49, gave his occupation as farmer and his birthplace as Virginia. His wife, Hannah Boyd, age 45, gave her birthplace as Kentucky. They listed ten children. The oldest two were boys whose birthplace was given as Tennessee. Their names were Paschall C. and Hiram G. The next four children, James F., Joseph B.B., Miranda and Alfred were listed as having been born in Kentucky. The four youngest, Mordicia, Calvin V., Berstamente and Darinada O. were listed as having been born in Tennessee. On December 5, 1853, Joseph Boyd bought approximately 950 acres of land from John L. Hughe in the S.M. Rainer Survey, Abstract No. 740 and the D. Anglin Survey, Abstract No. 2 for Fifteen Hundred Dollars (Volume G, Page 116, Collin County Deed Records).

At this time, there was no community known as Lavon. To the north, Miles Cope, his brother James and his father Mason had settled in 1848. The settlement took the name of Copeville in honor of Miles Cope, their first postmaster. Stambaugh and Stambaugh, History of Collin County, Texas, Page 74 lists Joseph Boyd as one of the early settlers in this community. To the south of the present town of Lavon, D. Anglin had established his headright in about 1846 and had started a settlement that later became known as Millwood. On May 21, 1851, when James Smith was made postmaster at Millwood, there was only one community that had a postmaster and that was McKinney, Joel F. Stewart, having been appointed on May 31, 1848. The land purchased by Joseph Boyd was an 800 acre tract in the D. Anglin Survey, the south part of which was very close to the Millwood settlement. The 150 acre tract was bound on the west and north by Bear Creek and on the south by the south boundary line of the S.M. Rainer Survey and the north boundary line of D. Anglin Survey and on the east by the line between the Wayne and Irene Watkins farm and the Hill farm, which is now being developed by W.R. "Sport" Feagin, as ranchettes. This includes the southeast corner of the present Boyd homeplace and Tollett-Geren homeplace. It is believed that this 150 acres was purchased by Joseph Boyd in order to get the hill on which the Geren home now sits, as a home site, since this terrain is very similar to the home site that Joe Boyd and his family left in Tennesnsee.

Joseph and Hannah's oldest child did not move to Texas with them. He remained in Henry County, Tennessee, where some of his descendants now live in Paris, Tennessee. The second Oldest, Hiram G. Boyd, did move to Texas with the family. In 1857, the settlement of Millwood consisted of two homes, a blacksmith shop and a general store. James Smith, the first postmaster, lived in one of the houses and Hiram Boyd in the other. In 1857, a saw mill was built in Millwood and this became one of the major towns in the county. The first flour mill was built by the postmaster, James Smith, and was powered with a 30 foot inclined wheel which was the footing for eight oxen to walk, thereby creating the power. This mill burned about the time of the Civil War. Col. Johnson owned the first store in Millwood with J.D. Nailor as Clerk. Just before Christmas in 1862, four brothers in a robbery of Johnson at his home, murdered him. Jim Reed, the Sheriff of Collin County, tracked them down and hanged three of them. The old road through Millwood is believed to be the earliest road ever established in the county that is still in existence.

On August 9, 1860, when the census was taken at Millwood, Texas, Joseph Boyd and wife, Hannah, listed four children, Alfred R., Mordicia M.C., Calvin V. and Buster M. as living at home.

The seventh child born to Joseph and Hannah Boyd was named Mordicia. He was born in Tennessee in 1840. On March 25, 1861, he volunteered to protect the frontier of Texas north of a line running west from Plano and east to Jefferson. He pledged to be ready at the call of the Governor. The organization was called the Farmersville Calvary Company No. 1, 15th Brigade under the command of Harrison Brummitt. On March 1, 1862, Mordicia M. Boyd, together with his older brothers James F. and Alfred R. Boyd volunteered as privates in Capt. James D. Nailor's company in the 16th Regiment of the Texas Cavalry Volunteers, commanded by Col. William Fitzhugh, which had been called into service by the Confederate states.

According to the marriage records of Collin County, Mordicia M. Boyd was married four times. First, January 6, 1862, to Rebecca Martin. Second, November 13, 1866, to Mary J. Graves. Third, May 4, 1877, to C.C. Harless. Fourth, on July 2, 1879, to Nancy Katherine Warden Baugh. Nancy Katherine's first husband had been killed at Shiloh, where the Old Turnpike crossed

East Fork two miles west of Millwood, while assisting the Sheriff in the arrest of a man wanted for bank and train robberies in Missouri. In the latter part of December, 1874, M.M. Boyd purchased 60 acres of land from A.J. Lewis in the S.M. Rainer Survey for $800 and there established the home where his and Nancy Katherine Warden's children were born. This is just east of the present town of Lavon and just across Bear Creek north of the Joe Boyd homestead.

Four children were born to Mordicia M. and Nancy Katherine Boyd. William Francis born May 30, 1880; Bessie Candus Boyd born April 10, 1882; Todd Henry Boyd born February 7, 1884, and Claudie May Boyd born May 3, 1885. All of the children except Todd Henry were born on the homeplace. Mordicia and Nancy Katherine took their two children, William Francis and Bessie Candus, in the latter part of 1883 and moved to Red River County near Clarksville for one year. It was there that Todd Henry was born February 7, 1884. Mordicia died in Red River County in the latter part of 1884 and Nancy Katherine brought her three young children back to the family homestead just east of Lavon where Claudie May was born on May 3, 1885. She later married Tom James and they had four children, Hezzey Edward, Yanch Allen, John I. and Anie Ione. After Tom James' death, Nancy Katherine married Tom Boone. Their children were Freeman Boone and Connie Walker Boone.

BOYD-STIMSON FARM

With the marriage of William Francis Boyd, the grandson of the original imigrant Joe Boyd, and Fannie Belle Stimson, the granddaughter of the original imigrant, Isaac Stimson, both the Boyd and Stimson families qualified for the 1974 Texas Family Land Heritage Program, conducted by Commissioner John C. White of the Texas Department of Agriculture. Thirteen Collin County farms qualified for this program and are listed in the first edition of the registry for the program. The Boyd-Stimson farms are listed as follows:

Boyd-Stimson Farms — 1853 and 1856 — Lavon, Nevada, Copeville and Josephine Communities.

Founders: Joseph Boyd of Tennessee (1853), Daniel M. Stimson of Virginia (1856).

1974 Owners: Mr. and Mrs. Roland Boyd, Mrs. O'Reda B. McCartney, McKinney.

Today's Boyd-Stimson Farms incorporate parts of land settled by Joseph Boyd (950 acres, December 5, 1853), and land bought by Daniel M. Stimson (116.5 acres, November 3, 1856). The farm also includes lands purchased by another ancestor, Mordicia M. Boyd, in the latter part of 1874. Stimson's father-in-law, John Abston, a veteran of the Battle of King's Mountain during the American Revolution, is buried on the farm, which originally produced cotton, corn, wheat, oats, bois d'arc posts, cattle and hogs. The Barry family, believed to be the most famous of polo players in the world, originated on the farm. During World War II, German POWs from Rommel's Afrika Corps, worked the land to provide food for American soldiers. The farm now yields cotton, wheat, oats, hay, maize, cantaloupes, cattle and goats.

The original imigrant in the Stimson family to Collin County, Isaac Stimson, together with his wife Rachel O., together with other members of their family, who died from 1858 to 1877, are buried in a small family burial plot in a grove of trees just west of the Ridgeview Cemetery, southwest of McKinney. Daniel M. Stimson was buried in the Abston Cemetery with the Abston family north of Lavon.

The six generations of the Stimson family who have lived, or are living in Collin County, are as follows: Isaac Stimson, Daniel M. Stimson, Fannie Belle Stimson Boyd, Roland Boyd, William Maston Boyd and Brad and Blake Boyd.

The six generations of the Joseph Boyd family who have lived, or are living in Collin County, are as follows: Joseph Boyd, Mordicia M. Boyd, William Francis Boyd, Roland Boyd, William Maston Boyd and Brad and Blake Boyd.

Also, another branch of the Joseph Boyd family of which six generations have lived, or are living in Collin County, is as follows:

Joseph Boyd, Mordicia M. Boyd, Todd Henry Boyd, Teresa Margaret Boyd, Billy Virgil Cryer and Bobby Nail Cryer Lokey.

STIMSON FAMILY

Erasmus Stimson who had been born in England April 14, 1762, came to America and settled in Pittsylvania County, Virginia. He and his wife, Lucy, had seven children. Their youngest child was Isaac who was born January 30, 1799, in Pittsylvania County, Virginia. Isaac and his wife, Rachel first moved to Kentucky, then to Texas. They had twelve children born from 1819 to 1839. They were, in order of their births, Edward C., Martha J., Amanda P.F., Abigail O., Daniel M., Maryan E., Isaac W., Lucy F., Rachel B., Soerateas H., Clemantine P. and Josea F. The family arrived in Collin County in 1853 and settled southwest of McKinney. They came to Texas with the Abston family. The two families were slave owners and it is believed that they migrated to Texas to find a more favorable climate for slave ownership. On August 15, 1864, Sarah Abston paid taxes on fourteen slaves. Isaac Stimson paid taxes on eight slaves. His son, Daniel M. Stimson paid taxes on two slaves. John Abston, who was very old at the time of the migration, had fought in the American Revolution at the Battle of Kings Mountain. He is buried in the Abston Cemetery (or Elias Belew Cemetery one mile north of Lavon). The fifth child of Isaac and Rachel Stimson was Daniel M., born April 26, 1827. He first married Sarah F. Abston, a daughter of John. They had six children, John W., Isaac P., Rachel A., Sarah O.J., Dan and Jim. After Sarah's death, Daniel M. married Susan Foster Hunter. They had one child, Rufus. After Susan's death, he married Mary Hewitt who was teaching school in Rockwall. They had two children, Nora who married A.P. Barry from Georgia; and Fannie Belle who married William Francis Boyd, son of Mordicia M. and grandson of Joseph Boyd.